# Law, Governance and Technology Series

Volume 23

The *Law-Governance and Technology Series* is intended to attract manuscripts arising from an interdisciplinary approach in law, artificial intelligence and information technologies. The idea is to bridge the gap between research in IT law and IT-applications for lawyers developing a unifying techno-legal perspective. The series will welcome proposals that have a fairly specific focus on problems or projects that will lead to innovative research charting the course for new interdisciplinary developments in law, legal theory, and law and society research as well as in computer technologies, artificial intelligence and cognitive sciences. In broad strokes, manuscripts for this series may be mainly located in the fields of the Internet law (data protection, intellectual property, Internet rights, etc.), Computational models of the legal contents and legal reasoning, Legal Information Retrieval, Electronic Data Discovery, Collaborative Tools (e.g. Online Dispute Resolution platforms), Metadata and XML Technologies (for Semantic Web Services), Technologies in Courtrooms and Judicial Offices (E-Court), Technologies for Governments and Administrations (E-Government), Legal Multimedia, and Legal Electronic Institutions (Multi-Agent Systems and Artificial Societies).

More information about this series at http://www.springer.com/series/8808

Douglas Walton

# Argument Evaluation and Evidence

Springer

Douglas Walton
Centre for Research in Reasoning,
Argumentation and Rhetoric (CRRAR)
University of Windsor
Windsor, Canada

ISSN 2352-1902 ISSN 2352-1910 (electronic)
Law, Governance and Technology Series
ISBN 978-3-319-19625-1 ISBN 978-3-319-19626-8 (eBook)
DOI 10.1007/978-3-319-19626-8

Library of Congress Control Number: 2015940890

Springer Cham Heidelberg New York Dordrecht London


Printed on acid-free paper

Springer International Publishing AG Switzerland is part of Springer Science+Business Media (www.springer.com)

*For Karen, With Love.*

# Acknowledgments

The research for this book was supported by Social Sciences and Humanities Research Council of Canada Insight Grant 435-2012-0104 on the Carneades Argumentation System. My collaborator on the grant, Tom Gordon, has contributed to the research in the book in many ways. Chapter 3 is a substantially revised and rewritten version of my paper "A dialogue system specification for explanation," originally published in *Synthese*, 182(3), 2011, 349–374. The original work for Chap. 3 was supported by a Research Grant, Argumentation in AI and Law, from the Social Sciences and Humanities Research Council of Canada. I would like to thank the members of CRRAR for comments made when I read an earlier draft of this chapter to them, especially Steven Patterson and Jin Rongdong, whose comments led to some especially significant improvements.

Chapter 3 is a substantially revised and lengthened version of my paper "A dialogue system specification for explanation" that originally appeared in *Synthese*, 182(3), 2011, 349–374. I would like to thank Springer Verlag for giving me permission to reprint this work. Chapter 4 is a substantially revised and rewritten version of the paper "On a razor's edge: evaluating arguments from expert opinion," originally published in *Argument and Computation*, 5(2–3), 2014, 139–159. This work was reprinted by permission of the publisher, Taylor & Francis Ltd., and I would like to express my thanks for that.

Chapter 5 is a substantially revised and rewritten version of my paper "An argumentation model of forensic evidence in fine art attribution," originally published in *AI and Society*, 28(4), 2013, 509–530. I would like to thank Springer Verlag for giving me permission to reprint this work. I would like to thank Bob Pinto, Phil Rose, and Chris Tindale for helpful comments and discussions when this paper was presented at a meeting of the Centre for Research in Reasoning, Argumentation and Rhetoric (CRRAR) in September 2012. Parts of Chap. 6 were read as a paper to CRRAR in February 2014. For helpful comments I would like to thank Tony Blair, Hans Hansen, Cate Hundleby, Neil Simpson, and Michael Sin. Martin Kemp sent me a set of detailed comments on this chapter that enabled me to make some significant improvements and correct some serious errors.

Research for Chap. 7 was made possible by a grant from the Social Science and Humanities Research Council of Canada. I would like to thank David Godden for inspiring me to take up this topic and for collaborating with me on an earlier paper ("Redefining knowledge in a way suitable for argumentation theory," presented at the OSSA 2007 Conference) that paved the way for this one. Chapter 7 is a substantially revised and rewritten version of the paper "Reasoning about knowledge using defeasible logic," originally published in *Argument and Computation*, 2(2–3), 2011, 131–155. This work was reprinted by permission of the publisher, Taylor & Francis Ltd., and I would like to express my thanks for that.

For discussions on topics related to chapters of the book, I would like to thank Floris J. Bex, J. Anthony Blair, Thomas F. Gordon, Marcello Guarini, Hans V. Hansen, Cate Hundelby, Ralph Johnson, Erik C. W. Krabbe, Fabrizio Macagno, Steven Patterson, Robert C. Pinto, Henry Prakken, Eddo Rigotti, and Andrea Rocci. I would like to thank Giovanni Sartor for the many discussions on legal argumentation we had both during his graduate seminar and during private talks in the Law Faculty of the European University Institute in Florence in 2012. This visit to Italy was funded by a Fernand Braudel Research Fellowship from January to April 2012. This book has also derived considerable benefit from the five-year period (2008–2013) when I held the Assumption Chair of Argumentation Studies at the University of Windsor. I would like to convey my special thanks to Christopher W. Tindale who, as Director of CRRAR, provided research facilities and a stimulating intellectual work environment for me to continue working on this project as a Distinguished Research Fellow of CRRAR during 2013 and 2014.

For their helpful comments on an earlier version of the book manuscript, I would like to thank Floris Bex, Pompeu Casanovas, and Scott Brewer. For much-valued help with proofreading and for creating the index, I would like to thank Rita Campbell.

# Contents

# Chapter 1
# Introduction to Argument and Explanation

**Abstract** This chapter defines the key notions of evidence and argument to prepare the way for the subsequent chapters. It uses a simple and intuitive example to motivate the reader and to explain how the modeling of the notions of evidence and argument in the subsequent chapters will progress. This chapter is built around the Sherlock Holmes case of the Study in Scarlet written by Sir Arthur Conan Doyle to illustrate Holmes' method of using evidence to arrive at a conclusion by a series of steps by which the evidence accumulates. It uses this example (1) to explain and show how both arguments and explanations contain reasoning, (2) to show how arguments and explanations are woven together in evidential reasoning, (3) to introduce the form of argument called inference to the best explanation, (4) and to show the importance of this form of reasoning for the study of evidential reasoning and argumentation.

This book shows through illustrative and instructive examples how evidence is used in pro and contra argumentation in natural language argumentation on controversial issues, and how the relationships between argument and evidence can be clarified using an argumentation model. In the first three chapters the book poses a series of key problems of evidential reasoning and argumentation. Each problem is posed in a clear and simple way so that anyone can understand the problem, and some argumentation-based tools are applied to the problems in a non-technical manner, paving the way to the solutions achieved in the remaining chapters by applying some recently developed computational models of argumentation made available in artificial intelligence. Hence the book progresses from confronting these problems to introducing argumentation-based tools needed to deal with them, and finally offering solutions to them, along the way building a useful and increasingly sophisticated general method for evaluating arguments.

Section 1.1 provides an outline of the argumentation in the book. Section 1.2 assembles some facts concerning the much disputed case of a cloth stored in a church in Italy that has been claimed by many to be the burial shroud of Jesus of Nazareth. The cloth has markings on it caused by bloodstains forming an image of what appears to be a man who has been crucified. Many books have been written on this case and a good deal of forensic evidence has been assembled by scientists who have tested the materials of the cloth. In Sect. 1.2, some of the basic pro and con



D. Walton, *Argument Evaluation and Evidence*, Law, Governance and Technology Series 23, DOI 10.1007/978-3-319-19626-8_1

arguments in the case are articulated and the structure of the evidential reasoning in the case is modeled using an argument diagram. An argument diagram, also called an argument map in artificial intelligence, is a visual structure representing the premises and conclusions in a sequence of argumentation along with the inferential links joining them together. The Turin shroud case is used in Sect. 1.1 to introduce the use of argumentation methods.

Section 1.3 introduces a basic type of reasoning that will be important in the rest of the book, abductive reasoning, often called inference to the best explanation (IBE). We will use these terms interchangeably in the book. Section 1.4 introduces a fictional case of evidential reasoning in which a clever piece of detective work was carried out by Sherlock Holmes, to the amazement of his associate Dr. Watson. This case concerned the first meeting between Holmes and Watson, described in the story *A Study in Scarlet.* Section 1.5 shows how the Study in Scarlet case combines argument and explanation. Section 1.6 presents an example of an explanation built by a group of students working together to learn about the Darwinian theory of evolution in a science class. Section 1.7 gives another example of an explanation of the same phenomenon by a different group of students. These examples are used to show how argument, explanation and evidence need to be combined in a unifying structure.

Section 1.8 shows how the argumentation in the Study in Scarlet case can also be modeled as showing Holmes partly also using a series of explanations to reason backward from conclusions to premises. Section 1.9 carries on with the same case modeled in a third way where the sequence of evidential reasoning contains an important part where one argument attacks another. Section 1.10 gives the reader some indications of how the methods, concepts and tools introduced will be applied to a series of other cases, and the problems they give rise to in the subsequent chapters. This section summarizes ten characteristics of the methods used to analyze the examples.

## 1.1 Outline of the Book

Schiappa (1995, 2002, 51) has advocated the centrality of argument evaluation "as a direction and purpose for argumentation studies", suggesting by implication that there currently exists no method of argument evaluation in this field. This book argues that there now is such a method that has been developed in artificial intelligence (a field of computer science) and proves it by applying the method with a convincing degree of success to many examples. The book also improves the method by showing how it can be extended to employ the concept of evidence as one of its main components.

Argumentation studies has emerged from several disciplines (including philosophy, speech communication, logic and artificial intelligence), and has led not only to considerable theoretical research but also to software systems for displaying argument structures that can be used to facilitate argumentation. Argument mapping tools are becoming much more popular in recent years (Scheuer et al. 2010), helping a user to identify and analyze arguments using a visual interface that displays premises and conclusions and sequences of argumentation. The next main problem is to build practical methods of argument evaluation using mapping tools that can be applied to real cases where evidence is used to evaluate arguments used in personal decision-making, law, scientific inquiry and public debate. This book presents a formal and computational model of argumentation that has been developed by computer scientists (working with the author) showing how it can be used to evaluate real arguments. The book illustrates by examples how this tool can be applied to cases in the public domain where scientific evidence presented by experts has to be evaluated by an audience of non-experts. One example is a controversy about whether a painting can be attributed to Leonardo da Vinci, based on forensic evidence collected by experts who disagree. Another example concerns a statistical correlation found between weather patterns in the southern Pacific and flu pandemics, which raised the question of whether there might be a causal connection between these two events, such as migrating bird patterns.

A major problem that is at once theoretical and practical in nature in the field of argumentation studies is to clarify the relationship between the concepts of argument and evidence. This book shows how evidence is used in pro and contra argumentation on controversial issues, and how the relationships between argument and evidence can be clarified on an argumentation model. The book poses a series of key problems of evidential reasoning and argumentation, and offers solutions achieved by applying recently developed computational models of argumentation made available in artificial intelligence. Each problem is posed in a clear and simple way so that anyone can understand the solution, whether or not the reader is an expert in argumentation studies or artificial intelligence. The book progresses from confronting these problems and offering solutions to them, along the way building a general theoretical framework that shows how evidential reasoning and argumentation can be combined.

Using current argumentation methods, this book progresses from confronting these problems and offering solutions to building a general theoretical framework that shows how evidential reasoning and argumentation need to be combined. The book provides a hands-on survey explaining to the reader how to use methods and concepts of argumentation theory that are increasingly being developed in a more sophisticated way through being formalized in computational argumentation systems. Among the tools featured are argument diagrams (also called argument maps), explanation diagrams, methods of combining arguments with explanations, argumentation schemes, and formal computational models of dialogue. For example, argumentation schemes have been applied to collaborative argumentation in examples of arguing to learn (Nussbaum 2008; Nussbaum and Edwards 2011; Macagno and Konstantinidou 2013). It is shown how computational systems can not only be used to model arguments, but also explanations, as well as systematic inquiry procedures in which evidence is brought to bear in a sequence of argumentation used to prove an ultimate claim. It applies argument mapping tools for making argument diagrams that are useful for representing and summarizing arguments visually. Such argument mapping tools are now used to structure educational interactions (Andriessen and Schwarz 2009). Argument mapping tools are designed to help a user visualize the premises and conclusions of arguments in a graphic structure, and display a sequence of connected argument chained together to support an ultimate conclusion. Empirical research has shown that argument mapping is a useful learning and teaching methodology (Dwyer et al. 2013). The book shows how the use of these tools and methods requires a new approach to the concepts of knowledge and explanation suitable for diverse settings, such as legal argumentation and science education. This book surveys the main methods and tools of argumentation theory that are so far showing promise as being the most useful ones for application to diverse fields, including natural language argumentation and argumentation in specialized domains such as law and science.

The book applies formal models of dialogue that take an argument to be an interaction between two or more parties and that represent different conversational settings of an argument. It is now well recognized that argumentative interactions play an important role in computer-supported collaborative learning (Baker 2003, 47; Nussbaum 2011). Two other notions that are fundamentally important for understanding teaching are the concepts of explanation and knowledge, assuming that education is the transmission of knowledge from the teacher to the students, and that much of what a teacher does can often better be described as explanation rather than argument. The book shows convincingly through a series of examples analyzed using argumentation methods that both arguments and explanations can only be properly understood if configured using formal models of dialogue. Moreover, the book concentrates on one especially important species of argumentation called inference to the best explanation (also often called abductive reasoning) and shows how it needs to be modeled by combining arguments and explanations in a hybrid dialogue structure.

It is widely acknowledged that there is a growing dependence on expert opinion evidence in important matters of public deliberation and in the way evidence is treated in the courts, so much so indeed that any study of evidential reasoning now needs to take this aspect of it into account. For this reason much of the book concerns arguments for and against expert opinions, in a framework in which expertise is defined both in the relationship of an expert to a body of knowledge and in the relationship of an argument from expert opinion to the audience to whom it was addressed as an argument presenting evidence. Through the use of case studies and computational tools from artificial intelligence, the book examines a series of examples of evidence being used in this way, arguing that it can be analyzed as a dialectical procedure with an opening stage, an argumentation stage and a closing stage. By applying these tools, the last chapter that puts forward a theory of evidential reasoning of the kind used in scientific inquiry that links evidential reasoning to arguments that pass through a sequence of argumentation that goes through several stages, typically from a problem formulation stage, to a discovery stage, to a stage where a claim to knowledge is based on a standard of proof.

A theme of the book is that evidential reasoning based on expert opinion testimony needs to be evaluated by basing this kind of argumentation on the assumption that an expert possesses knowledge in a particular field or domain of expertise. What makes an expert "an expert", on this view, is possession of knowledge. The problem solved by the case study evidence put forward and analyzed in the book is that evidential reasoning can be modeled using resources from argumentation theory, especially argumentation schemes, argument mapping tools, formal dialectical models of evidential procedures, and the combining of these tools as applied to significant problem cases.

This chapter introduces the reader to the investigations in the other chapters of the book by explaining (1) how argumentation theory as a distinctive approach to evidential reasoning basically works, and (2) how some standard argumentation tools are applied to evidential reasoning. These twin aims are carried out by analyzing two simple but realistic examples. The chapter also provides definitions and explanations of key terms and concepts used in argumentation theory that are applied to cases of evidential reasoning in the rest of the book. However, by using such examples the chapter also introduces the reader to some main problems in this emerging field of study.

Chapter 2 analyzes two case studies of murder trials in which the evidential reasoning employed is based on inference to the best explanation and shows to how to model this kind of pro-con argumentation using argument diagramming tools, argumentation schemes, and explanatory story-based scripts. On this approach, one intelligent agent reconstructs the motive of another by drawing an inference from facts and commitments of the other agent using abductive reasoning. This chapter extends the theory of (Walton and Schafer 2006), which provided an argumentation framework for reasoning forward from motive to action, and reasoning backward from action to inferred motive. The use of argument diagrams and explanation diagrams in the chapter provides a way of dealing with the circularity in the use of IBE noticed by Pardo and Allen (2008, 233): a hypothesis explains the evidence, but the evidence helps to justify the hypothesis. This work provides a basis for moving forward to confronting the technical problem of combining argument and explanation in such cases, solved in Chap. 3.

Inference to the best explanation is a form of argumentation that combines argument and explanation, leading to the next three problems. The first problem is how to define the notion of explanation in a way that can make it useful for argumentation studies. The second problem is how to build a set of criteria that can be used to determine in a particular text of discourse whether something should be interpreted as an argument or an explanation. The third problem is how to evaluate explanations so that one explanation can properly be said to be better than another.

Chapters 1 and 2 show how common cases of evidential reasoning are based on abductive reasoning, or inference to the best explanation, and we have seen how inference to the best explanation can be evaluated as a form of argument by asking the appropriate critical questions matching the scheme for the abductive type of argument. Inference to the best explanation works by putting forward an explanation that purports to account for the facts in a given case. At this point we are confronted with three questions of high generality and importance in argumentation, in artificial intelligence and in philosophy: (1) What is an explanation? (2) How can it be determined by objective criteria whether an explanation is successful (good)? (3) How can it be judged whether one explanation is better than another? These questions are answered in Chap. 3.

Many of the examples studied in this book involve scientific evidence presented by experts in a framework where an expert opinion needs to be used by people who are not themselves experts. Chapter 4 takes an argumentation approach to build a method for evaluating such arguments from expert opinion. The method uses the argumentation scheme for argument from expert opinion along with its matching set of critical questions. It shows how to use this scheme in three formal computational argumentation models that provide tools to analyze and evaluate instances of argument from expert opinion. This chapter offers solutions to key problems of how to apply argumentation tools to analyze and evaluate arguments from expert opinion. It is shown (1) how to use these tools to construct an argument diagram to represent pro and con arguments in a given argument from expert opinion, (2) how to evaluate the arguments and critical questions shown in the diagram, and (3) how to use this structure within a formal computational model to determine whether what the expert says is acceptable or not.

In Chap. 5 a formal and computational argumentation system is used to model the argumentation in a case of conflict among art experts on the attribution of an unsigned portrait of a young woman to Leonardo da Vinci. Forensic investigations were carried out by forensic experts and experts on art history. To begin with, the leading expert opinions were in direct conflict, but as technical investigations took place and new forensic evidence came in, the hypothesis that the painting was a genuine Leonardo[1] became more widely accepted. Chapter 5 presents an analysis of the structure of the interlocking argumentation in the case using a series of argument diagrams to track structure of the mass of evidence. It can be seen that the contested attribution of the painting takes the form of a series of conflicts among experts on art history and forensic evidence.

Chapter 6 extends the analysis of arguments from correlation to cause given in the current argumentation literature where the notion of a cause is analyzed as a set of conditions that are individually necessary for the occurrence of an event, and taken together are sufficient for the occurrence of that event (Walton et al. 2008, Chap. 5). A causal inference is dependent on what is called a *field*, meaning a constellation of factors that hold in an individual case, but where there are conditions of uncertainty, lack of knowledge and even inconsistency, because the situation is highly complex, and the state of the investigation into it can vary. Field-dependence means that argument from correlation to cause is analyzed in the examples as a defeasible form of argument that is subject to critical questioning and counter-arguments.

Chapter 6 is built around analyzing the arguments from correlation to cause in three illustrative examples. It is shown that arguments from correlation to cause are initially scientific arguments used to collect evidence and draw conclusions in

[1] According to Martin Kemp (private email), it is best not to call him 'da Vinci', which was not a stand-alone surname at this time.

an investigation, for example by experiments, but then they are also used both by scientists and non-scientists for all kinds of purposes. In Chap. 6 it is shown that argument from correlation to cause is inherently reasonable, and is indeed a common heuristic form of reasoning that we could not do without in scientific research, public policy formation, and most notably in clinical investigations and medical decision-making. But it is also shown that it is a form of argument that is highly variable in dependability, sometimes notoriously leading users to commit the *post hoc* fallacy.

The problems solved in the preceding chapters leads to an underlying problem of great theoretical generality – the problem of how evidential reasoning leads to knowledge. In Chap. 7, CAS is extended to build a procedural view of inquiry in which evidence is marshaled to support or defeat claims to knowledge. Through the use of this procedure, it is shown how the argumentation framework needs to be extended by an evidence-based theory of inquiry. This theory views the collection of evidence as a sequence of moves in a collaborative group inquiry in which agents evaluate what is known or not known.

A central problem of the book, to clarify the relationship between the concepts of argument and evidence, is posed in a pointed way throughout Chaps. 5 and 6. In these chapters the notion of evidence is prominent in the example of forensic evidential reasoning in the case of a da Vinci painting and in a series of examples of evaluating scientific arguments from correlation to causation. CAS defines the concept of an argument, but it is only in Chap. 7 that it is extended to provide some guidance on how to model the concept of evidence in an inquiry. The problem of clarifying how evidence is related to argument generally is reserved for Chap. 8, because it is an issue of such high generality, even though, as the book shows, it is also a central practical problem for argumentation studies as a field.

The book builds the exposition around engaging examples that anyone can understand and models the argumentation in the examples using visual displays. Building on the body of evidence provided by studying these examples, the book relates evidential reasoning in explanation to evidential reasoning in argumentation. Using argument visualization tools to display the structure of arguments and explanations in the examples, it shows how the four fundamental concepts of argumentation theory can be fitted together within a comprehensive and coherent argumentation theory. The four concepts are those of argument, explanation, evidence and knowledge.

## 1.2 The Shroud of Turin

The shroud of Turin is a long linen cloth kept in the Cathedral of St. John the Baptist in Turin Italy. It is believed by many to be the burial shroud of Jesus of Nazareth. It shows a striking image of a man's face and the whole front of his body as it might be laid out after crucifixion. There are marks on the face and body consistent with wounds of the kind that suggest the manner of Christ's crucifixion. When the image was photographed, its negative presented a much clearer and more impressive picture that convinced many that what has been preserved is an image of Christ on his burial shroud. The image of the face itself is very impressive. It looks comparable to many images of the face of Jesus found in popular representations. The image of the man represented on the shroud has a mustache, beard, and long hair. The man appears to be muscular and tall. The image itself could be classified as presenting a visual argument (Birdsell and Groarke 1996), a so-called multimodal argument, but we will not try to analyze this aspect of it here.

The shroud is a rectangular cloth that is more than 4 ft long by more than 3 ft wide. Reddish-brown stains that look like bloodstains are found on the cloth showing what appear to be wounds on the body shown in the image on the cloth. One wrist on the cloth shows what appears to be a round wound that could have been from piercing. Other marks that appear on the body look like they could have been from wounds on the torso and legs. Proponents of the authenticity of the image argue that these markings on the shroud are blood drippings of the kind that could occur during crucifixion.

The presence of the shroud in Turin, Italy was attested to in the fourteenth century, but before that time there are no historical records indicating its whereabouts, before that time, or even if it existed previously. Although there are other reports of a shroud thought to be the burial shroud of Jesus before that time, there is no firm evidence that these reports to refer to the same one that is in Turin.

The issue of whether the image depicted on the shroud is a genuine representation of Christ has been a subject of intense debate. Some experts think that the shroud was a medieval forgery, while other writings have argued for authenticity. Forensic investigations included a radiocarbon dating of the shroud in 1980, when the Catholic Church finally agreed to make a small sample of the cloth available for scientific testing. A team of scientific experts on radiocarbon dating at the University of Oxford said that the date of the shroud is between 1260 and 1390. Tests conducted independently by teams of radiocarbon dating experts at the University of Arizona and the Swiss Federal Institute of technology corroborated this dating. This evidence suggested that the shroud is a medieval forgery. These dates match the first known appearance of the shroud recorded from the known facts of its provenance. However, others argued that the sample chosen for testing was introduced in the Middle Ages as a repair fragment.

The controversy suggested by the description of the shroud of Turin case given above has led to further scientific investigations and much writing and argumentation on the subject. But in order to provide the reader with an interesting case that can be used to introduce some basic tools, methods and approaches typical of argumentation, let's take the description of the argumentation presented in the paragraph above as a case study. It is a realistic enough case, despite its incompleteness, to give the reader some idea of how an argument diagram can be used to represent the structure of argumentation in any given text of discourse. Any text of discourse in natural language will contain vagueness, ambiguity, confused or unclear reasoning that is difficult to follow, much less to represent analytically as a logical sequence of reasoning. So there are always decisions to be made on how to model the argumentation in a given text of discourse, and in some cases the best way

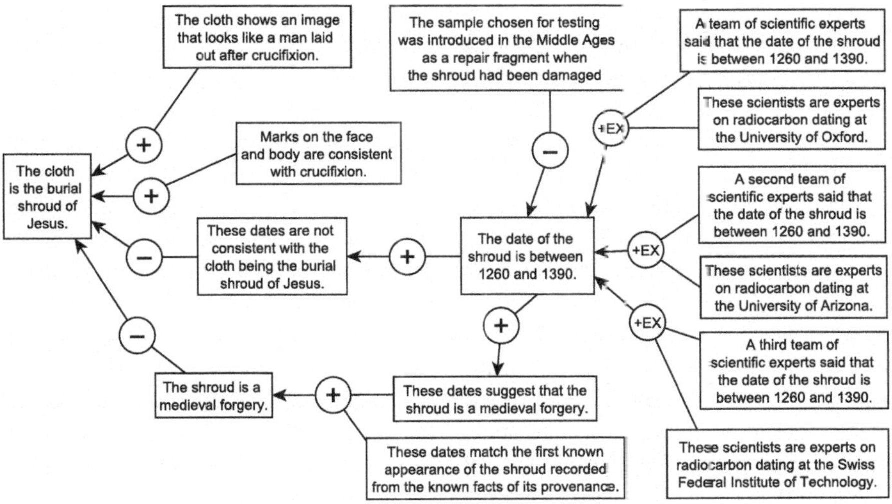


**Fig. 1.1** An argument diagram of the shroud of Turin case

to proceed is to recognize the possibility of several different interpretations that need to be considered. Although this particular example is not without its difficulties, it is at any rate free enough of them to be useful for our purposes.

In the argument diagram shown in Fig. 1.1, the ultimate claim that is at issue in the dispute is represented in the text box at the far left of the diagram. The proposition in the text box states that the cloth is the burial shroud of Jesus. The arguments displayed to the right of this textbox all lead by sequences of arrows into the single proposition. The arguments are represented by the circles, and some information about the nature of the argument is contained by notation within each circle.

If you look over the whole argument diagram you can see that it can be broken down into three parts. At the top there are two proarguments (indicated by the plus sign in the nodes) supporting the ultimate conclusion. In the middle there is a complex sequence of argumentation that composes a con argument (indicated by the minus sign in its node) attacking the ultimate conclusion. At the bottom there is another con argument, connected with the argument in the middle, that also attacks the ultimate conclusion. Let's examine each of these arguments in detail to see how they work.

The one pro argument at the top is based on the premise that the cloth shows an image that looks like a man laid out after crucifixion. This premise reports an observation about how some visual image appears to a viewer. The proargument just below it is based on the premise that marks on the face and body are consistent with crucifixion. This premise is also based on observations about how the image on the cloth appears to someone who views it, making the claim that signs on the face and body of the man shown in the image are consistent with crucifixion. We will not attempt here to classify these two types of arguments, but merely indicate that they are pro arguments supporting the ultimate conclusion. It might be noted that they are not very strong arguments by themselves, in the absence of further evidence. Further evidence is presented in the remaining two arguments, but these two arguments each go against the claim made in the ultimate conclusion.

The middle argument is based on three arguments from expert opinion shown in the column at the far right of the argument diagram. Each of these three arguments has the notation + EX displayed in its argument node. This notation represents the form of argument called argument from expert opinion. In its simplest form as a heuristic, this type of argument states that since an expert has asserted some particular proposition, this proposition may tentatively be accepted, even though its acceptance needs to be seen as provisional, depending on further evidence that might come in to the case being considered A *heuristic* is an inferential device that enables a person to rapidly jump to a tentative conclusion where a decision needs to be made in a situation of uncertainty. Heuristics are "fast and frugal" in use of cognitive resources (Gigerenzer et al. 1999). An example is the use of trial and error when no better way of solving a problem is currently available.

Heuristics, often apply to fast changing situations where a habitual response to a familiar situation may be the right thing to do even though there is little time to think about it, for example a fast decision to brake while driving on the freeway. The problem with heuristics is that the conclusion drawn may turn out to be wrong, as one could see in retrospect, or if one had time to collect and process more evidence (Walton 2010). Acceptance of a conclusion based on a heuristic inference is provisional.

This qualification about the acceptance being provisional means that such an argument is inherently defeasible in nature. A *defeasible argument* is one which provides some evidence in support of acceptance of a claim, even though that acceptance may have to be withdrawn later when new evidence enters a case. In this instance the three arguments from expert opinion all appear to be fairly strong. None of them offers the names of these scientists who tested the cloth using radiocarbon dating. But each of the teams of scientists were supposedly members of a research group on radiocarbon dating at a respectable university. If we needed to, we could track them down and find out who they were, and what their qualifications were in their respective scientific fields. Their carbon dating tests were carried out independently of each other, and so the three arguments as a group present significant evidence supporting the claim that the date of the shroud is between 1260 and 1390. Once this conclusion is accepted, it leads by a pro-argument to the next conclusion that these dates are not consistent with the cloth being the burial shroud of Jesus. What we have here is a chaining of two arguments together, where the conclusion of the first argument is reused as a premise in a second argument. Next, we can see that the conclusion of the second argument is reused as a premise in the third argument, which is a con argument attacking the ultimate conclusion that the cloth is the burial shroud of Jesus. In other words, this argument chains three arguments together, and when we put them all together they make up a strong con argument against the ultimate conclusion.

Next, let's look at the argument at the bottom of Fig. 1.1. It too reuses the earlier conclusion drawn by arguments from expert opinion that the date of the shroud is between 1260 and 1390, but takes it in a different direction. It uses this earlier conclusion as a premise to support the conclusion that these dates suggest that the shroud is a medieval forgery. This premise goes along with the other one shown at the bottom of the argument diagram in order to make up a pro argument leading to the conclusion that the shroud is a medieval forgery. This argument is not a very strong one. The two premises taken together merely suggest the hypothesis that the shroud is a medieval forgery. But even so, enough evidence is given by the premises – one of which is ultimately supported by the three arguments from expert opinion – to suggest that the conclusion that the shroud is a medieval forgery seems like a reasonable hypothesis to derive from these premises by inference.

There is one further argument that remains to be considered, namely the con argument shown at the top middle, based on the premise that the sample chosen for testing was introduced in the Middle Ages as a repair fragment when the shroud had been damaged. This seems to be a pretty strong argument against the claim that the date of the shroud is between 1260 and 1390, because the latter claim is based solely on expert opinion evidence, and if the experts only tested a fragment of the shroud that could have been introduced in the Middle Ages, none of the radiocarbon dating tests would show that the cloth did not come from a time earlier than the Middle Ages. It could still be possible that the cloth came from the time of the crucifixion of Jesus. So this con argument is a fairly serious one. If we accept its premise, it defeats reasonable acceptance of the conclusion that the date of the shroud is between 1260 and 1390, which is a necessary link in the chain of argumentation going from the expert opinion evidence across the middle of the argument diagram to the ultimate conclusion. However, no further evidence was given, according to the information about the case presented in the description above, to support this premise. But if some evidence for it were given, for example based on expert opinions of scientists who had examined the shroud in the repair fragment, it could be a very strong counterargument, and might defeat the network of pro-arguments supporting the ultimate claim at issue.

Here we need to note some terminology. A *single argument* is an argument that has only one premise. A *linked argument* is an argument that has two or more premises, in the simplest case just two premises, where the premises go together to support the conclusion. For example at each of the arguments from expert opinion displayed in the rightmost column of Fig. 1.1 is a linked argument. A *convergent argument* is an argument that has two or more premises, in the simplest case just two premises, and each of the premises supports the conclusion on its own, independently of the other premises. For example consider the two pro-arguments at the top left of the diagram. One is based on the premise that the cloth shows an image that looks like a man laid out after crucifixion. The other states that the marks on the face and body are consistent with crucifixion. Each of the arguments stands on its own as offering some evidence to support the ultimate conclusion by means of a pro-argument. A *serial argument*, in the simplest kind of case, is one that connects two simpler arguments together such that the conclusion of the first argument is reused as a premise in the second argument. But then it is possible to have a more complex type of serial argument in which the conclusion of the second argument is reused as a premise of a third argument, and so forth. To put this definition in a more compact way, the serial argument is simply a chaining of arguments one to another, as illustrated by the argument along the middle of Fig. 1.1. Finally a *divergent argument* is an argument that draws two conclusions from the same premise. For example if we look at the middle of Fig. 1.1, the premise that the date of the shroud is between 1260 and 1390 is used in two different pro-arguments leading to two different conclusions.

## 1.3 Abductive Reasoning

Abductive reasoning is a contested concept that has had various different meanings attributed to it. Sometimes abductive reasoning has been contrasted with deductive and inductive reasoning, suggesting that it is a kind of defeasible reasoning, but not the same kind associated with inductive reasoning of the kind used in probability and statistics. The historical components of the term are *ab* and *ducere,* meaning 'from' and 'to lead'. Normally an inference of the kind we are so familiar with logic representing an argument leads forward from a set of premises to a conclusion. In contrast, an abductive inference goes backward from a given conclusion in a search sequence to find premises that the conclusion might have been based on. This meaning is familiar in knowledge-based systems in computer science. For example, in an expert system, a user may want to ask the system what premises in its knowledge base were used by the system to arrive at its conclusion. In a knowledge-based system, the system not only has the capability to chain forward from premises in its knowledge base to some conclusion that has been queried. It also has the capability to chain backward to show which propositions in its knowledge base the line of reasoning originated from. This form of chaining backward is sometimes called a trace explanation. This brings us to the next meaning of abductive reasoning.

Peirce (1965, 375) described abductive reasoning as a procedure in which "we find some very curious circumstance, which would be explained by the supposition that it was a case of a certain general rule, and thereupon adopt that supposition." The words 'supposition' and 'adopt' suggest the tentative nature of abduction. As noted above, you can accept an abductively derived conclusion as a provisional commitment even if it is subject to retraction in the future. A general rule is a generalization about the way things can normally be expected to go in a familiar kind of situation. An example quoted below (Peirce 1965, 375) illustrates scientific abduction used in paleontology.

> Fossils are found; say, remains like those of fishes, but far in the interior of the country. To explain the phenomenon, we suppose the sea once washed over this land. This is another hypothesis.

We all know that fishes normally live in water, even though that general rule could be subject to some exceptions. But the notion that fish could live in an interior region where there is no body of water is puzzling, suggesting the need for an explanation. A plausible hypothesis is that there must have been water there at an earlier time. If there is no other explanation of the fish fossils being in the interior region, this hypothesis would seem to be the best explanation by default.

Notice that in the wording in Peirce's description of abductive reasoning quoted just above, as well as in his description of the fossils example, Peirce used the word 'explain'. Abductive inference in the more recent literature is often equated with inference to the best explanation. Harman (1965, 88–89) for example, wrote that inference to the best explanation "corresponds approximately to what others have called abduction". This pronouncement itself suggests that there have been differences of opinion on how to conceive abductive reasoning. One kind of case Harman (1965, 89) cited as a paradigm of abductive reasoning, however, is that of a detective who puts a mass of crime scene evidence and evidence about motives and other internal states together to arrive at the conclusion that the butler did it, in a murder case. In this chapter, we will take abductive reasoning to be equivalent to inference to the best explanation. The chapter will advocate a particular method for modeling explanations in such cases in criminal law.

The notion of an argument will be defined as a directed graph that typically takes the form of a tree structure in which the ultimate proposition to be proved or disproved appears as the root of the tree (at the far left of the figure) and diagrammatic representations of arguments shown in the chapter. The premises and conclusions making up the chain of arguments comprising the reasoning are shown as text boxes containing propositions. Propositions, or equivalently statements, are affirmative sentences that are true or false, accepted or rejected, or that have some comparable partitioning of values of this sort. An additional aspect of arguments, as they are conceived in this chapter, is that they have forms. They can fit deductive forms of argument, inductive forms of argument, or defeasible argumentation schemes that are not deductive in nature and do not fit the category of being inductive, according to the standard notion of probability. The notion of an explanation will also be defined as incorporating reasoning, but reasoning used for a different purpose – not to prove or disprove some claim that is at issue, but to convey understanding of something to a questioner in a dialogue.

## 1.4 The Study in Scarlet Case

The author of the Sherlock Holmes stories, Sir Arthur Conan Doyle (1859–1930), was a physician as well as a writer of crime stories. As a medical student at the University of Edinburgh, he was aware of the extraordinary observational and diagnostic abilities of Dr. Joseph Bell, Professor of Surgery at the Royal Infirmary. Bell was noted for drawing accurate and detailed conclusions, overlooked by others, from his observations about the physical and behavioral characteristics of patients. David Schum (1994, 478–480) has drawn a number of comparisons between Holmes' description of how he applies this kind of reasoning in criminal investigations to the procedure of hypothesis formation that Charles S. Peirce (1839–1914) called abductive reasoning. In many places in the Sherlock Holmes stories, Doyle attributes to his fictional character Holmes the ability to reason backward from observations to a hypothesis, contrasting it with a more commonly used capability to draw conclusions by reasoning forward from premises to a conclusion (Schum 1994, 479–480). One of the examples cited by Schum (1994, 480) and also by Hintikka and Hintikka (1982, 61) concerns the occasion on which Holmes and Watson first met, where Watson was astonished by Holmes' surprising and correct conjecture that Watson had recently been in Afghanistan.

In *A Study in Scarlet* Holmes explained the science of deduction by which he makes a series of observations in a case, lays the evidence out, and applies the rules of deduction to the problem to arrive at a conclusion on who committed a crime. Watson, returning from Afghanistan after being wounded on a military campaign, had been interviewed by Holmes as a person to share a flat at 221B Baker Street. Watson attributes this remark to being a lucky guess, but Holmes replies, "I *knew* you came from Afghanistan" (Doyle 1932, 20). He explained that from long habit, the train of reasoning he used "ran so swiftly through my mind that I arrived at the conclusion without being conscious of the intermediate steps". Holmes then proceeds to reconstruct the sequence of steps that he went through in his train of reasoning in this instance as follows (Doyle 1932, 20–21).

> Here is a gentleman of a medical type, but with the air of a military man. Clearly an army doctor, then. He has just come from the tropics, for his face is dark, and that is not the natural tint of his skin, for his wrists are fair. He has undergone hardship and sickness, as his haggard face says clearly. His left arm has been injured. He holds it in a stiff and unnatural manner. Where in the tropics could an English army doctor have seen much hardship and got his arm wounded? Clearly in Afghanistan.

This sequence of argumentation begins with a linked argument, composed of two premises and a conclusion.

Premise: He is a gentleman of a medical type.
Premise: He has the air of a military man.
Conclusion: He is an army doctor.

The next part of the argument is made up of two premises and a conclusion, and then from that conclusion a further one is inferred.

Premise: His face is dark.
Premise: His wrists are fair.
First Conclusion: That is not the natural tint of his skin.
Second Conclusion: He has just come from the tropics.

The inference from the two premises to the first conclusion is a linked argument. The inference from the first conclusion to the second appears to be an enthymeme based on an implicit premise, 'A person who has such a tint of a skin that is not natural must have just come from the tropics'.

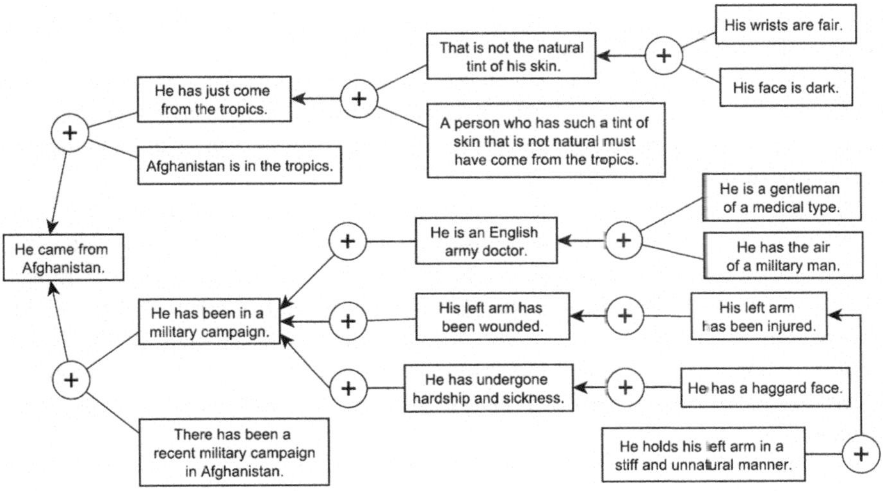


**Fig. 1.2** A standard argument map of Holmes' sequence of reasoning

The next argument in the train of reasoning is made up of a single premise and a conclusion.

Premise: He has a haggard face.
Conclusion: He has undergone hardship and sickness.

From this conclusion, and the previous conclusion that he is an army doctor, the implicit conclusion can be drawn that Watson has been in a military campaign.The next argument is also a single argument.

Premise: He holds his left arm in a stiff and unnatural manner.
Conclusion: His left arm has been injured.

From the previous conclusion that he is an army doctor, combined with the present conclusion that he has been injured, a new inference can be drawn that his left arm has been wounded.

Finally, Holmes asks the question: 'Where in the tropics could an English army doctor have seen much hardship and got his arm wounded?' The answer yields the final conclusion of the sequence, 'He came from Afghanistan'.

The sequence of reasoning is displayed in the argument diagram Fig. 1.2, where the final conclusion is shown at the far left. Along the way, Holmes has also inserted two assumptions based on common knowledge into his train of reasoning. One is the assumption that there had been a recent military campaign in Afghanistan in which English soldiers had participated. A second is the assumption that Afghanistan is in the tropics. None of these assumptions is in dispute, as far as the story related by Conan Doyle is concerned. However, the last proposition is dubious, for as most of us are aware these days, Afghanistan is a northern country that should not be classified as tropical. But let's not quarrel with Doyle's assumption on this point. From the point of view of the common knowledge of the times, Afghanistan might have seemed to have a "tropical" climate of the kind that could result in a tan, compared to the less sunny English climate.

The problem is how Holmes put all these arguments and assumptions together in his train of reasoning used to draw his final conclusion. To see how it is done, we need to put all the derived conclusions that Holmes drew together, and add the two unstated assumptions to them.

A glance at Fig. 1.2 shows how the argumentation breaks down into two main arguments. One concerns Holmes' observation of Watson's skin color variations, and his drawing of the conclusion that Watson has just come from the tropics. The other concerns Watson's apparent war injuries, and Holmes' linking of his observations of them, used to infer that Watson had taken part in the recent military campaign in Afghanistan. These two lines of reasons lead to Holmes' surprising conclusion (at least surprising to Watson) that Watson had just come from Afghanistan.

## 1.5 Abductive Reasoning in the Study in Scarlet Case

There is another plausible hypothesis that can be used to identify the train of reasoning that Holmes used to put these seven propositions together to derive his final conclusion that Watson came from Afghanistan. This hypothesis is that he used abductive reasoning.

On this hypothesis, Holmes chose the best explanation of the seven propositions above that he took to be factually correct according to his observations and inferences. If there were no recent military campaigns, other than the one in Afghanistan, that Watson could have participated in as a military doctor, the explanation of these facts that Holmes chose would be the only plausible one.

First, notice that Holmes' reasoning is based on factual observations that he made when introduced to Watson. The following six factual propositions are shown (roughly) in a column that goes down the right side of Fig. 1.2.

1. His wrists are fair.
2. His face is dark.
3. He is a gentleman of a medical type.
4. He has the air of a military man.
5. He has a haggard face.
6. He holds his left arm in a stiff and unnatural manner.

These six propositions present us with a set of facts supported by observations of Watson, and then inferences are drawn from them. In this respect, the structure of the reasoning in the case resembles the same kind of reasoning based on observations used in medical diagnosis or in scientific invention of a hypothesis.

Second, notice that the inferences drawn from these facts can be seen as explaining them. The observations that his wrists are fair and his face is dark pose an anomaly that calls out for an explanation. The hypothesis that he has just come

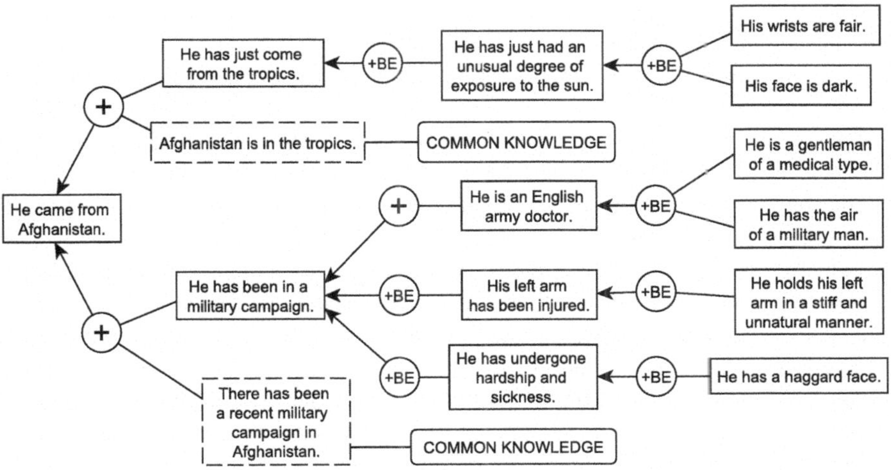


**Fig. 1.3** IBE structure of the reasoning in the Study in Scarlet case

from the tropics would explain these facts. The observations that he is a gentleman of the medical type and that he has the air of a military man can be explained by the hypothesis that he is an army doctor. The observation that he holds his left arm in a stiff and unnatural manner can be explained as an injury, which in turn could be explained as a wound that he suffered in a military campaign. The observed fact that he has a haggard face can be explained by his recently having undergone hardship and sickness.

This different way of modeling the structure of the argumentation suggests most of the nodes representing the arguments in these figures could be fitted to the scheme for abductive reasoning or inference to the best explanation (IBE). Abductive reasoning on the approach of Josephson and Josephson (1994) is equated with inference to the best explanation (IBE). On their account (Josephson and Josephson 1994, 14), IBE has the following form, where *H* is a hypothesis.

- *D* is a collection of data.
- *H* explains *D*.
- No other hypothesis can explain *D* as well as *H* does.
- Therefore *H* is probably true.

Figure 1.3 shows how the evidential structure of the Watson case can be modeled using IBE. The notation + BE indicates a pro argument use of inference to the best explanation.

In some instances in this book we will insert implicit (unstated) premises in an argument diagram. But in other instances, for reasons of simplicity and ease of exposition, we will omit implicit premises in argument diagrams. In Fig. 1.3, two premises are not explicitly stated: (1) the statement that Afghanistan is in the tropics, and (2) the statement that there has been a recent military campaign in Afghanistan. The choice of putting in such implicit premises or not is a matter of how much depth one wants to go into in building an argument diagram, and what the purpose and the audience are for the diagram.

Looking down the right side of Fig. 1.3, the six observational facts of the case are listed in the right column. To the left of each of the four subsets of these propositions, inferences from the best explanation of each subset are drawn. From the observation that his wrists are fair and his face is dark, the explanation offered is that he has just had an unusual degree of exposure to the sun. On the basis of the scheme for inference to the best explanation, this proposition is drawn as a conclusion. In turn, from this conclusion, the secondary conclusion that he has just come from the tropics is drawn by using the argumentation scheme for inference to the best explanation. In other words, since his having had such an unusual degree of exposure to the sun calls out for an explanation, the explanation that he has just come from the tropics can be inferred. These days there would be an alternative explanation, exposure to a sun lamp, but such devices did not exist during the time of Arthur Conan Doyle.

Further examples of using implicit assumptions in an argument diagram are two explanations as hypotheses: (1) the data that Watson has dark face and fair wrists is claimed to be explained by the hypothesis that he just had an unusual degree of exposure to the sun, and (2) the assumption is made that no other hypothesis can explain this collection of data as well as this hypothesis. The choice of putting in such implicit premises or not is a matter of how much depth one wants to go into in building an argument diagram, and what the purpose and the audience are for the diagram.

The observed facts of his being a gentleman of the medical type and his having the air of a military man are explained by the assumption that he is English army doctor. The explanation of his holding his left arm in a stiff and unnatural manner is explained by his being injured. His having a haggard face is explained by his having undergone hardship and sickness, which in turn can be explained by his having been in a military campaign. All the inferences shown in Fig. 1.3 have been modeled as instances of inference to the best explanation, except for three of them. The inference from his being an English army doctor to the conclusion that he has been in the military campaign does not appear to fit the argumentation scheme for inference to the best explanation. So in Fig. 1.3 it has been labeled as being an argument. The other two arguments, at the extreme left of Fig. 1.3, also are not labeled with any particular argumentation scheme. Both of them are based on a premise of common knowledge. These propositions are shown to lead to two main conclusions: he has just come from the tropics and he has been in the military campaign. These two main conclusions, along with the two items of common knowledge about Afghanistan, lead to the ultimate conclusion that he came from Afghanistan.

To see how Holmes drew this conclusion we have to look once again at the question he asked: ‘Where in the tropics could an English army doctor have seen much hardship and got his arm wounded?’ Here four factors are mentioned: tropics, English army doctor, hardship and wounded arm. These factors correspond to the bottom three text boxes in the middle column of Fig. 1.3, taken with the top textbox in the left column. These observations bring out an interesting feature of this case: at three of the horizontal levels of the figure, there is a chaining of abductive reasoning using two IBE argument steps.

There remains another aspect of the Watson case to be discussed. It is an instance of a special type of argument known in the literature as an evidence-accumulating argument, or a cumulative argument. As each of the items of observational evidence is introduced, there is a cumulative effect, a buildup of evidence. However, it is not a simple or straightforward procure in which evidence for the ultimate conclusion (He came from Afghanistan) becomes stronger as each item in the list of six is introduced. Instead there is a complex sequence of argument links to intermediate conclusions, and from there further steps to the ultimate conclusion. There are two masses of evidence, as indicated in Fig. 1.3 by the argument at the top left labelled + and the one at the bottom left, also labelled +. These are cumulative. In the text, first the top one is introduced, and then the second argument provides additional evidence to corroborate it.

## 1.6 An Example of an Explanation in Science Education

We can see from the last section that argument and explanation are combined and woven together in complex ways within the evidential reasoning in a given case when using IBE. How to sort out the complexities of these connections will not be fully sorted out until Chap. 3, but still, it will help at this point to use some simple examples from the field of science education to give the reader an idea of how such connections work.

Sandoval and Reiser (2004) conducted experimental classroom studies to explore the inquiry practices that students followed while using a software tool called ExplanationConstructor that supported their efforts to construct and evaluate explanations. The first version was implemented in a Chicago high school where the students were introduced to Darwin's theory of evolution in a lecture describing his ideas.

The purpose of the lab was to help students notice variations, to consider the effects and to graph patterns of them to help them understand the data. Questions were posed to students, and they sought answers in groups of three or four students. The students tried to propose explanations and to decide which items of data were relevant evidence to support their claims. The investigators examined the students' decisions to see whether or not they used ExplanationConstructor, and how they arrived at decisions. The investigators located significant points where the students articulated new questions to pursue a line of inquiry or propose a new explanation.

The ExplanationConstructor software tool was structured so that it was made easy for the students to cite data to support an explanation by making the potential evidence immediately visible on the screen. By this means the students could construct inferences, in effect arguments, using the data to support or attack an explanation that had been offered. The explanations were evaluated by four criteria (Sandoval and Reiser 2004, 362).

- Thoroughness and clarity of explanation were evaluated by configuring each explanation as a story connected together by a sequence of causes and effects. Explanations were evaluated on how clearly such causal chains were described.
- An explanation was evaluated as stronger to the extent that it linked data, such as measurements or weather conditions, to support parts of the explanation.
- An explanation was evaluated as better to the extent that it considered alternative explanations and showed why they should be rejected in favor of the one selected.
- Because an explanation is weakened by missing data, any given explanation was evaluated as weaker if it failed to document its limitations.

Sandoval and Reiser see their work as answering the repeated call among science educators to move towards making argumentation a central practice in teaching. They found two conditions in their classrooms that tended to support the kind of collaborative inquiry using argumentation that they wish to encourage: small group settings for collaborative learning and use of a software environment for argumentation support.

Berland and Reiser (2008, 28) showed how the practices of explanation and argumentation are complementary in educational settings, even in learning environments that differentially emphasize these practices. They identified three goals for constructing and defending scientific explanations: (1) using scientific evidence and concepts to make sense of a phenomenon being studied, (2) articulating these understandings, and persuading others to accept an explanation by supporting it with evidence from a scientific knowledge base. The third component is especially prominent at the stage where students have already articulated their understanding of the phenomenon through explanation and need to use persuasion to convince their community of its scientific accuracy (Berland and Reiser 2008, 30). (3)They see that these goals can only be carried out through an argumentation process of evaluating and defending claims and counterclaims. Thus in their view, explanations and arguments are interwoven with each other in practice and are necessary to support each other by the use of evidence.

Berland and Reiser (2008, 39) presented the following example as a typical response from the students of a kind that weaves reasoning, evidence and claims through the explanation. This example was elicited as a response from a group of students who were asked to use data from a knowledge base to answer the question of why most of the galpagos finches died in the mid-1970s, even though some survived the catastrophe. The students were given a database containing knowledge about the relationships between finch traits and their survival.

> The rainfall decreased a lot which created the plants to not grow as much, so the Chamae, Portulaca, and Cactus had softer seeds so birds fought in competition for those plants. Since those plants were very scarce there was one other plant called the Tribulus, which had harder and lengthier seeds so the best chance for survival was to adapt to the Tribulus and be able to eat the seeds without dying.

This example is a good one for the model of explanation that will be set out in Chap. 3. On this model, a successful explanation has been achieved when there has been a transfer of understanding from the party giving the explanation to the party asking for it. This model reflects Scriven's (2002, 49) description: "Explanation is literally and logically the process of filling in gaps in understanding, and to do this we must start out with some understanding of something." This transfer of understanding works by the explainer helping the explainee to fill gaps in a sequence of events and actions based as the common knowledge shared by both parties. This notion of understanding is in turn based on scripts of a kind employed in artificial intelligence research (Schank 1986).

A script is a connected sequence of events or actions that both parties understand in virtue of their common knowledge about the ways things can be generally expected to happen in situations both are familiar with. In the famous restaurant script (Schank 1986), a man enters a restaurant, goes to a table, picks up a menu, orders soup, eats the soup when it arrives, pays the bill when it arrives, gets up and leaves the restaurant. Suppose that part way through this script, he unexpectedly gets up from his chair and pulls his pants down. That would be an anomaly, suggesting the need for an explanation. But then suppose we are told that he spilled hot soup on his legs. Now we understand what happened, or at least we can, once some further gaps in the sequence are filled in.

How the sequence of events in the example of the explanation given above about the survival of the finches can be visually represented as a script is shown in Fig. 1.4. The sequence of events is partly, but not entirely causal in nature. Nevertheless it represents a natural sequence of events that all of us can understand showing how each event led in a way that we can understand to an outcome of it in the circumstances of the case, based on our common knowledge. We understand that as the rainfall decreased, the plants did not grow as much, because of our common knowledge understanding that plants require water to grow. We can also easily understand how some of the plants had softer seeds than others, and why the birds would generally find it easier to eat the softer seeds as opposed to the harder seeds. We also understand that because the birds were concentrating on eating the softer seeds and there were not as many seeds available, the birds fought in competition for the softer seeds. Of course, we all understand how once the birds kept eating the softer seeds, under conditions of decreased rainfall, fewer seeds would be available and some of the birds would likely die from starvation. We also understand how there could be an exception to this trend in the case of some birds who were able to adapt to eating harder seeds from the Tribulus plant.

The event calculus is a logical language for representing reasoning about actions and events in fluent sequences that change over time, designed by Kowalski and Sergot (1986), with stories (scripts) in mind. A *fluent*, in artificial intelligence, is a condition that can change over time. For example the predicate ON(block, table, $t_1$) can hold at time $t_1$ when the block is on the table, but fails to hold at a later time $t_2$ when the block has been removed from the table. The event calculus is generally used to model fluent sequences in which actions and events are linked together in a script.

Looking at the visual representation of the sequence of events shown in Fig. 1.4, it is easy to grasp how it explains why some of the birds died and others survived. So it is easy to appreciate why this explanation is coherent and fits with the scientific

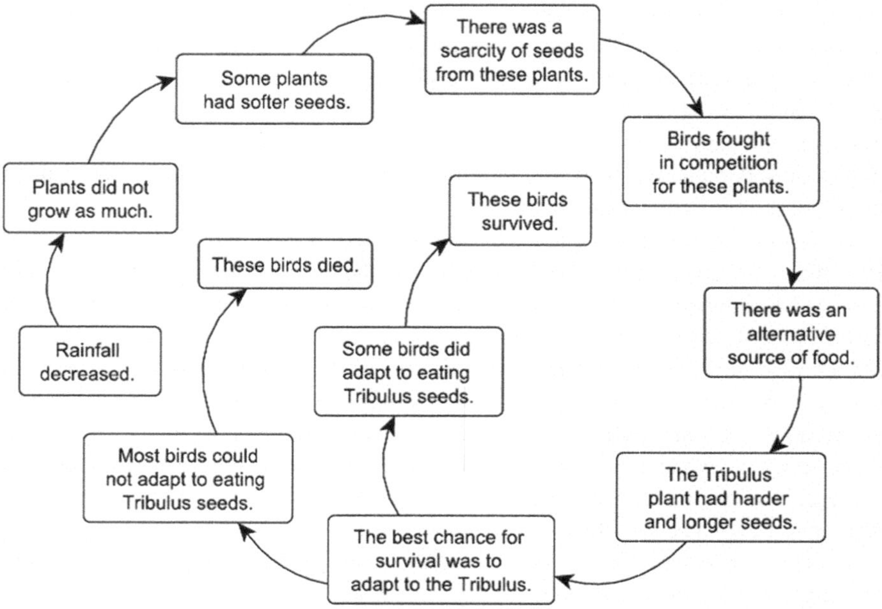


**Fig. 1.4** Script-based model of the first student explanation

facts in such a manner that it explains why some of the birds died while others survived. From the point of view of science education, where the goal is to find a good explanation that could be used to teach students how scientific method works, this explanation has some good qualities. But we also need to see some of its limitations.

## 1.7 Combining Argument and Evidence with Explanation

The explanation of the survival of the Galapagos finches presented above was judged to be coherent, and consistent with the scientific data, but a failure of the explanation was judged to be that the students did not make clear which parts of it were based on the scientific evidence and which parts represented inferences that they had drawn themselves. The second explanation (Berland and Reiser 2008, 40) differed from the first one in that the students not only explained what happened, but also presented the supportive evidence and reasoning.

> We believe that the reason some of the finches survived was because they ate the plant that was able to survive without water called Tribulus. The charts of cactus, Portulaca, and Chamae all show a major decrease to zero, from wet 73 to wet 77 except for the Tribulus plant. The Tribulus plant decreased quite a lot but not enough to disappear all the way. It survived after the drought in the dry season in 77. The research of four birds that survived

> showed that they all ate Tribulus. Which means that the drought didn't affect the Tribulus plant, which didn't affect the ground finches that ate it. According to the information we found, our hypothesis is correct. They both said that the Tribulus was the best surviving plant of the drought in 77, which didn't affect those who ate it.

According to Berland and Reiser (2008, 40), the second example presents a coherent and plausible account of why many of the finches disappeared but some survived.

But why was the second explanation thought to be better than the first one? A failure of the first one was that the students did not make clear which parts of it were based on scientific evidence. The second explanation was better because the students not only explained what happened, but also presented evidence supporting arguments, which in turn supported components of the explanation they had offered. If you simply look through the second explanation, and compare it with the first, you can see that the second one is much stronger because of the way scientific evidence is woven through it and connected by arguments to parts of the explanation that might otherwise be questionable.

The problem posed by the findings of Berland and Reiser is one of judging when one explanation is better than another, and isolating objective reasons why the one can reasonably be taken to be superior to the other. This is the problem taken up in Chap. 3. Basically the problem is to find some way of modeling the relationships between the evidence in a given case and the explanations offered to explain some apparently anomalous event in the case. The problem will turn out to be essentially one of filling in the pathways of argumentation between the evidence in the explanation. The main tool that will be used to solve this problem is the introduction of the hybrid theory that will combine arguments with explanations. The main working tool that will be used to model cases where arguments and explanations are connected is to present the evidential reasoning in any given case as a graph structure. Methods of this sort are already widely used in argumentation studies in artificial intelligence.

Schum (1994) showed in a technically sophisticated way how evidential reasoning can be modeled using a tree structure that can be visualized using an argument diagram. As will be shown in subsequent chapters, this approach has become the basic method used to analyze and evaluate evidential reasoning in argumentation. In this chapter, this methodology has been introduced in a minimal way that is easy to follow and that contains few specialized assumptions, technical notations, or other features that restrict it to special domains. But there is enough there so that we can move forward with it, bringing out other features as it is applied to more complex examples.

This chapter used a diagrammatic method to represent arguments and explanations, as well as relationships between them. Using argument diagrams, also called argument maps, is a method that has been widely adopted in argumentation to visually represent the structure of an argument. An argument diagram of the kind illustrated in this chapter typically takes the form of a tree structure in which there is a single proposition representing the ultimate claim at the root of the tree. The other propositions, comprising the premises and other conclusions drawn from them along the way, lead through the tree and converge toward this root proposition. Another tool that was used in this chapter to help represent arguments in a visual format is the application of argumentation schemes, or forms of argument of a particular type that link premises to conclusions. For example, in Fig. 1.1 the argumentation scheme for argument from expert opinion was represented in a circular argument node in the diagram.

An argument diagram can be drawn manually using pencil and paper, but there are many software drawing tools that can be used to assist a user to draw diagrams of various kinds, and these tools can also be used to represent the structure of an argument or an explanation, e.g. Gliffy (www.gliffy.com), Lucidchart (https://www.lucidchart.com) and yEd (http://www.yworks.com/en/products_yed_about.html). There are also computer supported argument visualization tools available specifically designed to represent the structure of arguments. These tools have now become widely used argumentation methods for clarifying, analyzing, summarizing and evaluating arguments. There are now more than sixty known software systems of this kind specifically designed for argument visualization (Scheuer et al. 2010).

Rationale (http://rationale.austhink.com/) is a software tool for building argument maps for many uses. For example it can be used to help students learn skills of critical thinking or to prepare for a debate by systematically building arguments useful for persuasion. A Rationale argument map is drawn in the form of a structure with the conclusion to be proved shown at the top of the page with the sequence of argumentation supporting it shown below it. Another system called Agora (http://agora.gatech.edu/) uses deductively valid forms of argument as its argumentation schemes. Rationale uses defeasible schemes such as argument from expert opinion or argument from testimony. Hoffman (2011) explains how such software tools can assist collaborative learning.

Chapter 3 will show how at a higher level of generality how arguments and explanations are woven together in evidential reasoning.

## 1.8 Backward Abductive Reasoning

Abductive reasoning is often described in the literature in terms of the contrast between forward and backward reasoning. Normally in logic we are used to viewing an argument as a forward moving sequence from a set of premises to a conclusion. Abductive reasoning is often described as a backward moving sequence from a conclusion to pick out one or more premises on which the conclusion is based. Forward reasoning is also typically explained as the use of a set of premises chained forward using a sequence of reasoning to prove the conclusion. In contrast, backward reasoning is explained as a sequence of explanations from one event or phenomenon to another. In fact Conan Doyle (1932, 138) in *A Study in Scarlet* has Holmes describe his famous method of evidential reasoning as having a backward movement in his thoughts.

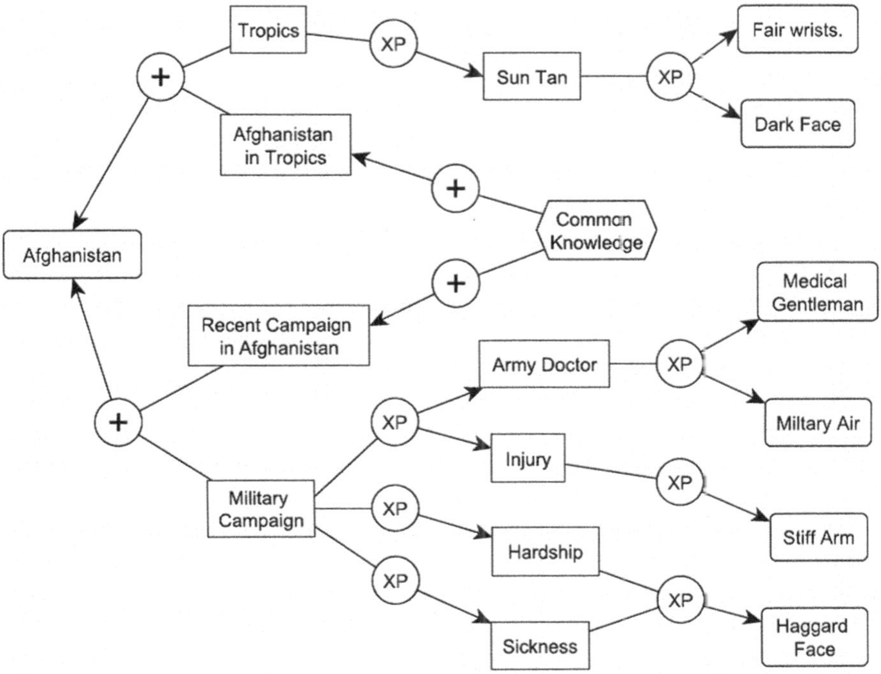


**Fig. 1.5** Backward IBE structure of the reasoning in the Study in Scarlet case

> In solving a problem of this sort, the grand thing is to be able to reason backward. That is a very useful accomplishment, and a very easy one, but people do not practice it much. In the everyday affairs of life it is more useful to reason forward, and so the other comes to be neglected. There are fifty who can reason synthetically for one who can reason analytically.... Let me see if I can make it clearer. Most people, if you describe a train of events to them, will tell you what the result would be. They can put those events together in their minds, and argue from them that something will come to pass. There are few people, however, who, if you told them a result, would be able to evolve from their own inner consciousness what the steps were which led up to that result. This power is what I mean when I talk of reasoning backward, or analytically.

There is a way to model the abductive reasoning used in the Watson case as a backward sequence of explanations of the kind that can be contrasted with the forward sequence of argumentation shown in Figs. 1.2 and 1.3. This way of modeling the abductive reasoning in the Watson example, shown in Fig. 1.5, represents it as a structure that combines arguments with explanations, and that moves backwards from the set of factual observations made by Holmes in the case to propositions inferred from these observations by inference to the best explanation.

The basic facts to be explained in the case, as observed by Holmes, are shown in rounded rectangles. The propositions drawn by inferences from such explanations, or from common knowledge, are shown in rectangles with square corners. The notation XP in a round node represents an explanation. The plus sign contained in a round node indicates a pro argument.

According to this model of the evidential reasoning in the case, Holmes' observation of Watson's contrasting fair wrists and dark face can be explained by Watson's having a sun tan. The sun tan can in turn be explained by Watson having been in the tropics. Taken together with the proposition based on common knowledge that Afghanistan is in the tropics, this explanatory sequence leads to the conclusion that Watson came from Afghanistan. But this is just one of the arguments leading to that conclusion.

The other argument can also be shown as a sequence of backward abductive reasoning in Fig. 1.5. Holmes' observations that Watson is a gentleman of medical type and that he has a military air can be explained by the hypothesis that he is an English army doctor. His stiff arm can be explained as an injury. His haggard face explains his appearance of hardship and also his appearance of sickness. All four of these findings are in their turn explained by the hypothesis that Watson has been in a military campaign. This hypothesis, along with the premise based on common knowledge that there was a recent campaign in Afghanistan, is used to argue that Watson recently came from Afghanistan.

As we look over these two arguments presented as backward reasoning based mainly on explanations, but also on arguments in some instances, they can be integrated together as follows. The top argument presents some reason to accept the conclusion that Watson recently came from Afghanistan, but by itself it is only a weak and inconclusive argument supporting this conclusion. But when the bottom argument is brought forward, and seemed to corroborate the top argument, the two combined are strong. This form of argumentation is sometimes called a *cumulative argument*, a chain of argumentation in which there is a procedure of evidential aggregation as new arguments corroborating previous arguments are added to a sequence of evidential reasoning. In this instance, the argument at the top supports the conclusion that Watson was in Afghanistan. But then there is a separate line of argumentation shown at the bottom that also supports the same conclusion. The evidence builds up in a sequential order in this case as new observations are made by Holmes. First he observes the fair wrists and the dark face of Watson. Then he observes that Watson appears to be a medical gentleman with a military air. These new observations boost up the evidential value of the first ones. Then Holmes observed that Watson has a stiff arm that he carries in an unnatural manner. This observation provides still more evidence to boost up the direction that Holmes' line of reasoning is taking, leading to his ultimate conclusion that Watson came from Afghanistan. The last step in the evidential sequence is Holmes' observation of Watson's haggard face, a piece of evidence that fits in with the previous ones to boost up the plausibility of Holmes' hypothesis even further. This step-by-step procedure of boosting up the plausibility of the ultimate conclusion that Holmes derives in the case is often described in the literature as a cumulative chain of argumentation.

## 1.9 Undercutters and Rebutters

Pollock (1995) drew a distinction between two kinds of refutations he called rebutting defeaters, or rebutters, and undercutting defeaters, or undercutters (Pollock 1995, 40). A rebutter gives a reason for denying a claim. An undercutter casts doubt on whether the claim holds by attacking the inferential link between the claim and the reason supporting it. Pollock used the red light example (1995, 41) to illustrate his distinction.

> For instance, suppose $x$ looks red to me, but I know that $x$ is illuminated by red lights and red lights can make objects look red when they are not. Knowing this defeats the prima facie reason, but it is not a reason for thinking that $x$ is *not* red. After all, red objects look red in red light too. This is an *undercutting defeater* (Pollock's italics).

If I see a red object it would seem that the proposition that what I see is red is immediately evident, would require no argument to support it. Some would say that in such a case, I am justified in claiming that I known the object is red, and that nobody can tell me otherwise. However, Pollock showed in his remarks quoted above that my claim to see a red patch in such a case is based on a defeasible argument. The argument, as reformulated below, can be called the argument from perception.

Major Premise: If an agent $\alpha$ capable of perception has an $\Omega$ image (an image of a perceptible property $\Omega$) then it can defeasibly be inferred that what the agent perceives can be classified as $\Omega$.
Minor premise: An agent $\alpha$ capable of perception has an $\Omega$ image.
Conclusion: The object can be classified as $\Omega$.

This rule seems to apply well to Pollock's example. If I see an object that looks red to me, that is evidence that it is red, and therefore I can draw the conclusion that the object is red. But then suppose, as Pollock suggests, that I find out that the object is illuminated by a red light. This new evidence functions as an undercutter in Pollock's sense, because, as Pollock pointed out, red objects look red in red light too. However it is important to recognize this new evidence does not rebut the claim that the object is red, because it might be red for all I know. It merely undercuts the argument that it is red by casting the argument into doubt, undermining its support for the conclusion that the object is red.

Next it can be shown that there is another way of modeling the abductive reasoning in the Study in Scarlet case that offers a different model to show how the second argument interacts with the first one. This way of modeling the interaction between the two arguments is shown in Fig. 1.6, where the node containing the minus sign is an undercutter. The undercutter undercuts the pro argument above it. Pollock's argument from perception appears to be very useful as a potential argumentation scheme for helping us to deal with many different kinds of evidential reasoning, for example evidential reasoning deriving conclusions from witness

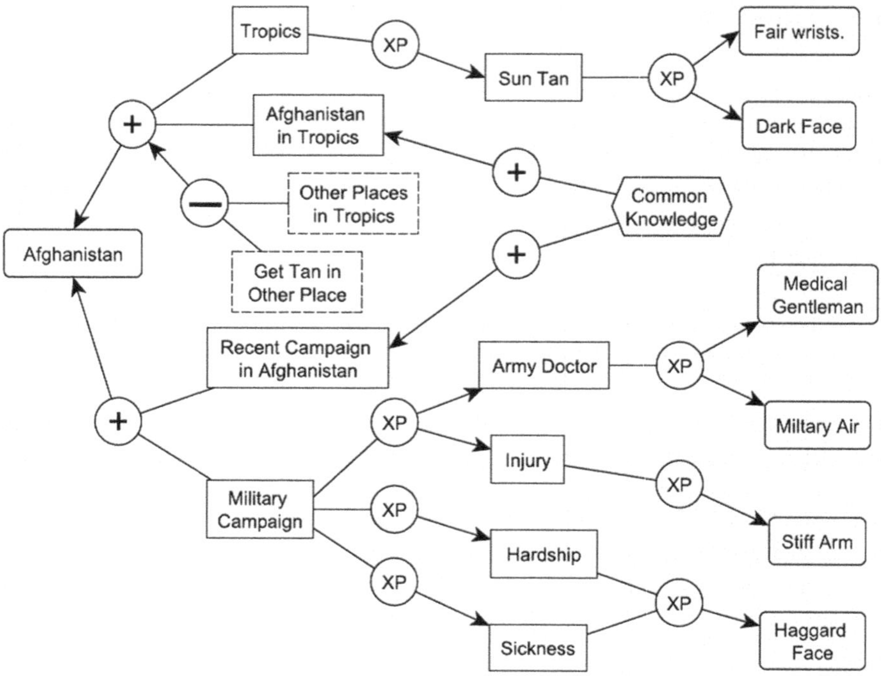


**Fig. 1.6** Arguments in the Study in Scarlet case as backward undercutters

testimony evidence. It also seems to have many implications for helping us to work towards defining a defeasible notion of knowledge that could be useful for evaluating scientific reasoning based on empirical observations leading to a hypothesis. But the problem is that, for several reasons, a version of the argument is stated in a carefully circumscribed way that makes it useful only within narrow circumstances. As noted by Prakken et al. (2003, 38), Pollock's conception of defeasible knowledge-based reasoning is based exclusively on inference rules of classical deductive logic, and inductive rules that require the use of numerical probabilities of the kinds used in statistics. For this reason it becomes tricky to extend it to the kinds of arguments we are interested in that are based on appearances. This can be shown by considering two examples.

To begin with, the weakness of the argument at the top of Fig. 1.6 requires some comments. The problem with the argument at the top is although it narrows down the possibilities by suggesting that Watson could only have gotten his sun tan by having recently been in the tropics, there might be many places in the tropics where he could have gotten a sun tan. This line of reasoning has left a loophole open. In Fig. 1.6, this opening in the line of argumentation is shown by inserting two implicit premises, indicated by the dashed border of the text boxes in which the two propositions appear: there are other places in the tropics, and he could have gotten the tan in one of these other places. These two premises are combined to form an argument labeled in Fig. 1.6 as an undercutter. An undercutter is a form of argument that attacks another argument not by attacking its premises or its conclusion, but by attacking the inferential link, the argument itself that connects the premises with the conclusion.

Then, as shown in Fig. 1.6, the argument at the bottom attacks the undercutter by providing a sequence of argumentation that weighs against the argument that Watson could have gotten his sun tan in some place in the tropics other than Afghanistan. This new argument itself is a defeasible argument, so it does not conclusively rule out the hypothesis that Watson could have gotten his tan at some other place in the tropics. But it does give a reasonably strong argument that counterattacks the previous arguments shown above it. In short the relationship between the two arguments, represented in this way, shows the second one to countervail the undercutting argument in the first one.

The following example was used in (Prakken 2003, 858) to link Pollock's argumentation scheme for argument from perception to common types of arguments used in reasoning about legal evidence. This example can be expressed in the following form (Walton 2006, 5).

Major Premise: If something looks like an affidavit, then it is an affidavit.
Minor Premise: This object looks like an affidavit.
Conclusion: This object is an affidavit.

Suppose a document is in a folder containing evidence to be used in a trial. It may be reasonable to assume that in these circumstances the document really is an affidavit, or at least can be accepted tentatively as an affidavit subject to closer examination. Clearly such an argument is defeasible however, for if upon closer examination, the document appears to be a clever forgery of some sort, and not a real affidavit, the conclusion that it is an affidavit will have to be withdrawn. The original argument concluding that the document may be taken to be an affidavit is not entirely worthless. It is not rebutted in Pollock's terms, but is countervailed by the new finding.

However, this example shows some elements that are different from Pollock's red light example. In this example something is classified as an affidavit, because of its appearance as a document, perhaps at first glance, under the circumstances that the document was not examined carefully but merely inserted into a folder and admitted as legal evidence, on the assumption that the document is genuine. But there are legal requirements that a document must meet in order to qualify as being classifiable as an affidavit. The document has to be written in a certain form, contain signatures in the right places, and so forth.

For these reasons, Pollock's version of the argument from perception was generalized into a different format for use as an argumentation scheme applicable to evidential reasoning for example of the kind used in legal trials and forensic investigations in which evidence is collected and assessed in (Walton 2006). This version of the scheme was called argument from appearance (Walton 2006, 6). Below a modified version of it is given.

Major Premise: If an image $\Omega$ suggests an object O that could be classified under verbal category C, then the object should be classified under verbal category C.
Minor Premise: This image suggests an object O that could be classified under verbal category C.
Conclusion: This object O should be classified under verbal category C.

For our second example, we can return to the case of the shroud of Turin. Two of the arguments shown in the argument diagram of Fig. 1.1, the reader may recall, were based on argument from appearance. One of these arguments was based on the premise that the cloth shows an image that looks like a man laid out after crucifixion. The statement may be true, and may accurately reflect how the image appears to anyone who looks at it.

The other argument was based on the premise that marks on the face and body are consistent with crucifixion. This argument too may look initially like it could be based on argument from appearance, but it is better classified as being an abductive argument of the kind that was traditionally called argument from sign. For example if a hunter sees animal prints in the snow, and says that these track show that a bear passed this way, it can be defeasibly inferred that a bear passed this way. Of course this reasoning could also be possibly classified as an argument from expert opinion, if we assume that the hunter was an expert of some sort on animal tracks. However, setting this possibility aside, the example seems like a good instance of inference to the best explanation. Given the appearance of the tracks left in the snow, the best explanation of how they got there may be that a bear passed this way and left the prints in the snow.

So to return to the argument based on the premise that the cloth shows an image that looks like a man laid out after crucifixion, this argument fits the form of argument from appearance. But it also suggests some of the dangers of this form of argument, because appearances can be misleading, and some appearances are more reliable than others as premises for argument drawing a conclusion about what the image in the appearance really represents. While it may be true that the image on the cloth looks very much like a man laid out after crucifixion, and when produced as a photographic negative, the image of the man's head that appears on the cloth would strongly suggest to a believer that she is looking at the face of Christ, these appearances could be misleading. Things may look the way they do because the creator of the cloth designed the imprint on the cloth to present an image that would look very much like what a believer would expect the crucified Christ to look like.

## 1.10 Conclusions

The three main examples in this chapter have shown that argument from appearance is closely related to inference to the best explanation, and should be regarded as a defeasible form of argument subject to critical questioning. The following two critical questions are proposed as appropriate for the scheme for argument from appearance.

(CQ1) Could the image Ω that has the appearance of an object O looking like it could be classified under C be misleading for some reason?

(CQ2) Although it may look like O can be classified under C, could there be grounds for indicating that it might be more justifiable to classify it under another category?

These examples suggest that great care needs to be taken with the formulation of the scheme for argument from appearance and with issues of how it applies to real arguments used in evidential reasoning. Finally, some more general discussion of how undercutters are used in the chain of evidential reasoning shown in Fig. 1.6 is helpful.

The way Holmes posed the question suggests that he might have used a process of elimination. Holmes asked the question, “Where in the topics could an English doctor have seen much hardship and got this arm wounded?” Along these lines, we might assume that it was common knowledge that there were no recent military campaigns, other than the one in Afghanistan, that Watson could have participated in as a military doctor. If there were no other such campaigns, then Holmes could use elimination to draw the conclusion that Watson could only have come from Afghanistan. But there is no evidence to support this hypothesis, and so the other hypothesis should be considered.

Both ways of interpreting Holmes’ evidential reasoning as a backward sequence of explanations combined with arguments to show how the second argument is related to the first are possible. It could be noted that the second way is reminiscent of a formal structure called an abstract argumentation framework (Dung 1995). An argumentation framework is a graph structure made up of (1) a set of elements, modeled as nodes of a graph, and (2) a set of relations, represented as arrows in the graph joining the nodes. The nodes represent arguments and the arrows represent a so-called attack relation whereby one argument attacks another. An example can be given by looking at instances where an undercutter argument attacks another argument. Since the undercutter argument has attacked the other argument, that argument is now considered “out” (not accepted). However, suppose the undercutter is in turn attacked by another undercutter, the first undercutter is now “out”. Therefore we can conclude that the original argument labelled + is now “in” (accepted). One development of CAS has been the introduction of the capability to model exceptions as undercutters in this fashion.

Notice however that argument attack is only one aspect of the kind of argumentation that needs to be dealt with in the examples studied so far. As shown by these examples, what is characteristic of argumentation is that in any given case, the pro arguments as well as the con arguments need to be brought to bear on the issue to be resolved. Both sides need to be considered, and the strengths and weaknesses of the arguments on both sides need to be taken into account.

This chapter has shown by the two main examples studied that evidential reasoning has a graph structure that can be visualized using an argument diagram representing a sequence of argumentation that displays ten characteristics.

- The ultimate premises are based on observations, witness testimony, expert testimony, or whatever supposed facts are admitted as evidence.
- The inferences are drawn from premises taken to be accepted or acceptable.
- The inferences sometimes, but not always, can be fitted to argumentation schemes.
- There is an ultimate proposition to be proved or disproved.
- This proposition is supposed to be supported by reasoning in argumentation meeting some standard of proof, even if that standard may not be stated explicitly.
- In some instances, arguments are combined with explanations.
- IBE is a type of argument that is especially important in evidential reasoning.
- Argument from perception is a type of argument that is especially important in evidential reasoning.
- Argument from expert opinion is a type of argument that is especially important in evidential reasoning.
- Distinguishing between two ways of attacking an argument, by using undercutters and rebutters, is especially important in evidential reasoning

All ten of these leading characteristics of evidential reasoning will be shown to be important in the subsequent chapters. The remaining chapters will take up problems posed by more complex examples, one at a time, and propose solutions. All of the chapters, taken in order, converge on the underlying main problems of reconfiguring the relationships between the fundamental concepts of argument, explanation, knowledge and evidence.

## References

Andriessen, J., and B. Schwarz. 2009. Argumentative design. In *Argumentation and education*, ed. N. Muller Mirza and A. Perret-Clermont, 145–174. Dordrecht: Springer.

Baker, M. 2003. Computer-mediated argumentative interactions for the co-elaboration of scientific notions. In *Arguing to learn*, ed. J. Andriessen, M. Baker, and D. Suthers, 47–78. Dordrecht: Kluwer.

Berland, L.K., and B.J. Reiser. 2008. Making sense of argumentation and explanation. *Science Education* 93(1): 26–55.

Birdsell, D.S., and L. Groarke. 1996. Toward a theory of visual argument. *Argumentation and Advocacy* 33(1): 1–10.

Doyle, A.C. 1932. *The complete Sherlock Holmes: The memorial edition.* Garden City: Doubleday, Doran & Co.

Dung, P.M. 1995. On the acceptability of arguments and its fundamental role in nonmonotonic reasoning, logic programming and n-person games. *Artificial Intelligence* 77(2): 321–357.

Dwyer, C.P., M.J. Hogan, and I. Stewart. 2013. An examination of the effects of argument mapping on students' memory and comprehension performance. *Thinking Skills and Creativity* 8: 11–24.

Gigerenzer, G., P.M. Todd, and ABC Research Group. 1999. *Simple heuristics that make us smart*. Oxford: Oxford University Press.

Harman, G. 1965. The inference to the best explanation. *Philosophical Review* 74: 88–95.

Hintikka, J., and M.B. Hintikka. 1982. Sherlock Holmes confronts modern logic: Towards a theory of information seeking through questioning. In *Argumentation: Approaches to theory formation*, ed. E.M. Barth and J.L. Martens, 55–76. Amsterdam: Benjamins.

Hoffman, M. 2011. Cognitive effects of argument visualization tools. In *Proceedings of the 9th international conference of the Ontario Society for the Study of Argumentation*, 1–12. Windsor: OSSA.

Josephson, J.R., and S.G. Josephson. 1994. *Abductive inference: Computation, philosophy, technology*. New York: Cambridge University Press.

Kowalski, R., and M. Sergot. 1986. A logic-based calculus of events. *New Generation Computing* 4(1): 67–95.

Macagno, F., and A. Konstantinidou. 2013. What students' arguments can tell us: using argumentation schemes in science education. *Argumentation* 27(3): 225–243.

Nussbaum, E.M. 2008. Collaborative discourse, argumentation, and learning: Preface and literature review. *Contemporary Educational Psychology* 33(3): 345–359.

Nussbaum, E.M. 2011. Argumentation, dialogue theory, and probability modeling: Alternative frameworks for argumentation research in education. *Educational Psychologist* 46(2): 84–106.

Nussbaum, E.M., and O.V. Edwards. 2011. Critical questions and argument strategems: A framework for enhancing and analyzing students' reasoning practices. *Journal of the Learning Sciences* 20(3): 443–488.

Pardo, M.S., and R.J. Allen. 2008. Juridical proof and the best explanation. *Law and Philosophy* 27(3): 223–268.

Peirce, C.S. 1965. Collected papers of Charles Sanders Peirce. In *Elements of logic*, vol. 2, ed. C. Hartshorne and P. Weiss. Cambridge, MA: Harvard University Press.

Pollock, J.L. 1995. *Cognitive carpentry*. Cambridge, MA: The MIT Press.

Prakken, H. 2003. Logical dialectics: The missing link between deductivism and pragma-dialectics. In *Proceedings of the fifth conference of the International Society for the Study of Argumentation*, ed. Frans H. van Eemeren et al., 857–860. Amsterdam: SicSat.

Prakken, H., C. Reed, and D. Walton. 2003. Argumentation schemes and generalisations. In *Reasoning about evidence,* 32–41. Proceedings of the 9th international conference on artificial intelligence and law. Edinburgh/New York: ACM Press.

Sandoval, W., and B.J. Reiser. 2004. Explanation-driven inquiry: Integrating conceptual and epistemic scaffolds for scientific inquiry. *Science Education* 88(1): 345–372.

Schank, R.C. 1986. *Explanation patterns: Understanding mechanically and creatively*. Hillsdale: Erlbaum.

Scheuer, O., F. Loll, N. Pinkwart, and B.M. McLaren. 2010. Computer-supported argumentation: A review of the state of the art. *Computer-Supported Collaborative Learning* 5(1): 43–102.

Schiappa, E. 1995. *Warranting assent: Case studies in argument evaluation*. Albany: SUNY Press.

Schiappa, E. 2002. Sophisticated modernism and the continuing importance of argument evaluation. In *Arguing communication and culture: Selected papers from the 12th NCA/AFA conference on argumentation*, ed. G.T. Goodnight, 51–58. Washington, D.C: National Communication Association.

Schum, D.A. 1994. *Evidential foundations of probabilistic reasoning*. New York: Wiley.

Scriven, M. 2002. The limits of explication. *Argumentation* 16(1): 47–57.

Walton, D. 2006. *Character evidence: An abductive theory*. Dordrecht: Springer.

Walton, D. 2010. Why fallacies appear to be better arguments than they are. *Informal Logic* 30(2): 159–184.

Walton, D., and B. Schafer. 2006. Arthur, George and the mystery of the missing motive: Towards a theory of evidentiary reasoning about motives. *International Commentary on Evidence* 4(2): 1–47.

Walton, D., C. Reed, and F. Macagno. 2008. *Argumentation schemes*. Cambridge: Cambridge University Press.

# Chapter 2
# Inference to the Best Explanation

**Abstract** Chapter 2 studies the problem of how to model evidential reasoning of the most common kind in criminal trials using the tools presented in Chap. 1. Chapter 2 analyzes two case studies of murder trials in which the evidential reasoning employed is based on inference to the best explanation and involves motive evidence. The chapter uses argument diagramming tools, argumentation schemes, and explanatory story-based scripts to model the evidential structure of the use of inference to the best explanation in both cases. Both cases are from textbooks used to teach students how to grasp the basics of pro-contra argumentation used in evidential reasoning in a criminal trial of a highly typical sort. The chapter offers the beginnings of a solution to the technical problem of combining argument and explanation in such cases, pointing the way forward to Chap. 3, where a method of evaluating explanations is built up.

This chapter studies the problem of how to model evidential reasoning of the most common (and apparently simple kind) in criminal trials. It has direct applications to evidential reasoning of the kind used by a detective or by a forensic investigator. It has indirect applications to many cases of scientific reasoning from a set of facts, such as observations and experimental findings, to a hypothesis. It also shows how typically in a criminal case the issue turns on two competing stories, and that for this reason in order to evaluate claims about motives it is necessary to go to a deeper level of analysis in which explanations are embedded within arguments.

Section 2.1 introduces the reader to the basic concepts needed to understand what follows in the subsequent parts of the chapter. This section defines the basic notions of argument, reasoning, abductive reasoning, and explanation as these terms are used in the rest of the chapter. It presents a standard textbook example from Wigmore (1931) that gives the reader an idea of how abductive reasoning is used in a typical criminal case as a way of providing and evaluating evidence. It gives a small example of a Wigmore chart that Wigmore (1931) used to represent part of the evidence in a criminal trial, and also it shows how a modern argument diagram typically represents this part of Wigmore's argument. Section 2.2 presents a longer example of a case outline provided by Wigmore in his book, *A Student's Textbook of the Law of Evidence*, and analyzes the evidential reasoning in the case using an argument diagram of the hybrid sort that contains both explanation and


D. Walton, *Argument Evaluation and Evidence*, Law, Governance and Technology Series 23, DOI 10.1007/978-3-319-19626-8_2

evidence. Section 2.3 presents a strikingly similar case from a fifth century BC Sophist manual, attributed to Antiphon, which was used to teach the method of pro-contra argumentation to represent the arguments on both sides in a trial. This argument structure is analyzed using a comparable diagram. Both cases are clear examples of inference to the best explanation used in a criminal trial. These two case studies are used in the subsequent parts to investigate how arguments can be combined with explanations in IBE.

Section 2.4 uses another case to illustrate the use of argument from motive to action, and develops the theory that the reverse of this reasoning, which goes backward from action to motive, is built on inference to the best explanation. Section 2.6 presents a story diagram used to visually represent the account that is the basis of the explanation in the disappearing sailor case, and Sect. 2.7 does the same thing for the Antiphon case. Section 2.8 discusses the problem of how to fit stories and arguments together, using the two cases and their argument diagrams as the basis of the discussion. Section 2.9 shows how arguments and explanations are connected to each other through the forward and backward process of reasoning characteristic of evidential argumentation about motives. It shows how this relation suggests a way of best connecting arguments and explanations in argument diagrams of the kind represented in the disappearing sailor and Antiphon cases. Section 2.10 presents argumentation schemes for both types of reasoning given in Sect. 2.4, along with a standard argumentation scheme for abductive reasoning that models it as inference to the best explanation.

## 2.1 Basic Concepts, Methods and Definitions

To show how a typical example of abductive reasoning in criminal cases works, it is best to begin with a textbook example from (Wigmore 1940, 420). This example shows how Wigmore generally framed cases of legal evidence in criminal law as instances of inference to the best explanation (IBE).

> The fact that *a* before a robbery had no money, but after had a large sum, is offered to indicate that he by robbery became possessed of the large sum of money. There are several other possible explanations - the receipt of a legacy, the payment of a debt, the winning of a gambling game, and the like. Nevertheless, the desired explanation rises, among other explanations, to a fair degree of plausibility, and the evidence is received.

This example shows very clearly how this type of argument is extremely common in evidential reasoning in criminal law cases. In this case the evidential reasoning is derived from making a choice among three (or possibly more) competing explanations of the facts, and then drawing the conclusion by equating it with the explanation selected as the best choice. Hence according to the definition proposed above, it fits into the category of abductive reasoning

As noted above, the concept of an argument is defined using a directed graph structure in which premises and conclusions make up the nodes of the graph. On this definition, an argument can easily be represented as what is nowadays called

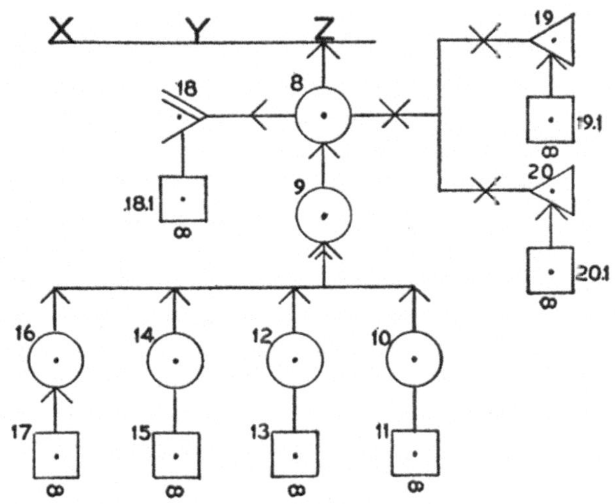


**Fig. 2.1** A small example of a Wigmore chart (Wigmore 1931, 56)

an argument map or argument diagram. Wigmore was one of the early exponents of the use of such argument diagrams to represent evidential reasoning in legal cases. Indeed, there is evidence that he may be taken to be one of the founders of the use of this technique to model argumentation, or even the originator of it, although claims of this sort can be difficult to prove or disprove. Wigmore called building an argument diagram of this sort "charting", or composing an evidence chart.

The diagram shown in Fig. 2.1 is a part of a larger example of a Wigmore chart he gave us (Wigmore 1931, 62) to represent the evidential reasoning in the case of Commonwealth v. Umilian. In this case, as described by Wigmore (1931, 63), two men were working together as farm laborers in 1899. One man disappeared and was never found alive. Three months later his headless mutilated body was found enclosed in a bran sack in an unused well 500 ft from the barn where both had been working. The skull was found some time later in the cellar of the barn. The defendant, the other man who worked together with the victim, had ample opportunity to commit the murder, and no other person had the opportunity to do it without being discovered. Later investigations discovered that the defendant had deeply hostile feelings towards the victim and had made threats against him (Wigmore 1931, 64).

The mass of evidence analyzed by Wigmore in his fairly elaborate chart that is in effect an argument diagram of the evidential reasoning in this case is too substantial and complex for us to attempt to re-create it as a modern argument diagram for the purposes of this investigation. What is of interest for us to examine is a selected part of the evidence in this case given by Wigmore as an example to illustrate how his chart method works. The chart method is quite elaborate, with all kinds of specialized notation (Goodwin 2000), but at least this one example can be used to give the reader some general idea of what a Wigmore chart looks like.

Z is one of the ultimate probanda to be proved in the case, namely the statement that the defendant killed the victim. Circles represent evidentiary facts. For example the circle labeled 8 represents the proposition that the defendant had a revengeful murderous motive. The dot in the circle represents the belief that the proposition represented by the circle actually obtains. Arrows represent inferences. For example, the arrow from circle 8 to Z represents the inference from the motive to the conclusion Z. Wigmore also represented explanations on his charts, but he saw explanations as counterarguments that attack, undermine or "explain away" a given argument. On his charts, an open angle represents an explanation of this sort. For example, open angle 18 at the left hand side of circle 8, represents "the fact that the accused did actually marry the woman, this fact tending to explain away the revengeful emotion, as probably having ceased to exist" (Wigmore 1931, 56–57). The square represents testimonial evidence. The infinity symbol represents a fact judicially admitted by the tribunal (53). The letter X, placed across a line, means that the inference represented by the line has probative value, in the estimation of the charter (34). A modern style of part of the argumentation in Wigmore's case is shown in Fig. 2.2.

The modern style argument diagram shown in Fig. 2.2 and the Wigmore chart shown in Fig. 2.1 are basically similar in their structural essentials. The nodes represent pieces of evidence in the form of propositions. The arrows represent inferences from some nodes to other nodes. The inferences are chained together into sequences that form a structure nowadays called a directed graph (defined in this chapter, Sect. 2.8), where the sequence of arrows moves toward and culminates in an ultimate claim (conclusion) to be proved or disproved. However, the modern style argument diagram is easier to read for explanatory purposes because it does not require the memorizing of elaborate notation. In the example shown in Fig. 2.2, a pro argument is represented by a circular node containing a plus sign and a con argument is represented by a circular node containing a minus sign.

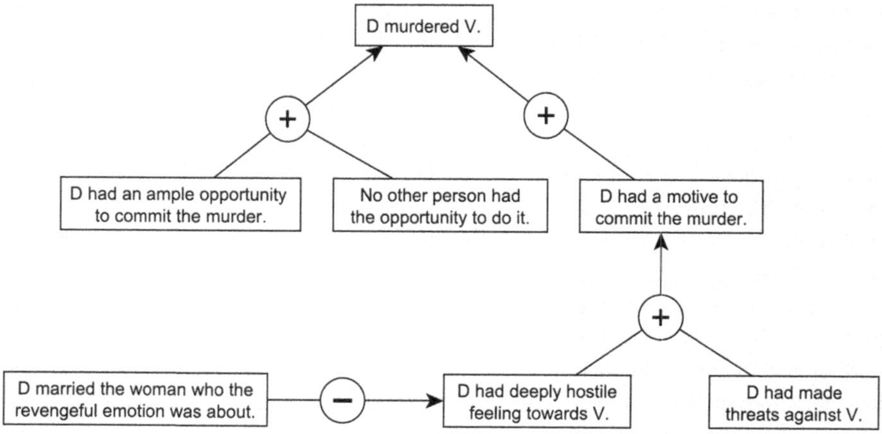


**Fig. 2.2** A modern-style argument diagram of part of Wigmore's argument

In Chap. 1 all the argument graphs had the ultimate conclusion drawn at the left, with the network of argumentation flowing into it from right to left. This will be the convention mainly used from Chap. 3 onwards. However, in this chapter and Chap. 3, and generally in cases where arguments are combined with explanations, the argument graphs are shown with the ultimate conclusion at the top, with all the subsidiary arguments flowing into it from the bottom to the top, following Wigmore's style.

## 2.2 The Case of the Disappearing Sailor

In his book, *A Student's Textbook of the Law of Evidence*, Wigmore (1935, 311) presented a case outline that has some interesting aspects from an evidential point of view.

> A seaman S on the bark "Nancy Lee" from Hull to Sydney had been constantly surly and insubordinate to the second mate M, against whom he had a grudge, arising in some prior voyage in another vessel. M on this voyage had two or three times knocked down S for disobedience. On January 14 S had the trick at the wheel in M's watch; the others of that watch were furling the topsail. When the next watch came on, S himself was at the wheel. Next day M could not be found, nor was he ever seen again on the remaining 60 days of the voyage, though the vessel was thoroughly searched. S is tried for the murder of M. There was considerable other evidence against him, and none against anyone else. M might have jumped overboard, or he might have fallen overboard, but there was no evidence tending to show either such fact.—The "corpus delicti," i.e., death of M by criminal agency, is sufficiently evidenced; though a few courts would rule in the negative.

Wigmore begins his description of the case by presenting several key evidential facts. The seaman S had been constantly surly and insubordinate against the second mate M, against whom he had a grudge. The grudge arose in some prior voyage in another vessel. On this voyage M had knocked down S two or three times for disobedience. These and the other facts represented in the initial part of the text appear to be evidence leading up to some sort of claim. The claim becomes evident in the middle part of the text where Wigmore states that S is tried for the murder of M. But just before that Wigmore describes an anomalous situation that calls out for an explanation. The next day M could not be found, and although the vessel was thoroughly searched, M was never seen again. It is highly unusual for a sailor on a vessel on a voyage of this sort to simply disappear one day without any apparent reason. Because of the factual evidence presented by Wigmore at the beginning of his description of the case, however, an explanation automatically presents itself to the reader. The suspicion is immediately raised in the reader's mind whether S could have murdered or disabled M and thrown him overboard.

At the end of Wigmore's description of the case, he presents four alternative explanations with reasons for dismissing three of them. One is that M might have jumped overboard. A second is that M might have fallen overboard. The second and the fourth fall under the heading of criminal agency, as Wigmore notes. One of these is that S might have murdered M. The other is that someone else on the vessel might have killed M. However, Wigmore points out that there was no evidence tending to prove any of these three hypotheses. On this basis Wigmore comments at the end of the quoted text that the death of M by criminal agency is "sufficiently evidenced", even though a few courts would rule otherwise.

The reasoning in this case can be visually represented using a structure that represents it as an instance of IBE. The top of the diagram in Fig. 2.3 represents the explanation part of the case at the top, and displays the evidential structure of the case in the bottom part. What is especially of interest is how the two parts connect together.

At the top, in one of the text boxes, the anomalous situation to be explained appears. This is the statement that the first mate of a ship had disappeared during a voyage. The three facts supporting the statement, according to Wigmore's presentation of the case, are shown just above the statement. The arrows connecting these four statements could be viewed as representing arguments, but they do not have to be interpreted this way. Just below this part, it is stated that four explanations are possible. M might have died by criminal agency, he might have fallen overboard, or he might have jumped overboard. This part of the diagram is explanatory in structure, and so the arrows are taken to indicate a sequence of explanatory reasoning in this structure. This analysis is built on the theory that reasoning can take place both in arguments and explanations, but the purposes for which the reasoning is used are different (Walton 1990b).

The bottom part of the diagram displays the argumentation. It is easily recognizable as a typical argument map, containing a sequence of premises and conclusions joined together by argument links that chain forward to an ultimate conclusion, the statement that S murdered M. Supporting the ultimate conclusion is the sequence of argumentation laid out below it. The statements that S had an opportunity and that he had a motive are displayed in text boxes with dotted borderlines, indicating that they are implicit premises. They were not explicitly stated by Wigmore in his description of the case, but they need to be inserted to make the chain of argumentation make sense. Arguments are presented below each of these statements.

The arguments appear in the circles represented as nodes of the graph structure, and each argument has a label. For convenience of the commentary, each pro or con argument is numbered. So we can see, for example, by looking at the lower right side of Fig. 2.3 that pro argument +4 has the premise that S had a grudge against M when M disappeared. There is only one con argument, −1, but it applies to three of the four explanatory hypotheses. Looking over Fig. 2.3 as a whole, the main feature to be observed is that a part of the diagram at the top has an explanatory function comprising the fact to be explained, and listing the different explanations that could explain this fact. In this instance there are four explanations listed. Three of these are rejected on the basis that there is no evidence supporting any of them. However, the fourth is supported by a mass of evidence depicted in the sequence of reasoning below the text box containing the hypothesis that S murdered M. In conventional representations of the use of evidence in criminal and forensic investigations, the

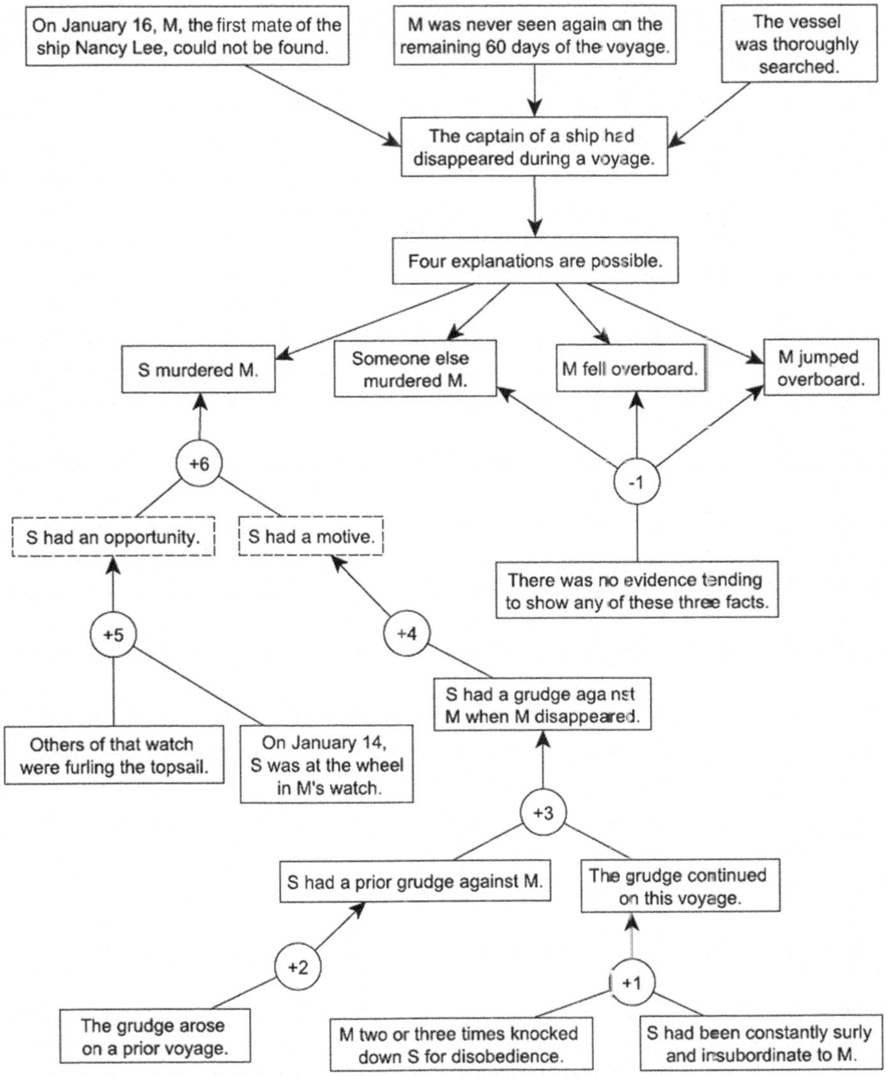


**Fig. 2.3** A diagram of the evidential reasoning in the disappearing sailor case

expression 'motive, opportunity and means' is often used to represent three kinds of evidence to lead to a convincing conclusion. However these three factors are insufficient to prove an accusation of murder in order to meet the standard of proof used in criminal law, the beyond reasonable doubt standard. In addition to motive opportunity and means, proving a claim to the standard is normally taken to require proof that the defendant actually carried out the action in question. Even though the mass of evidence shown in the description of Wigmore's disappearing sailor case might not be sufficient to prove that S murdered M in a trial, it does present some fairly strong evidence, as indicated by Wigmore's comment that the death of M by criminal agency is sufficiently evidenced in the case, even though some courts would not convict on this evidence.

The problem posed by the case is: what is the connection between argument and explanation once the evidential structure of the case is configured according to its representation shown in Fig. 2.3? In the more usual cases of the kind studied by Bex (2011), evidence, in the form of arguments, supports propositions that are parts of the explanation sequence. This case is different, however, in that it joins together argument and explanation in a way that suggests that the whole structure of the reasoning joining the explanation part to the argument part is an instance of inference to the best explanation. The disappearance of M cannot plausibly be explained by the hypothesis that one of the other persons on the ship sneaked up onto the deck while S was there and somehow disposed of M by throwing him overboard. Excluding these possible explanations leaves only one further candidate, the explanation that S murdered him by throwing him overboard, or by rendering him unable to resist and then throwing him overboard. This explanation is a highly plausible one, for as shown in the evidential chain of reasoning displayed in Fig. 2.3, S had a motive for committing the murder. Not only was there plenty of evidence supporting the conclusion that S had such a motive, there was no evidence against anyone else, presumably including the lack of evidence that anyone else had a motive to murder M. Looked at in this way, the evidence in this case can be structured very well using the model of inference to the best explanation. But a part of the problem is to try to figure out whether the argumentation scheme for inference to the best explanation should apply to the structure of the reasoning displayed in the whole diagram in Fig. 2.3, or whether it applies in some more specific locale, for example to one of the argument nodes in the bottom of the diagram.

## 2.3 The Antiphon Case

Curiously, the disappearing sailor case, taken from a student's textbook on evidence, can be shown to have a structure similar to a famous ancient case also intended to be used to teach skills of trial argumentation to students. This case, described in (Walton et al. 2014), is one of a series of classic cases of arguments used by ancient Greek rhetoricians and skeptical philosophers for instructional purposes to illustrate aspects of an approach to argumentation that has a distinctive method of looking at the evidence on both sides of a disputed claim.

Antiphon, a fifth-century Sophist, provided a series of texts meant for use to teach the method of pro-contra argumentation in a trial. In this case, the basic facts are as follows (Diels and Kranz 1952, 87 B1: 2.1.2). The victim has been murdered. The defendant is his known enemy. A slave accompanying the murdered man, before dying from blows inflicted on him in the assault, testified that their assailant was the defendant. The first part of the case described by Antiphon (quoted below from

Diels and Kranz 1952, 87 B1: 2.1.4) rules out a number of alternative hypotheses about who might have committed the crime.

> It is not plausible that professional criminals killed this man, as no one would give up an obvious and achieved advantage for which he had risked his life, and the victims were found still wearing their cloaks. Nor again did anyone who was drunk kill him, since the murderer then would be identified by his fellow guests. Nor would the victim be killed because of a quarrel, since people would not quarrel in the dead of night and in a deserted spot. Nor was it a case of a man aiming to kill someone else and killing the victim, because then his attendant would not have been also killed.

Antiphon's description of the case goes on to argue for a positive hypothesis: "Who is more likely to have attacked him than an individual who had already suffered great injuries at his hands and could expect to suffer greater ones still?" (2.1.5). Three other arguments presented by Antiphon as supporting evidence (Diels and Kranz 87 B1: 2.1.5, 6–7) are quoted below from (Walton et al. 2014, 91).

> Since the defendant was an old enemy of the murdered man and had brought several unsuccessful cases against him; since he had been indicted by the dead man on several cases, all of which he lost at the cost of much property; and since he bore a grudge for this, then it "was natural for him to plot against him, and it was natural for him to seek protection from his enmity by killing his opponent".

The prosecutors summed up their case against the defendant by arguing to the jury that they cannot acquit the defendant because the evidence both from witness testimony and from the circumstances of the case proved his guilt.

The reasoning in this case can be modeled using the argumentation scheme for inference to the best explanation to build an argument map comparable to the one used on the disappearing sailor case displayed in Fig. 2.3. In Antiphon's case five possible explanations are considered and four of them are rejected using con arguments. However, the argumentation in the Antiphon case is different from the argumentation in the disappearing sailor case in one respect. In the Antiphon case, the four explanations that are rejected are offered first, and then the positive sequence of argumentation supporting what is taken to be the best explanation is presented. Nevertheless, the similarity between the instances of inference to the best explanation in the two cases is brought out in Fig. 2.4.

The argumentation in this case begins with the phenomenon that provided the anomaly raising the need for an explanation, the finding that the victim (V) was found on his way from a banquet. The first part of the case described by Antiphon consists of the four explanations of the crime facts supplied in the quotation above: (1) professional criminals killed V, (2) someone who was drunk killed V, (3) V was killed because of a quarrel, and (4) it was a case of the man aiming to kill someone else and killing the victim. Each of these four possible explanations is rejected, and the arguments supporting each rejection are shown in the four con arguments −1 to −4, displayed horizontally along the top part of Fig. 2.4. But there is a fifth explanation.

The next part of the argument diagram to be considered is the sequence of argumentation under the selected hypothesis, the statement that D murdered V. At

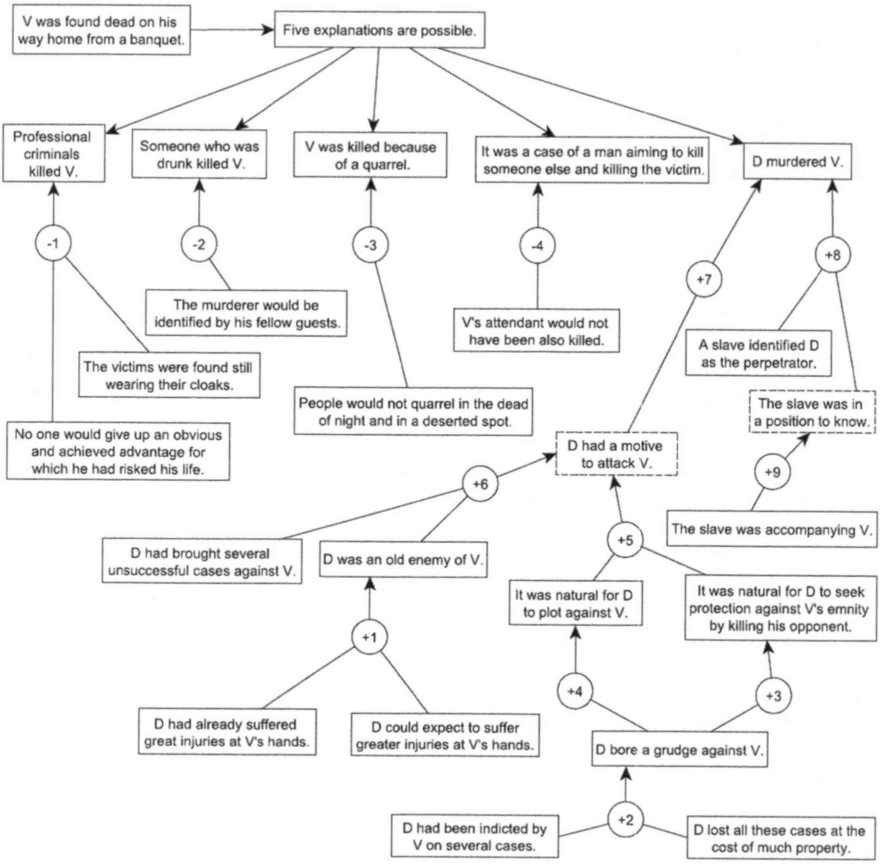


**Fig. 2.4** An argument diagram of the evidential reasoning in the Antiphon case

this point the similarity between the argumentation structure shown in Fig. 2.4 and the structure shown in Fig. 2.3 is readily apparent. There is a sequence of possible explanations across the top, and under the selected explanation a sequence of argumentation flows downward to the bottom of the argument diagram. Another similarity is that the sequence of argumentation in both cases depends on motive evidence. Under the implicit premise that D had a motive to attack V, shown by the dotted border line around the statement in the argument diagram, a marshaling of the evidence to support this premise is displayed as six connected pro arguments.

The argument diagram representing the structure of the reasoning in the Antiphon case given in (Walton et al. 2014, 92) is similar in some respects to the part of the argument shown in Fig. 2.4 representing the sequence of argumentation on the right of Figure 2.4 leading into the proposition stating that D murdered V. But it is also different from the other diagram in certain respects. The other diagram displays the evidence at the bottom of the diagram under a horizontal line and has the argument from motive to action (the defendant attacking the victim) at the top of the figure, above the line. Figure 2.4 is most distinctively different in that it displays the explanation structure with the multiple choices of explanations as part of the diagram. Thus the latter diagram is designed to give a fuller model of the evidential structure in the case that shows how argumentation and explanation are connected. Thus it is meant to give more of a basis for revealing how IBE is used in the case. So while the two diagrams have something in common, they are meant for different purposes.

An interesting difference between the two cases can be explained as follows. In the disappearing sailor case, there was only lack of evidence providing the reason for rejecting each of the alternative explanations. In the Antiphon case, separate arguments are provided as reasons to reject each of the four alternative explanations. As an example to illustrate of the use of IBE, therefore, the Antiphon case is somewhat the better one. A striking similarity is that both cases depend on the use of motive evidence to support the charge of murder. And in both cases there is an extensive network of argumentation supporting the claim that the defendant had a particular motive. This feature is of special interest to illustrate the evidential structure of motive evidence, especially on the approach that argument from fact to motive has an argumentation scheme and represents an especially interesting instance of the use of IBE in criminal cases.

## 2.4 Studying How Schemes Can be Fitted into Argument Diagrams

Figures 2.3 and 2.4 are standard argument diagrams used to represent the argumentation in the disappearing sailor case and Antiphon case, except for certain features. One of these features is that they attempt to combine argument and explanation by adding an explanation part at the top of each diagram. The other feature is that they have nodes connecting the set of premises to the conclusion in any given instance of an argument. These special features enable us to extend the analysis in some interesting ways. How that can be done is the subject of this section.

Each scheme has a set of critical questions attached to it that enable an argument fitting the scheme to be questioned or criticized. The scheme represents basic ways an argument having this form can be responded to. The critical questions are devices used to help a respondent in a discussion come up with some idea of how she might probe into the argument presented to her more deeply by spotting its weak or questionable points. However, arguments can be attacked or rebutted in different ways, and the critical questions do not represent all the possible ways of attacking an argument. There are different ways of representing a scheme. Two variations are worth mention here. The first is that it is possible to represent critical questions as additional assumptions that can be added to the ordinary premises in a scheme. This feature is very valuable because it means that the critical questions can be represented on a standard argument diagram. The second variation is that each scheme can be represented in a more complex manner that has more premises included, or it can also be represented in a simpler manner as a so-called heuristic scheme (Walton 2010). The heuristic scheme represents a faster transition from the premises of the scheme to the conclusion in which the reasoner does not hesitate by taking additional premises or complexities into account.

One of the schemes recognized in the literature is called argument from witness testimony. This scheme can be represented in the following heuristic format: witness W asserts that proposition A is true; W is in a position to know whether A is true or not; therefore A may tentatively be accepted as true (subject to critical questioning and further investigations). Such a scheme can be inserted into the node representing an argument in an argument diagram provided that the given argument fits the requirements of the scheme. Adding argumentation schemes to an argument diagram contributes to making the diagrammatic representation of the given argument more useful as a device for analyzing and evaluating the argument by proper standards.

As an example, the reader should look at the top right of Fig. 2.4 where node +8 in the diagram represents a particular argument. The premise of the argument is the statement that a slave identified D as the perpetrator. The additional implicit premise that the slave was in a position to know has been added to the diagram. The dotted border around the perimeter of a text box containing this proposition indicates that it is an implicit premise that was not explicitly stated in Wigmore's original text describing the case, but that can be justifiably added in order to help render argument +8 in a more complete fashion that helps us make more sense of it. Of course we have to realize that this proposition is merely an added assumption that has been put in by the argument analyst, but nevertheless it can help us to better evaluate the argument. Once this implicit premise has been inserted, the argument +8 fits the scheme for argument from witness testimony.

The argument +7 comprised of one premises and a conclusion, shown at the middle of Fig. 2.4, is an instance of argument from motive to action. The argumentation scheme for argument from motive to action can be formulated in a complex representation, based on the comparable form of inference described by Leonard (2001, 442).

Conditional Premise: If agent $\pi$ had a motive for bringing about action $\mu$ then $\pi$ is more likely to have brought about $\mu$ than otherwise.
Motive Premise: $\pi$ had a motive to bring about $\mu$.
Conclusion: $\pi$ brought about $\mu$.

For example we could have put a notation in the node containing +7 for the argumentation scheme for arguing from a fact to a motive. This form of inference, as structured by Leonard, with two premises and a conclusion can be modeled as an argumentation scheme for argument from motive to action. But it can also be configured in a simpler heuristic format as follows: $\pi$ had a motive for bringing about action $\mu$, therefore $\pi$ brought about $\mu$.

But now there is a problem with Fig. 2.3. +6 has been drawn as a linked argument containing two premises, the premise that S had an opportunity and the premise that S had a motive. If we want to use the heuristic form of argument from motives to action to represent the argumentation scheme in node +6, we have to reconfigure argument +6 as a convergent argument. In other words, we have to reconstruct it as two separate arguments. One is the argument that S had a motive, therefore S murdered M. The other is the argument that S had an opportunity, therefore S murdered M. Then we might also possibly have another argumentation scheme for argument from opportunity, stating that if someone that an opportunity to carry out a particular action, then it is more likely that he carried out this action, all else being equal.

So here we have two choices about how to represent +6 in the argument diagram in Fig. 2.3. One of these choices of interpretation can utilize the scheme for argument from motive to action. So far then, we have seen how an argument that goes from a motive to an action can be configured with this argumentation scheme. But we are still left with the problem of how to argue the other way around, from facts about actions and circumstances to a motive.

Abductive reasoning can be used to establish the existence of a motive by drawing an inference from premises concerning facts of a case to a conclusion that a motive exists (Walton and Schafer 2006). A sequence of reasoning leads from a set of circumstances in a case to a hypothesis that postulates the existence of a motive. Some of the reasoning in the case of Idaho v. Davis (53 P. 678 Idaho 1898) can serve as an example of an argument from actions to a motive. This case concerned the struggle between sheep herders and cattlemen to control land. The prosecution offered three facts as evidence to prove that D, a cattleman, killed W, a sheep herder. The structure of evidential reasoning in the case is shown in Fig. 2.5.

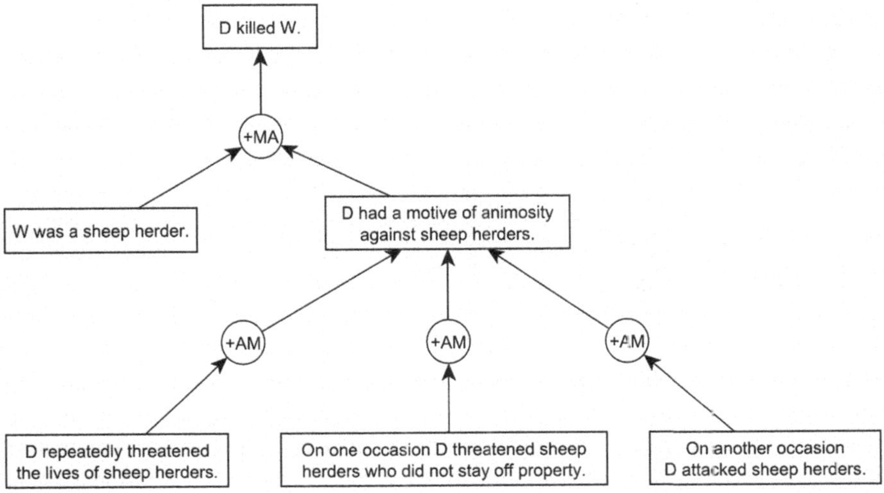


**Fig. 2.5** An argument diagram for the sheep herders example

Note that this case also provides an illustration of the use of argument from motive to action. The scheme for argument from action to motive is labelled as AM in the three bottom argument nodes. The top node is labelled + MA to indicate a pro argument from motive to action. However, the example also raises a problem about how best to model the schemes for argument from motive to action and argument from action to motive. Should the scheme have one premise or two? Normally argument from motive to action would seem to only require one premise (postulating a motive), but in this instance it requires two. Also, instead of modeling argument from action to motive to action as three separate arguments, as indicated in Fig. 2.5, it might seem that this form of argument is better seen as a single use of this scheme based on a collection of data representing facts of a case. To see how these problems can be approached, it is useful to put these two schemes into a more general theoretical framework by introducing the argumentation scheme for practical reasoning.

In the scheme below, the first-person pronoun 'I' represents a rational agent that has goals, some (normally incomplete) knowledge of its circumstances, the capability of acting to change these circumstances and the capability to perceive and remember the consequences of its actions. The heuristic format of practical reasoning, called practical inference, can be represented by the following scheme (Walton et al. 2008, 323).

Major Premise: I have a goal *G*.
Minor Premise: Carrying out this action *A* is a means to realize *G*.
Conclusion: Therefore, I ought (practically speaking) to carry out this action *A*.

Walton and Schafer (2006) developed a computational system to model forward-moving sequences of practical reasoning from a goal to an action of the following form.

*Com* $\pi$ ((GOAL G) & *Know* $\pi$ (bring about $\mu \rightarrow$ bring about G)) $\rightarrow$ *Com* $\pi$ (bring about $\mu$)

The arrow $\rightarrow$ represents a defeasible inference from a set of premises to a conclusion. The *Com* operator represents an agent $\pi$'s commitments (the set of propositions she accepts). If $\pi$ is committed to a goal, as indicated by $\pi$'s actions (including speech acts), and $\pi$ is also committed to some actions it knows will bring about the goal, then as a rational agent it should be committed to the act of carrying out these actions (subject to reservations concerning other aspects of the circumstances). More generally, $\pi$ should carry out the action expressed in the conclusion, according to the constraints of the plan it has adopted, and according to circumstances that are imperfectly known and subject to change over time.

The basic idea behind the Walton and Schafer system is that argument from motive to action can be modeled as a species of practical reasoning from goal to action. On this theory, a motive can be defined as a species of goal that in turn represents a species of commitment of a rational agent. The rational agent is essentially a practical reasoner. On this theory, there can also be a backward sequence of practical reasoning from action to goal. The characteristic backward sequence of practical reasoning from an action to a goal is modeled by Walton and Schafer by applying the following conditional rule to warrant any argument from action to goal.

($\pi$ (bring about $\mu$) & *Know* $\pi$ (bring about $\mu \rightarrow$ bring about G)) $\rightarrow$ *Com* $\pi$ (GOAL G)

Suppose for example that we have evidence that $\pi$ has carried out $\mu$, and we have evidence that it knows (or reasonably thinks) that bringing about $\mu$ is the means to achieving its goal G. Based on this evidence, we can infer by reasoning from action to goal that $\pi$ is committed to G.

A general observation needs to be made here that argumentation from an agent's stated or known goal, and its knowledge of its circumstances, to its action is a relatively straightforward form of practical reasoning. Once evidence is brought forward to show that a given agent has a particular goal as one of its commitments, and evidence is brought forward that the agent is aware that within its circumstances there is a particular means that is necessary or useful to carry out this goal, then it can be relatively straightforwardly inferred by practical reasoning that the agent has a reason to take action to carry out this means. Forward practical reasoning of this kind is not so problematic to model. However, backward practical reasoning from evidence about an agent's actions, along with evidence about the agent's circumstances, to draw a conclusion about what the agent's goal might have been, is an important speculative kind of conjecture. The reasons for this opinion were already well articulated in the philosophical literature about the problem of other minds. It has always been regarded as a problem to reason backwards from an agent's actions to a hypothesis about the agent's goals, motives or intentions that can be presumed to have been the agent's reasons for carrying out these actions. The basic problem is that goals motives and intentions are internal states of an agent, and only the agent itself can have direct access to these internal states. So any inference drawn by one agent about the goal or motive of another agent has seemed, according to the traditional philosophical accounts, to be a kind of speculative leap. The solution to the problem proposed by Walton and Schafer is to see backward practical reasoning from an agent's actions to its presumed goals as a species of abductive reasoning.

Abductive reasoning, on this approach, is equated with inference to the best explanation (IBE). According to Josephson and Josephson (1994, 14), abductive inference has the following form, showing its structure as inference to the best explanation. *H* is a hypothesis.

- *D* is a collection of data.
- *H* explains *D*.
- No other hypothesis can explain *D* as well as *H* does.
- Therefore *H* is probably true.

A central problem for this way of modeling abductive reasoning is to analyze the notion of explanation contained in it. On the definition of this contested concept preferred here, an *explanation* is an account of some event or action that is problematic for the explainee to understand, and the explainer presents a story (script) that makes the event (action) understandable to the explainee. A theory of explanation built along these lines will be presented in Chap. 3.

On the abductive theory advocated here, argument from action to motive is modeled as a species of inference to the best explanation that goes from premises that represent a collection of data (factual evidence) to offer an explanation of this set of facts that uses backward practical reasoning to go from an agent's action to a conclusion about the agent's goal. The goal is equated with a motive. Following the theory of Walton and Schafer, a motive is defined as a special kind of commitment that can lead to action. On this theory, argument from action to motive is a complex kind of argumentation based on abductive practical reasoning.

A fundamental insight of Thagard and Shelley (1997) is that abductive reasoning can be performed visually, has a visual component, and is therefore iconic or diagrammatic in its structure. Thagard and Shelley (1997, 7) used the example in which a person finds a scratch on her car door and forms a mental image of a car driving up beside hers and then its driver opening its car door that scratches hers. Thagard and Shelley described the explanation in such a case as a kind of "mental movie" in which the person imagines her door being scratched and forms a mental image of the sequence of actions that led to this outcome. They suggest that the explanation in such a case can be represented as a graph taking the visual form of a diagram that represents a sequence of connected actions and events. Thagard and Shelley (1997, 8) modeled such sequences as graphs, and propose the hypothesis that graphs can be used to reveal the structure of visual abductive reasoning. They also offered examples of the formation of hypotheses in archaeology that visually explain unusual properties of artifacts and skeletal remains (Thagard and Shelley 1997, 9–10). This graph-theoretic way of modeling abductive reasoning will be a basic method of this book, as will be made explicit in this chapter, Sect. 2.8.

There still remains an even more pervasive underlying problem of how to configure the argumentation in the disappearing sailor case and the Antiphon case as instances of inference to the best explanation. Clearly that is the basic structure of the whole chain of argumentation shown in Figs. 2.3 and 2.4, but where does the argument node for IBE fit into some node or nodes in these two figures? Or does the IBE scheme somehow fit all over the diagram as it flows from the explanatory part at the top to the argumentation part at the bottom?

## 2.5 The Hybrid Theory

There are two main approaches in artificial intelligence and law on reasoning with criminal evidence, the argumentation approach and the script-based stories approach. The argumentation approach is well illustrated by the use of argument diagrams in the disappearing sailor case and the Antiphon case. In this stories approach, an account of what supposedly happened in a case is constructed using a narrative sequence of events or actions called a script. According to the theory presented in (Schank and Abelson 1977), scripts are based on common knowledge that human agents possess about routine events and ways of doing things that they follow in everyday life and that are often so familiar to them that they don't have to think about them. The canonical example familiar in the literature is the case of the man who opens the door, enters the restaurant, walks over to a table, sits down, orders some food, for example a bowl of soup, eats the soup, gets up from the table, walks over to the cash register, takes some money out of his pocket and gives it to the person at the cash register, and leaves the restaurant by once again opening the door. This sequence of actions is understandable to all of us.

However, suppose some unusual event happens part way through the script. The man is sitting there normally eating his food, but then suddenly he pulls his chair back, stands up and pulls his pants down. This event is anomalous. It appears puzzling to us and calls out for some sort of explanation. But then suppose someone explains to us that the soup was very hot, and that the man accidentally spilled it on his pants. In such a case, the explanation is successful because we can now understand what happened. We know that hot soup spilled on one's legs can be very unpleasant, even painful or dangerous. So we can now grasp the new script that explains what happened.

A failure of understanding comes from a gap in a script, or a puzzling deviation from a script that represents a normal activity of the kind we are familiar with. A gap or deviation may constitute an anomaly for the audience to whom the script is described, if they do not understand what happened. In the restaurant example, what happened was anomalous and called out for an explanation, because the audience observing the incident did not realize the soup was so hot, or perhaps did not even see that it had fallen onto the man's legs.

To grasp the difference between the argumentation approach and the script-based story approach, it is necessary to see that an argument is inherently different from an explanation. The purpose of an argument is to offer evidence to prove or support some proposition that is a claim made but is subject to doubt by the audience. The purpose of an explanation is to help the audience who does not understand something to come to understand it based on common knowledge and on other factual knowledge in the case. The purpose of an argument is to get the audience to come to accept something that is doubtful or unsettled to them whereas the purpose of an explanation is to get them to understand something that they already accept as a fact.

Understanding, in this sense, should not be equated with confidence that one has understood something, for this "feels-right" confidence can often be misleading, and is often associated with bias. The sense of understanding meant here is reconstructive and communicative. It is based on a framework of two or more parties reasoning together who share some common knowledge about how things normally go in stereotypical situations.

There is a useful test to judge whether a given text of discourse should properly be said to express an argument or an explanation. Is the proposition to be proved or explained an accepted fact, or is it something that is in doubt? If it is an accepted fact, it doesn't need to be proved, but only to be explained. If it is something that is in doubt, it doesn't need to be explained, but only to be proved, supported by evidence, or disproved. If its purpose conforms to the latter need, it should be classified as an argument. The problem is that in some cases the natural language text of discourse may be vague, ambiguous, or simply lack enough context to enable an audience to properly determine whether it should be taken as an argument or an explanation. This kind of situation is not a practical problem in most cases however, provided one is aware of its existence.

Responding to a request for explanation of such an anomaly is best seen as a kind of repair process used to help an audience come to understand something that for some reason they found anomalous or did not understand. A story is a set of statements, offered by one party in a dialogue in answer to questions put by the other. A story could be a set of statements that links some statements to others by inferential relations linking an agent's goals to his actions. A story does not have to be internally consistent, but if an inconsistency is found, questions can be asked, and the story might have to be repaired or given up.

These concepts of script-based stories and explanations have been applied to evidential reasoning in criminal law. Pennington and Hastie (1993) gave numerous lengthy examples of criminal cases in which plausible reconstructions of the sequence of events and actions in the form of stories provide competing explanations of what supposedly happened in the case. A plausible story describes a general pattern of actions and events of kinds that we are all familiar with. One story can be more plausible than another. Alternative stories about what happened before, during and after a crime can then be compared according to their plausibility and the amount and quality of evidence they explain. The prosecution has one story, the defense has a different story, and the two stories conflict with each other by offering competing explanations of what supposedly happened in the case.

To solve this problem Wagenaar et al. (1993) devised a special type of story used to represent legal reasoning called an anchored narrative. Bex (2011) has proposed a hybrid framework for reasoning with arguments, stories and criminal evidence, a formal framework that shows how the plausibility of the story can be evaluated by giving arguments that ground the story on evidence that supports or attacks it.

One of the most important aspects of the use of stories in criminal cases is that a story can be tested against other evidence, such as circumstantial evidence or testimonial evidence, The process of checking a story in relation to relevant evidence that bears on it is called "anchoring" by Wagenaar et al. (1993, p. 39). It is important to recognize that a plausible story may not be very well supported by the evidence whereas a less plausible story may be supported by more evidence. When the witness has presented a story as his or her account of what supposedly happened in a case at trial, the story can also be questioned in cross-examination in a way that may make it fall apart. The notion of an anchored narrative is more complex than that of a script, because it also involves justifying parts of the account that are questionable, or may even be dubious. In cases of inference to the best explanation, argument and explanation are woven together. For this reason, where IBE is used in criminal cases at trial, such as the disappearing sailor case and Antiphon case, the problem is to see how IBE fits argument and explanation together in the evidential reasoning in the case.

A hybrid theory that formally models arguments combined with explanations is available in (Bex 2011). In this model the relations between events, actions and evidence in a story are connected by causal rules. This model (Bex 2013) also allows for comparison of multiple incompatible stories in a case. A *story* as defined by (Bex 2011, 59), is a particular, coherent, chronologically ordered sequence of states and events. To be coherent (Bex 2011, 76) a story must meet three requirements: (1) it must fit a story scheme, a causal sequence of events and states comprehensible to common knowledge which the particular story fits, (2) it must be internally plausible and (3) it must be internally consistent, based on his causal theory. A causal theory is defined as (1) a finite sequence of propositions representing hypothetical events connected to each other by causal inference rules, (2) where each inference in the sequence fits the DMP rule of inference. A story scheme is formally defined as a collection of propositions and a set of inference rules for classical logic with a defeasible *modus ponens* rule for a conditional operator $\Rightarrow$ that represents defeasible generalizations. Since argumentation schemes can be represented as defeasible *modus ponens* rules, in principle this structure allows for the possibility of utilizing argumentation schemes. There is also an evidential part of the theory that allows for factual evidence in a case to support or attack the plausibility and coherence of a story.

The formal hybrid theory $HT = (ET, CT)$ is a combination of a causal-abductive theory $CT$ and an evidential argumentation theory $ET$. The formal hybrid methodology uses $ET$ and $CT$ to construct hybrid argument-explanation graphs showing how evidence supports or attacks stories combined with arguments. The hybrid theory can also model abductive causal reasoning. In the abductive part of the theory $CT = (H, T, F)$, $T$ is a set of causal rules, $H$ is the set of hypotheticals, literals occurring in the antecedent of some rule in $T$, and $F$ is the set of explananda, the proposition or story to be explained. The basic idea behind Bex's theory of abductive inference is that if we have a rule *cause* $\rightarrow$ *effect* in $T$ and we observe *effect*, we are allowed to infer *cause* as a hypothetical explanation of the effect. Such an explanation can be a single proposition or a causally connected story consisting of chains of causal rules. The explananda follow from the hypotheticals and the causal theory.

In the *argumentation theory* $ET = (R, K)$, $R$ is a set of evidential rules and $K = K_E \text{ U } K_A$ is a knowledge base, where $K_E$ is a consistent set *evidence* and $K_A$ is a set of *commonsense assumptions* based on common knowledge of the way events can normally be expected to run in a familiar kind of situation. The logic for $ET$ is similar to the logic of ASPIC+ (Prakken 2010), which integrates rule-based argumentation with structured arguments. Evidential arguments can be built by taking evidence or assumptions from $K$ and rules from $R$ as premises and chaining applications of defeasible *modus ponens* to produce tree-structured argument graphs.

In inference to the best explanation, multiple explanations are generated, comparatively evaluated according to criteria that express the degree to which they conform to the evidence and their plausibility. Arguments based on evidence can be used to show that an explanation is consistent or inconsistent with the evidence.

Arguments may also be used to reason about the plausibility of an explanation, as the validity and applicability of causal rules can become the subject of an argumentation process. Arguments about the plausibility of explanations are based on plausible reasoning, carried out by using commonsense knowledge about how the world generally works in familiar situations.

The examples of evidential reasoning using inference to the best explanation introduced in Chap. 1 showed however that in order to work towards building such a formal model and apply it to real cases of natural language discourse, it is necessary to show how arguments and explanations can be combined. For example the analysis of the explanation in the Galapagos finches example shown in Fig. 1.4 shows that the students' explanation why most of the finches died even though some survived is based on arguments supporting the explanation, and these arguments in turn are based on evidence found by scientific research. The hybrid theory is applicable to this task because it provides a systematic method for evaluating explanations that is fully compatible with argumentation. Therefore computational systems of argument evaluation need to be extended to be able to deal with cases of inference to the best explanation where arguments and explanations are combined. What will be done in this book is to take a semiformal approach at this point that adopts the general framework of the hybrid theory in a simplified way and combines it with other formal systems that also need to be extended to building a general method for the evaluation of arguments and evidence in real cases.

In Chap. 1 it was shown by the examples that even though one argument diagram may need to be highly complex to represent implicit premises and conclusions by building an analysis of the given argument in depth, it is best to begin with a simple argument diagram that represents and summarizes the main steps in the sequence of argumentation. For example, it was stated that for reasons of simplicity and ease of exposition six implicit premises were omitted in the six IBE arguments. The same kind of approach was shown in the script-based model of the student explanation in the Galapagos finches example shown in Fig. 1.4. The arrows in this graph did not all represent causal transitions from one event or action to another. For example the first step was from the decreasing rainfall to the plants not growing as much. This is a causal step but the next step goes to a text box saying that some plants had softer seeds. The failure of the plants to grow as much as normal did not cause the plants to have softer seeds. Nevertheless, we see there is a connection between the two states that needs to be part of the story. For our purposes, we want a script representing a story to intuitively model how the connections between the events or actions in the story intuitively hang together. For this purpose we used a semiformal representation, a graph that shows how one step in the story leads to another, and as in Fig. 1.4, how a tree structure can represent alternative outcomes of the prior sequence of steps. For the purpose of this approach, a *story* is defined (1) as a set of a finite sequence of propositions representing hypothetical events connected to each other (2) where each step (represented as an arrow in the explanation diagram) from one proposition to the next represents a natural transition from one event or action to the next, and where the naturalness of the transition derives from the common knowledge of the participants (including both the agents in the sequence and the audience who is supposed to comprehend the sequence). What makes the sequence hang together is not always or exclusively a set of causal inference rules, or other logical inference rules, such as DMP, but the shared knowledge of the audience and the teller of the story about the way things can normally be expected to go in a kind of situation both are familiar with (Walton and Macagno 2005). For example they can be expected to understand that pointing a gun at someone and pulling the trigger is a way of killing that person if the gun is loaded, that this sort of action is very dangerous, serious, and may cause injury or death of the other party. In the classic script example, the audience can be expected to understand that (normally, subject to exceptions) if you order a hamburger in a restaurant, you are expected to pay for it, and if you don't there will be repercussions. These are not just causal rules, but sequences of actions and events that normal people (for example, those in jury) can be expected to know about.

At the present stage of the research, artificial intelligence systems for modeling reasoning based on common knowledge have not yielded systems that can be applied to the modeling of stories directly, but several projects have been underway for some time that show promise of being so used. The best known of these is called Cyc, a system produced by Cycorp.[1]

The objective of the Cyc project is to codify the millions of items of knowledge that compose human common knowledge in machine-usable form. For example the propositions 'Every tree is a plant' and 'Plants eventually die' are represented in its knowledge base. The knowledge base contains over one million propositions, rules and common sense notions. The logic of Cyc is based on predicate calculus, and it can carry out deductive inferences such as *modus ponens*, *modus tollens*, and quantificational inferences. Cyc has an ontology that enables it to draw inferences based on classifications. Hence from the two example propositions above, Cyc can draw the conclusion that trees eventually die. Cyc has an inference engine, a computer program that can combine the items in its knowledge base to generate conclusions that can then be included in its knowledge base as well. Cyc can also use this inference engine to answer questions on whether something is in its knowledge base or not.

## 2.6 A Story for the Disappearing Sailor Case

Let's look back to Fig. 2.3 and try to see where the argumentation scheme for inference to the best explanation should be represented on the argument diagram. In Fig. 2.3 four facts are represented at the top of the diagram, which shows the evidence in favor of (or against) each of the four competing explanations of the facts. Inference to the best explanation, as a form of argument, is complex. It involves four parts. First, there is the part of describing some supposedly factual situation. Second, there is the attempt to explain the facts by offering competing hypotheses.

[1] http://www.cyc.com/why-cyc

Third, there is the task of judging which of the explanations is the best. Fourth, the inference is drawn that the selected explanation is the hypothesis representing the conclusion to be drawn from the first three parts of the abductive reasoning.

When we look back over Fig. 2.3 and try to place the scheme for inference to the best explanation on the diagram, the best thing to say is that the scheme fits at no particular node in the diagram. It applies to the diagram as a whole. The reason is that the four parts of the inference to the best explanation described above fit all over the various aspects of the argument diagram shown in Fig. 2.3. There are the facts of the case described at the top. There is the attempt to explain the facts by offering four competing hypotheses. There is the task of judging which one is the best of the four explanations, carried out in this instance by laying out the evidence beneath each of the four hypotheses. Since as shown below node −1, there was no evidence tending to show the three other explanations are supported as hypotheses, so the hypothesis that S murdered M is selected. The reason for its selection is that the argument diagram below this hypothesis supports it by a body of evidence connected together into a reasoned chain of argumentation supporting the hypothesis.

In this case the rationale for selecting the one hypothesis and rejecting the three competing ones is that the selected hypothesis is supported by a body of evidence that fits together into a sequence of argumentation in an appropriate way, whereas the other three hypotheses have no evidence in support of them. So in this case, making a decision on which hypothesis to select is a straightforward task. The reason that the one hypothesis is a better explanation than the others is essentially that this hypothesis is the only one supported by evidence. In this case the criterion for selecting one hypothesis as better than another is evidential support, or the lack thereof.

There is also another way to look at structure of inference to the best explanation in the disappearing sailor case, suggesting the presence of another criterion for selecting the chosen hypothesis. Partly what makes the argumentation for the chosen hypothesis so compelling is not just its structure as a body of evidence connected as a chain of argumentation. Another factor is that this body of evidence hangs together as a coherent story. As an experiment let's reconstruct the description of what supposedly happened as displayed in the argumentation sequence and try to work it into a coherent story representing what supposedly happened in the case. One way of displaying the story is shown in Fig. 2.6.

In story sequences the arrows do not always represent causal relationships between one description of an event and another one, or merely temporal relationships between two events. In many instances that can be a good way to interpret an arrow in a story diagram. On the theory of (Bex 2011, 1), the relation between the events in a story are expressed as causal rules that draw an inference from a cause to an effect, and this is the type of argumentative reasoning that is taken by Bex to characterize evidential reasoning. But a different approach to modeling of the story in the disappearing sailor case is illustrated in Fig. 2.6.

This story represents a sequence of actions or events that are connected up in a pattern that is understandable to all of us because of the common knowledge we have about the normal way things can be expected to go in a familiar situation. Each arrow represents a normal transition of the kind that we understand from one event

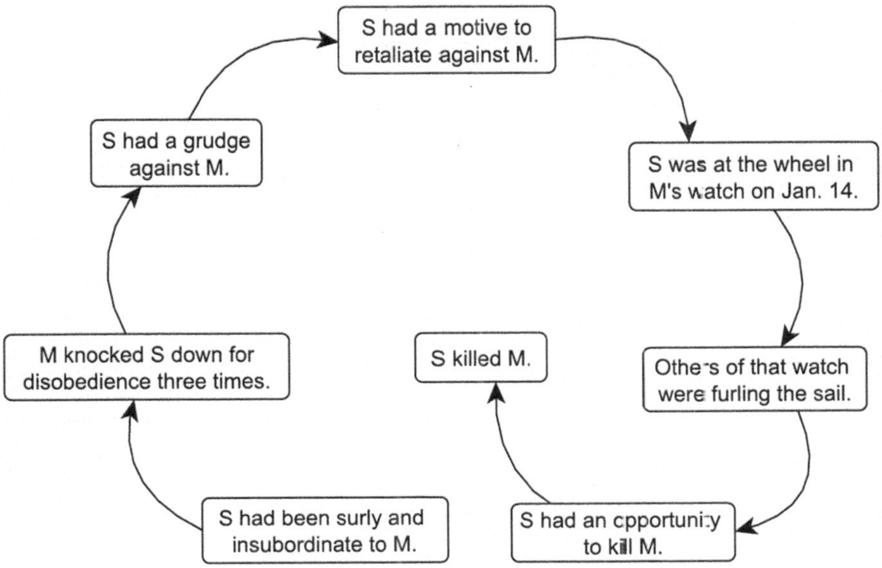


**Fig. 2.6** A story diagram for the disappearing sailor case

to another. If we look at the story diagram in Fig. 2.6, the sequence of events make sense to us. S had been surly and insubordinate to M, and hence M had knocked S down for disobedience three times. We can understand this transition, because being knocked down for disobedience would be an outcome that might normally be expected for surliness and insubordination on a ship. Understandably, the outcome of S's having been treated this way by M was that S had a grudge against him. Once again, we can understand this as a normal sequence of events of the kind that might possibly happen in the situation. We can see that in the rest of the chain of events as well, each step follows in a pattern we can understand from the previous step, and so forth. Once all the steps are in place, as shown in Fig. 2.6, the story makes sense as a whole. Most of us do not have experience of being on a ship, much less experience of being on a ship like the Nancy Lee, but still we know enough about seagoing life that we can easily understand the sequence of events as an explanation of what presumably happened in the case. This way of modeling the story is less formal and broader than the hybrid theory of Bex. But in Chap. 3 it will be shown how the two approaches can be combined.

## 2.7 A Story for the Antiphon Case

Next let's model part of the story in the Antiphon case visually using a graphic story. In the Antiphon case, five competing explanations are set out side by side along the top of Fig. 2.4. Comparably to the disappearing sailor case, the hypothesis

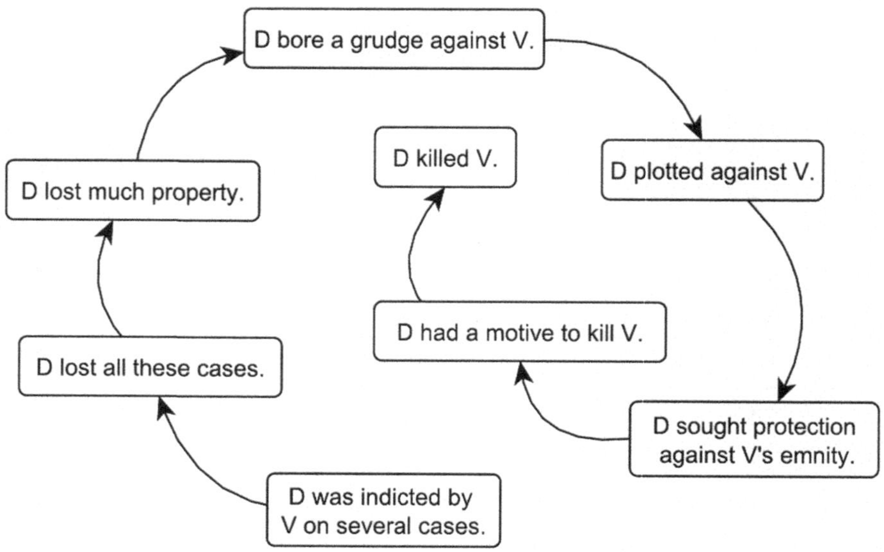


**Fig. 2.7** A story diagram for the Antiphon case

that is selected as the best explanation is shown with a chain of argumentation underneath that acts as evidence supporting this hypothesis. However, in contrast to the disappearing sailor case, in the Antiphon case, there is some evidence supporting each of the other hypotheses. Following our analysis of the disappearing sailor case, let's try to see if the chain of argumentation supporting the chosen hypothesis can be modeled as a coherent story. Both cases are similar in an important respect. In both cases one party bore a grudge against the other, and this grudge was the basis of the motive that the one party had for killing the other. This sequence of events is represented in the story script in Fig. 2.7. So far the relationship between the argument diagram and story scheme in the two cases seems to be roughly similar. However, there is a difference that needs to be taken into account.

In the Antiphon case four counterarguments −1 to −4 are presented as evidence attacking each of the four rejected hypotheses. Also, each of these four counter-arguments can be reconstructed as a story. The first one states two propositions: (1) No one would give up an obvious and achieved advantage for which he had risked his life, and (2) the victims were found still wearing their cloaks. It offers these two propositions as premises in a counterargument to the hypothesis that professional criminals killed V. Can this counterargument also be represented as a story? It seems that it can. We can all understand that professional criminals act from a motive of profit, and a cloak might be worth money to them. If we can put ourselves in the situation of someone in the ancient world, there is enough of the commonality of what can be expected in a situation of this sort that we can understand that it would be expected for the professional criminals to take the cloak. So this story, even though it is very short one, does give us at least some reason to have reservations about the hypothesis that professional criminals killed V. The explanation of professional criminals killing V does not hang together as a coherent story.

Let's move on to consider the second counterargument. The explanation here is that someone who is drunk killed V, but this explanation is attacked by the counterargument that the murderer would be identified by his fellow guests. This is not a very plausible story as it stands. But perhaps it could be made more plausible by filling in some implicit assumptions. According to the facts of the case the victim was on his way home from a banquet where, presumably, the participants would be drinking wine. The suggestion appears to be that, since this incident took place in an isolated location, the murderer would have been one of the participants in the banquet. If so, it would be likely that the murderer would be somehow identified by being linked to the victim as a fellow participant in the banquet. The story is very sketchy, however. It is not quite clear what the connections are. This story does seem to provide some sort of attempted explanation of why the hypothesis that a drunken banquet participant killed V can be rejected, but it does not seem to be a strong counterargument because the explanation does not hang together as well as it should.

Comparable remarks can be made about the explanations offered in counterargument −3 and −4. Here too, we can reconstruct the arguments as explanations, but as explanations they are weak and sketchy compared to the much more coherent explanation given for the chosen hypothesis. If this is a reasonable analysis of the argumentation in the Antiphon case it can be seen that although this case is similar to the disappearing sailor case in some important respects, it also goes beyond the disappearing sailor case in its depth, and is dissimilar in a certain respect. Instead of pitting one fairly strong explanation against competitors that are not supported by any story, it pits one fairly strong explanation against competitors that do have stories attached to them. However, compared to the chosen explanation, the competing explanations are less complete, less elaborate, and less plausible.

## 2.8 Graph Structures for Explanations and Arguments

The argument diagramming technique illustrated in Figs. 2.3 and 2.4 shows a certain way of modeling arguments comparable to the way Thagard and Shelly (1997) modeled abductive reasoning. It models arguments using argument graphs consisting of argument nodes linked to statement nodes. In the mathematical field of graph theory, a directed graph is a structure made up of a set of nodes (vertices, points) connected by a set of edges (arcs, directed edges, arrows). An unordered graph can be simply defined as an unordered pair G = (N, A), where N is the set of nodes and A is the set of arrows. A directed graph can then be defined as a set of ordered pairs of nodes and arrows. Note that directed graphs can contain cycles of the sort shown in Fig. 2.8.

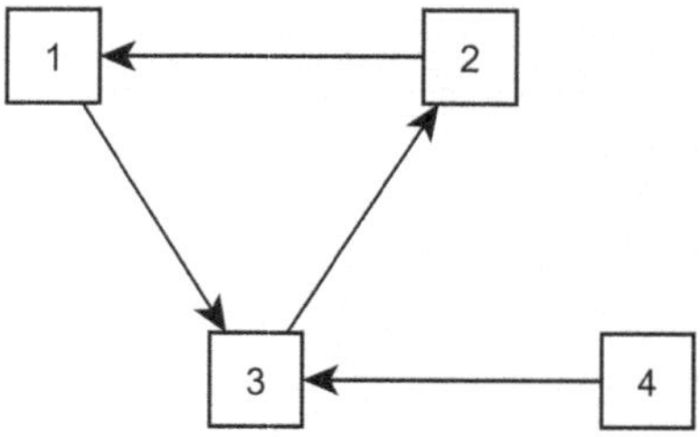


**Fig. 2.8** A cycle in a directed graph

In Fig. 2.8, the cycle is shown as the sequence of nodes 1, 3, 2, 1. A bipartite graph is a graph in which the nodes can be separated into two independent sets $N_1$ and $N_2$ such that every arrow in the graph connects a vertex in $N_1$ to one in $N_2$. It has been shown that a bipartite graph can equivalently be defined as one that does not contain any odd length cycles. Figures 2.5 and 2.6 in drawn in the style of CAS to represent arguments take the form of bipartite graphs in which there are two independent sets of nodes. The rectangle nodes represent propositions (premises or conclusions) and the circle nodes represent arguments. The premises and conclusions of an argument graph are represented as rectangular (text box) nodes. Argument nodes are of two types, pro and con, indicated by the plus or minus sign in the argument node. The name of an argumentation scheme may also be inserted into an argument node. Such argument graphs define the structure of arguments in a particular stage of dialogue. In Chap. 4 it will be shown how argument graphs of this sort can be evaluated.

Explanations are also modeled as directed graphs, as shown in Figs. 2.6 and 2.7., but in a different way. The examples shown in these two figures are linear graphs, but it is also normal to have branching graphs representing explanations. The statements appearing in the text boxes, such as the ones shown in Figs. 2.6 and 2.7, represent propositions describing actions or events. The actions or events appearing in the text boxes are connected together as a graph in an order representing the natural way the proponent of the argument and the audience would expect such a sequence of events to normally proceed. Any sequence that appears to be different, such as one that exhibits an inconsistency or a missing link in the sequence that is unexplained, will appear to the audience to be an anomaly. For this reason an anomalous sequence of this sort will naturally give rise to a request for an explanation. Such a sequence of events and actions representing an explanation hangs together as a holistic network that is more plausible if it is more coherent, and fulfills eight criteria for plausible reasoning in a good explanation (see just below). Explanations are not subject to attack or support in the same way arguments are, but they can be examined critically and questioned, especially if part of the explanation is not plausible or if there are gaps in the explanation that need to be filled before it can describe a natural sequence of events that makes sense. On the other hand, explanations are similar to arguments, because they can be attacked and supported by evidence that is independent of and external to the explanation. This evidence comes from propositions that are taken to be factual by the audience, and that are accepted by the audience as such. Hybrid graphs can be used to model cases where arguments are used to support or attack an explanation.

Arguments and explanations of the kinds we have studied in the examples so far are typically based on plausible reasoning. For example, it is interesting to recall that in the very first example of IBE that we considered, the short example from (Wigmore 1940, 420), Wigmore described how the conclusion is derived by commenting that the desired explanation arose from among other explanations to a fair degree of plausibility. Eleven characteristics of plausible reasoning are listed in (Walton et al. 2014). Eight of them are relevant to the task of evaluating one explanation as more plausible than another, based on the reasoning contained in the explanation.

1. Plausible reasoning is based on common knowledge.
2. Plausible reasoning is defeasible.
3. Plausible reasoning is based on the way things generally go in familiar situations.
4. Plausible reasoning can be used to fill in implicit premises in incomplete arguments.
5. Plausible reasoning is commonly based on appearances from perception.
6. Stability is an important characteristic of plausible reasoning.
7. Plausible reasoning can be tested, and by this means, confirmed or refuted.
8. Probing into plausible reasoning in a dialogue is a way of testing it.

These characteristics can be applied to the way of modeling an explanation as a story illustrated in this chapter. The second one makes possible the feature that an explanation that is supposed to be plausible can be supported or attacked by arguments joined to the explanation. The fifth one shows the connection of plausible reasoning with witness testimony in many instances.

In important respects, as we have seen, arguments and explanations are very different, and need to be treated differently as components of evidential reasoning. There is a clear contrast with the graph structures used to model arguments and the scripts used to represent explanations. When using argument mapping tools to analyze and evaluate a particular argument, one has to be very careful to stick very closely to the wording of the text of discourse in the given case. As we saw, in some instances implicit premises that were not explicitly stated in the given text of discourse need to be added in. Each implicit additional premise or conclusion added into an argument diagram must be carefully justified by citing evidence from the text of discourse showing the inference from that evidence to the propositions selected, based on a shared common knowledge of the audience and the proponent of the argument. Building an argument diagram to interpret and analyze a given argument requires a very careful procedure in which each inference from a set of premises to a conclusion can either be represented by an inference rule like DMP or an argumentation scheme, or else it must clearly represent an inference that can be justifiably drawn based on the given text of discourse and appropriate rules of inference. Arguments are subject to attack by counterarguments, and subject to support by corroborating arguments or by evidence, such as that based on testimony.

## 2.9 The Forward and Backward Relation

From a practical point of view of those working in the field of argumentation, either inside or outside legal argumentation, the question is what method can be used to model inference to the best explanation? Such a method would seem to require merging argument and explanation together, for after all inference to the best explanation is not only an extremely common form of argument, but also involves the concept of explanation. The problem is how to combine the two concepts together in some kind of practical working method of dealing with abductive reasoning (Pardo and Allen 2008).

The Wigmore diagrams do have a device for combining arguments and explanations. And looking at the examples that Wigmore used, he certainly had a grasp of the working use of inference to the best explanation, and regarded this type of evidential argumentation as fundamentally important. But Wigmore viewed explanations in a special kind of way, for purposes of drawing up evidential charts, as being a way of counter-attacking an argument by "explaining it away". This approach really won't suit our purposes here, for two reasons. One is that we have a much more robustly developed concept of explanation, and according to this concept arguments are distinctively different from explanations in the way they are used. The other is that Wigmore charts are much more complex than the kinds of argument diagramming tools currently used in artificial intelligence and in argumentation studies, and although they certainly can be used to diagram evidential legal argumentation, there are now better tools available. From the point of view of the way argument diagrams are currently used both in argumentation studies and by automated argument assistant tools that have diagramming component, Wigmore's method of combining arguments and explanations does not seem to be especially useful.

To see how arguments and explanations are related to each other in a way that can give us a clue on how to coordinate them in argument diagrams and explanation diagrams based on scripts, let's look back to the argument diagram of the sheep herders example presented in Fig. 2.5. This argument diagram has the proposition 'D killed W' as its ultimate conclusion. Supporting this proposition is an argument from motive to action, and supporting one premise of this argument there are three arguments from action to motive. The sequence moving forward to the ultimate proposition shown at the top of the diagram is naturally interpreted as an argument that presents evidence supporting the ultimate conclusion. But if we look at the argument backward, in other words proceeding in a sequence from top to bottom, it can also appear to represent an explanation of why D killed W. It provides this explanation by stating that there is a motive of animosity against sheep herders, adding that W was a sheep herder. It then provides some evidence to support the proposition that D had a motive of animosity against sheep herders. This lower part of the diagram is really an argument, as opposed to an explanation, but still it is helpful in supporting the explanation.

The part of the diagram shown at the top can be seen as an explanation if it is viewed backwards from the argument point of view. How can it work in both a backward and forward way to have these two different functions? The reason is that a motive can be used to prove or give evidence to support a proposition about an agent's actions, but a motive can also be used to explain why an agent carried out a particular action.

Comparable observations can be made about the argument diagrams of the disappearing sailor case and the Antiphon case shown in Figs. 2.3 and 2.4. In Fig. 2.3, the part of the argument diagram shown at the lower left is an argument supporting the proposition that S murdered M. But when viewed from a backward perspective, it can be seen as providing two explanations. One is an explanation of how S murdered M by showing that he had an opportunity to do so. The other is an explanation of why S murdered M, by showing that he had a motive to do so. These two explanations are combined in the story diagram shown in Fig. 2.6 that combines motive and opportunity into an orderly temporal sequence leading up to the proposition that S has killed M.

Similarly Fig. 2.4, the argument diagram that shows the evidential reasoning in the Antiphon case, as a sequence of argumentation displayed beneath the proposition that D murdered V that explains why D might have carried out this action by attributing a motive to him. The precise nature of this motive and the events that led up to it are presented in the rest of this argument, and also in the story diagram shown in Fig. 2.7. Seen in a backward way, the part of the argument diagram at the right bottom of Fig. 2.4 performs an explanatory function comparable to the explanation diagram shown in Fig. 2.7.

This backward and forward relationship is typical of the use of practical reasoning in everyday conversational argumentation in natural language (Walton 1990b). In trying to decide what to do in everyday deliberations, we often base the reasoning on some kind of goal that we have formulated which it is reasonable to have, and then search around for means to contribute to the realization of this goal. Having found this means, a rational agent can then proceed to carry out an action, or sequence of actions, that will implement this means. Such an example of forward reasoning in deliberation is an instance of practical reasoning used as an argument to justify a conclusion that a particular action should be carried out. But the same kind of practical reasoning can be applied backward when one is trying to figure out what the goal or motivation of another agent might be by observing its actions in a given set of circumstances. In this kind of case, the reasoning goes from the actions as evidence and derives a conclusion about what are taken to be the goals of the agent who carried out those actions.

## 2.10 Conclusions

The solution to the problem posed by the cases studied in the chapter is to be found in matching up the forward and backward movements of the practical reasoning in the cases, following the evidential structure set in place by Walton and Schafer (2006). The argumentation sequence moves forward in both main cases to the ultimate conclusion that the defendant committed murder. The explanation sequence moves backward from the action allegedly carried out by the defendant, murdering the victim, to an attribution of a motive. The motive and the action hang together, along with the other parts of the story, as a plausible explanation of why the murder was committed. These examples show the usefulness of having an argumentation scheme for abductive reasoning, and thereby modeling it not just as a form of reasoning but also as a form of argument.

To manage the examples of inference to the best explanation discussed in this chapter, we need an argumentation scheme for abductive reasoning with a matching set of critical questions. The scheme offered by the Josephsons (Josephson and Josephson 1994, 14), as shown in this chapter, Sect. 2.4, has the following form, where *H* is a variable representing a hypothesis and *D* is a variable representing a given set of data or (presumed) facts. It basically says that if *D* is a collection of data, and hypothesis *H* explains *D*, and no other hypothesis can explain *D* as well as *H* does, then *H* is plausibly true. The Josephsons did not specifically use an argumentation model and so did not claim that the form of inference to the best explanation they had identified was an argumentation scheme. However, the device they used to evaluate instances of inference to the best explanation (1994, 14) was formulated as a set of questions.

1. How decisively does *H* surpass the alternative explanations?
2. How good is *H* by itself, independently of the alternatives?
3. How reliable are the data?
4. How much confidence is there that all plausible explanations have been considered?
5. Are there practical considerations, including the costs of being wrong?
6. How urgent is the need is to come to a conclusion at all before seeking further evidence?

According to the Josephsons, the conclusion to be inferred using this scheme is selected by choosing the best explanation of the data.

There is also a more recent account (Walton et al. 2008, 329–330) that does present inference to the best explanation as an argumentation scheme with a matching set of critical questions. In fact, two such schemes are offered. The backward scheme is the one comparable to the analysis of abductive reasoning given by the Josephsons. The term ‘account’ in this scheme can be taken here as equivalent to the term ‘explanation’. An explanation is defined in (Walton 2005) as an account of some connected sequence of events or actions that helps to transfer understanding from one party to another through a process of communication. An account is equated with what is called a story, a notion analyzed through the concept of a script that has come to us from studies in artificial intelligence (Bex 2011). The literature in artificial intelligence and law shows how the use of stories both to explain and to argue can be tested against evidence, such as circumstantial and testimonial evidence.

**Backward Argumentation Scheme**

PREMISE 1: $D$ is a set of data or supposed facts in a case.
PREMISE 2: Each one of a set of accounts $A_1, A_2, \ldots, A_n$ is successful in explaining $D$.
PREMISE 3: $A_i$ is the account that explains $D$ most successfully
CONCLUSION: Therefore $A_i$ is the most plausible hypothesis in the case.

But there is also a forward scheme that utilizes a graph structure well known to argumentation theorists because it is the basic structure of the commonly used argument diagrams illustrated in Chap. 1 and this chapter.

**Forward Argumentation Scheme**

PREMISE 1: $D$ is a set of data or supposed facts in a case.
PREMISE 2: There is a set of argument graphs $G_1, G_2, \ldots, G_n$, and in each argument graph $D$ represents premises of an argument that, supplemented with plausible conditionals and other statements that function as missing parts of enthymemes, leads to a respective conclusion $C_1, C_2, \ldots, C_n$.
PREMISE 3: The most plausible (strongest) argument is represented by $G_i$.
CONCLUSION: Therefore $C_i$ is the most plausible conclusion in the case.

The forward scheme is more difficult to grasp until more is explained in Chap. 3 about how diagrams can consist of graphs that combine arguments with explanations. Also given in (Walton et al. 2008, 330) is a list of critical questions matching the first scheme, but also easily adaptable to the second one.

**Critical Questions for IBE**

$CQ_1$: How satisfactory is $A_i$ itself as an explanation of $D$, apart from the alternative explanations available so far in the dialogue?
$CQ_2$: How much better an explanation is $A_i$ than the alternative explanation so far in the dialogue?
$CQ_3$: How far has the dialogue progressed? If the dialogue is an inquiry, how thorough has the search been in the investigation of the case?
$CQ_4$: Would it be better to continue the dialogue further, instead of drawing a conclusion at this point?

Note that the scheme offered by Walton, Reed and Macagno depends on two devices, the use of argument graphs and the use of formal models of dialogue. In Chap. 3 a theory of explanation is ventured that combines these two devices, showing how both arguments and explanation can be modeled by a hybrid graph structure that combines arguments with explanations.

The story shown in Fig. 2.6 is a successful explanation of what happened, based on the evidential facts, because it hangs together as a believable story that explains in a comprehensible way what might quite plausibly have happened in the case. It offers an explanation supporting the hypothesis that S murdered M. It is good

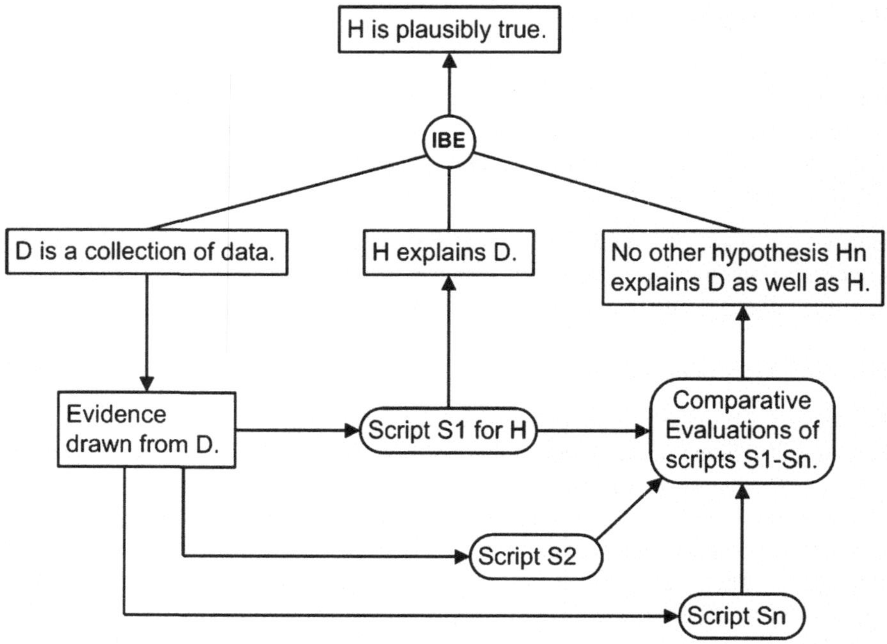


**Fig. 2.9** Fitting arguments and explanations together with IBE

enough to support the claim that it is the best explanation of the facts of the case, of those considered. Accordingly, it can now be seen and appreciated how an instance of abductive reasoning moves forward by an argument based on the IBE scheme to the conclusion that the selected hypothesis is plausibly true.

A schematic outline of this structure is shown in Fig. 2.9. The premises of the IBE argument are evidentially based on a comparative evaluation of the explanations based on the competing scripts (as many as there are, if any). The scripts are collected from the evidential data in the case. During the process of examination of any or all of the stories that may ensue, new propositions are added to or deleted from D. If there is a tie between equally plausible stories, the IBE cannot go through.

In the disappearing sailor case and the Antiphon case, the competing explanations to the selected one are either nonexistent or else sketchy and incomplete. The selected explanation was clearly the most comprehensive one. In these cases, relative to the evidence made available in the description of the case, the one explanation stands out as obviously the most plausible and well supported one. No information was given in these cases on how well each of the explanations that were offered stood up to critical questioning on examination. And the selected cases are clearly more comprehensive in covering relevant events and in filling in gaps. In these cases there was not much of a contest between the selected story and its competitors. That is not a disadvantage of using these cases for the purposes they were designed to investigate in this chapter, because their comparative simplicity enables the reader not to get lost in the details of trying to outline the mass of evidence in a fully described criminal case.

In the standard literature, IBE is described as a form of reasoning different from argument. One of the main lessons brought out by this chapter is that IBE is better seen as a type of argument. But when seen in this way, a particularly subtle aspect of the structure of IBE becomes apparent. It combines argument with explanation. Although there are different ways of defining abductive reasoning in the different disciplines, this book will take the approach that abductive reasoning is most fruitfully defined as inference to the best explanation, and secondarily, that inferences drawn by abductive reasoning represent not only a form of argument, but a form of argument incorporating explanation within it. This approach at first seems to make IBE much more complicated, but nevertheless the complication is worth it, because it opens the way to a much more practical and realistic model of IBE revealing how the power of IBE resides in its being based on human understanding and common knowledge concerning expectations of the ways things can normally be expected to go in familiar situations. Because it links IBE in this way to the way the human mind carries out routine actions by encapsulating them in familiar sequences, this approach has considerable power in helping artificial intelligence to build autonomous agents to use goal-based intelligent practical reasoning. Chapter 1 began with simple cases where abductive reasoning is used as a form of evidential reasoning as it could take place in a single mind. But Chap. 3 moves on to consider multiagent instances of inference to the best explanation where IBE is seen as a form of argumentation that needs to be evaluated in light of communicative speech acts in multiagent explanation settings.

To get any further with seeing how argument and explanation should be fitted together in cases of inference to the best explanation in evidential reasoning, it is necessary to provide an analysis of the concept of explanation. This analysis must provide a model of explanation that fits with the requirements of the examples of IBE studied in Chap. 1 and this chapter, and offer a method of explanation evaluation aid in judging whether one explanation is better than another.

## References


Bex, F.J. 2011. *Arguments, stories and criminal evidence: A formal hybrid theory*. Dordrecht: Springer.

Bex, F.J. 2013. Abductive argumentation with stories. Workshop on formal aspects of evidential inference (International Conference on AI and Law, 2013, Rome). http://www.florisbex.com/papers/BexStoriesValues.pdf. Accessed 22 Feb 2013 at this site.

Diels, H., and W. Kranz. 1952. *Die Fragmente der Vorsokratiker*. Berlin: Weidmannsche Verlags-buchhandlung.

Goodwin, J. 2000. Wigmore's chart method. *Informal Logic* 20(3): 223–243.

Josephson, J.R., and S.G. Josephson. 1994. *Abductive inference: Computation, philosophy, technology*. New York: Cambridge University Press.

Leonard, D.P. 2001. Character and motive in evidence law. *Loyola of Los Angeles Law Review* 34(2): 439–536.

Pardo, M.S., and R.J. Allen. 2008. Juridical proof and the best explanation. *Law and Philosophy* 27(3): 223–268.

Pennington, N., and R. Hastie. 1993. The story model for juror decision making. In *Inside the juror: The psychology of juror decision making*, ed. R. Hastie, 192–221. Cambridge: Cambridge University Press.

Prakken, H. 2010. An abstract framework for argumentation with structured arguments. *Argument & Computation* 1(2): 93–124.

Schank, R.C., and R.P. Abelson. 1977. *Scripts, plans, goals and understanding*. Hillsdale: Erlbaum.

Thagard, P., and C. Shelley. 1997. Abductive reasoning: Logic, visual thinking, and coherence. In *Logic and Scientific Methods*, ed. M.-L. Dalla Chiara et al., 413–427. Dordrecht: Kluwer, http://cogsci.uwaterloo.ca/Articles/Pages/%7FAbductive.html

Wagenaar, W.A., P.J. van Koppen, and H.F.M. Crombag. 1993. *Anchored narratives: The psychology of criminal evidence*. Hemel Hempstead: Harvester Wheatsheaf.

Walton, D. 1990a. *Practical reasoning: Goal-driven, knowledge-based, action-guiding argumentation*. Savage: Rowman & Littlefield.

Walton, D. 1990b. What is reasoning? What is an argument? *Journal of Philosophy* 87(8): 399–419.

Walton, D. 2005. *Abductive reasoning*. Tuscaloosa: The University of Alabama Press.

Walton, D. 2010. Why fallacies appear to be better arguments than they are. *Informal Logic* 30(2): 159–184.

Walton, D., and F. Macagno. 2005. Common knowledge in legal reasoning about evidence. *International Commentary on Evidence* 3(1): 1–42.

Walton, D., and B. Schafer. 2006. Arthur, George and the mystery of the missing motive: Towards a theory of evidentiary reasoning about motives. *International Commentary on Evidence* 4(2): 1–47.

Walton, D., C. Reed, and F. Macagno. 2008. *Argumentation schemes*. Cambridge: Cambridge University Press.

Walton, D., C.W. Tindale, and T.F. Gordon. 2014. Applying recent argumentation methods to some ancient examples of plausible reasoning. *Argumentation* 28(1): 85–119.

Wigmore, J.H. 1931. *The principles of judicial proof*. Boston: Little, Brown and Company.

Wigmore, J.H. 1935. *A student's textbook of the law of evidence*. Chicago: The Foundation Press.

Wigmore, J.H. 1940. *A treatise on the Anglo-American system of evidence in trial at common law*, vol. 1, 3rd ed. Boston: Little, Brown and Company.

# Chapter 3
# A Dialogue System for Evaluating Explanations

**Abstract** This chapter presents a theory of explanation by building a dialectical system that has speech act rules that define the kinds of moves allowed, such as putting forward an argument, requesting an explanation and offering an explanation. Pre and post-condition rules for the speech acts determine when a particular speech act can be put forward as a move in the dialogue, and what type of move or moves must follow it. This chapter offers a dialogue structure with three stages, an opening stage, an explanation stage and a closing stage, and shows how an explanation dialogue can shift to other types of dialogue known in argumentation studies such as persuasion dialogue and deliberation dialogue. Such shifts can go from argumentation to explanation and back again. The problem of evaluating explanations is solved by extending the hybrid system of (Bex, Arguments, stories and criminal evidence: a formal hybrid theory. Springer, Dordrecht, 2011) which combines explanations and arguments to include a method of testing stories called examination dialogue. In this type of dialogue an explanation can be probed and tested by arguments. The result is a method of evaluating explanations.

Arguments are different from explanations. Arguments are supposed to be used to prove a disputable claim whereas explanations are supposed to be used to convey understanding to an audience, or to someone who has encountered an anomaly, something he or she is puzzled about and does not understand. To use this distinction to be able to tell the difference we have to define putting forward an argument and putting forward an explanation as two distinctively different types of speech acts. Both these speech acts need to be embedded in a framework in which two rational agents communicate with each other for some communicative purpose, requiring a formal dialogue model.

Dialogue models of argumentation of the kind developed in Walton and Krabbe (1995) are now proving their worth as tools useful for solving many problems in argumentation studies, artificial intelligence, and multi-agent systems. Many formal dialogue systems have been built (Bench-Capon 2003; Prakken 2005, 2006), and through their applications (Verheij 2003), we are getting a much better idea of the general requirements for such systems, and how to build them. Reed (2006) has provided a dialogue system specification that enables anyone to construct a formal dialogue model of argumentation by specifying its components and how they are


D. Walton, *Argument Evaluation and Evidence*, Law, Governance and Technology Series 23, DOI 10.1007/978-3-319-19626-8_3

combined (Reed 2006, 26). This dialogue system specification provides a more convenient method for setting up formal dialogue systems of kinds that are useful for modeling argumentation in computing and that are currently being built for various applications (Wells and Reed 2012). According to the argument of this chapter, a variant on Reed's dialogue system specification can also be applied to dialogue systems for explanation, and it offers a logical and philosophical basis for the notion of explanation employed in case-based systems of explanation (Leake 1992; Schank et al. 1994).

Dialogue models of explanation in computing are based on examples of dialogical sequences of questions and answers in which one party tries to explain to another how some machinery works (Cawsey 1992; Moore 1995). The dialogues incorporate user feedback that enables the explanation process to recover from misunderstandings. A more abstract prototype dialogue theory of explanation CE has been built in (Walton 2007a). According to this theory, both asking for and providing an explanation consist of special types of moves (speech acts) that have pre and post condition rules in dialogues. The hybrid model of Bex (2011) will turn out be especially important, because it combines arguments and explanations. This chapter builds on these models, using them to provide practical methods for evaluating explanations.

## 3.1 Two Examples

We begin this section with two examples of explanations of the kind that might be classified under the category of everyday explanations that we all encounter and use on a daily basis in conversational exchanges. These examples give the reader an idea of the target we are aiming at in providing a theory of explanation.

The first example, an explanation by a science teacher to an audience of students (Unsworth 2001, 589), is used in science education. The explanation assumes that the students are expected to know that coal is widely used as an energy source, that it is black and fairly hard, and that it is found in the earth. It also assumes that the students may not be familiar with the process of how coal is formed in the earth. Here is the explanation given by the teacher to the students: "Coal is formed from the remains of plant material buried for millions of years. First the plant material is turned into peat. Next the peat turns into brown coal. Finally the brown coal turns into black coal". The explanation is concise. It only represents a brief sequence of events that take the form of a script. But it relies on some implicit elements as well, in addition to the ones already mentioned. It is assumed that the students know what coal is, that they know what plant material is, that they know what peat is, and that they know that one material can change into another in the earth. The anomaly for the students that gives rise to their lack of understanding is that they also know that plant material is soft and brown, whereas they know that coal is hard and black. How could something that is hard and black come from something that is soft and brown? It is this anomaly that provokes the need for an explanation. Showing the intervening link of the peat helps the students come to understand enough about the process so that the anomaly is resolved. If not, and they ask further questions, very likely the science teacher can tell them more about the process, assuming that he or she has further scientific knowledge about the subject that they lack.

The reader will recall from Chap. 1, Sect. 1.6 how a comparable sequence of events in the case of the survival of the Galapagos finches was visually represented as a script. This script- based device of the explanation diagram used our common knowledge about how plants require water to grow, and so forth, to display the structure of an explanation of why some of these birds died and others survived. It was shown in Chap. 1, Sect. 1.6 using Fig. 1.4 how such an explanation diagram represents a natural sequence of events that all of us can understand, and once such a natural sequence is set out schematically, it provides a structural framework for modeling an explanation.

In another example, somebody asks why the radiators are usually located under the windows in a room, when windows are the greatest source of heat loss. The explainer assumes that the two of them share common knowledge about many implicit assumptions not stated in the explanation as given. For example, the explainer assumes that the questioner already knows that when warm and cold air are combined in an enclosed space, the warm air tends to rise and the cold air tends to fall. The question presents an anomaly. If the windows are the greatest source of heat loss, then putting the radiators under the windows in a room would seem to be wasteful of energy. So why is it so commonly done? To grasp the anomaly, you have to be aware of the common knowledge that building practices generally avoid doing things that are wasteful of energy. The following explanation is offered. The windows are the coldest part of the room, so when air in the room contacts the windows, it falls to the floor. After being heated by the radiator, however, it rises. This continuing procedure takes the form of a convection current in which the air continuously circulates around the room. This circular sequence of events presents a script or story as shown in Fig. 3.1.

But now suppose that the radiator were to be placed on the inside wall. In this case, the inside wall would stay warmer and there would be a noticeable temperature difference in the two areas that would not be comfortable for those in the room. In the script for this contrasting part of the explanation, we have an inside of the room that is too hot to be comfortable and a part near the windows that is too cold to be comfortable. In this script there is no convection current such as the one shown in Fig. 3.1. It is the contrast that provides the explanation. The respondent, in his explanation, puts forward a connected account showing how placement of the radiator under the window in a room generally leads to a convection current that circulates the warm and cold air around the room, mixing it together and providing a moderate temperature throughout the room that makes it comfortable for the occupants. The explanation works by contrasting this script with one for placing the radiator on the inside wall. No explanation diagram is given here for this contrasting script, for it would be a very simple one showing a warmer side of the room and a colder side with no air flow sufficient to restore the imbalance.

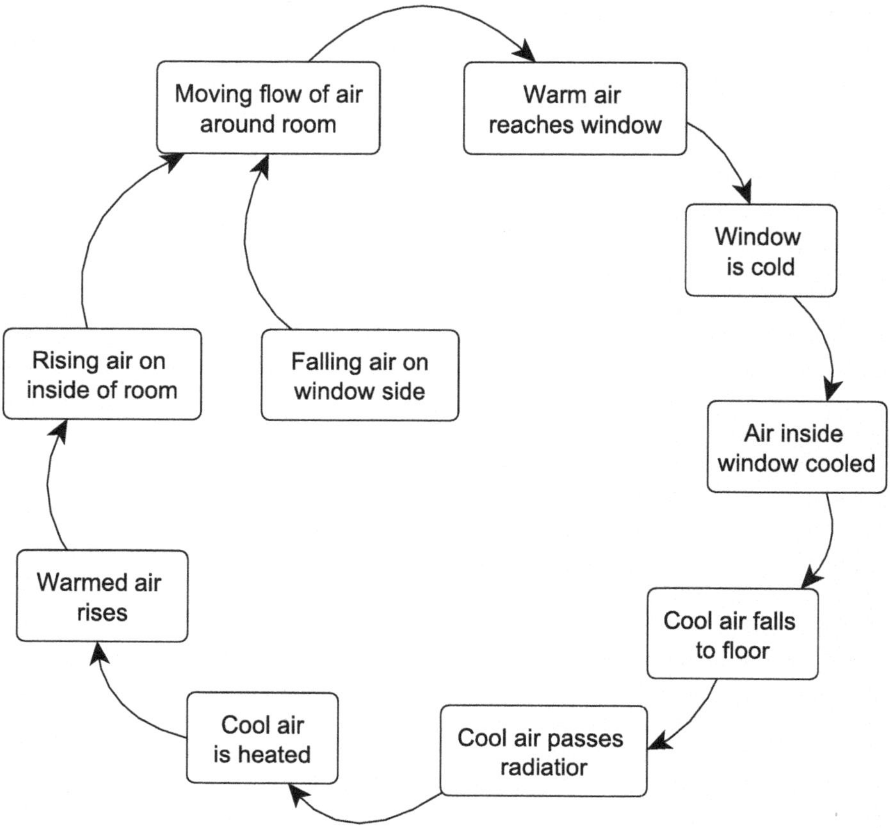


**Fig. 3.1** The radiator script

The question expresses an anomaly posed by the situation of the hot radiator under the window making a lot of heat wasted, if the windows are the greatest source of heat loss. This doesn't make sense because conservation of energy is a well-known goal in designing human habitation. Unnecessary heat loss is a bad thing, and so why the normal placement of radiators would lead to such apparently unnecessary heat loss is puzzling. The explanation solves the puzzle by giving an account of heat circulation in a room, showing that the heat loss is not as great as the questioner initially appeared to assume, and that putting the radiator elsewhere in the room would have negative consequences.

The aim of this chapter is to build a dialectical system of explanation primarily meant to be applicable to everyday examples like these two out of the following components.

- Opening Move: this move starts the explanation process when a request for an explanation is made by one party.
- Speech Act Rules: these rules define the different speech acts (kinds of moves) that are allowed in the dialogue.

- Pre and Post Condition Rules: these rules determine, respectively, (a) the conditions under which a speech act can be put forward as a move in the dialogue, and (b) which type of move (or moves) must follow it.
- Success Criterion: it determines when an explanation is successful, i.e. when transfer of understanding can be taken to have been achieved.
- Closing Move: this point occurs either when the explanation that was offered is successful, or when no explanation can be given, and therefore the dialogue should end. The former occurs when the dialogue has proceeded through a testing stage (if required) showing that the success criterion has been met.

As indicated by the success criterion, a successful explanation has been achieved when there has been a transfer of understanding from the party giving the explanation to the party asking for it. The purpose of offering an argument to another party is to give the other party a reason to accept a claim doubted by that other party. It is a proposition that is at issue, or is unsettled. The purpose of offering an explanation is to help the other party who indicates by his questioning that he doesn't understand something. If the explanation is to be helpful, it should help the questioner to come to understand something that he did not understand before. A successful explanation should make the questioner come to understand, by relating what he fails to understand to what he already understands. This statement of the goal of an explanation is a normative ideal, however. In real instances one party can mislead the other by giving an explanation that she knows to be wrong, or by accepting an inadequate explanation. Alternatively the party who receives the information may say she understands, or may even think she understands, but be wrong. It is assumed in the model that both participants will follow rules for co-operative dialogue, but as we will see, this Gricean assumption can be violated in real instances of explanations, and so real cases need to be tested for success.

But there are some hard questions posed by this way of defining the notion of explanation. How is it to be determined when such a transfer has taken place? What is understanding? This question seems like an especially hard one, as it could be rephrased as, 'How can we understand understanding?' Another question is how it can be tested whether an explanation is successful.

There are some important limitations to the scope of this chapter. One is that there is not enough space to apply the system to an extensively developed set of case studies of real explanations found in texts of every day discourse of the kind that can be found in (Cawsey 1992; Moore 1995; Leake 1992). The other is that although studying explanations in special fields is an important part of the topic, there is no space here to include topics like scientific explanation and historical explanation. However, in the problems for further research section, there are suggestions for further research on these matters, and some problems are posed that suggest how to extend the findings of the chapter in these directions.

## 3.2 Basic Components of an Explanation Dialogue

Von Wright (1971) described explanations that convey understanding of an action or event. Understanding, in this sense, should not be taken to refer merely to a feeling of personal confidence that one has understood something. Since then the notion of understanding has become a component in case-based explanation in artificial intelligence (Schank 1986; Schank and Abelson 1977; Schank and Riesback 1981; Schank et al. 1994). These case-based models of explanation are dialectical in that they involve a transfer of understanding between two parties who can communicate with each other. They also involve a sense of 'understanding' that is reconstructive in the sense that one party in a dialogue can use understanding of familiar situations to fill gaps in the understanding of another. In this sense, understanding should be taken to have a dialectical meaning that can be modeled in a framework of two parties reasoning together who share some common knowledge about how things normally go in stereotypical situations. To grasp this dialectical sense of understanding, we look to the formal dialogue models used to represent various aspects of argumentation (Reed 2006).

To grasp how transfer of understanding can be modeled in a formal rule-governed dialogue structure, we need to build on Hamblin's notion of the commitment store of a participant in a dialogue as analyzed in Walton and Krabbe (1995). As each partner in a dialogue makes a move, statements are inserted into his/her commitment store, or deleted from it. For example, if a party asserts statement *A*, then *A* is inserted into her/his commitment set. A commitment store is basically just a set of statements, but inferences can be drawn from these statements representing implicit commitments. If an agent is committed to one statement, then the other party to the dialogue can often assume justifiably that he must be committed to other related statements as well. Of course, she can always ask him. But in many cases she can assume that he is committed to some statement indirectly, based on what he said. For example, suppose Bob went to a pizzeria and ordered a pizza. It can normally be assumed that he is committed to paying for the pizza before he leaves the pizzeria. Also, the retraction of one's commitment often requires a stability adjustment, meaning that other statements implying this commitment will also have to be retracted in order to preserve consistency (Walton and Krabbe 1995, 144–149). In a rigorous persuasion dialogue (RPD), the moves and responses are restricted tightly by the rules so that what is allowed is precisely indicated as a small number of options at each move. For example, only yes-no questions can be asked, and the only answer allowed is yes or no. In a permissive persuasion dialogue (PPD), participants have more choices regarding what kinds of moves they can make at each turn, and how many things they can say at a given move (Walton and Krabbe 1995, 126). Also, responses to a previous move are less strictly determined. For example, a party may be allowed to put forward an argument and ask a question at the same move. In either type of dialogue, commitment sets do not always have to be consistent, but if one party's commitment set can be shown by the other party to be logically inconsistent, the first party needs to remove the inconsistency, and perhaps also retract other commitments related to it.

The rules governing the operations of commitment sets in formal dialogue systems (Wells and Reed 2012) are used as a basis in this chapter to show a way toward representing transfer of understanding in an explanation dialogue. At the beginning of an explanation dialogue, each party is assumed to have a knowledge base that operates more or less like a commitment store in an argumentation dialogue. Each knowledge base is a set of statements, including particular statements and general statements that can act as rules to draw inferences by applying them to other statements. The participants must also share a common knowledge base containing general and particular common knowledge about the event that is to be explained. This common knowledge base contains common-sense procedural knowledge that enables a language user to understand how things typically happen in stereotypical situations, enabling her/him to fill in missing elements not explicitly stated in a given text of discourse.

As shown in Chap. 2, Sect. 2.5, these commonly known normal ways of doing things in familiar situations were codified in early work in AI (Schank and Abelson 1977) using what they called scripts. This theory was based on the hypothesis that much common sense reasoning is based on unstated assumptions in a text of discourse that can be added in to fill gaps to make chains of reasoning explicit. The standard illustration is the restaurant example, a version of which was presented in Chap. 2, Sect. 2.5. Consider the following less exciting version consisting of the following set of seven explicit statements. (1) John went to a restaurant. (2) The hostess seated John. (3) The waitress gave John a menu. (4) John ordered a lobster. (5) He was served. (6) He left a tip. (7) He left the restaurant. The account implicit in this set of statements can be made explicit by filling in gaps through drawing plausible inferences. We can infer defeasibly that lobster was listed on the menu. Maybe it was a special item not listed on the menu, and the waitress told John about it. Still, from statements (3) and (4) in the list, we can derive the implicit statement by inference that lobster was listed on the menu. Normally restaurant customers get their information about what is available from the menu they are given. It is also reasonable to infer defeasibly that John ate the lobster. We can fill in gaps by inserting implicit statements based on implicit assumptions about the normal ways of doing things when a person goes to a restaurant.

A more flexible way to represent familiar routines that represent common knowledge is to use smaller modules called MOPs, or memory organization packages (Schank 1986). These also represent stereotyped sequences of events, but are smaller than scripts and can be combined in a way that is appropriate for the situation when they are needed. For example, the space launch MOP includes a launch, a space walk and a re-entry (Leake 1992, 73) as parts of a package of connected events. MOPs are used in case-based reasoning (CBR), a pragmatic approach to explanation used in AI. CBR is the process of solving new problems based on the solutions of similar past problems. A mechanic who fixes an engine by recalling the cases of another car with a similar problem uses CBR. Scripts and MOPs can be used to build or amplify a story, a connected sequence of events or actions that hangs together, is ordered as a sequence, and that contains gaps that can be filled in. In such a case, the explanation that was given may not only need to be filled out by making implicit parts of it explicit, some parts of it may have to be justified by producing arguments to back them up. Here we are dealing not just with explanations, but also with arguments used to support an explanation.

Each participant's understanding of the anomaly being discussed will change and evolve over the course of a dialogue. At the beginning of an explanation dialogue both participants share a common knowledge base containing the MOPs needed for the explanation queries and attempts that will follow. As the part of the dialogue where the explanation is asked for and provided proceeds, MOPs will be brought forward from the knowledge base that was there at the beginning. The MOPs are inserted for use by the participants and deleted when they are not in use. Hence they operate in a way comparable to the way that commitment stores operate in an argumentation dialogue.

The MOPs at the beginning of a dialogue represent the way things can normally be expected to go in kinds of situations that are familiar to both parties. During the later part of the dialogue one party puts forward an account of something that happened, a kind of story that may or not be true in reality, but that neither party wants to dispute. The other party may find something puzzling in the account, something that does not look normal or quite right, and ask for an explanation of the perceived anomaly. As the dialogue proceeds, statements will be inserted into or deleted from each party's knowledge base as each of them makes moves in the dialogue. What triggers the need for an explanation is that one party fails to understand something in the account that the other is taken to understand. Then the other party is expected to amplify the account in a way that will provide the required understanding.

CBR explanation systems have already been implemented that roughly fit the dialogue framework so far sketched out. For example, ACCEPTER (Leake 1992) is a computer system for story understanding, anomaly detection and explanation evaluation. Explanations are directed towards filling knowledge gaps revealed by anomalies. ACCEPTER has two special features. (1) Explanations are built from uncertain inferences based on plausible reasoning. (2) Context (including explainer beliefs and goals) is crucial to explanation evaluation. The examples of stories processed by ACCEPTER include the death of a race horse, the death of a basketball star, the explosion of the space shuttle Challenger, the recall of Audi 5000 cars for transmission problems, a fictional story about a lame racehorse that wins a race, and an account of an airliner that leaves from the wrong departure gate (Leake 1992, 38). Although ACCEPTER fits some parts of the explanation dialogue system built below, it does not fit all of them. Some problems in building the system will especially bring out features that arguably do not fit with ACCEPTER.

In this chapter, the aim is not to build a formal dialectical model representing any particular type of explanation, nor is it to build an implemented explanation system for computing like ACCEPTER. Rather the aim is to build a general stencil or format, a dialogue system specification for explanation. Reed (2006) has already specified the general requirements for a dialogue system specification as follows. A dialogue is a set of moves from a first one to a last one, where the two parties (in the simplest case) take turns making moves. The system needs to set out what locutions (speech acts) are permitted for the participants to make at each move. The pre-conditions are the conditions that must be met before one of the locutions can be legally uttered. The specification also needs to set out conditions defining what counts as an acceptable reply (next move) to any given type of move. These are called the post-conditions of a move. A dialogue system can be captured completely according to Reed (2006, 26) by specifying the pre-conditions and post-conditions of every possible locution, along with two other factors. One is the set of rules governing the participants' commitment stores and the other is a list of the termination states of the dialogue: "Pre and post conditions can be completely specified by listing those dialogic obligations, commitment store entries and structural conditions that their locutions depend upon or establish". Reed's specifications are intended to apply to formal dialogue systems for argumentation, and the question is whether comparable conditions can be adapted to a dialogue system for explanation.

We model all the types of dialogue as having three stages, an opening stage, an argumentation stage and a closing stage. The model of explanation dialogue proposed here will have three corresponding stages, an opening stage, an explanation stage and a closing stage. The goal of an explanation type of dialogue is for there to be a transfer of understanding from the one party to the other. At the opening stage, the participants agree to take part in a certain type of dialogue, and to follow the rules and conventions of the dialogue, which they both understand and accept. At this stage, it should be clear, for example, that they are engaging in an explanation dialogue, as opposed to some other type of dialogue like an argumentation dialogue, or some dialogue in which information is simply to be exchanged. During the explanation stage, a request for an explanation is made, and then the other party responds to the request. Following these moves, the two parties make other kinds of moves that are ideally supposed to lead to the closing stage, where the explanation is judged to be successful or not.

In the explanation dialogue system CE of Walton (2007a, b), the closing stage had two rules. The first states that if the explainee makes the reply 'I don't understand' in response to an explanation offered by the explainer, the dialogue can continue. The second rule states that if the explainee makes the reply 'I understand' in response to an explanation, the dialogue ends at that move. This attempt to provide closure rules was based on the assumption that the criterion for the successful completion of the dialogue is the explainee's being satisfied with the explanation given by the explainer. The problem with this criterion is that the explainee could be faking, or could simply be mistaken. Even though he says he now understands what he formerly did not, this may simply not be true. Even though he has the psychological feeling that he understands, it may well be that he does not really understand the explanation that was offered. In other words, we need a better test for the success of an explanation other than its being acceptable or feeling right to the explainee. The new system of explanation dialogue Explainer built in the next section has a different criterion.

## 3.3 The Explainer Dialogue System

For it to be clear that the two participants are starting an explanation dialogue, four requirements must be met. The first two are more general and the second two are more specific, requiring an introduction of some other notions. The first requirement is that the two parties to the dialogue share understanding of some things, and especially that they share and accept some common knowledge about the way things normally work in some domain they are familiar with. The second requirement is that one party, called the explainer, is presumed to have understanding of something that the second party, called the explainee, lacks. In the example of the teacher explaining to students how coal is formed, it is presumed that the teacher has scientific understanding of this process and that the students do not. This example also shows that the situation is not so simple. For example, it is assumed that there is more than one student in the class. But to make as simple a structure as possible for the basic notions, the dialogue system specification assumes that there are only two participants in a dialogue representing the roles of explainer and explainee. We need to stress though that in real cases of explanations, what is represented as one party in the dialogue may in fact be a large group.

The third requirement is that there has to be an account that both parties have access to. In the radiators example the explainer puts forward a connected account showing how placement of the radiator under the window in a room generally leads to a convection current that circulates the warm and cold air around the room, mixing it together and providing a moderate temperature throughout the room that makes it comfortable for the people in it. Normally in an explanation dialogue the account is given by the explainer to the explainee, but in any case, both of them have to have access to it. An account is a set of statements in which there are inferences from some statements to others but it needs to be stressed that there can also be implicit statements drawn by inference from the explicit statements. In the radiators example, the explainer assumes that the explainee already knows that when warm and cold air are combined in an enclosed space, the warm air tends to rise and the cold air tends to fall. Just as in the first example, the person offering the explanation expects that the person to whom the explanation was directed already knows quite a bit about a kind of situation familiar to both of them. In the dialogue system, accounts are based on scripts, MOPs or stories.

The fourth requirement for the opening stage of an explanation dialogue is that the explainee has to detect an anomaly in the account, something that doesn't fit in with the account. An anomaly is something the explainee does not understand in an account, even though she understands the rest of the account. For example, it may be an inconsistency, or a statement in the account that appears implausible. The explainee's question in the radiators example presents an anomaly. If the windows are the greatest source of heat loss, then putting the radiators under the windows in a room would seem to be wasteful of energy. So why is it so commonly done? To grasp the anomaly, you have to be aware of the common knowledge that building practices generally avoid doing things that are wasteful of energy. It would be anomalous for rooms to be normally configured with radiators under the window if, as it appears, this leads to wasteful heat loss.

The explanation stage is initiated by the explainee's putting forward a special type of speech act. There can be various kinds of explanation questions that ask for different kinds of explanations. However, the system Explainer is meant to be a simple and basic dialogue system specification on which specialized and more complex systems can be built, and so there is only one kind of explanation speech act in it. It has the form 'ExplanAnom*x*', where *x* is an anomaly in an account that has been given by the other party. The speech act 'ExplanAnom*x*' makes a request to the explainer to provide understanding concerning the anomaly *x*. The explanation dialogue is opened by the explainee's putting forward the speech act 'ExplanAnomA1', where A1 is an instance of *x*. The dialogue proceeds to the second move when the explainer makes an attempt to explain the anomaly. At the third move, the explainee can accept the explanation or not. But other responses are also allowed. The explainee may still not understand what she needs to understand, and so she may have to ask further questions about aspects of the explanation that appear puzzling.

Moulin et al. (2002, 174–176) showed that there are three kinds of explanations that are common in AI, trace explanations, strategic explanations and deep explanations. Let's begin with trace explanations. In expert systems, the system produces an explanation in response to a user's how or why questions by producing an execution trace, a sequence of inferences leading from statements in the knowledge base to the statement queried. Strategic explanations place an action in context by revealing the problem-solving strategy of the system used to perform a task. Deep explanations require two separate knowledge bases and a transfer from the system's base to the user's that fills in gaps in the user's knowledge base. The system has to know what the user knows, to fill in the gaps. It is this third type that best fits the dialogue model.

A chain of inferences in an account is called a sequence of reasoning. Of the three kinds of explanations mentioned above, the simplest is the trace explanation, and we use this type as an illustration of an account here. In a trace explanation, a statement *A* that has been queried is traced by chaining backward in a knowledge base to the set of facts (statements) and rules (of inference) in the knowledge base. *A* is derived by a chain of inferences from the facts, where the process is viewed as forward chaining. Looked at in reverse, such a chain of arguments is an explanation. This kind of explanation fits the covering law model, as long as the inferences in the chain are only of the deductive or inductive sort. But there are other kinds of explanation. In other cases, an account can take the form of a script, an account that has gaps in it because not all the connections in the account are stated explicitly. These gaps have to be filled in by making assumptions about common knowledge shared by a speaker and hearer.

A speech act is a type of move made by one or the other party as a dialogue proceeds. One speech act is the request by one party to the other party to offer an explanation of an anomaly. For each type of move, there are pre-condition rules that set the conditions under which a party is allowed to make that type of move, and post-condition rules that set the allowable replies to each type of move by the other party. Generally, the participants take turns as follows. The explainee makes the first move by asking for an explanation, and then the explainer gets a chance to respond by offering one. If the explainer offers one, the explainee can simply accept it by saying 'I understand', but if she replies by saying she does not understand, she can then proceed to ask questions about it. At this point, the dialogue shifts to a different type of dialogue as explained in the section on the closing stage below. Below are the basic speech acts of Explainer.

Assertion: Putting forward a statement, *A*, *B*, *C*, ..., is a permissible locution, and truth-functional compounds of statement-letters are also permissible locutions.[1]
Factual Question: The question '*A*?' asks 'Is it the case that *A* is true?'
Explanation Request: The speech act 'ExplanAnom*x*' makes a request to the explainer to provide understanding concerning some anomaly *x*.
Explanation Attempt: a response to a previous explanation request made by the explainee that purports to convey understanding to the explainee.
Inability to Explain Response: 'I can't explain it', concedes that the explainer has no explanation at this point to offer of the statement asked about.
Positive Response: A response claiming that the hearer understands an explanation.
Negative Response: A response claiming that the hearer does not understand an explanation.

Below are the pre-condition rules for these speech acts.

Pre-condition Rule for an Explanation Request: In order for the speech act 'ExplanAnom*x*' to be put forward, the statements replacing the *x* variable must constitute an anomaly.
Pre-condition Rule for an Explanation Attempt: The previous move by the other party must be a request for an explanation.
Pre-condition Rule for an Inability to Explain Response: The previous move by the other party must be a request for explanation.
Pre-condition for the Positive Response: The previous move by the other party must be an explanation attempt.
Pre-condition for the Negative Response: The previous move by the other party must be an explanation attempt.

Below are the post-condition rules for the speech acts.

Post-condition Rule for an Explanation Request: An explanation request must be followed at the next move by an explanation response.
Post-condition Rules for an Explanation Attempt: An explanation response must be followed at the next move by the other party's saying 'I understand it' or 'I don't understand it'.

[1] Assertions include only statements (propositions), and do not include promises, commands, and so forth.

Post-condition for the 'I understand it' Response: to be determined below.
Post-condition for the 'I don't understand it' Response: to be determined below.

The last two post-condition rules are not formulated yet, because of the problem of closure. There can be two different ways of determining when the closing stage has been arrived at. On one view, the closing stage is reached when the explainer has offered an explanation and the explainee is satisfied with it. The dialogue system for explanation CE (Walton 2007a, b) was built on the following two rules for the success of an explanation attempt.

CESR1. If after any explanation attempt is made, the explainee replies by saying, 'I understand', the explainer's clarification attempt is judged to be successful.
CESR2. If after any explanation attempt is made, the explainee replies by saying 'I don't understand', the explainer's explanation attempt is judged to be unsuccessful.

These success rules are used in CE to define the closing stage of an explanation dialogue, based on the assumption that the closing stage is reached once the explanation attempt carried out in the dialogue is judged to be successful or unsuccessful.

The problem with this way of setting up rules for the closing stage is that in many of the most significant cases, determining success or failure on the basis of whether the explainee says she understands the explanation offered is not enough to close the dialogue. The "feels-right" explanation is often associated with bias (Trout 2002, 223–228). On another view, the dialogue should only be closed when the explanation has been tested, and has been found to have passed the tests that should be required of it. Only then can it be said whether the explanation is truly successful or not. But what is the test? In science, ideally, the test is to collect all the data required to conclusively test the explanation experimentally. But for practical purposes, with many of the explanations we give in everyday conversations that are good enough for what is required, resources are not available for collecting more data necessary for a satisfactory tentative explanation to be offered. In many instances, for practical purposes, collecting more data to test the explanation further would be too costly, or would just not be useful because of the limitations of the present needs and circumstances. On this view, testing the explanation by critically probing into gaps and questionable parts in it, based on what is already known, would be good enough to provisionally accept it. Examination dialogue can fit either of these methods of testing. It can proceed by critical questioning in argumentation or by the collection and examination of further data, for example by experimental testing.

The context concerning what the purpose of the explanation is supposed to be plays a role in deciding which of the two views is applicable. If the context is that of a scientific inquiry, further testing by collecting of data may be the best criterion for closure. If the explanation is part of an everyday conversational exchange, conducting experimental tests or launching into a detailed scientific explanation might not be appropriate. These moves may even impede the transfer of understanding. Thus we should not take a 'one shoe fits all' approach to this problem.

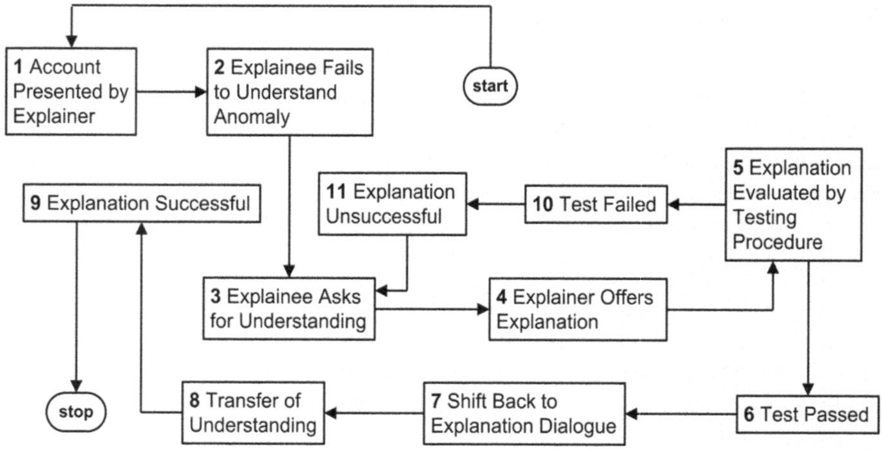


**Fig. 3.2** Typical dialogue sequence in explainer

In order to keep to the most general approach of building a simple system as a starting point for developing other more complex models of explanation dialogue, we have proposed a middle view between the two views outlined above. This view is tailored to seeing explanation as based on defeasible reasoning that leads to a plausible explanation based on the known facts, but is open to correction or improvement as more data is brought in to fill out an account or support it by external evidence. On this view, an explanation is successful if it is tested by the explainee's critical questioning that probes into its weak spots, or by examining further data, to see if it survives this testing process by answering all the questions satisfactorily. An explanation is unsuccessful if it fails this testing process.

The closure rules are meant to solve the problem of the failure cycle illustrated by the possibility of the feedback cycle {3, 4, 5, 10, 11, 3}, illustrated in the typical explanation sequence in Fig. 3.2, and the problem of the unsuccessful explanation in the example of the science teaching dialogue presented in Sect. 1.6. For an explanation dialogue to be successful, understanding has to be transferred from the explainer to the explainee. What is the evidence that this transfer has been achieved? The need to evaluate an explanation, and the extent to which it needs to be tested, vary with the context. In a science class, the anomaly may be posed by a simple misunderstanding that can be explained briefly, and that everyone is satisfied with. In a context of scientific research, the anomaly may be a wicked problem and the explanation of it may be lengthy, complex, and involve experimental testing. Thus the closure rules must allow for such pragmatic variations.

The closure rules need to fit the 14-step sequence that leads to closure set out in Sect. 3.5. If both parties are satisfied with the explanation offered, that can be the end of the dialogue. There may be no need to go into more depth. However, if either party is not satisfied, he or she can ask more questions, extending the dialogue. If the explainee is not satisfied, she can ask more questions, and may need to (step 5).

The explanation should proceed in this direction, ideally until the explanation finally makes sense to the explainee. This may never happen, so in practice some limit will need to be set on the time or cost. The explanation is only successful however, if the anomaly is removed and the explainee understands what she asked about. If the explainer is not satisfied that the explainee really understands, then as shown at step 7, there may need to be a shift to a testing procedure.

This way of handling explanation attempts suggests the following closure rules.

Closure Rule 1: If both parties are satisfied, the dialogue can be closed.

Closure Rule 2: If the explainee is not satisfied, she should ask further questions, continuing the dialogue until it has reached a point where either (a) she is satisfied or (b) her questioning must be closed off for practical reasons.

Closure Rule 3: If the explainer is not satisfied, the explainee's understanding of the explanation is subjected to a testing procedure.

Closure Rule 4: The testing procedure terminates when either (a) the explainer is satisfied or (b) his questioning must be closed off for practical reasons.

Closure Rule 5: When the testing interval ends, there is a shift back to the continuation of the original explanation dialogue.

Closure Rule 6: The explanation dialogue terminates when either (a) there has been a transfer of understanding of the kind required or (b) it must be closed off for practical reasons.

We now return to Scriven's hypothesis which says that that the success of an explanation needs to be tested.

Figure 3.2 outlines how a sequence of explanation dialogue typically runs in the system, and the explanation offered is evaluated as successful or not. The sequence begins with two requirements set at the opening stage of the dialogue. The first is the explainer's offering an account, a set of assumed facts or accepted statements that are connected together by inferences (box 1 in Fig. 3.2). The second is that the explainee has found an anomaly in the account, something in it that he does not understand (box 2). Then (box 3) the explanation stage is set into motion, where the explainee asks a question asking for understanding of the anomaly, and the explainer offers an explanation that attempts to provide the requested understanding (box 4). Then (box 5) there is a shift to an interval in which the explainer's comprehension of the explanation is tested by the explainer's asking a series of probing questions designed to see if the explainee now understands the account or not. If the test is passed (box 6), it can be taken that the required understanding has been achieved, and the dialogue can then shift back from the testing procedure to the main explanation dialogue (box 7). If transfer of understanding has been carried out (box 8), the explanation can be evaluated as successful (box 9).

What happens if the test carried out during the testing interval has failed (box 10)? This shows that the explanation was unsuccessful (box 11). So now what should be done? Should the dialogue stop there? The solution shown in Fig. 3.2 is that the dialogue can be continued. The explainee can try to rephrase the question by indicating better what he failed to understand, in light of the previous examination dialogue (box 3). Then the explainer can offer a different explanation, modified to better suit the needs of the explainee (box 4). This explanation improvement cycle shown in Fig. 3.2, {3, 4, 5, 10, 11, 3}, can go around several times, as the two parties move collaboratively to better and better explanations until enough success has been achieved so that transfer of understanding has taken place. Failure occurs when the two parties remain stuck in this feedback loop because the examination dialogue keeps failing. In such a case, once the shift is made back to explanation dialogue, the explanation dialogue still fails. How can the parties break this failure cycle? The answer will be given in the next sections.

## 3.4 Examples of Abductive Reasoning in Trials

Bex (2011, 141–160) has modeled the dynamics of the process of proof in a trial as a dialogue game in which each side, the defense and the prosecution, builds the story representing what it claims has happened. During the argumentation stage of trial, the story is supported by evidence, and then during the trial each side will attack the story of the other side by putting forward arguments. On Bex's theory, the players in the game build a hybrid theory by taking turns to perform speech acts in a communication language. Rules representing the dialogue protocol determine when each player is allowed to make a particular type of move, and how the other player needs to respond to that move in order to keep the dialogue going forward. The current winner of the game is the player who is committed to the explanation that is currently considered to be the best one at that point (Bex 2011, 147). Of two competing explanations, the one is judged to be better than the other if it covers more evidence and is contradicted by less or equal evidence that the other (Bex 2011, 148). The criteria offered for determining when one explanation is better than another provide measures designed to answer the critical question 'How decisively does the current story surpass the alternative stories?' (149). Bex offers legal cases to explain how the hybrid theory is applied to real examples.

A paper (Bex and Walton 2012) that extended the hybrid theory of (Bex 2011) used one civil case study and two criminal cases studies to show how evidential reasoning can work by comparing stories on either side of a case. The most important feature of these case studies for our purposes here is that they use inference to the best explanation as the central form of argument that weighs stories in a trial. To evaluate the argumentation in such cases, the model uses proof standards and burdens of proof. Here we will use two of the three cases to show how the hybrid theory combines argument and explanation, and show how this suggests a way forward to building formal dialogue models that can combine speech acts for putting forward arguments based on evidence with speech acts for asking explanation questions.

In the case of Anderson v. Griffin (397 F.3d 515), outlined in Bex and Walton (2012, 120–121), the driveshaft of a tractor-trailer broke while the truck was proceeding down an Interstate highway, severing the brake connection. Debris on the highway was kicked up, striking a pickup truck behind the tractor-trailer. The two trucks collided and a car following the pickup truck struck the wreckage from their collision, injuring the two people in the car. The plaintiff (the two people in the car), sued the truck dealer, the person responsible for maintenance of the tractor- trailer. The plaintiff and the defendant each presented a story to support their side of the case. According to the plaintiff's story (Bex and Walton 2012, 120), 3 weeks earlier, the company who owned the tractor-trailer noticed a looseness in the driveshaft and asked the truck dealer to tighten it but the dealer failed to tighten one of the joints, and it broke. This story was supported by the truck dealer's records. According to the defendant's story, the debris kicked up by the chains hanging from the tractor-trailer could have been the cause of the crash.

How the two stories compete with each other, and how each of the argument supporting or attacking them is based on the evidence in the case is shown in Fig. 3.3. For the notation used in the diagram see Fig. 1.5. The two stories, each of which offers an explanation why the driveshaft broke, are presented as rounded nodes joined by open arrows. The conventions governing this diagram are comparable to the ones used in Fig. 1.5. Similar to Fig. 1.5, the story runs along the top of the diagram, but also continues to the middle and right, where the road debris story supports the element of the driveshaft story at the top. The arguments are represented by rectangular nodes (text boxes) leading by closed arrows to another node or to a line joining two nodes. Such closed arrows denote evidential (argument) links. The circular nodes indicate arguments. In some instances, the argument supports an element of a story, while in other instances the argument supports the link joining one element of the story to another. For example the rectangular node containing the evidence from the truck dealer's records supports the statement which is part of the story along the top that the truck dealer did not repair the driveshaft. In other instances, an argument supports the link between the one element in a story and another. For example, the expert opinion evidence from the plaintiff's expert supports the story link between the statement that the truck dealer did not repair the driveshaft and the statement that the driveshaft broke. Note that as with the examples treated previously, the arguments only fit argumentation schemes if implicit premises are made explicit. For example, the argument based on the expert opinion evidence from the plaintiff's expert supports part of the story shown along the top of Fig. 3.3, but only if the implicit premises are added that the plaintiff's expert is an expert in a particular domain of knowledge and the other premise that the domain of knowledge is the same as that concerning repairs to a driveshaft on a truck. The arguments toward the bottom part of the diagram support or attack the stories shown in the more or less the upper part of the diagram. The arguments can either support or attack parts of the story. Such arguments can use other schemes such as argument from analogy (Brewer 1996).

The plaintiff's story is represented by the open arrows joining the three rounded nodes along the top of the diagram going from right to left. According to this story, the driveshaft broke because the truck dealer did not repair it properly. The defendant's story is represented by the open arrows joining the three rounded nodes

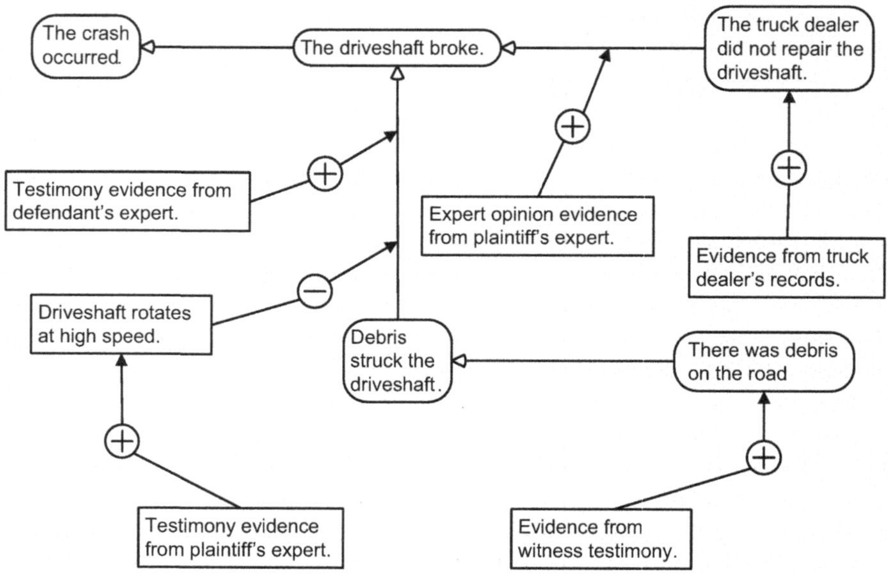


**Fig. 3.3** Competing stories and evidence in the Anderson v. Griffin case

below, claiming that the driveshaft broke because it was struck by debris from the road. Here we can see the relation between the story and the arguments used to support or attack parts of the story based on the factual evidence of the case.

Because this case is a legal trial, there are rules determining what counts as evidence, and there are rules determining burden of proof. It is a civil case, and so the standard of proof required is that of the preponderance of the evidence. This standard essentially means that the one argument is evidentially weighed against the other, and if the argumentation on the one side can be judged to be significantly stronger than the argumentation on the other side, the stronger argument prevails. At the closing stage of the trial the adjudicator, a third party (judge or jury), will determine whether the argumentation on the plaintiff's side has met this burden of proof or not. Studying legal cases of this sort can give us a lot of insight into how abductive argumentation based on evidence is evaluated. Essentially how it works is that the global burden of proof, or burden of persuasion as is called in law, is set at the opening stage. In a jury trial, the judge has to make it clear to the jury what legal standard is applicable in the jurisdiction of the case, and has to explain to the jury how that standard needs to be applied. Then during the argumentation stage, the actual courtroom proceedings, the burden of proof, legally called the evidential burden or the burden of producing evidence, shifts back and forth from one side to the other. At the closing stage, and evaluation of the outcome is arrived at, based on what happened in the two earlier stages.

In this case a detailed explanation of how this shifting of the burden of proof should take place has been presented in (Bex and Walton 2012, 122), but a brief summary of this explanation will help to explain how the stories, the arguments and evidence are woven together in three stages. At the opening stage, the burden of proof is on the side of the defendant (the truck dealer). Unless he successfully attacks the plaintiffs' explanation, or provides a better explanation of why the crash occurred, the jury will rule for the plaintiff. In fact what happened was that the defendant offered the alternative explanation that debris must have struck the driveshaft. Now the evidential burden shifts back to the plaintiff's side. Each time some evidence is brought forward by each side to support its story, or to raise damaging questions about the story of the other side, the evidential burden shifts back and forth. What happened in this case was that the plaintiff argued that a piece of road debris would be highly unlikely to strike the driveshaft with enough force to break it, given that the driveshaft rotates at such a high speed (27 times a second). At the closing stage of the trial, the jury ruled in favor of the plaintiff, so apparently they concluded after deliberations that the plaintiff's explanation was sufficiently better than the defendant's, the implication being that the preponderance of evidence standard had been met, once the arguments on both sides had been weighed against each other.

In the second case (US v. Beard, 354 F. 3d 691 – Court of Appeals, 7th Circuit 2004) the defendant, John Beard, appealed an earlier conviction in which he had been found guilty of carrying a gun while committing a drug offense. Police were watching a parking lot in which two cars were parked side-by-side. Here are the basic facts of the case (Bex and Walton 2012, 126).

> Beard got out of one of the cars, entered the other car for a few minutes, and then returned to his car. Both cars left the scene and were later stopped by the police. In Beard's car police found drugs in a secret compartment behind the rear seat and a loaded derringer in the closed center console of the front seat, concealed under some papers. In the other car they found cash. Beard did not own the car. He had borrowed it eight months before from its owner, and had been seen driving it from time to time during this period. However, he was not the only person who used the car during that period. The papers concealing the derringer did not seem to have belonged to Beard either. They did not pertain to him.

The issue was whether the derringer belonged to Beard. There are two possible scenarios. Conceivably Beard placed the gun in the console, or conceivably one of the others who used the car during the eight month period placed it there. The remarks quoted above suggest that the hypothesis that someone who borrowed the car placed a loaded gun in the console and covered it with papers to conceal it is not a very likely possibility. As will be suggested in some remarks quoted from the court transcript below, it seems implausible that someone would conceal a gun in the console of a car and then forget about it. At the appeal, Beard's lawyer offered no explanation for the presence of the derringer in the car. The reason suggested for this failure, by the trial notes (written by Judge Posner), is worth quoting from Bex and Walton (2012, 129).

> The lawyer seems to have thought that since the government had the burden of proof, and Beard was privileged not to testify (and he did not testify), it was irrelevant that the jury was given no alternative to the government explanation as to whose gun it was.

This explanation given by the court is worth quoting, because it shows that the argumentation in a case like this needs to be evaluated by looking at competing explanations, and depends on evaluating the plausibility of alternative explanations, if any are offered. The problem is that the defense failed to carry out a reasonable search for evidence that would support an alternative explanation of the facts of the case. Poking holes in the government's case is not good enough. The defense must put forward a competing explanation that is at least plausible enough to raise reasonable doubt about the government's explanation. Since the defense failed to do this, they lost the appeal.

No one supposed that the derringer was the property of the car's owner – that she hid a loaded gun in the center console when she lent Beard the car. Hence there remain only two possible explanations of the facts. One is the explanation that Beard placed the gun in the console. The other is the explanation that someone who borrowed the car from Beard placed it in the console. The remarks quoted from the court transcript in Bex and Walton (2012, 128–129) compares the two explanations.

> Since others besides himself used the car during the eight months that he possessed it, conceivably the gun was left there by one of these users, but that is highly unlikely. It would mean that someone who borrowed the car from Beard placed a loaded gun in the console, covered it with papers to conceal it, and then — what? Forgot about it? That is possible, but it was not so likely a possibility as to compel a reasonable jury to acquit Beard.

The problem for the defense is that it provided no evidence to support this alternative story, and without such support, the prosecution's argument, although weak, is enough to prevail. It is possible that someone borrowed the car from Beard, placed a loaded derringer in the console, covered with papers to conceal it, and then forgot about it. But it does not seem very likely, without further details to substantiate such a story.

Essentially the prosecution's argument can be summed up as follows (Bex and Walton 2012, 126).

> Premise 1: The gun was being carried during a drug offense.
> Premise 2: Drug dealers bring guns to a deal to instill fear in their business associates, or if they feel the need for protection.
> Conclusion: It is reasonably clear that the gun was Beard's.

Premise 2 is a generalization apparently based on previous generally known cases about how drug dealers generally conduct their operations. It tells us that drug dealers have reasons to carry a gun during a drug offense, and it can be inferred from this as an interim conclusion that drug dealers commonly bring a gun along during a drug deal. These assumptions suggest the conclusion that Beard took the derringer along during this drug deal and concealed it in the console of the car. The argument on the other side appears to be nonexistent.

There was no circumstantial evidence that the gun belonged to Beard. Instead, the supporting evidence for the prosecution's argument was common knowledge about how things normally go in drug deals. So how could it be decided by the jury, on this basis, that Beard was guilty of carrying a gun during a drug offense to the criminal law standard of beyond a reasonable doubt? The best way to answer this question is to model the reasoning used by the court as an instance of inference to the best explanation (Bex and Walton 2012, 15–16).

> The choice had to be made between two explanations of the facts of the case. What needed to be explained was how the gun got into the console between the seats in the car. One of the three possible explanations is that the derringer was the property of the car's owner, and that she had the loaded gun in the console when she lent Beard the car. This explanation was ruled out by the court. We are not told why, but possibly it was because the car owner had no previous criminal convictions and was not related to the drug trade. The second explanation is that Beard put the derringer in the console because he had the goal of instilling fear in a business associate or the goal of protection during a dangerous drug deal. This seems to be a fairly plausible explanation, because it had been decided by the previous court that Beard was guilty of conducting the sale of drugs, and it is known from previous cases that there is common knowledge about how drug dealers conduct these exchanges.

A third explanation, that somebody else who used car during the 8-month period placed the derringer in the console, was also considered by the court (Bex and Walton 2012, 16). The problem with this explanation is that it is not very plausible that someone would place a loaded gun in the console, cover it with papers to conceal it, and then forget about it. Therefore, according to the detailed analysis of the argumentation in the case given by Bex and Walton, the decision was arrived at on the basis of evaluating and comparing these three explanations and arriving at a conclusion on the basis of inference to the best explanation. It can still be asked how the court could have arrived at the conclusion of guilt beyond a reasonable doubt when the evidence was so slim. Nevertheless from a normative point of view, it is clear that the structure of the reasoning the court used to arrive at its conclusion can be seen as an instance of inference to the best explanation.

As a closing remark, it should be added that two of the explanations are best modeled as stories that depend on having implicit assumptions drawn from common knowledge. The story that Beard put the gun in the console can be analyzed as an instance of the argumentation scheme for practical reasoning. It is presumed that Beard had a goal of protecting himself in a dangerous environment, and since this goal can be achieved by carrying an available gun, the plausibility of the conjecture that Beard put the derringer in the console is supported. This practical reasoning argument is based on the plausible generalization that drug dealers bring guns to a deal to instill fear in order to have protection from dangerous associates. This generalization in turn can be supported by common knowledge about how drug deal exchanges work. Once these implicit premises are stated and brought into the practical reasoning structure of the argument, the story that Beard put the gun in the console becomes quite plausible. On the other side, the story that somebody other than Beard put the gun in the car, covered it with papers to conceal it, and then forgot about it, is not very plausible. Once again, the reasons for evaluating it in this way come out when some implicit assumptions are added in to the network of argumentation. One of these is the assumption that it is unlikely that anyone would forget a gun and leave in a car, given that a gun is a significant object that a person would be not very likely to forget about.

## 3.5 A Hybrid Explan System

A third problem is how the Explainer system can deal with the failure cycle displayed in Fig. 3.2 depicting the typical sequence of dialogue in Explainer. Failure occurs when the two parties remain stuck in this feedback loop because the examination dialogue keeps failing. In such a case, once the shift is made back to explanation dialogue, the explanation dialogue still fails. How can the parties break this failure cycle? The solution to this problem is to be found by incorporating a double dialectical shift from explanation dialogue to examination dialogue and then back again, and by providing a success criterion for the original explanation dialogue that can be achieved through the success of the intervening examination dialogue.

The problem of the failure cycle {3, 4, 5, 10, 11, 3}, shown in Fig. 3.2, occurs where the examination dialogue interval turns out to be unsuccessful at point 11 in the sequence. What should happen here? For example, in the science teaching dialogue on coal, suppose the student examines the explanation offered by the teacher as well as she can, and the teacher answers her questions as well as he can, but the examination dialogue fails to throw any light on the explanation offered. The student is not convinced that the teacher's explanation has stood up to critical scrutiny and concludes that the teacher does not know what he is talking about. The teacher is convinced that the student has not asked the right questions in her examination interval and still has not understood how his explanation has resolved the anomaly she questioned in it. Perhaps keeping trying to reopen the examination dialogue might eventually lead to success, but there needs to be some sequence of moves leading up to closure to solve the problem of how to formulate the post-condition rules of Explainer that were left open in Sect. 3.4.

The solution to the problem lies in more fully formulating the closure conditions for examination dialogue when such a dialogue is embedded in an explanation dialogue. The criterion suggested by Scriven's test is that the explainee must have proved her capacity to answer new questions, but we now have to add to this test. For the examination dialogue to be good enough to be closed off before the shift, both parties have to have performed well enough. The explainee has to have asked the right questions to show that she has understood the explanation well enough to probe into it critically, and the explainer has to have dealt with questioning well enough to show that he really knows what he is talking about. When this has taken place in a given case is discussed in Dunne et al. (2005) and Walton (2006). In real cases, however, there are often practical limits on the process imposed by costs and circumstances.

The solution is provided by breaking the structure of an explanation dialogue into a characteristic sequence of fourteen substages leading to the closure of the explanation dialogue. The sequence is linear, up to substage 4, but then there is a choice point so that the sequence becomes a tree with two branches. The explanation dialogue can be closed off in two ways, depending on which branch is followed.

1. The explainer has put forward some account, a coherent story about event.
2. The explainee finds an anomaly in the account, and assumes that the explainer understands it and can explain it.
3. The explainee asks for an explanation of the anomaly, and the explainer replies by attempting an explanation.
4. The explainee is satisfied with the explanation or not. Either option can lead to a continuation of the dialogue.
5. If the explainee is not satisfied, she can ask further questions about the account.
6. This option leads to a continuation of the explanation dialogue where the explainer is questioned by the explainee.
7. If the explainee is satisfied, the explainer can ask further questions to test whether she really understands the account or not.
8. This option leads to a shift to a testing interval in which the explainee is questioned by the explainer.
9. If the explanation fails the test, then the original explanation dialogue is closed.
10. If the examination dialogue is successful, there is a dialectical shift back to the explanation dialogue.
11. The results of the gain in understanding can now be carried over to the continuation of the original explanation dialogue.
12. If the results of the gain in understanding from the examination dialogue are sufficient for a transfer of understanding of the kind required by the original explanation dialogue, the explanation is successful.
13. If the results of the gain in understanding are insufficient, the explanation is unsuccessful.
14. The original explanation dialogue is now closed.

According to this way of plotting the path of the explanation dialogue to closure, both parties need to have passed dialectical tests. Both need to have contributed to the dialogue well enough so that light is thrown on the understanding of both. The account of the explainer has to stand up to scrutiny, and the scrutiny undertaken by the explainee has to show that she understands how the account works, what its implicit elements are, and how they fit in with the parts explicitly stated. Also, both parties have to prove that they can critically evaluate the account by asking and responding to probing questions about what appear to be the weak points in it. Explainer incorporates a modified version of Scriven's test that takes both performances into account.

The solutions to these three problems proposed in Sects. 3.4 and 3.5 make it possible to construct a hybrid dialogue system specification for explanation that meets the requirements set out above. So far, the model of explanation dialogue presented seems simple, and in some instances that is the way it should be. For example, in a classroom setting, suppose the teacher offers an explanation to a student. The teacher's explanation attempt is successful if the student understands the explanation given to him. If not, the explanation has not been successful, and the teacher is obliged to start again by rephrasing or amplifying the explanation in some way. On the other hand, even this apparently simple example has some dialectical complications. For the exchange to represent a good example of collaborative learning, the student could reply by pointing out some specific aspect of the explanation that is not comprehensible to him. For example, he could say that he does not understand some of the terminology or concepts that are part of the explanation. Or he could argue that the explanation does not fit with how he understands comparable situations that he is more familiar with that are similar to the event being explained by the teacher. In other words, what has happened in such a case is that the burden has shifted onto the teacher to continue the conversation by clarifying his earlier explanation and rephrasing it in terms that are more acceptable or familiar to the student.

In other words, it is too simple to base the success or failure of an explanation attempt on whether the explainee understands, or claims to understand, the explanation given by the explainer. If there is a failure, the burden should not always reside on the side of the explainer. The explainee should have the right to require that the explainer continue the conversation. What the explainee needs to do is to make two kinds of moves (speech acts) to continue the dialogue from that point. It will help the dialogue along if the explainee can cite some specific respect in which the explanation has failed for him, for one of a range of reasons. It could be that the explainee finds an apparent inconsistency in the explanation. Or it could be that the explainee finds some gaps in the explanation. Or it could be that there is something about the explanation which does not fit with the explainee's factual knowledge of the sequence of events that are supposedly being explained. Once the two parties focus in on some specific difficulties of this kind, such findings will help the dialogue move forward in a way that may make for a more successful explanation, a much better explanation that is more plausible, more comprehensible, and better worked-out in its details. Or it could go the other way.

These matters become even more complex in cases of abductive reasoning because in these cases arguments and explanations are woven in together. In order to build a formal model of dialogue to represent such cases, such as the examples of inference to the best explanation presented in the first two chapters of this book, the dialogue has to contain not only moves that take the form of explanations, but also moves that take the form of arguments. This means that the Explainer system presented here has to be combined with one or more of the standard models of argumentation already so well-known as central in the argumentation literature, such as models of argumentation in persuasion dialogue, deliberation dialogue, negotiation, and other contexts of use of argumentation that have been extensively studied. This is where the hybrid theory comes in and needs to be applied, because its most powerful advantage as a model is that it shows how arguments and explanations should be combined so that they can each support each other in examples like those in the two previous chapters, that involve abductive reasoning.

In particular, the hybrid system has a formal dialogue structure mapped out that allows arguments and explanations to be combined. One of its strongest capabilities is that it provides a formal framework for evaluating explanations as strong or weak, where the most important criterion is how it will give an explanation that is supported by evidence. In general, the hybrid system will rule that if you are comparing two explanations of the same set of facts, the chief determinant of which is the better explanation will be which one of them is based on the strongest arguments supported by the evidence, consisting of the relevant set of facts in the case, and the rules of inference applicable to those facts. Many of these rules will be defeasible arguments based on common sense generalizations describing the ways things can be generally expected to go in virtue of common knowledge applicable to the circumstances of the case.

A hybrid system requires not just a system of explanation dialogue comparable to the Explan system with protocols that determine how each of them can put forward requests for explanations, and the other party needs to respond. A hybrid system to account for abductive reasoning, and in general for allowing a critic to judge whether one explanation is better than another or not, needs to have protocols that determine how the explainee can and should respond to any explanation put forward by the explainer by questioning, criticizing or even attacking by counterarguments any aspect of the explanation that is not clear to him.

In other words, what is needed are rules (protocols), comparable to rules for burden of proof of the kind required in persuasion dialogue, that determine on which side the burden should be to continue the conversation by making particular kinds of moves in order to properly respond to an explanation that has been offered to him. The explainee doesn't have to simply accept the explanation, but on the other hand it may be best to model the dialogue in such a way that he is not allowed to simply reject it either by saying that he doesn't understand. Instead it is better if there is an obligation on him to continue the conversation by pointing out the particular respect that he fails to understand, and even better, give some reasons why he doesn't understand it. If we can provide protocols for dialogues that contain both arguments and explanations that govern these kinds of back-and-forth moves between the two parties, we will have a formal dialogue model that is much more powerful than any simple model of explanation dialogue that does not take counter arguments and critical questions based on arguments into account. It is clear therefore that a hybrid system is needed, and it needs to be a system that can cope adequately with providing a framework and protocols for supporting and attacking explanations with arguments.

Hamblin (1970, 265–276) built the system called a Why-Because System with Questions to model argumentation between two communicating agents called White and Black. By convention, White makes the first move, and after that point the two agents must take turns making moves, containing what he called locutions, but which are nowadays considered to be speech acts. The language is that of propositional calculus and at each move a speaker can put forward a statement to make a claim (Hamblin 1970, 265). As each party makes any kind of move of the kinds allowed by the dialogue rules, statements are either inserted into or retracted from its commitment set. A commitment set is a repository that is kept in memory throughout the dialogue and updated at each move.

The list of speech acts in this type of dialogue is presented below. The variables $A, B, C \ldots$ stand for statements. Assertion, or making a claim, is one type of speech act that can be put forward in a move in such a dialogue. For example if Black asserts that snow is white then the proposition that snow is white will be inserted into

Black's commitment store. An assertion is defined as a type of speech act containing a statement that has been put forward in a move in the dialogue by an agent. The speech act of making an assertion has three components: (1) it is attributed to an agent that made the assertion, (2) it contains a statement that was asserted, and (3) the assertion move makes the claim that the agent is committed to. When an agent asserts a statement, it goes into its commitment set. Speech acts of the following four kinds are allowed to be put forward in moves. Another kind of speech act is the asking of a question. One particularly important kind of question is the so-called why-question, which in the Why-Because System with Questions is essentially a request for an argument to support a claim.

*Assertion*: 'Assertion *A*' is the speech act of putting forward a statement as an assertion.
*Retraction*: 'No commitment *A*' is the speech act of retracting a commitment, assuming that agent was previously committed to *A*.
*Yes-No Question*: 'Question '*A, B, C,* . . . ,?' is the speech act of asking whether the hearer accepts that one of the statements *A, B, C,* . . . is true.
*Why-Question Requesting Support*: 'Why *A*?' is a request for the other agent to supply an argument that would give it reason to accept *A*.

Hamblin (1970, 166) also considered a burden of proof rule that could be added to the system: if agent a1 asks agent a2 'Why *A*?', then if a2 is committed to *A*, a2 must present an argument for *A* or a2 must retract its commitment to *A*.

In natural language discourse asking a why-question is ambiguous. Asking such a question could be a request for justification of a speaker's previous claim, bringing the burden of proof rule into play, but it could also be a request for an explanation. In the Why-Because System with Questions Hamblin defined a why-question as being a request for an argument needed to support a claim, because he was not at that point concerned with explanations. But it is possible to construct a dialogue system for explanation based on Hamblin's dialectical framework, one that is meant to model explanations. One speech act in an explanation system is the asking of a why-question, now seen as the request by one party to the other party to offer an explanation of something the first party claims not to understand. Comparable to the list of speech acts for the Why-Because System with Questions above, for each type of move, there need to be pre-condition rules that set the conditions under which an agent is allowed to make a particular type of move, and post-condition rules that specify the allowable replies by the other agent.

Generally, the participants take turns as follows. The explainee makes the first move by asking for an explanation, and then the explainer gets a chance to respond by offering one. If the explainer offers one, the explainee can simply accept it by saying 'I understand'. If she replies by saying she does not understand, she can then proceed to ask further questions about it. The dialogue is closed when this sequence of questioning has been exhausted. Here we combine these two systems to create a new hybrid system we call the Why$^2$ System. The leading characteristic of this new hybrid system is that it has two kinds of why-questions. One is a request to provide an argument while the other is a request to provide an explanation.

Below are six kinds of especially significant speech acts in this new hybrid dialogue system, carried forward from the basis speech acts of the Explainer system (see p. 80).

*Assertion*: Putting forward a statement, $A$, $B$, $C$, ..., is a permissible locution, and truth-functional compounds of statement-letters are also permissible locutions.
*Factual Question*: The question '$A$?' asks 'Is it the case that $A$ is true?'
*Argument Request*: The speech act 'Why$^1$ $A$?' makes a request to the explainer to provide an argument that supports $A$.
*Explanation Request*: The speech act 'Why$^2$ $A$?' makes a request to the explainer to provide understanding concerning $A$.
*Explanation Attempt*: a response to a previous explanation request made by a1 that purports to convey understanding of $A$ to a2.

These speech acts combining arguments and explanations need to be put into a formal dialectical hybrid system that could be used to analyze texts combining arguments and explanations.

The theory of abductive reasoning of Walton (2004) took a comparable approach by viewing the process of explanation as a procedure that joins two or more types of dialogue together. Typically, for example, in a persuasion dialogue arguments are put forward by both sides in order to resolve a conflict of opinions, and many of these arguments take the form of abductive reasoning, itself regarded as a species of argumentation. But then, in order to evaluate the arguments contained in the persuasion dialogue, the comparison needs to be made to determine which of two competing explanations is better. Or to cite another kind of typical example, one side might argue that an explanation offered by the other side is inherently weak because it contains gaps or inconsistencies. Then the defending side might try to fill the gaps or argue that the apparent inconsistency is not a real one. The general problem is one of how to model this kind of evidential situation in relation to the types of dialogue currently recognized in the argumentation literature, such as persuasion dialogue, inquiry dialogue, deliberation, negotiation, and so forth. Clearly one step forward is to recognize that explanation involves some special kind of dialogue in its own right in which a burden of explanation shifts back and forth between the explainer and the explainee as the explainer criticizes the explanation put forward by the explainer, and the explainer has a chance to respond to these criticisms.

## 3.6 The Shift to Examination Dialogue

Scriven (1972, 32) provided a different way of testing the success of an explanation in the following quoted remark, expressed in the form of a dialogue.

> How is it that we test comprehension or understanding of a theory? We ask the subject questions about it, questions of a particular kind. They must not merely request recovery of information that has been explicitly presented (that would test mere knowledge, as in knowing the time or knowing the age of the universe). They must instead test the capacity to answer new questions.

Based on this remark, we now formulate *Scriven's Test*: the success of an explanation is judged by the explainee's capacity to answer new questions, shown in an extension of the dialogue sequence where probing questions are put to the explainee.

Using Scriven's test for the success of an explanation, the closure rules for CE need to be modified. The explainee needs to show real understanding, and not merely claimed understanding. But how is real understanding to be judged? How can Scriven's test be implemented in some method that would tell us when real understanding has been achieved so that the explanation can be judged to have been successful? The proposal made here is to use something called an examination dialogue. The examination dialogue is embedded into the original explanation type of dialogue to provide a continuation of it in which the explanation offered and accepted in the explanation is tested.

Examination discourses (*perastikoi logoi*) were defined by Aristotle (1928) in *On Sophistical Refutations* (165b4–165b6) as consisting of questions and replies designed to test an answerer's claims to knowledge. Such a dialogue is "based on opinions held by the answerer and necessarily known to one who claims knowledge of the subject involved." The aim of this kind of dialogue, according to Aristotle (*On Sophistical Refutations* 172a33), is to "attempt to test those who profess knowledge." Socrates' use of his skills of examination in the Platonic dialogues provides the classic examples. Lawyers are familiar with the use of examination skills in trials, for example in questioning an expert witness. But we also need to use examination skills in practical affairs of everyday life. For example, this type of dialogue takes place when you communicate with your physician, or other expert advisers, when they give you advice or recommend a particular course of action when you are trying to decide what to do.

An analysis of the structure of examination dialogue was presented in Walton (2006). Examination dialogue was shown to have two goals, the extraction of information and the testing of the reliability of this information. The first goal is carried out by the asking of questions in order to obtain information from the respondent, and by an exegetical function used to obtain a clear account of what the respondent means to say. The testing goal is carried out with critical argumentation used to judge whether the information elicited is reliable. To perform this function, the information is tested against the respondent's other statements, known facts in the case, and other information thought to be true. This type of dialogue was shown in Walton (1996) to be most prominent in both legal and non-legal arguments based on expert opinion. It was also shown to be central to dialogue systems for questioning and answering in expert systems in artificial intelligence. The examples studied also included exegetical analyses and criticisms of religious and philosophical texts as well as legal examinations and cross-examinations conducted in a trial setting.

Dunne et al. (2005) have built a formal model of examination dialogue in which one party, called the questioner, elicits statements from another party called the responder. The questioner has the aim of discovering the responder's position on some topic being discussed. The questioner may do this either to gain insight into the responder's understanding of the topic, or to expose an inconsistency in the responder's position. Their system is designed to model the process in which one party scrutinizes the other party's position to reveal internal inconsistencies in it. The examiner wins if she shows that the responder is committed to an inconsistency. This finding is achieved if the party being questioned replies that he denies a particular proposition or has no comment on it, but then the examiner shows that he has already revealed through his previous replies, or by evidence already accepted in the case, that he is committed to this proposition. According to their classification, examination dialogue is embedded in an information-seeking dialogue, and it is also seen, in some cases, as a prelude to persuasion dialogue (Dunne et al. 2005, 1560). Further work (Bench-Capon et al. 2008) has shown how commitment in examination dialogue can be modeled using value-based argumentation frameworks.

There can be dialectical shifts, or changes of context from one type of dialogue to another during the same continuous sequence of argumentation (Walton and Krabbe 1995). Consider the case of a contractor and a homeowner engaged in negotiation dialogue on a proposal to install a concrete basement in a house where the contractor begins to inform the homeowner about the city regulations on thickness of concrete for house basements. The standard example (Parsons and Jennings 1997) is the case where two agents have a joint intention to hang a picture. One has the picture and a hammer, and knows where the other can get a nail. They have a deliberation dialogue but can't agree on who should do which task. They then shift to a negotiation dialogue in which the one agent proposes that he will hang the picture if the other agent will go and get the nail. There can be many different kinds of dialectical shifts of this kind in everyday discussions. In some cases, the new dialogue contributes to the success of the previous one. This kind of case is classified as a functional embedding of the one dialogue into the other. In other cases, the one dialogue is an interruption in the first one, but there is no serious problem because the first dialogue can easily be resumed once the second one has finished. However, in some cases, the advent of the second dialogue blocks the progress of the first one, or seriously interferes with it, and presents a serious obstacle to its progress. These kinds of cases are classified as illicit dialectical shifts (Walton and Krabbe 1995). However, the shift in examination dialogue from information-seeking to persuasion dialogue, of the kind noted by Dunne et al. (2005), is an embedding of a highly typical and especially significant sort.

It was shown in Walton (2006) that examination dialogue can be of two basic types, and each one was named after terms used in Greek philosophy. Guthrie (1981, 155) drew a distinction between two types of examination, defining peirastic discussion as "testing or probing" and exetastic discussion as "examining critically". Guthrie described the distinction between these two types of examination as a component of the Aristotelian method of dialectical discussion used for testing and investigating (155).

In the peirastic type, the aim is merely to get an account representing what the respondent is supposedly claiming, based on the available textual evidence of the discourse. In this type of dialogue the one party in a dialogue tries to make sense of what the other has said by interpreting and reconstructing what was said.

The exetastic type is more argumentative. The questioner probes into the weak points of the answerer's account, asking critical questions, and even questioning statements and implicit assumptions in the account. The aim of this process is to reveal implausible statements, internal inconsistencies, logical weaknesses and gaps in the account. Both types of examination can be used to test an explanation, but the second type is the harder test to pass.

The goal of an explanation dialogue is a transfer of understanding from the one party to the other. This goal defines what it is for an explanation attempt to be successful in that type of dialogue. It is assumed that both parties accept this goal as part of the opening stage when they agree to take part in an explanation. This implies that both parties desire a transfer of understanding to take place, and that both will be co-operative in politely following the rules of the dialogue. The general goal of an examination dialogue is quite different. Its twin goals are to extract information from the respondent and to test the reliability of this information. Examination dialogue is more adversarial than explanation dialogue. The examiner uses questions to test the reliability of the information obtained from the respondent. To carry out such a test, one means at the disposal of the questioner is to try to trap the respondent into committing to an inconsistency, or into committing to a statement that is not plausible. These moves may make the respondent look foolish, or may even make it appear that the respondent is lying. Thus examination dialogue can become quite aggressive in some instances and even appear to be hostile. In some instances it even shifts to interrogation dialogue, an even more adversarial type of dialogue with different goals (Walton 2003).

An interesting aspect of explanation dialogue to study concerns cases where the dialogue goes wrong, and participants show that they are not well-intentioned or cooperative. These include cases where one party seeks to mislead the other, either by giving a false explanation or by accepting an inadequate one. They even include cases where one party seeks to maliciously waste the other party's time and energy by being whimsical or acting capriciously. These same sorts of difficulties can occur in the applicability of explanation models to computer systems. The computer system, even if it is designed and created with good intentions, may be bug-ridden, and so act in a manner that appears irrational or malicious to an independent observer. In other cases, something disguised as an explanation may really function as a different type of dialogue.

For these reasons, examination dialogue can provide a means of testing whether a transfer of understanding has really taken place or not in an explanation dialogue. If the explainee merely desires to convince the explainer that such a transfer has taken place when it has not, the explainer might be able to expose this failure by probing into the explanation by shifting to an examination dialogue. On the other side, if the explainer seeks to confuse, to obfuscate, to prevaricate, or even to intimidate the explainee, rather than to transfer understanding, the explainee can critically probe into the offered explanation to reveal the defects and problems in it, and possibly even reveal it as spurious. Hence we now turn to a consideration of how explanations can be tested to see whether they are really successful or not, by means of a shift to an examination dialogue.

A careful distinction needs to be drawn between an explanation and a clarification, as distinctive types of dialogues (Walton 2007b). Both explanation and clarification involve transfer of understanding from one party to another in a dialogue, but explanation can be of an event, or of an anomaly of any sort. A clarification dialogue occurs where one party has made some move in the dialogue, a verbal move or speech act, and there is something that is unclear to the second party. Then the second party, at his next move, declares that he does not understand what was said, and then he requests that the first party provide the understanding needed to remove the obscurity. The purpose of a clarification dialogue is to achieve clarity about something that is unclear (obscure) to the one party. Removing obscurity is one kind of transfer of understanding, but there are many other kinds as well. While an explanation responds to a perceived anomaly, a clarification responds to an obscurity. Another difference is that an explanation arises from an account, very often of some reported event, whereas a clarification arises from a previous message in a dialogue. Schlangen (2004, 137) brings out this point very well when he writes that what examples of clarification have in common is that unlike normal questions, they are "not about the state of the world in general, but about aspects of previous utterances". Further work needs to be done on giving an illustration, which appears to be different from explanation and clarification. These issues are included in the problems for further research section below.

An objection can be posed by imagining the hypothetical case of a science teacher who is excellent in every way, except that his knowledge base is riddled with falsehoods. His students, who know no better, accept his explanations, and let's even assume that when examined on them, they answer the questions well, showing that they understand the explanations the teacher offered. The objection that might be raised when considering this hypothetical case is that it shows that Explan makes the success of an explanation too explainee-relative. The objection suggests that in addition to the success conditions, truth conditions should need to be met in order to make an explanation a good one. The solution to this problem is provided by the shift from the explanation dialogue to the exetastic type of examination dialogue when required. In this type of dialogue, questions are raised on whether the statements in the given explanation are true, or factually accurate. An exetastic dialogue, like an anchored narrative, is argumentative. It probes critically into the weak points in an account. It requests justifications (supporting arguments) for claims made. For example in a scientific explanation, this kind of examination includes consideration of whether the explanation in question fits with existing data, including the use of experimental results to test the explanation.

## 3.7 How to Determine the Best Explanation

This section sets out a method of comparatively evaluating two competing explanations to see which is better. This is done by judging, based on a dialogue, how plausible each of them is as a story that fits the facts of a given case and the common knowledge shared by the participants in the dialogue. This set of accepted propositions (commitments) is set in place as the knowledge base at the opening stage, and modified according to the commitment rules as the dialogue proceeds. On the account given in Walton (2011) there are eight criteria that can be used to judge how good a given story is as an explanation compared to another story.

1. how well it performs its function of helping a questioner to make sense of something,
2. whether it is internally consistent or not,
3. whether an alleged inconsistency can be dealt with,
4. how well it is supported by the factual evidence,
5. how plausible the account is generally,
6. how comprehensive it is in covering relevant events and actions,
7. how detailed it is in filling in gaps, and
8. how well it stands up to critical questioning and examination.

Factors 1–8 are determined in a given case within the dialogue framework of the case in accord with the rules of the dialogue and requirements of the Explainer system.

The problem posed by factor 8 is solved by embedding an examination dialogue into the explanation dialogue in the given case. In legal explanations in a courtroom setting, there are rules for examinations and cross-examinations. In scientific explanations, the process of examination involves close scrutiny of the data provided by nature, and the designing and running of experiments to test a hypothesis. By solving these problems, the system specification builds a process model of explanation in which two parties take turns making moves according to procedural rules. The rules set out a normative model for explanation so that any example of a real explanation can be evaluated as reasonable or not according to standards set by the stages, the rules, and the goal of the dialogue. For example, circular explanations can be evaluated as unsuccessful on the basis that they fail to transfer understanding in the way required of a successful explanation in the Explainer system.

However, the test example of the explanation of why some of the finches in the Galapagos Islands died in the mid-1970s described in Chap. 1, Sects. 1.6 and 1.7, shows how the eight criteria of the goodness of an explanation listed above need to be supplemented. Sandoval and Reiser (2004, 362) showed how explanations need to be evaluated by script-based criteria, such as how well the story in an explanation ties together as a coherent sequence of events. They also proposed a criterion that an explanation should be evaluated stronger if it links evidence to support parts of the explanation. Also, Berland and Reiser (2008, 28) identified that one of the goals for constructing and defending a scientific explanation as that of persuading others to accept the explanation by supporting it with evidence from a scientific knowledge base. These factors are vitally important to take into consideration when evaluating the worth of an explanation, and they were well illustrated in the second student explanation described in Chap. 1, Sect. 1.7, where the students did not do an especially good job of backing up their explanation with specific facts drawn from scientific evidence. How the explanation in this case was supported by argumentation which itself was supported by the factual scientific evidence in the case cited by the students was shown graphically in Fig. 1.4.

These considerations suggest that two further criteria should be added to the list of eight above: (9) how well the explanation, especially if challenged, is supported by arguments, and (10) how well the arguments are supported by factual evidence. The criteria of Sandoval and Reiser also suggested two other criteria. One is the extent to which alternative explanations have been considered and why they should be rejected in favor of the selected explanation. This criterion is especially important when considering cases of IBE, where the ultimate conclusion drawn is that the explanation being considered is the best of all the candidates. Another criterion suggested by Sandoval and Reiser is whether an explanation has documented its own limitations by considering whether it might be weakened by missing data. These criteria are especially important to emphasize the connection between argument and explanation, and to show how both argument and explanation need to be evaluated in light of the supporting evidence, and also in light of how extensive the inquiry was in which the evidence was collected.

To sum up, there are twelve general criteria that should be used to evaluate the worth of an explanation.

1. how well it performs its function of helping a questioner to make sense of something,
2. whether it is internally consistent or not,
3. whether an alleged inconsistency can be dealt with,
4. how well it is supported by the factual evidence,
5. how plausible the account is generally,
6. how comprehensive it is in covering relevant events and actions,
7. how detailed it is in filling in gaps,
8. how well it stands up to critical questioning and examination,
9. how well the explanation was supported by arguments.
10. how well the argument was supported by factual evidence, and
11. which alternative explanations have been considered, and why were they rejected?
12. how well the explanation documented its own limitations by considering whether it might be weakened by missing data.

These criteria work together to offer a general procedure of how to evaluate explanations comparatively when evaluating the comparative goodness of each of the explanations in relation to the facts admitted as evidence in a case. The script-based story diagram is used as the basis for modeling a story and comparing it to a competing story. But beyond that, the hybrid diagram displays both the script and the argumentation and evidence supporting the notes and links in the script, and attacks the weak points in it based on evidence, of the kind illustrated in Fig. 3.1. This is the best method for the displaying the structure of an explanation. By this means one can gain an appreciation both of how well the explanation hangs together as a coherent script, and how well it is supported or undermined by the arguments and factual evidence in the case. These lessons can now be applied to the Galapagos finches example studied in Chap. 1 (Sect. 1.6), to show how the two explanations can

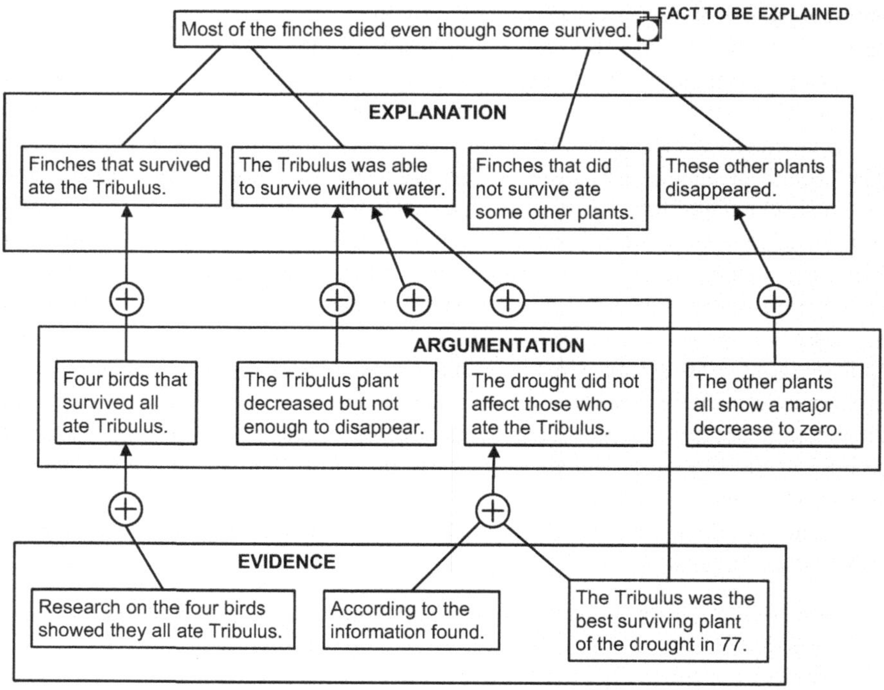


**Fig. 3.4** The evidence-based structure of the second student explanation

be evaluated so that one is shown to be better than the other. The first explanation was also a good one, but the second was better. Why it was better can be shown using the hybrid argument-explanation graph in Fig. 3.4.

The superiority of the second explanation is that the three components of claim, evidence and reasoning can be clearly differentiated. On their analysis, the first sentence presents a claim, and the next three sentences, identified by the phrase 'research shows', are presented as evidence to support the claim. On their analysis, the last three sentences clarify logical connections between the evidence and the claim.

Figure 3.4 shows a way of modeling the explanation in a way that emphasizes the importance of the second criterion for the success of an explanation given by Sandoval and Reiser (2004, 362): an explanation is better to the extent that it links data, such as measurements or weather conditions, to support parts of the explanation. In the analysis shown in Fig. 3.4, the explanation is modeled as a contrastive explanation. The original fact to be explained was why most of the finches died even though some survived. This obviously requires a contrast between two factual situations, most of the finches died, but some of them survived. The purpose of the explanation is to explain this contrast.

Figure 3.4 shows how a successful explanation is given, according to the second criterion of Sandoval and Reiser, by a sequence of reasoning that goes through three levels. At the top level the basic explanation is given in two parts, where each part explains one half of the contrasting factual situation. The explanation on the left shows that the finches that survived ate the Tribulus and the Tribulus was able to survive without water. This is only part of the explanation, however. We also have to look at the right side, which states that the finches that did not survive ate some other plants, and these other plants disappeared. By putting these two contrasting situations together, explanation is achieved by enabling the reader to get some grasp of the explanation of the initial fact to be explained. Because the reader has common knowledge of how such a situation would go, he or she would know that when these other plants disappeared, the finches would not have a food source, and this would explain why they did not survive. Similarly, the reader would know, based on common knowledge, that the other finches survived because their food source, the Tribulus, was still available, because in a situation of drought it could still survive.

It is interesting to note that this top part of the explanation is not as complete as the script-based information given by the previous student group. This explanation was better, as judged by the third criterion of a good explanation set out by Sandoval and Reiser. This criterion stated that an evaluation is better, on grounds of firmness and clarity, if it is configured as a story connected together by a sequence of causes and effects. The explanation given by the first group was better in this regard, as shown in Fig. 3.4. This explanation brought out other causally intervening events. For example, the other plants had softer seeds, so birds fought in competition for those plants, whereas the Tribulus had harder and longer seeds, so the finches that had the best chances for survival were the ones that could adapt to eating the Tribulus seeds.

## 3.8 A Method of Evaluating Explanations

An important test of the plausibility of a story is how it fares when examined in a dialogue between the two sides in the case, the questioner and the respondent. The respondent's commitments in such a dialogue are evidenced by his or her actions and recorded utterances (speech acts) in the dialogue. Every dialogue, on this theory has a commitment set, a log of propositions accepted by the participant, in the database (commitment set) of that participant. Using this database, and the common knowledge shared by the participants in the dialogue, the stories on either side can be critically tested in an examination dialogue that probes into the weakest links in the story. Under a successful scrutiny of this sort, the story becomes more plausible or less plausible, depending on how the questions are answered.

Consider once again the case of the disappearing sailor from Wigmore (1935, 311) studied in Chap. 2, Sect. 2.2. What becomes apparent when we compare the two stories in Figs. 2.6 and 2.7 with their respective argument graphs shown in Figs. 2.3 and 2.4 is that each of the stories fits roughly (but overall) to the long argumentation in the bottom part of the figure going into the ultimate *probandum*. This matching of the argument and story in both cases suggests the conclusion that even though the method and purpose of the argument is different from that of the story, the two are structurally isomorphic. In other words a participant in a trial, a lawyer, a judge, a witness or jury member, if he or she wants to persuade somebody who fits into one of the other roles as his or her audience, she can have a choice as to whether to use an argument or a story for that purpose. For example an attorney attempting to summarize what he or she takes to be the most significant evidence in the case at the end stage of the trial might use an argument structure to show how the sequence of argumentation leads from the admissible evidence to the ultimate claim he or she needs to win the case, the ultimate *probandum*. On the other hand if the evidence might seem to be subtle, possibly confusing, or simply difficult to summarize in a way that will have a strong persuasive impact on the jury, a story might be used. Either route could achieve the same end, depending on which is thought to be more suitable for the audience. Stories are often more intuitive and compelling, perhaps because they better fit the normal way we so often think and reason in everyday life. Stories have a heuristic value. They require less work and calculation than following what might be a long, subtle and complex sequence of argumentation. Stories can be long, complex and subtle too, but if a story is coherent and the sequence of events in it fits a familiar pattern, they can be much more persuasive.

Stories are more intuitive and compelling to the extent that they are based on a network of plausible reasoning in which each step in the story graph proceeds naturally to the next step, and the whole sequence fits together in accord with the common knowledge of the participants in the dialogue on the way things can normally be expected to go in a kind of situation they are familiar with. According to the account given in Walton et al. (2014, 27) plausible reasoning has the following eleven main characteristics.

1. Plausible reasoning proceeds from premises that are more plausible to a conclusion that was less plausible before the plausible argument.
2. Something is found plausible when hearers have examples in their own minds.
3. Plausible reasoning is based on common knowledge.
4. Plausible reasoning is defeasible.
5. Plausible reasoning is based on the way things generally go in familiar situations.
6. Plausible reasoning can be used to fill in implicit premises in incomplete arguments.
7. Plausible reasoning is commonly based on appearances from perception.
8. Stability is an important characteristic of plausible reasoning.
9. Plausible reasoning can be tested, and by this means, confirmed or refuted.
10. Probing into plausible reasoning in a dialogue is a way of testing it.
11. Plausible reasoning admits of degrees determined by testing, but of a kind different from those of the standard probability values and Bayesian rules used in Pascalian probability.

Another important consideration is to link understanding to explanation. Evaluating explanations depends on comparing stories on a basis of comprehensibility (understanding) and evidential support. Plausible reasoning links comprehensibility together with evidential support, and both factors are linked together with other factors. Explanations can be comparatively evaluated as better or worse based on six criteria.

1. How well they enable the questioner to resolve the anomaly that led to the need for an explanation. A good explanation enables the questioner to come to understand something he did not understand when he asked for an explanation.
2. How plausible they are. A plausible explanation is one that fits in with the normal and expected ways events and actions go in situations we are familiar with.
3. How well they are supported by evidence. Do plausible arguments support them?
4. How consistent they are. If an apparent inconsistency is found, can it be resolved or explained?
5. How comprehensive and detailed they are in covering relevant events and actions. Does one explanation explain some important fact that the other cannot?
6. How well they stand up to critical questioning and examination. Do plausible arguments attack them, and are they strong enough to stand up against the arguments that support them?

Ultimately however, explanations can only be fully evaluated by situating them in a dialogue setting where an explanation is put forward by one party, the explainer, and reacted to by another party, we have called the explainee. If the explanation is fully comprehensible to the explainee and he accepts it, because he understands it, then the explanation is successful and acceptable, and the dialogue can be closed off. However in many instances, for example in collaborative learning in educational settings, the explanation may be greatly improved, and the explainee's comprehension of it greatly enhanced if the explainee ask questions that pinpoint what aspects of it he does not understand. Such a dialogue can continue, and it is the thesis of this chapter that such an explanation can become better than it was before as a successful dialogue of this type continues. It was also contended in this chapter that such a dialogue can start out as a persuasion dialogue in which abductive reasoning or inference to the best explanation is used by both parties, and then continue to an explanation dialogue in which the explanation is critically questioned during an examination dialogue. The examination dialogue provides the basis for judgment to be made on which is the best one of the explanations that have been offered by the competing sides in the original persuasion dialogue.

The dialectical structure to provide a normative model for performing such evaluations of arguments and explanations when they are intertwined in this way is quite a complex undertaking which requires formulation of a protocol governing the speech acts of explanation and argument, and providing rules that determine the pre and post-conditions for each of the different types of moves containing speech acts. This chapter has provided a basis for continuing the exploration and building of dialectical structures combining arguments and explanations.

The system as a whole is quite a complex one, and therefore unwieldy in some ways when it comes to attempting to apply it to real cases where inference to the best explanation is used. In Sect. 3.4 two legal cases, Anderson v. Griffin and US v. Beard, were used to show how this dialectical structure can be applied to real cases in a legal setting. In both cases, each side presented an explanation in the form of a story, and the story was exposed to examination and criticism during the argumentation in the trial. It was this argumentation sequence during the argumentation stage of the trial that brought out the evidence that was marshaled on both sides as a basis for determining which side should be judged to be the winner of the original persuasion dialogue. To model the abductive argumentation in such a trial, as we see in these examples, a burden of persuasion is set at the opening stage by law, depending on whether the case is a civil or criminal one. In a civil trial, the burden of proof set at the opening stage is generally that of the preponderance of the evidence. In a criminal trial the burden of proof is that of beyond reasonable doubt. A winning argument by one side or the other has to provide argumentation based on evidence that meets the appropriate burden of proof set by law at the outset of the trial procedure. As we saw through the analyses of Bex and Walton of the argumentation in these two cases, the evidential burden of proof shifted back and forth between the two sides as the trial progressed through the argumentation stage to the closing stage where a decision was made by the judge or jury. Note that in instances of dialogue of this type there are two main protagonists engaged in a persuasion dialogue but there is also a third-party who decides at a metalevel, once the closing stage has been reached, which side has won. Since both cases were based on use of inference to the best explanation, the evaluator, the judge or jury, had to reach this decision by determining which side had produced the best (or better) explanation.

As noted above, such legal cases are complex and require that a mass of connected arguments and explanations be analyzed and evaluated. Of course we have a method of analyzing such cases, namely the application of the hybrid argument-explanation graphs. But the graph really tracks the sequence of arguments and explanations. By itself it does not provide a method of evaluating explanations comparatively in order to determine which explanation is better. The dialogue method has the potential to carry out such a determination, but as noted in the previous paragraph it is a complex method that is, at its current state of development, complex and unwieldy. Fortunately there is a shortcut method available that has already been recognized in the argumentation literature and that can be applied to such cases.

A profile of dialogue is defined (Walton 1989, 3) as a manageably short local sequence of moves embedded in a longer (global) sequence of moves in a dialogue. A longer sequence could be global, meaning that it stretches continuously from the opening stage of the dialogue to the closing stage. If the selected local sequence fits into such a longer sequence, it can help to analyze features of the local argumentation displayed. The idea is that the profile of dialogue can function as a working tool for the study of argumentation because it is manageable as an alternative to dealing with all the formal protocol of a complex dialogue structure. So defined, profiles of dialogue have proved to be useful for analyzing fallacies and other puzzling and problematic phenomena of natural language argumentation. As the following moderately abstract example shown in Table 3.1 illustrates, the profiles technique can also be applied to instances of the use of inference to the best explanation by tracking the shifting of the burden of proof (the evidential burden)

**Table 3.1** Example dialogue for testing abductive reasoning

| Proponent | Respondent |
|---|---|
| 1. Here is an IBE argument | 1. Is there an alternative explanation? |
| 2. If so, you need to provide it | 2. Here is an alternative explanation |
| 3. Why is your explanation better than mine? | 3. It fits better with the facts |
| 4. In what way does it fit better with the facts? | 4. It is better supported by the evidence |
| 5. What evidence? | 5. Here is some evidence |
| 6. OK, but it also contains an inconsistency | 6. What is the inconsistency? |
| 7. These two parts are inconsistent | 7. This inconsistency can be explained |
| 8. How can you explain it? | 8. Here is an explanation |
| 9. Even so, my explanation is more plausible | 9. How can you prove that? |

back and forth through a sequence of dialogue exchanges. In such a sequence, as we have seen in the examples studied in Chaps. 2 and 3, it is assumed that there is some global burden of proof or burden of persuasion set at the outset that can be used to determine the success requirements of any argument or explanation that is offered during the next stage, the so-called argumentation stage, of the dialogue. As the dialogue proceeds, this evidential burden shifts back and forth from one side to the other. The evaluator of the arguments and explanations put forward in the dialogue, at the closing stage, has the task of tracking back through the shifts to see whether the pre and post-moves at any shift conform to the dialogue protocol governing the legitimacy of the speech act put forward by the one side, and the reaction of the other side at its next move.

In this dialogue the proponent starts out at her first move putting forward an argument that fits the scheme for inference to the best explanation It could be any argument of this kind, such as the ones discussed in Chaps. 1 and 2. At his first move, the respondent asks one of the questions matching the scheme for inference to the best explanation, the question of whether there is an alternative explanation. Now the notion of burden of proof kicks in. The proponent, at her second move, states that in order to contest her initial abductive argument, the respondent needs to provide such an alternative explanation. Let's say that the respondent at his next move provides some alternative explanation. At her third move, the proponent once again invokes the notion of burden of proof, by asking the respondent to show why his explanation is better than the one she originally offered. At his next move, the respondent offers an appropriate reply, saying that his explanation fits better with the facts. Once again, the proponent appeals to burden of proof, at her fourth move, by asking the respondent to show in what way his explanation supposedly fits better with the facts. The respondent replies in an appropriate way, claiming that his explanation is better supported by the factual evidence in the case. This is a reasonable reply, but the proponent's reply to her is also reasonable. She again appeals to the requirement of burden of proof at her fifth move by asking him to specify the evidence. Let's say that, as shown at the respondent's fifth move, he supplies some evidence to support his explanation. At her sixth move the proponent attacks the respondent's explanation by claiming that it contains an inconsistency. This move seems to shift the initiative back to the respondent side, but the respondent now invokes the notion of burden of proof again by asking the proponent to specify the inconsistency. At her seventh move, the proponent provides some evidence for her claim that there is an inconsistency. She specifies two parts of his explanation that are inconsistent. In his reply, his seventh move, the proponent claims that the inconsistency can be explained. At her eighth move the proponent invokes something like the notion of burden of proof, except that in this instance, it could be better called a burden of explanation. She asks him to offer an explanation that would resolve the inconsistency. At his eighth move, the proponent fulfills this obligation of the burden of explanation by offering an explanation for the apparent inconsistency claimed by the proponent at her seventh move. But at her ninth move, the proponent counterattacks by arguing that her explanation is more plausible. This time the respondent invokes the burden of proof by asking her how can she prove that?

This dialogue illustrates two aspects of how any argument fitting the scheme for inference to the best explanation should be evaluated. First, it shows how the notion of burden of proof is involved affecting nearly all the moves in the dialogue or arguably, even all of them. It appears appropriate for the participants using the notion of burden of proof to direct how the other party should reply to a particular move. And in all instances, the replies given seem to be appropriate, meaning that they would appear to be the kinds of moves that would fit reasonable requirements on the shifting of the burden of proof at any given moment. Second, all the moves seem reasonable, either as speech acts put forward or as responses to such speech acts by the other party in a dialogue that combines argument and explanation. For this reason the dialogue shown in Table 3.1 can be classified as a normative profile of dialogue.

A novelty of the dialectical theory of explanation presented in this chapter is that it not only introduces the notion of burden of explanation to argumentation theory, but it also introduces the idea of the burden of responding to an explanation to back up the challenge to it by producing counterarguments based on evidence. This means that if the respondent replies to an explanation saying it does not make sense to him, this can certainly be a legitimate response, but it needs to be backed up by specifically indicating the particular respect in which the explanation fails to make sense. For example if the explanation is challenged by saying that it is incoherent, or inconsistent, or it doesn't account for the factual circumstances of the case, then some evidence has to be brought forward explaining the incoherence, pointing out the specific inconsistency, or bringing forward some factual evidence that appears to refute the explanation.

## 3.9 Problems for Further Research

The following problems for further research are singled out as the most important.

1. How can the hybrid system help us to determine whether something in a text is an argument or an explanation?

2. How can we build a useful typology of types of explanations for use in the hybrid system?
3. How well does the hybrid system apply to explanation of human actions, for example in history and law?
4. Can the hybrid model analyze understanding in science, and apply it to case studies of scientific explanations and use of inference to the best explanation in scientific discovery of hypothesis?

With respect to problem 1, it can be said, broadly speaking, that the goal of an argument is to remove doubt, whereas the goal of an explanation is to convey understanding of an anomaly in a given account. But how do we determine whether the purpose of some discourse fits one or the other of these goals? We have to examine the text of the case carefully for textual indicators of the kind studied by Snoeck Henkemans (1997). However, the key to doing this lies in the pre and post-conditions for the speech acts. An argument is not only put forward in a different way from an explanation, but is reacted to in a different way as well. How can the hybrid system be helpful for this job, when it is carried out in a way comparable to the work on identifying arguments in texts?

The aim of this investigation was not to provide a typology of different types of explanations. There was no space here for this project, even though it is a prerequisite for building formal dialogue systems based on different kinds of explanation questions, like how questions, why questions, questions asking about human actions, and so forth. With respect to problem #2, it needs to be said that there are typologies of explanation questions, but there is little agreement among them, and none of them seems especially useful for developing the hybrid system in this direction. Perhaps the reason for the heterogeneous variety is that they come from different fields, like logic, computing, linguistics and psychology, and they seem to have different purposes in mind for using explanations. It can be suggested, however, that a good place to start is the categorization scheme for types of explanations given by Kass and Leake (1987), based on and their large collection of examples of anomalies and explanations.

The classification of different types of explanations given in the categorization scheme of Kass and Leake (1987, 3–4) provides a hierarchy of types of explanations divided at the top level into three types of explanations.

- Explanations involving intentional actions, for example an explanation of a person's decision to drop out of school. Such explanations involve plans and goals.
- Explanations involving material forces, for example, an explanation of an unexpected snow storm caused by material forces. This type of explanation also includes cases like device problems and the lack of a resource necessary for an event to take place.
- Explanations involving social forces, for example an explanation of an increase in the crime rate. This type of explanation does not involve plans and goals, and excludes explanations of goal-directed actions by institutions. It involves behavior that results from the interactions of many independent agents whose actions are not coordinated.

Kass and Leake (1987, 3) note, however, that in some cases more than one type of explanation may be applicable. For example, if we are trying to explain why the government wastes money, we might offer an intentional explanation, like "they think they can solve every problem by throwing money at it", or we might offer a social explanation, such as "the interaction of branches of government causes huge overhead". This categorization scheme, along with the many examples of everyday explanations collected by Kass and Leake is a good place to begin the study of different types of explanations. The category of intentional actions brings us to problem #3.

There is huge literature on problem 3, both in computing, especially in the field of planning, and in philosophy, especially philosophy of history. Collingwood (1946) called the simulative process used by the historian "re-enactment" (Dray 1995). Dray (1964, 11–12) , described the components of Collingwood's theory of re-enactment: in these words: "Clearly the kinds of thoughts which Collingwood's theory requires are those which could enter the practical deliberations of an agent trying to decide what his line of actions should be". There are some nice resources in argumentation and computing that arise from the argumentation scheme for practical reasoning (Atkinson et al. 2006). Explanation of human actions, of the kind especially common in history and law, is typically based on goal-directed reasoning. One agent explains the actions of the other by attributing presumed goals to the other. Goal-based or means-end reasoning, called practical reasoning, is used in planning in AI (Bratman et al. 1988). Value-based argumentation frameworks employ schemes for practical reasoning in a dialogue framework (Bench-Capon 2003).

Pera's dialectical model of science (Pera 1994), provides an elegant way of extending Explainer to confront problem 4, but any attempt to move in the direction of applying the hybrid system to scientific explanations also takes us to the problem of precisely defining the notion of scientific understanding. In a case of scientific explanation, say explaining friction as a macro-phenomenon by talking about the micro-properties of surfaces, "it is clear that we are now constrained to explanations using the primitives and laws of physics" (Scriven 2002, 50). It is the phenomena of everyday experience that need to be understood in a special way, and it is the laws and primitives of physics that are taken to be understood. Hence, as Scriven points out, scientific explanation is not reduction to the familiar, but transfer of a special kind of understanding required by a special kind of explanation.

There is a growing literature on helping us to better understand the special notion of understanding in the natural sciences (Friedman 1974; Trout 2002; Moulin et al. 2002). Finocchiaro (1980) has used case studies of scientific discovery to show how scientific explanation can be viewed as a dialectical process of growth of understanding as questions are asked and hypotheses are offered as answers that require experimental testing. The Explainer system offers a syntactic structure for explanation dialogue by specifying the form each move must take at each of the three stages of such a dialogue, and by giving pre and post-conditions for each move in such a dialogue, but it does not yet define a precise semantics for the system. A semantic structure is also needed that specifies the units of understanding, and how they are sent as messages in the dialogue from the one party to the other.

So far this structure has not yet been provided, in any precise way. The best we have been able to do so far is to use existing resources of case-based reasoning to model in a general way how understanding is successfully transferred. This process is successfully carried out when an anomaly in an existing script is queried by one party and then resolved by the other party by patching up the existing script to fit it all together better so that it now makes sense to the questioner. The outcome should be a change from a script that was previously fragmented (in the understanding of the questioner) to a script that is fitted back together.

It can be noted that legal explanations also have a three-party dialogue structure consisting of the pro side, the contra side, and a third party trier, a judge or a jury. The third party listens to the arguments put forward and queried by the other two parties and weighs them as weaker or stronger. In audience-specific value-based models of persuasion dialogue (Bench-Capon et al. 2007), the audience is identified with an ordering of values. A given argument is assessed by the audience in accordance with its preferred values. In Gordon and Walton (2009), the audience weighs the relative strength of arguments presented to them, and an argument evaluation structure associates an audience with a stage of dialogue and assigns proof standards to propositions. When the hybrid model is extended by adding a third party audience, this audience uses standards for the success of an explanation to judge whether the given explanation is more satisfactory or less satisfactory. Precisely how legal explanations can best be modeled in three-party dialogues along these lines, however, remains a problem for further research.

## 3.10 Conclusions

This chapter has defined the components needed for a dialectical explanation system, and showed how to combine these components to produce the system specification. It offers a dialogue structure with three stages, an opening stage, an explanation stage and a closing stage.

One problem encountered was that of the failure cycle that can occur in the closing stage, and this problem was solved by carefully specifying the rules for the closing stage. Another problem was to devise a means for testing the success of an explanation. These problems were solved by adopting a hybrid dialogue system for combining and evaluating stories and arguments. The problems were solved by extending the hybrid system of Bex (2011) into a dialectical framework in which a set of explanations can be comparatively evaluated to determine which is best. If two or more of the explanations are tied, the system can also reveal the strengths and weaknesses of each of the competitors, so that additional evidence can be collected and used to further the evaluate the explanations.

Figure 3.5 is a UML graph structure explaining in outline how the dialectical procedure of evaluating an explanation works. The first step in the sequence is for the one party, called agent a1, to perform the speech act of requesting an explanation. The second step is for the respondent, agent a2, to provide an explanation, or at least

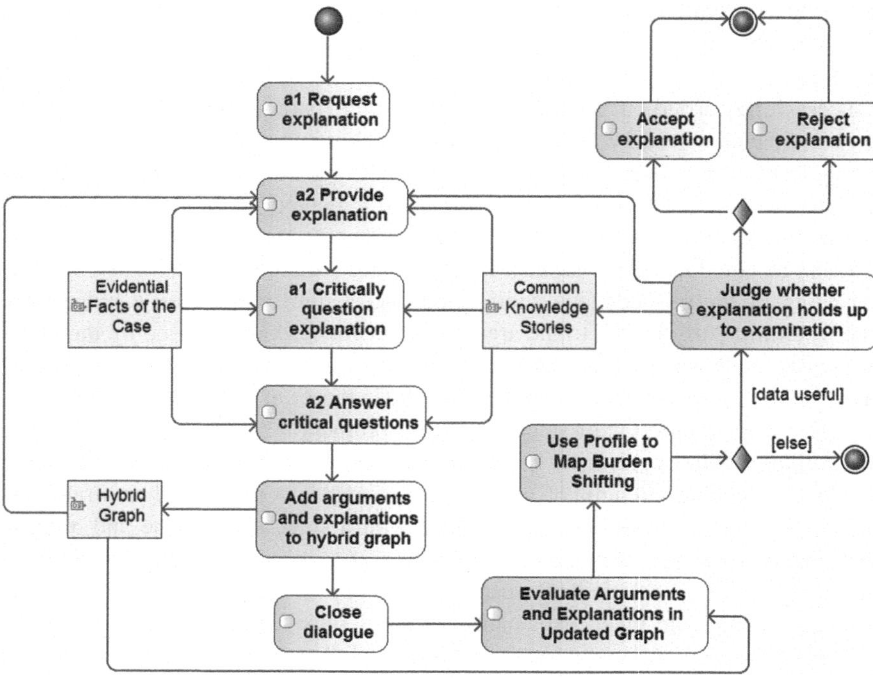


**Fig. 3.5** The dialogue procedure for evaluating an explanation

to make an explanation attempt. At the third step a1 critically questions and attacks the explanation, for example by pointing out weak points where the story is not possible, or by attacking the story, showing that it is not based on evidence, or there is evidence that can be drawn from the circumstances of the case showing that the story is not plausible. At the fourth step, a2 attempts to provide answers to these critical questions, and to reply to the objections by posing counter-arguments. At the fifth step, all these arguments and explanations are collected together in a hybrid graph that represents the accumulation of arguments, explanations and evidence at any particular point. The sequence of the first five steps goes through a cycle that leads back to the second step where a2 provided an explanation. All the moves made during this five-step dialogue sequence will have (hopefully) enriched the explanation, making it more subtle and complex, and making it more plausible. On the other hand, a2's criticisms may have pointed out so many weak transitions and gaps in the explanation that it has now come to be highly questionable, and may even be seen as implausible. The probing examination that has taken place during this sequence of steps in the argumentation stage of dialogue may even have showed that the explanation is implausible because of an internal inconsistency which a1 is unable to explain. At any rate, after cycling through this sequence several times, the dialogue will eventually reach the closing stage. When it has reached this stage the outcome may need to be decided by a third-party evaluator, or may have to be made by limitations of cost and time. If there is no third party, it may be made by a1 and a2 reaching an agreement on when to quit.

Having reached the closing stage of the initial sequence, the dialogue moves on to an evaluation stage. The hybrid graph built up during the first six steps is carried forward to this evaluation stage, and used in conjunction with the profile of dialogue tool illustrated in Table 3.1 to evaluate, using the hybrid system protocol alongside the profile tool, which of the competing explanations has held up better as a result of the examination procedure carried out during the first five steps of the dialectical procedure as a whole. Using these tools the dialogue is evaluated to determine which of the competing explanations, assuming several explanations have been offered, is the best one. If only one explanation has been offered, and no competing explanation has been offered by the opposing side, as in the Beard case, then the explanation that has been offered wins by default. The final step in the evaluation procedure is to accept the best explanation and reject all the alternative explanations that were offered.

Below is a summary of the standard sequence of events in a dialogue system for explanations.

- Two parties have a conflict of opinions in a persuasion dialogue and each party has a story which it puts forward as part of an inference to the best explanation to try to show that its opinion represents the best explanation of some sequence of events that supposedly took place.
- However, each of the parties argues that its explanation is the better one, and in order to prove this they attack the explanation of the opposed party by asking critical questions and posing counterarguments.
- Following the dialogue protocol, each party asks a question requesting an explanation of the account given by the other side, and the other side replies by arguing that its explanation is better, partly by questioning and attacking the opposed explanation.
- During this sequence of argumentation factual evidence concerning the circumstances of the case is brought forward and used to support one's own explanation and attack the explanation offered by the other side.
- During the argumentation stage, different kinds of evidence are brought forward and evaluated. For example, the testimony of a witness may be cross-examined to find weaknesses in it suggesting that the story of the witness is not plausible.
- At some point it is judged that the argumentation has continued to the point where sufficient opportunity has been given for the conflict to be resolved.
- The dialogue reaches the closing stage where the mass of argumentation forming a large hybrid graph can be evaluated, so that it can be determined if one side has met its burden of persuasion.

The model of explanation built in this chapter is a system specification that can be used to build specific dialectical systems meant to be applicable to realistic cases of explanations of different kinds. The intent is to produce a dialogue system specification that is very general so that it can accommodate many different formal models of explanation dialogue that fit the general pattern of the system, and many different dialectical contexts of use, such as everyday conversational explanations, scientific explanations, explanations in special scientific fields such as computing, historical explanations, legal explanations, and so forth. Kass and Leake (1987) built up a corpus, the Yale explanation corpus of 170 anomalies, with one or more explanation for each, yielding a total of over 350 explanations. The method put forward in this chapter is designed to be practically useful so that it can be applied to real examples, such as the cases given in Chaps. 1, 2 and 3. The method needs to be improved by research in two directions. The first is to collect more real examples of explanations, and instances of inference to the best explanation, and to apply the method to these examples, thereby making the method more detailed and sophisticated. The second is to refine the formal structure of the method by showing how it fits the hybrid model of arguments and stories (Bex 2011), and especially by showing how the hybrid model can be extended so that it can be applied in a more detailed way to the method. By this means, it is hoped that a formal argumentation model that can include this method as a component can be built. In this book, our primary concern is to set out a systematic method for evaluating argumentation generally. But as the example so far have shown, since inference to the best explanation is such an important type of argument linking arguments to evidence, the general objective of the book can only be carried out by dealing with explanations as well as arguments.

## References

Aristotle. 1928. *On sophistical refutations*, Loeb classical library. Cambridge, MA: Harvard University Press.

Atkinson, K., T.J.M. Bench-Capon, and P. McBurney. 2006. Computational representation of practical argument. *Synthese* 152(2): 157–206.

Bench-Capon, T.J.M. 2003. Persuasion in practical argument using value-based argumentation frameworks. *Journal of Logic and Computation* 13(3): 429–448.

Bench-Capon, T.J.M., S. Doutre, and P.E. Dunne. 2007. Audiences in argumentation frameworks. *Artificial Intelligence* 171(1): 42–71.

Bench-Capon, T.J.M., S. Doutre, and P.E. Dunne. 2008. Asking the right question: Forcing commitment in examination dialogues. In *Computational models of argument: Proceedings of COMMA 2008*, ed. P. Besnard, S. Doutre, and A. Hunter, 49–60. Amsterdam: IOS Press.

Berland, L.K., and B.J. Reiser. 2008. Making sense of argumentation and explanation. *Science Education* 93(1): 26–55.

Bex, F.J. 2011. *Arguments, stories and criminal evidence: A formal hybrid theory*. Dordrecht: Springer.

Bex, F.J., and D. Walton. 2012. Burdens and standards of proof for inference to the best explanation: Three case studies. *Law, Probability and Risk* 11(2–3): 113–133.

Bratman, M., D. Israel, and M. Pollack. 1988. Plans and resource-bounded practical reasoning. *Computational Intelligence* 4(3): 349–355.

Brewer, S. 1996. Exemplary reasoning: Semantics, pragmatics and the rational force of legal argument by analogy. *Harvard Law Review* 109: 923–1038.

Cawsey, A. 1992. *Explanation and interaction: The computer generation of explanatory dialogues*. Cambridge, MA: MIT Press.

Collingwood, R.G. 1946. *The idea of history*. Oxford: Clarendon.

Dray, W. 1964. *Philosophy of history*. Englewood Cliffs: Prentice-Hall.

Dray, W. 1995. *History as re-enactment: R. G. Collingwood's idea of history*. Oxford: Oxford University Press.

Dunne, P.E., S. Doutre, and T.J.M. Bench-Capon. 2005. Discovering Inconsistency through examination dialogues. In *Proceedings IJCAI-05*, 1560–1561. Edinburgh.
Finocchiaro, M. 1980. Scientific discoveries as growth of understanding: The case of Newton's gravitation. In *Scientific discovery, logic, and rationality*, ed. Thomas Nickles, 235–255. Dordrecht: Reidel.
Friedman, M. 1974. Explanation and scientific understanding. *The Journal of Philosophy* LXXI: 5–19.
Gordon, T.F., and D. Walton. 2009. Proof burdens and standards. In *Argumentation and artificial intelligence*, ed. Iyad Rahwan and Guillermo Simari, 239–260. Berlin: Springer.
Guthrie, W.K.C. 1981. *A history of Greek philosophy*. Cambridge: Cambridge University Press.
Hamblin, C.L. 1970. *Fallacies*. London: Methuen.
Kass. A., and D. Leake. 1987. *Types of explanations*, Technical report ADA183253. U. S. Department of Commerce, Alexandria.
Leake, D.B. 1992. *Evaluating explanations: A content theory*. Hillsdale: Erlbaum.
Moore, J.D. 1995. *Participating in explanatory dialogues*. Cambridge, MA: MIT Press.
Moulin, B., H. Irandoust, M. Belanger, and G. Desbordes. 2002. Explanation and argumentation capabilities. *Artificial Intelligence Review* 17(3): 169–222.
Parsons, S., and N.R. Jennings. 1997. Negotiation through argumentation: A preliminary report. In *Proceedings of the second international conference on multi-agents systems*, ed. Mario Tokoro, 267–274. Menlo Park: AAAI Press.
Pera, M. 1994. *The discoveries of science*. Chicago: The University of Chicago Press.
Prakken, H. 2005. Coherence and flexibility in dialogue games for argumentation. *Journal of Logic and Computation* 15(6): 1009–1040.
Prakken, H. 2006. Formal systems for persuasion dialogue. *The Knowledge Engineering Review* 21(2): 163–188.
Reed, C. 2006. Representing dialogic argumentation. *Knowledge-Based Systems* 19(1): 22–31.
Sandoval, W., and B.J. Reiser. 2004. Explanation-driven inquiry: Integrating conceptual and epistemic scaffolds for scientific inquiry. *Science Education* 88(1): 345–372.
Schank, R.C. 1986. *Explanation patterns: Understanding mechanically and creatively*. Hillsdale: Erlbaum.
Schank, R.C., and R.P. Abelson. 1977. *Scripts, plans, goals and understanding*. Hillsdale: Erlbaum.
Schank, R.C., and C.K. Riesback. 1981. *Inside computer understanding*. Hillsdale: Erlbaum.
Schank, R.C., A. Kass, and C.K. Riesbeck. 1994. *Inside case-based explanation*. Hillsdale: Erlbaum.
Schlangen, D. 2004. Causes and strategies for requesting clarification in dialogue. In *Proceedings of the 5th SIGdial workshop on discourse and dialogue*, ed. Michael Strube and Candy Sidner, 136–143. East Stoudsburg: XXXX. Available at: http://acl.ldc.upenn.edu/hlt-naacl2004/sigdial04/pdf/schlangen.pdf.
Scriven, M. 1972. The concept of comprehension: From semantics to software. In *Language comprehension and the acquisition of knowledge*, ed. J.B. Carroll and R.O. Freedle, 31–39. Washington: W. H. Winston & Sons.
Scriven, M. 2002. The limits of explication. *Argumentation* 16(1): 47–57.
Snoeck Henkemans, F. 1997. *Analyzing complex argumentation: The reconstruction of multiple and coordinatively compound argumentation in a critical discussion*. Amsterdam: SICSAT.
Trout, J.D. 2002. Scientific explanation and the sense of understanding. *Philosophy of Science* 69(2): 212–233.
Unsworth, L. 2001. Evaluating the language of different types of explanations in junior high school texts. *International Journal of Science Education* 23(6): 585–609.
Verheij, B. 2003. DefLog: On the logical interpretation of prima facie justified assumptions. *Journal of Logic and Computation* 13(3): 319–346.
von Wright, G.H. 1971. *Explanation and understanding*. Ithaca: Cornell University Press.
Walton, D. 1989. *Informal logic*. Cambridge: Cambridge University Press.
Walton, D. 1996. *Argumentation schemes for presumptive reasoning*. Mahwah: Lawrence Erlbaum Publishers.

Walton, D. 2003. The interrogation as a type of dialogue. *Journal of Pragmatics* 35(12): 1771–1802.

Walton, D. 2004. *Abductive reasoning*. Tuscaloosa: University of Alabama Press.

Walton, D. 2006. *Character evidence: An abductive theory*. Dordrecht: Springer.

Walton, D. 2007a. Dialogical models of explanation. In *Explanation-aware computing: Papers from the 2007 AAAI workshop*, Technical report WS-07-06, 1–9. Menlo Park: AAAI Press.

Walton, D. 2007b. Clarification dialogue. *Studies in Communication Sciences* 7: 165–197.

Walton, D. 2011. Teleological argumentation to and from motives. *Law, Probability and Risk* 10(3): 203–223.

Walton, D., and E.C.W. Krabbe. 1995. *Commitment in dialogue*. Albany: State University of New York Press.

Walton, D., C.W. Tindale, and T.F. Gordon. 2014. Applying recent argumentation methods to some ancient examples of plausible reasoning. *Argumentation* 28(1): 85–119.

Wells, S., and C. Reed. 2012. A domain specific language for describing diverse systems of dialogue. *Journal of Applied Logic* 10(4): 309–329.

Wigmore, J.H. 1935. *A student's textbook of the law of evidence*. Chicago: The Foundation Press.

# Chapter 4
# Evaluating Expert Opinion Evidence

**Abstract** This chapter offers solutions to key problems of how to apply argumentation tools to analyze and evaluate arguments from expert opinion. It is shown (1) how to structure the argumentation scheme for argument from expert opinion, (2) how to apply it to real cases of argument from expert opinion, (3) how to set up the matching set of critical questions that go along with the scheme, (4) how to find the place of trust in configuring the schemes and critical questions, (5) how to use these tools to construct an argument diagram to represent pro and con arguments in a given argument from expert opinion, (6) how to evaluate the arguments and critical questions shown in the diagram, and (7) how to use this structure within a formal computational model to determine whether what the expert says is acceptable or not. One of the critical questions raises the issue of trust, and a central problem is to determine how the other critical questions fit with this one. The chapter studies how trust is related to argument from expert opinion in formal computational argumentation models.

Evaluating arguments based on scientific evidence frequently has to be carried out by people who are not themselves experts, and have to extract the evidence from expert scientific testimony. In the Galapagos finches example, first outlined in Chap. 1 Sect. 1.6, a group of students had the task of using data from scientists to answer the question of why most of the Galapagos finches died during the mid-1970s. The explanation by a second group of students was more successful because it linked the scientific research findings as evidence to the explanation of why some birds survived while others did not. In the issue of whether the driveshaft broke because debris from the road struck it, the civil case of Anderson v. Griffin, studied in Chap. 3, was decided on the basis of conflicting expert testimony. The expert for the one side claimed that the truck dealer's failure to repair the driveshaft was what made the driveshaft break, but the expert for the other side claimed that road debris struck the driveshaft and broke it.

Argument from expert opinion has long been included in logic textbooks under the heading of the fallacy of appeal to authority, and even though this traditional approach of so strongly mistrusting authority has changed, generally the argumentation approach stresses the value of critical questioning. For example, if you are receiving advice from your doctor concerning a treatment that has been



D. Walton, *Argument Evaluation and Evidence*, Law, Governance and Technology Series 23, DOI 10.1007/978-3-319-19626-8_4

recommended, it is advocated that you should try not only to absorb the information she is communicating to you, but also try your best to ask intelligent questions about it, and in particular to critically question aspects you have doubts or reservations about. This policy is held to be consistent with rational principles of informed and intelligent autonomous decision-making and critical evidence-based argumentation.

Sections 4.3 and 4.4 explain certain aspects of defeasible reasoning that are important for understanding arguments from expert opinion. Sections 4.5 and 4.6 show how to use the argumentation scheme for argument from expert opinion and its matching set of critical questions to evaluate expert opinion evidence. Sections 4.7 and 4.8 explain how a formal and computational system for argument evaluation can use argument weights to help evaluate arguments from expert opinion by taking critical questions and counterarguments into account. Following the good advice that real examples should be used to test any theory of argument, Sect. 4.9 models some arguments from expert opinion in a real case discussing whether a valuable Greek statue (kouros) that appears to be from antiquity is genuine or not. Section 4.10 summarizes the findings and draws some conclusions. By these means, this chapter makes the tools needed to evaluate the argumentation in a much more extensive real case where there was a conflict of expert opinions on whether a painting attributed to Leonardo da Vinci was genuine or not.

## 4.1 Arguments from Expert Opinion

Argument from expert opinion has always been a form of reasoning that is on a razor's edge. We often have to rely on it, but we also need to recognize that we can go badly wrong with it. Argument from expert opinion was traditionally taken to be a fallacious form of argument coming under the heading of appeal to authority in the logic textbooks. But research in studies on argumentation tended to show by an examination of many examples of argument from expert opinion that many of these arguments were not fallacious, and in fact they were reasonable but defeasible forms of argumentation. At one time, in a more positivistic era, it was accepted that argument from expert opinion is a subjective source of evidence or testimony that should always yield to empirical knowledge of the facts. However, it seems to be more generally acknowledged now that we do have to rely on experts, such as scientists, physicians, financial experts and so forth, and that such sources of evidence should be given at least some weight in deciding what to do or what to believe in practical matters. Thus the problem was posed of how to differentiate between the reasonable cases of argument from expert opinion and the fallacious instances of this type of argument. This problem has turned out to be a wicked one, and it has become more evident in recent years that solving it is a significant task with many practical applications.

The way towards a solution proposed in (Walton 1997) was to formulate an argumentation scheme for argument from expert opinion along with a set of critical questions matching this scheme. The scheme and critical questions can be used in a number of ways to evaluate a given instance of argument from expert opinion. The scheme requires this type of argument to have certain premises articulated as special components of the scheme, and if the argument in question fails to have one or more of these premises, or otherwise does not fit the requirements of the scheme, then the argument can be analyzed, and even criticized on this basis. The missing premise might be merely an unstated premise or an incomplete argument of the kind traditionally called an enthymeme. Or in another more problematic kind of case, the expert source might not be named. This failure is in fact one of the most common problems with appeals to expert opinion found in everyday conversational arguments, such as political arguments and arguments put forward in newsmagazines. One premise of the given argument is that an expert says such and such, or experts say such and such, without the expert being named, or the group of experts being identified with any institution or source that can be tracked down. In other instances, the error is more serious, as suggested by the fallacy literature (Hamblin 1970). In some instances fallacies are simply errors, for example the error to name a source properly. However in other instances fallacies are much more serious, and can be identified with strategic errors that exploit common heuristics sometimes used to deceive an opponent in argumentation (Walton 2010). Fallacies have been identified by van Eemeren and Grootendorst (1992) as violations of the rules of a type of communicative argumentation structure called a critical discussion. Such implicit Gricean conversational rules require that participants in an argumentative exchange should cooperate by making their contributions to the exchange in a way that helps to move the argumentation forward (Grice 1975). There is an element of trust presupposed by all parties in such a cooperative exchange.

Some might say that the problem is when to trust experts, and suggest that arguments from expert opinion become fallacious when the expert violates our trust in someone. Trust has become very important in distributed computational systems: a distributed system is a decentralized network consisting of a collection of autonomous computers that communicate with each other by exchanging messages (Li and Sighal 2007, 45). Trust management systems aid automated multiagent communications systems that put security policies in place to allow actions or messages from an unknown agent if that agent can furnish accredited credentials.

Haynes et al. (2012) reported data from interviews in which Australian civil servants, ministers and ministerial advisors tried to find and evaluate researchers with whom they wished to consult. The search was described as one of finding trustworthy experts, and for this reason it might easily be thought that the attributes found to be best for this purpose would have implications for studying the argument from expert opinion, of the kind often featured in logic textbooks. In the study by Haynes et al. (2012, 1) evaluating three factors was seen as key to reaching a determination of trustworthiness: (1) *competence* (described as "an exemplary academic reputation complemented by pragmatism, understanding of government processes, and effective collaboration and communication skills"); (2) *integrity* (described as "independence, authenticity, and faithful reporting of research"); and (3) *benevolence* (described as "commitment to the policy reform agenda"). The aim of this study was to facilitate political policy discussions by locating suitable trustworthy experts who could be brought in to provide the factual data needed to make such discussions intelligent and informed.

Hence there are many areas where it is important to use criteria for trustworthiness of an expert, but this chapter takes a different approach of working towards developing and improving arguments based on an appeal to expert opinion. This chapter takes an argumentation approach, motivated by the need to teach students informal logic skills by helping them to be able to apply argumentation tools for the identification, analysis and evaluation of arguments. Argument from expert opinion has long been covered in logic textbooks, mainly in the section on informal fallacies in such a book, where the student is tutored on how to take a critical approach. A critical approach requires asking the right questions when the arguer is a layperson who is confronted by an argument that relies on expert opinion.

Goldman (2001, 85) frames the problem to be discussed as one of evaluating the testimony of experts to "decide which of two or more rival experts is most credible". Goldman defines expertise in terms of authority, and defines the notion of authority as follows: "Person *A* is an authority in subject *S* if and only if *A* knows more propositions in *S*, or has a higher degree of knowledge of propositions in *S*, than almost anybody else" (Goldman 1999, 268). This doesn't seem to be a very helpful definition of the notion of an expert, because it implies the consequence that if you have two experts, and one knows more than the other, then the second can't be an expert. The good thing about the definition is that it defines expertise in a subject, in relation to the knowledge that the person who is claimed to be an expert has in that subject. But a dubious aspect of it is that it differentiates between experts and nonexperts on the basis of the number of propositions known by the person who is claimed to be an expert, resting on a numerical comparison. Another questionable aspect of the definition is that it appears to include being an authority under the more general category of being an expert. This is backwards from an argumentation point of view, where it is important to clearly distinguish between the more general notion of an authority and the subsumed notion of an expert (Walton 1997).

In a compelling and influential book, Freedman (2010) argued that experts, including scientific experts, are generally wrong with respect to claims that they make. Freedman supported his conclusions with many well documented instances where expert opinions were wrong. He concluded that approximately two thirds of the research findings published in leading medical journals turned out to be wrong (Freedman 2010, 6). In an appendix to the book (231–238), he presented a number of interesting examples of wrong expert opinions. These include arguments from expert opinion in fields as widely ranging as physics, economics, sports, and child-raising. Freedman went so far as to write (6) that he could fill his entire book, and several more, with examples of pronouncements of experts that turned out to be incorrect. His general conclusion is worth quoting: "The fact is, expert wisdom usually turns out to be at best highly contested and ephemeral, and at worst flat-out wrong" (Freedman 2010). The implications of Freedman's reports of such findings are highly significant for argumentation studies on the argument from expert opinion as a defeasible form of reasoning.

Mizrahi (2013) argues that arguments from expert opinion are inherently weak, in the sense that even if the premises are true, they provide either weak support or no support at all for the conclusion. He takes the view that the argumentation scheme for argument from expert opinion is best represented by its simplest form, 'Expert *E* says that *A*, therefore *A*'. To support his claim he cites a body of empirical evidence showing that experts are only slightly more accurate than chance (2013, 58), and are therefore wrong more often than one might expect (63). He even goes so far as to claim (58) that "we do argue fallaciously when we argue that [proposition] *p* on the ground that an expert says that *p*". He refuses to countenance the possibility that other premises of the form of the argument from expert opinion need to be taken into account.

From an argumentation point of view, this approach does not provide a solution to the problem, because from that point of view what is most vital is to critically question the argument from expert opinion that one has been confronted with, rather than deciding to go along with the argument or not on the basis of whether to trust the expert or not. One could say that from an argumentation point of view of the kind associated with the study of fallacies, it is part of one's starting point to generally be somewhat critical about arguments from expert opinion, in order to ask the right questions needed to properly evaluate the argument as strong or weak. Nevertheless, as will be shown below, trust is partly involved in this critical endeavour, and Freedman's findings about expert opinions being shown to be wrong in so many instances are important.

One purpose of this chapter is to teach students informal logic skills using argumentation tools. Another purpose is to show that the work is of value to researchers in artificial intelligence who are interested in building systems that can perform automated reasoning using computational argumentation. Argumentation is helpful to computing because it provides concepts and methods used to build software tools for designing, implementing and analyzing sophisticated forms of reasoning and interaction among rational agents. Recent successes include argumentation-based models of evidential relations and legal processes of examination and evaluation of evidence. Argument mapping has proved to be a useful tool for designing better products and services and for improving the quality of communication in social media by making deliberation dialogues more efficient. Throughout many of its areas, artificial intelligence has seen a prolific growth in uses of argumentation, including agent system negotiation protocols, argumentation-based models of evidential reasoning in law, design and implementation of protocols for multi-agent action and communication, the application of theories of argument and rhetoric in natural language processing, and the use of argument-based structures for autonomous reasoning in artificial intelligence.

The way forward advocated in the present chapter is to use formal computational argumentation systems that (1) can apply argumentation schemes (2) that are to be used along with argument diagramming tools (3) that distinguish between Pollock-style rebutters and undercutters (Pollock 1995). On this approach, the problem is reframed as one of how laypersons should evaluate the testimony of experts based on an analysis or examination of the argument from expert opinion and probe into it by distinguishing different factors that call for critical questions to be asked. On this approach, a distinction is drawn between the expertise critical question and the reliability critical question. Credibility could ambiguously refer to either one of these factors or both.

From an argumentation point of view, dealing with the traditional informal fallacy of the *argumentum ad verecundiam* (literally, argument from modesty) requires carefully examining lots of examples of this type of strategic maneuvering for the purpose of deception. This project was carried forward in Walton (1997) and brought out common elements in some of the most serious instances of the fallacy. In such cases it was found that it is hard for a layperson in a field of knowledge to critically question an expert, or the opinion of an expert brought forward by a third party, because we normally tend to defer to experts. To some extent this is reasonable, for example in law, where expert witnesses are given special privileges to express opinions and draw inferences in ways stronger than a nonexpert witness is allowed to. In other instances, however, because an expert is treated as an authority, and since as we know from psychological studies there is a halo effect surrounding the pronouncements of an authority, we tend to give too much credit to the expert opinion and are reluctant to critically question it. It may be hard, or even appear immodest, for a questioner to raise doubts about an opinion that is privy to experts in the field of knowledge if one is not oneself an expert in this field. Thus the clever sophist can easily appeal to argument from expert opinion in a forceful way that takes advantage of our deference to experts by making anyone who questions the expert appear to be presumptuous, and to be on dubious grounds. In this chapter however, the view is defended that argument from expert opinion should be regarded as an essentially defeasible form of argument that should always be open to critical questioning.

## 4.2 Formal Systems for Modeling Argumentation

The Bayesian approach to argument evaluation (Hahn et al. 2013) uses the Bayesian rules for negation, conjunction, disjunction and conditional probability that have been applied very successfully to games of chance and other statistical settings. A statement is assigned an initial probability value between 0 and 1, and then a formula (Bayes' Rule, explained below) is used to calculate a higher or lower probability value as new evidence comes to be known. A statement that is a tautology is always taken to have a probability of 1, while a statement that is a self-contradiction is always taken to have a probability of 0. The conditional probability rule can be defined using the negation and conjunction rules below. The negation rule states that the probability of $\sim A$ is calculated as 1 minus the probability of $A$. The conjunction rule states that the probability of $A$ & $B$ is calculated as the probability of $A$ multiplied by the probability of $B$, provided that $A$ and $B$ are independent. The disjunction rule states that the probability of $A \vee B$ is calculated as the sum of the probability of $A$ and probability of $B$, minus the probability of $A$ & $B$. The conditional probability rule states that the probability of $B$ given $A$ can be defined as the probability of $A$ & $B$ divided by the probability of $A$.

The law widely known as Bayes' rule of conditional probability can be derived from the rules for conjunction and negation.

$$Pr\,(A|B) = \frac{\mathrm{Pr}\,(B|A) \times \mathrm{Pr}(A)}{Pr(B)}$$

Using this rule, the probability of $A$ given $B$ can be calculated from knowing the probability of $B$ given $A$, along with prior values of $A$ and $B$. For example, if a source is thought to be an expert the statement it claims to be true will increase the probability of the conclusion, whereas if the source is thought to be biased it will decrease the probability of the conclusion.

Whether and to what extent Bayesian calculations are useful for evaluating legal argumentation or arguments used in everyday conversational argument is hotly disputed. There are many believers and many skeptics. The skeptics think that assigning precise probability values to premises and conclusions in such arguments is based on a false precision that leads to fallacies and paradoxes.

The most famous example is the conjunction fallacy. According to the Bayesian rule, the conjunction of two statements $A$ and $B$ is less than the probability of either $A$ or $B$ individually. But Tversky and Kahneman (1982) gave the following example to groups of the respondents. Linda is a 31-year-old outspoken and very bright bank teller who majored in philosophy. As a student she was concerned with issues of social justice, and she participated in antinuclear demonstrations. Which of two statements is more probable: (1) Linda is a bank teller, or (2) Linda is a bank teller and is active in the feminist movement. Most of those asked the question chose (2) as their answer. This was taken to suggest either that the respondents were illogical, according to the standard conjunction rule for statistical reasoning, or that the conjunction rule must somehow be wrong.

The Bayesian approach has many advocates, however, and they hold strong ground because the Bayesian rules are so widely used in many areas of science and business. Surely they should be applicable to law and everyday reasoning as well, one would think. On the other side there are now AI systems for argumentation that take a different approach. Three of these are summarized briefly below. None of them applies numerical values to premises and conclusions in arguments, at least so far in their development. So these systems, so far, are competitors to the Bayesian method, but there is always the possibility of some hybrid system combining the two approaches that may emerge in the future.

There are formal argumentation systems that have been computationally implemented that can be used to model arguments from expert opinion and to evaluate them when they are nested within related arguments in a larger body of evidence (Prakken 2011). An important property of these systems is that they represent argument from expert opinion as a form of argument that is inherently defeasible, and they formally model the conditions under which such an argument can be either supported or defeated by the related arguments in a case.

One such system is ASPIC+ (Prakken 2010), based on a Dung-style abstract argumentation framework that determines the success of argument attacks and that compares conflicts in arguments at the points where they conflict (Dung 1995). ASPIC+ is built around the notion of defeasibility attributed to Pollock (1995), which distinguished between two types of argument defeaters called undercutters and rebutters. This distinction was explained in Chap. 1, Sect. 1.6.

The formal argumentation system ASPIC+ is based on a logical language *L* consisting of a set of strict and defeasible inference rules used to build arguments from a knowledge base *K* that consists of a set of propositions that can be used as premises that can be combined with the inference rules to generate arguments (Modgil and Prakken 2014). An example of a strict inference rule would be the deductively valid rule of *modus ponens* of classical logic. An example of a defeasible inference rule would be the argumentation scheme for argument from expert opinion: *E* is an expert in domain *D*; *E* asserts that proposition *A*; *A* is within domain *D*; therefore *A* can be tentatively accepted subject to critical questioning. Arguments are trees containing nodes representing propositions from *L*, and edges from a set of nodes $\varphi_1, \ldots, \varphi_n$ to a node $\psi$ representing an argument from premises $\varphi_1, \ldots, \varphi_n$ to a conclusion $\psi$. ASPIC+ (Prakken and Sartor 1997) evaluates argumentation by using abstract argumentation frameworks (Dung 1995). In an abstract argumentation framework, the proponent starts with an argument he wants to prove and when the opponent has his turn, he must provide a defeating counterargument. In such a system each argument can be attacked by other arguments, which can themselves be attacked by additional arguments. The typical result is a graph structure representing a series of attacks and counterattacks in an argumentation sequence of the following sort: $a_1$ attacks $a_2$, $a_2$ attacks $a_3$, $a_3$ attacks $a_2$, and so forth. An argument is refuted if it is attacked by any other argument that is accepted and not refuted, and is accepted only if it survives all attacks against it.

The logical system DefLog (Verheij 2003, 2005) has been computationally implemented and has an accompanying argument diagramming tool called ArguMed that can be used to analyze and evaluate defeasible argumentation. ArguMed is available free on the Internet: (http://www.ai.rug.nl/~verheij/aaa/argumed3.htm) and it can be used to model arguments from expert opinion. The logical system is built around two connectives called primitive implication, represented by the symbol ~> and dialectical negation, represented by X.

There is only one rule of inference supported by primitive implication. It is the rule called *modus non excipiens* by Verheij (2003), widely called defeasible modus ponens (DMP).

*A* ~> *B*
*A*
Therefore *B*

The propositions in DefLog are assumptions that can either be positively evaluated as justified, or negatively evaluated as defeated. The system may be contrasted with that of deductive logic in which propositions are said to be true or false, and there is no way to challenge the validity of an inference. The only ways to challenge a deductively valid argument is to attack one of its premises or pose a counterargument showing that the conclusion is false. No undercutting, in Pollock's sense, is allowed.

To see how primitive implication works, consider how Pollock's red light example (Verheij 2003, 324) is represented in DefLog by taking the conditional 'If an object looks red, it is red', as a primitive implication. The reasoning in Pollock's example where the observer sees the object is red, and therefore concludes that it is red, is modeled in DefLog as the following DMP argument.

looks_red
looks_red ~> is_red
Therefore is_red

The reasoning in the second stage of Pollock's example is modeled as follows.

looks_red
illuminated by a red light
looks_red ~> X(looks_red ~> is_red)
Therefore X(is_red)

The third premise is a nested defeasible primitive implication containing a defeasible negation. It states that if the object looks red under the circumstances of its being illuminated by red light it cannot be inferred that it is red simply because it looks red. The conclusion is that it cannot be concluded from the three premises of the argument that the object is red. Of course it might be red, but that is not a justifiable reason for accepting the conclusion that it is red. How the red light argument above is visually represented in Verheij's argument diagramming system ArguMed can be shown using Fig. 4.1.

The first stage of the reasoning in Pollock's example is shown by the argument at the bottom of Fig. 4.1. It has two premises, and these premises go together in a linked argument format to support the conclusion that the object I see is red. Above these two premises we see the undercutting argument, which itself has two premises forming a second linked argument. This second linked argument undercuts the first

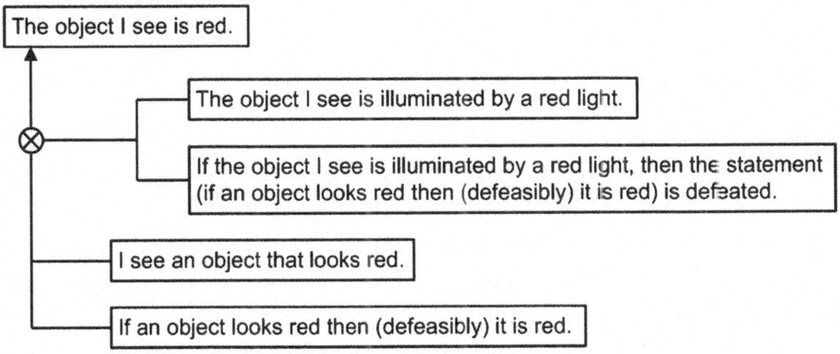


**Fig. 4.1** Pollock's red light example modeled in DefLog

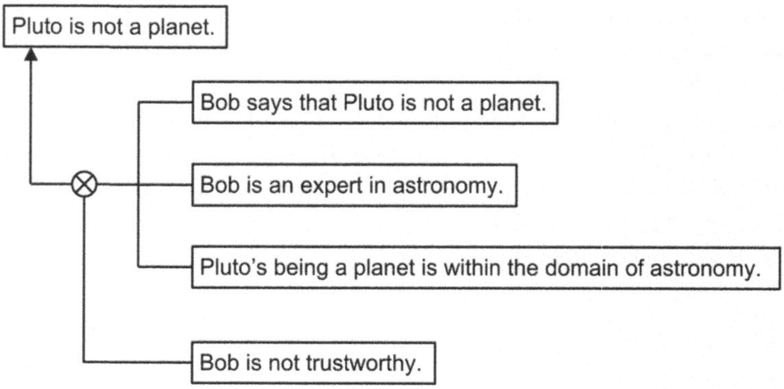


**Fig. 4.2** Argument from expert opinion as a defeasible argument in DefLog

one, as shown by the line from the second argument to the X appearing on the line leading from the first argument to the conclusion. So the top argument is shown as undercutting the bottom argument, in a way that visually displays the two stages of the reasoning in Pollock's example.

Next it is shown how an argument from expert opinion is modeled as a defeasible argument in DefLog by displaying a simple example in Fig. 4.2.

The argumentation scheme on which the argument represented in Fig. 4.2 is based will be presented in Sect. 4.5 below. Even though this form has not yet been stated explicitly the reader can easily see at this point that in the example shown in Fig. 4.2 a particular form of argument from expert opinion is being used. In this example the argument from expert opinion is shown with its three premises in the top part of Fig. 4.2. The proposition at the bottom, the statement that Bob is not trustworthy, corresponds to one of the critical questions matching this scheme for argument from expert opinion. Let's say that when a critic puts forward this statement, it undercuts the argument from expert opinion based on Bob's being an expert in astronomy. The reason is that if Bob is not trustworthy, a doubt is raised on whether we should accept the argument based on his testimony. More will be shown about how to model trustworthiness in another system below.

## 4.3 The Carneades Argumentation System

The Carneades Argumentation System (CAS), a formal and computational argumentation system (https://github.com/carneades) was named after a Greek sceptical philosopher. CAS formally models argumentation as an argument graph, a structure made up of nodes that represent premises or conclusions of an argument, and arrows representing arguments joining premise to conclusions (Gordon 2010). Formally, an argument graph is a bipartite, directed, labeled graph $\langle S, A, P, C\rangle$ consisting of four elements. $S$ is a set of statement nodes, $A$ is a set of argument nodes, $P$ is a set of premises, and $C$ is a set of conclusions. Rectangular nodes contain propositions that function as premises and conclusions of arguments. Circular nodes represent different kinds of arguments corresponding to argumentation schemes. A distinctive feature of CAS is that it distinguishes between pro and con arguments in an argument graph. A pro argument supports a conclusion or another argument. A con argument attacks a conclusion or another argument. In any CAS argument graph, one of statements is designated at the outset as the main issue (ultimate claim being supported or contested). This statement will always be the root of the argument tree in all the examples in this paper. shown at the extreme left of the argument diagram. An example of a CAS argument graph is given in Fig. 4.5.

An argument evaluation structure is defined in CAS as a tuple ⟨state, audience, standard⟩, where a proof standard is a function mapping tuples of the form ⟨issue, state, audience⟩ to the Boolean values true and false. An *issue* is a proposition to be proved or disproved in the system. A *state* is a point which the sequence of argumentation is in, and an *audience* is the respondent to whom the argument was directed in a dialogue. The audience determines whether a premise has been accepted or not, and argumentation schemes, along with the audience, determine whether the conclusion of an argument should be accepted given the status of its premises (accepted, not accepted or rejected). A proposition in an argument evaluation structure is *acceptable* if and only if it meets its standard of proof when put forward at a particular state according to the evaluation attributed to the audience (Gordon and Walton 2009).

Four standards were formally modeled in CAS (Gordon and Walton 2009). They range in order of strictness from the weakest shown at the top to the highest shown at the bottom. According to the scintilla of evidence standard, there must be at least one applicable argument. According to the preponderance of evidence standard, the scintilla of evidence standard must be satisfied, and the maximum weight assigned to an applicable pro argument must be greater than the maximum weight of an applicable con argument. According to the clear and convincing evidence standard the preponderance of evidence standard must be satisfied, the maximum weight of applicable pro arguments has to exceed a first threshold and the difference between the maximum weight of the applicable pro arguments and the maximum weight of the applicable con arguments exceeds a second threshold. According to the beyond reasonable doubt standard, the clear and convincing evidence standard needs to be satisfied, and the maximum weight of the applicable con arguments needs to be less than a third threshold. The three thresholds are not given a fixed numerical value. They need to be specified by the user. The modeling of the four standards is presented in a more rigorous fashion in Chap. 5, Sect. 5.4.

CAS optionally allows a user to assign numerical weights to arguments in an argument graph. The weights represent how strongly the user thinks the audience accepts an argument. Both standards of proof and the assignment of weights to arguments in an argument graph can be used to deal with deadlocks, cases where there is both a pro argument and a con argument for the same conclusion. Consider a case where there are two arguments from expert opinion, one pro conclusion and one con that same conclusion. An example of an argument graph representing this kind of case is shown in Fig. 4.5. Let's assume in such a case that the audience has accepted all the premises of both arguments, and each of the two arguments fits the scheme for argument from expert opinion. Both arguments are inherently reasonable. Here we have a deadlock. Is there any device that can be applied in CAS to break it? There are two devices used by CAS, proof standards and argument weights.

The argument weights allow the audience to provide input on which argument they find to be stronger. For example the audience may find the one expert to be better qualified, have better knowledge of the field or domain of expertise, and be less biased. The audience can use these findings to evaluate the one argument from expert opinion as being stronger than the other. The standards of proof can also be applied in such a case. If the one argument from expert opinion is sufficiently stronger than the other to meet the required standard of proof in the case, such as the standard of clear and convincing evidence, then clearly the stronger one is the argument that should be accepted. For example, if the pro argument is sufficiently stronger than the con argument so that when the two arguments are combined the pro argument meets its standard of proof despite being attacked by the con argument, then the pro argument should be accepted.

The weight of an argument is represented by a fraction between zero and one. Consider the example shown in Fig. 4.3. Let's start with the pro argument at the bottom. The audience accepts this argument with strength of 0.5, and accepts both premises, as indicated by p2 and p4 being colored green. In the printed version of the book, a green box will appear as a darkened (gray) box. So far then, it looks like p1 should be accepted. But we also have to consider the con argument at the top. The default standard of proof for arguments in CAS is set at preponderance of the evidence so if a1 is stronger than a2, a1 will win. But the sole premise of a1, p3, is not accepted by the audience. But it can be proved by a4, which has both premises accepted. Then p3 must be colored green, and accordingly p1 must also be colored green. What is shown is that a1 rebuts a2.

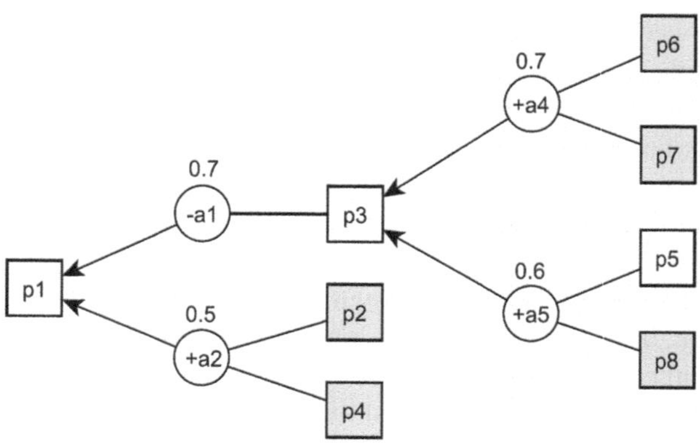


**Fig. 4.3** An example showing evaluating argumentation using weights

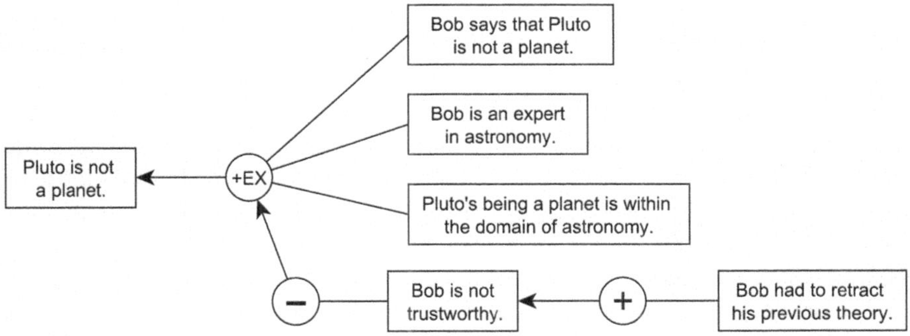


**Fig. 4.4** CAS version of the Pluto example

Next let's look at an argument that illustrates an undercutter, as contrasted with the rebutter exemplified in the argument in Fig. 4.3. CAS can also use argumentation schemes to model defeasible arguments such as argument from expert opinion, argument from testimony, argument from cause and effect, and so forth. The name of the scheme fits the round argument node in a CAS argument graph, as shown in Fig. 4.4.

If the scheme fits the argument chosen to be modeled, the scheme is judged to be applicable to the argument and the argument is taken to be "valid" (defeasibly). The name of the argumentation scheme in Fig. 4.4 is indicated in the node joining the three premises to the ultimate conclusion. EX stands for the argument from expert opinion, and the plus sign in the node indicates that the argument from expert opinion is used as a pro-argument. The statement 'Bob is not trustworthy' is the premise in a con argument, indicated by the minus sign in the node leading to the node containing the argument from expert opinion. This con argument is modeled by CAS as a Pollock-style undercutter. This means that it will defeat the original argument if supported by evidence, as is shown in the example in Fig. 4.4. ASPIC+, DefLog and CAS all use undercutters and rebutters to model defeasible argumentation, but the way that CAS does this in the case of argument from expert opinion is especially distinctive. This will be explained using an example in Sect. 4.7.

## 4.4 The Scheme and Matching Critical Questions

There can be different ways of formulating the argumentation scheme for argument from expert opinion. The first formulation of the logical structure of this form of argument was given in Walton (1989, 193), where *A* is a proposition.

*E* is an expert in domain *D*.
*E* asserts that *A* is known to be true.
*A* is within *D*.
Therefore, *A* may plausibly be taken to be true.

Matching the original version of this scheme six critical questions were informally presented (Walton 1989, 194–196). The first is whether the opinion put forward by the expert falls within his or her field of competence. The second is whether the source cited as an expert is really an expert, as opposed to being a source that was cited on grounds of popularity or celebrity status. The third is the question of how authoritative the expert should be taken to be. The fourth is whether there are other experts who disagree. The fifth is whether the expert's opinion is consistent with any objective evidence that may be available. The sixth is whether the pronouncement made by the expert has been correctly interpreted.

A more recent version of the scheme for argument from expert opinion was given (Walton et al. 2008, 310) as follows. This version of the scheme is closely comparable to the one given in Walton (1997, 210).

Major Premise: Source *E* is an expert in subject domain *S* containing proposition *A*.
Minor Premise: *E* asserts that proposition *A* is true (false).
Conclusion: *A* is true (false).

The difference between this scheme and the earlier one is that the assumption that the proposition *A* is within the domain *D* is stated as a separate premise in the original version, whereas in the later version it is included as part of the major premise.

It has also been noted that the scheme can be formulated in a conditional version that makes it have the structure of defeasible modus ponens (DMP) in DefLog. This conditional version can be formulated as follows (Reed and Walton 2003, 201).

Conditional Premise: If Source *E* is an expert in subject domain *S* containing proposition *A*, and *E* asserts that proposition *A* is true (false) then *A* is true (false).
Major Premise: Source *E* is an expert in subject domain *S* containing proposition *A*.
Minor Premise: *E* asserts that proposition *A* is true (false).
Conclusion: *A* is true (false).

Part of Mizrahi's argument (2013, 68) is that the conditional premise in the expanded version of the scheme for argument from expert opinion is "implausible" because it makes the claim that the fact that an expert says that proposition *P* is true makes it significantly more likely that *P* is true. However, he holds this opinion because, like Goldman, he takes the traditional view that such a conditional can only be deductive in nature, like the strict material conditional of classical deductive logic, or an inductive conditional that is statistical in nature. CAS offers a third possibility by admitting a form of *modus ponens* that is defeasible but not inductive in nature.

On this view the conditional version of the scheme has the following logical structure, where $P_1$, $P_2$ and $P_3$ are meta-variables for the premises in the scheme and *C* is a meta-variable for the conclusion.

If $P_1$, $P_2$ and $P_3$ then *C*
$P_1$, $P_2$ and $P_3$
Therefore *C*

It is important to emphasize that the scheme has to be seen as defeasible in nature when taken as an instance of the form of inference DMP. The assumption behind configuring the scheme in this defeasible manner is that generally speaking it is not justifiable to take the word of an expert as infallible, even though it is also generally reasonable to presume what an expert says is right in the absence of evidence to the contrary. To accept what an expert says as having to be right absolutely, beyond all questioning or possibility of doubt makes that form of argument inherently fallacious. Exploiting the tendency of some participants in argumentation to take what an expert says as sacrosanct has been identified fallacious form of argument from authority in which an arguer tries to get the best of a speech partner unfairly (Walton 1997). When you are trying to decide what to do in a given set of circumstances, or what proposition to accept, you can do much better if you tentatively accept what an expert says unless you have reason not to accept it, so long as you are prepared to critically question the advice given by the expert. In (Walton 1997) it is shown that it is important not to be intimidated by expert opinions because of the powerful halo effect of an expert pronouncement. The original critical questions matching the original scheme have been reformulated in a more precise way to match the newer version of the scheme. This new way of formulating the six basic critical questions (Walton et al. 2008, 310) has a name for each question. This way of formulating the six basic critical questions comes from the earlier version of the scheme given in Walton (1997, 223).

*Expertise Question*: How credible is *E* as an expert source?
*Field Question*: Is *E* an expert in the field *F* that *A* is in?
*Opinion Question*: What did *E* assert that implies *A*?
*Trustworthiness Question*: Is *E* personally reliable as a source?
*Consistency Question*: Is *A* consistent with what other experts assert?
*Backup Evidence Question*: Is *E*'s assertion based on evidence?

The important factor to stress once again is the defeasible nature of the argument. This defeasible aspect is brought out by seeing how the critical questions function as devices for evaluating an argument from expert opinion. If a respondent asks any one of the six critical questions, the original argument defaults. This means that the conclusion can no longer be taken to be accepted given that the premises are accepted, unless the question is answered adequately. But once the question has been answered adequately, the argument tentatively stands until further critical questions are asked about it. As more critical questions matching the scheme are answered appropriately, the argument from expert opinion gets stronger and stronger, even though it may have been weak to begin with.

## 4.5 Critical Questioning and Burdens of Proof

It is important to realize that the six basic critical questions are not the only ones matching the scheme for argument from expert opinion. Through research on argument from expert opinion and its corresponding fallacies, and through teaching students in courses in informal logic how to try to deal intelligently with arguments based on expert opinion, these basic six critical questions have been distilled out as the ones best suited to give guidance to students on how to critically and intelligently react to arguments from expert opinion. However, each of the basic critical questions has critical sub-questions beneath it (Walton 1997).

Under the expertise critical question, there are three sub-questions (Walton 1997, 217).

1. Is *E* biased?
2. Is *E* honest?
3. Is *E* conscientious?

Classifying and framing such critical questions is a matter of analyzing examples of fallacious arguments from expert opinion, to see where these erroneous arguments went wrong (Walton 1997). Once the errors were classified in a systematic way, sets of critical questions designed to pinpoint and cope with them were also classified.

The possibility that critical questions can continue to be asked in a dialogue that can go on continually between an arguer and a critical questioner poses problems for modeling a scheme such as argument from expert opinion in a formal and computational argumentation system. Can the respondent go on and on forever asking such critical questions? Open-endedness is of course characteristic of defeasible arguments. They are nonmonotonic, meaning that new incoming information can make them fail in the future even though they hold tentatively for now. But on which side should the burden of proof lie on bringing in new evidence? Is merely asking a question enough to defeat the argument, or does the question need to be backed up by evidence before it has this effect?

The defeasible nature of the argument from expert opinion can be brought out even further by seeing that evaluating an instance of the argument in any particular case rests on the setting in which there is a dialogue between the proponent of the argument and a respondent, or critical questioner. The proponent originally puts forward the argument, and the respondent has the task of critically questioning it or putting forward counterarguments. Evaluating whether any particular instance of the argument from expert opinion holds in a given case depends on two factors. One is whether the given argument fits the structure of the scheme for argument from expert opinion. But if so, then evaluation depends on what happens in the dialogue, and in particular the balance between the moves of the proponent and the respondent. The evaluation of the argument depends on pro and contra moves made in the dialogue. It is possible to put this point in a different way by expressing it in terms of shifting of the burden of proof. Once a question has been asked and answered adequately, a burden of proof shifts back to the questioner to ask another question or accept the argument. But there is a general problem about how such a shift should be regulated and how arguments from expert opinion should be modeled.

Chris Reed, when visiting at University of Arizona in 2001, asked a question. Is there any way the critical questions matching a scheme could be represented as statements of the kind represented on an argument diagram? I replied that I couldn't figure out a way to do it, because some critical questions defeat the argument merely by being asked, while others don't, unless they are backed up by evidence. These observations led to two hypotheses (Walton and Godden 2005) about what happens when the respondent asks a critical question: (1) when a critical question is asked, the burden shifts to the proponent to answer it and if no answer is given, the proponent's argument should fail, (2) to make the proponent's argument fail, the respondent needs to support the critical question with further argument.

Issues such as completeness of a set of critical questions are important from a computational perspective since they hold not only for the scheme for argument from expert opinion but for all schemes in general. But the question is not an easy one to resolve because context may play a role. For example an opinion expressed by an expert witness in court may have to be questioned in a different way from the case of an opinion being expressed in an informal setting, or one put forward as a conclusion in a scientific paper. Wyner (2012) discusses problems of this sort that have arisen from attempts to provide formal representations of critical questions. In Parsons et al. (2012) argumentation schemes based on different forms of trust are set out. In particular there are schemes for trust from expert opinion and trust from authority. These matters need to be explored further.

## 4.6 The Carneades Version of the Scheme and Critical Questions

The problem of having to choose between the two hypotheses led to the following insight that became a founding feature of CAS: which hypothesis should be applied in any given case depends on the argumentation scheme (Walton and Gordon 2005). In other words, the solution proposed was that a different hypothesis should be applied to each critical question of the scheme. This solution allows the burden of proof for answering critical questions to be assigned to either the proponent or the respondent, on a question by question basis for each argumentation scheme (Walton and Gordon 2011).

The solution was essentially to model critical questions as premises of a scheme by expanding the premises in the scheme. The ordinary premises are the minor and major premises of the schemes. The assumptions represent critical questions to be answered by the proponent. The exceptions represent critical questions to be answered by the respondent. The two latter types of critical questions are modeled as additional premises. On this view whether a premise holds depends not only on its type but also the dialectical status of the premise during a sequence of dialogue. Shifts of burden take place as the argumentation proceeds in a case where the parties take turns making moves. They do not represent what is called burden of persuasion in law, but are more like what is called the burden of producing evidence, or what is often called the evidential burden in law (Prakken and Sartor 2009).

In the current version of the CAS (https://github.com/carneades/carneades) there is a catalogue of schemes (http://localhost:8080/policymodellingtool/#/schemes). One of the schemes in the catalogue is the one for argument from expert opinion, shown below.

**id:** expert-opinion
**strict:** false
**direction:** pro
**conclusion:** *A*
**premises:**

- Source *E* is an expert in subject domain *S*.
- *A* is in domain *S*.
- *E* asserts that *A* is true.

**assumptions**:

- The assertion *A* is based on evidence.

**exceptions:**

- *E* is personally unreliable as a source.
- *A* is inconsistent with what other experts assert.

The trustworthiness critical question is represented by the statement that *E* is personally unreliable as a source, classified as an exception. This means that if the respondent in the dialogue asks whether *E* is personally reliable as a source (the trustworthiness question), the proponent's argument from expert opinion will not be defeated unless the respondent backs up her allegation with some evidence. Otherwise the proponent is entitled to respond by saying, "Of course the expert is personally reliable, and that holds unless you can provide evidence to the contrary".

In contrast, the backup evidence question is treated as an assumption. This means that if the respondent asks for backup evidence on which the experts can support her claim, the proponent is obliged to provide some evidence of this kind, or else the argument from expert opinion fails. We reasonably expect experts to base their opinions on evidence, typically scientific evidence of some sort, and if this assumption is in doubt, an argument from expert opinion appears to be questionable. Once we have classified each critical question matching a scheme in this way, a standardized way of managing schemes in computational systems can be implemented.

## 4.7 An Example of Argument from Expert Opinion

To get some idea of how CAS evaluates arguments from expert opinion, consider a typical case where *A* is a proposition that is subject to controversy and there are expert opinions both pro and con *A*. One expert Anita is pro *A*, while another expert Brad is con *A*. The proposition A is shown at the far left in Fig. 4.5, as always in a CAS argument graph.

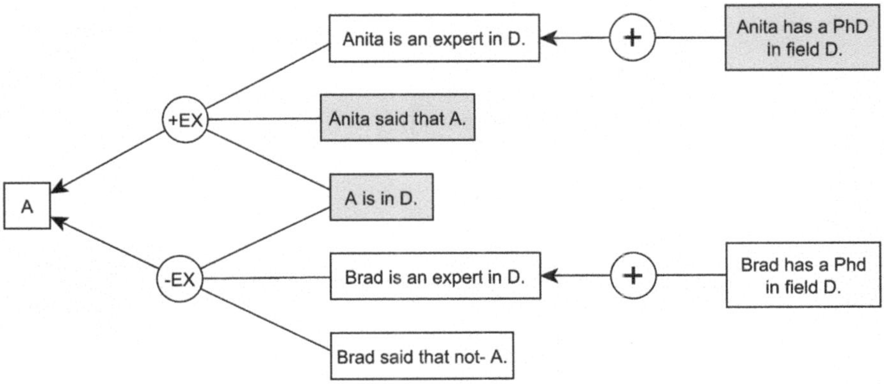


**Fig. 4.5** A case of the battle of the experts modeled in CAS

The classic case, called the battle of the experts, occurs where one expert asserts proposition *A* and another expert asserts proposition not-*A*. The two arguments are shown in the two circular argument nodes, both labeled as arguments from expert opinion. Each of the arguments fits the scheme for argument from expert opinion. The pro argument, shown at the top, has two of its premises accepted by the audience. These two propositions are shown in rectangles with green backgrounds. There is also one other proposition shown with a green background, indicating audience acceptance, namely the proposition that Anita has a PhD in field (domain) *D*. Let's say that the pro argument indicated with the plus sign at the top fits some argumentation scheme such as DMP, accepted by the audience. If so, CAS automatically shows the proposition that Anita is an expert in D with a green background. Therefore CAS also automatically shows the ultimate proposition to be proved, *A*, in a green rectangle. So far then, the pro argument at the top is adequate to show that the ultimate proposition is acceptable.

Next, what about the con argument at the bottom of Fig. 4.5? How does CAS take this argument into account? To see how, let us turn to Fig. 4.6, where *A* is shown in green, because it is now proved by the pro argument at the top. In the argument at the bottom, the premise that Brad is an expert in *D* is shown in a white rectangle, indicating that it is not accepted. But it is supported by an argument with the premise that is accepted, namely the premise that Brad has a PhD in field *D*, so CAS will automatically color the proposition that Brad is an expert in *D* green. All three premises in the con argument from expert opinion will now be shown in CAS as accepted by the audience. Once again the pro and con arguments are deadlocked. Here we have a classic case of the battle of the experts.

Now the con argument is deadlocked with the pro-argument, so CAS will automatically remove the green background from proposition *A*. Neither argument can prevail over the other at this point. There are various ways such a deadlock can be dealt with by CAS. One is to utilize the notion of standards of proof. Another is to assign a numerical weight to each argument, indicating how strongly the

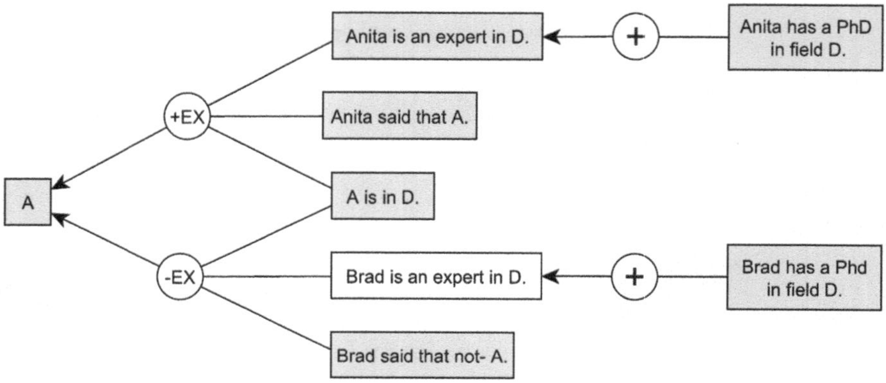


**Fig. 4.6** Extending the case by bringing in the audience

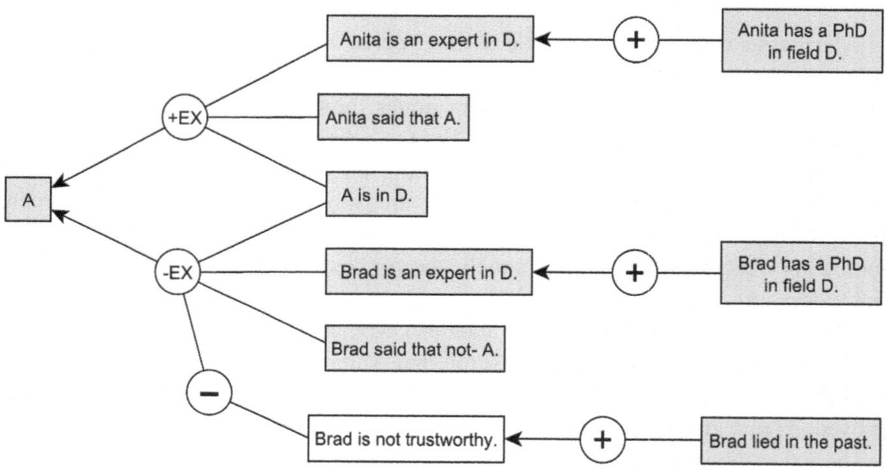


**Fig. 4.7** The trustworthiness critical question modeled as undercutter

audience accepts it. By combining these two means, or using them separately, one argument can be shown to be stronger than another. In CAS these alternatives can be combined. There are also other ways of breaking the deadlock. A new argument might come in that tilts the burden of proof against one side or the other.

For example let's see how the trustworthiness critical question might enter into consideration in the case of this sort. The trustworthiness question is classified as an exception, meaning that just asking it does not defeat an argument from expert opinion. To defeat the argument, some evidence needs to be given to support the allegation. Hence the evidential situation can be modeled by representing the trustworthiness question as a con argument. The con argument at the bottom of Fig. 4.7, is shown as attacking the con argument from expert opinion just above it. This is an instance of a critical question that is an exception being modeled as an undercutter.

As shown in Fig. 4.7, the allegation that Brad is not trustworthy is supported by an argument that has a premise stating that Brad lied in the past. Because this premise provides a reason to support the allegation that Brad is not trustworthy, the asking of the critical question defeats the argument from expert opinion in this instance. Hence Brad's argument from expert opinion is knocked out of contention, and so CAS automatically shows the ultimate conclusion in a green rectangle.

This example has been merely a simple one made up for purposes of illustration so the reader can get a basic idea of how CAS models arguments, how it visually represents them using argument diagrams, and how it evaluates them by using the notion of an audience. To get a better idea, as always in the field of argumentation studies, it is helpful to examine a real example.

## 4.8 The Case of the Getty Kouros

A kouros is an ancient Greek statue of a standing nude youth, typically standing with its left foot forward, arms at his sides, looking straight ahead. The so-called Getty kouros was bought by the J. Paul Getty Museum in Malibu California in 1985 for 7 million dollars. Although originally thought to be authentic, experts have raised many doubts, and the label on the statue in the museum reads "Greek, about 530 BC, or modern forgery". Evidence concerning the provenance of the statue is weak. It was bought by the museum from a collector in Geneva who claimed he had bought it in 1930 from a Greek dealer. But there was no archaeological data tracing the statue to Greece. The documentary history of the statue appeared to be a hoax because a letter supposedly from the Swiss collector dated 1952 had a postcode on it that did not exist until 1972 (True 1987). Figure 4.8 displays the structure of the two arguments from expert opinion, and the argument from the provenance evidence.

As also shown in Fig. 4.8, there was some evidence supporting the genuineness of the statue. It was made from a kind of marble found in Thrace. Norman Herz, a professor of geology at the University of Georgia, determined with a 90 % probability that the source of the stone the statue was carved from was the island of Thasos. Stanley Margolis, a geology professor at the University of California, showed that the dolomite surface of the sculpture had undergone a process in which the magnesium content had leached out. He concluded that this process could only have occurred over the course of many centuries (Margolis 1989). He stated that for these reasons the statue could not have been duplicated by a forger (Herz and Waelkens 1988, 311).

CAS can be used to model the structure of these arguments using the standards of proof, the notion of audience as a basis for determining which premises of an argument are accepted, rejected or undecided and the other tools explained in Sect. 4.4. We begin by seeing how one argument from expert opinion attacks another. Whether the ultimate conclusion should be accepted or not depends in CAS on the standard of proof that is to be applied (Gordon 2010). If the preponderance of

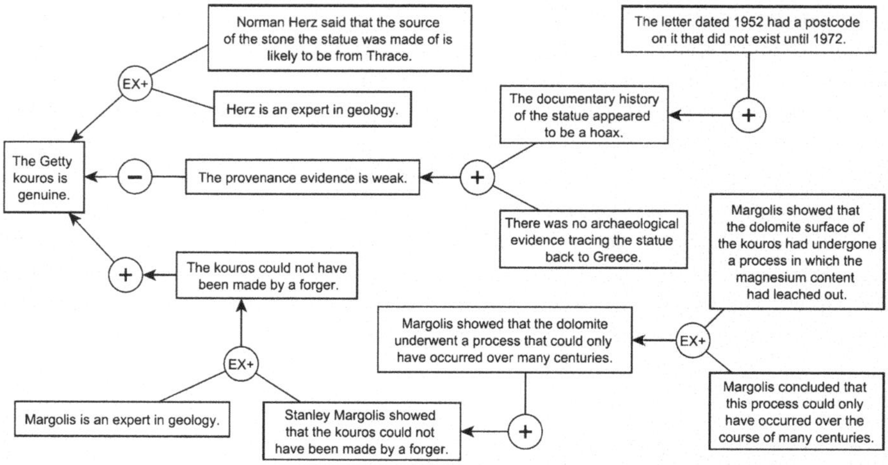


**Fig. 4.8** First two arguments from expert opinion in the Getty Kouros case

the evidence standard is applied, the pro arguments for the genuineness of the kouros could win. If a higher standard is applied, such as clear and convincing evidence, or beyond a reasonable doubt, the pro argument might fail to prove the conclusion. On this view, the outcome depends on the standard of proof for the inquiry and on how acceptable the premises are to the audience that is to decide whether to accept the premises or not. In this case the standard of proof required to establish that the kouros is genuine is high, given the skepticism that is always present in such cases on the part of the experts due to the possibility of forgery, and the cleverness of forgers exhibited in many comparable cases. The three main bodies of evidence required to meet this standard are (1) the geological evidence concerning the source of the stone statue is made of, (2) the judgment of experts concerning how close is the match between the artistic techniques exhibited in this statue and the comparable techniques exhibited in other statutes of the same kind known to be genuine, and (3) the provenance evidence.

## 4.9 Extending the Getty Kouros Case

The case can be extended by introducing some evidence provided by a third expert as shown in Fig. 4.9. In the 1990s a marine chemist named Miriam Kastner was able to artificially induce de-dolomitzation in the laboratory. Moreover, this result was confirmed by previous findings of Margolis.[1] These results showed that it is possible that the kouros was synthetically aged by a forger. This new evidence cast doubt on the claim made by Margolis that this process could only occur over the

[1]Michael Kimmelman, Absolutely Real? Absolutely Fake?, *New York Times*, August 4, 1991, accessed 29/8/2008.

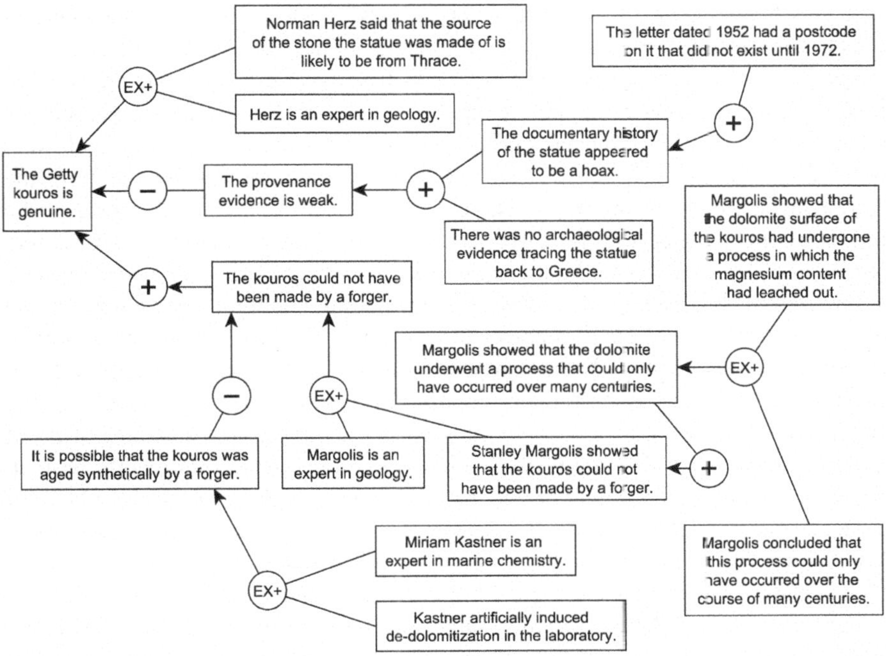


**Fig. 4.9** Third argument from expert opinion in the Getty case

course of many centuries, weakening the argument based on the appeal to the expert opinion of Margolis by casting doubt on one of its premises.

Modeling the example of the Getty kouros using CAS is useful for demonstrating a type of reasoning that the scheme for argument from expert opinion is intended to capture. It shows how one argument from expert opinion can be attacked by or supported by other arguments from expert opinion. However one subject that we will not deal with in exploring these examples is the role of accrual of arguments. We see that the pro argument from expert opinion based on the expertise of Herz in geology was supported by the corroborative pro argument from expert opinion based on the geological expertise of Margolis. It is implied that the first argument, while defeasible, must have had a certain degree of strength or plausibility to begin with, and then when the second argument based on the geological evidence came to be taken into consideration, the conclusion that the Getty kouros is genuine became even more plausible. But then, when the argument from expert opinion put forward by Margolis was attacked by the undermining argument based on an appeal to expert opinion from marine chemistry, the degree of acceptability of the conclusion must have gone down. These variations in the strength of the body of evidence supporting or attacking the ultimate conclusion that the Getty kouros is genuine suggest that some sort of mechanism of accrual of arguments is implicitly at work in how we evaluate the strength of support given by the evidence in this case. However it is known that accrual is a difficult issue to handle formally (Prakken 2005).

It has been shown in this chapter how to use CAS to evaluate arguments in which one argument needs to be re-evaluated as new evidence in the form of another argument that corroborates or attacks the first argument comes in. But this procedure is carried out manually by having the user mark propositions as accepted or not, based on input from the audience. A research project currently underway is to modify CAS so it can do such evaluations automatically by inputting the new evidence, propagating the revisions forward, and changing acceptance of the ultimate conclusion accordingly. But even so, by showing how evidential reasoning can be modeled in the Getty kouros case, we can still use CAS to update evidence.

Provenance evidence is especially important as a defeating factor even where the other two factors have been established by means of a strong body of supportive evidence. Looking at Fig. 4.9, it can be seen that the geological evidence is fairly strong, because it is based on the concurring opinion of two independent experts. However, given the weakness of the provenance evidence, the standard of proof required to establish that the Getty kouros is genuine cannot reasonably be met. Also, the situation represented in Fig. 4.9 represents a conflict, because the body of evidence under category 1 is conflicted with the body of evidence under category 3. What is missing is any consideration of the evidence under category 2.

If we were to take into account further evidence not modeled in Fig. 4.8, the evaluation of the evidential situation might not turn out to be too much different, since there was a recurring conflict of opinions on how close the match was between the Getty kouros and other statues of the same kind known to be genuine. Once we look at the further evidence shown in Fig. 4.9, the geological evidence is weakened by the introduction of new evidence concerning Kastner's artificial aging of the stone in the laboratory by de-dolomitization. In Fig. 4.9 the new evidence based on the argument from expert opinion of Kastner is shown at the bottom of the argument diagram. This new argument attacks the conclusion of the Margolis expert opinion argument that the kouros could not have been made by a forger.

This new evidence brings the geological evidence even further from the possibility of meeting the standard of proof required to establish that the Getty kouros is genuine. If other experts independent of Margolis were to confirm Kastner's result, it would make the argument from geology stronger. However the fact that it was Margolis who confirmed Kastner's result is good as well, in a certain respect, because he was the original expert who claimed that the statue could not have been duplicated by a forger. Now it would seem that he would have to admit that this is possible. Although we don't have any evidence of his reaction, his confirmation of Kastner's result suggests that there is reason to think that he would have reason to retract his earlier claim that the statute could not have been duplicated by a forger.

## 4.10 Conclusions

Schiappa (2002, 51) has strongly advocated the centrality of argumentation evaluation as giving a direction and purpose for research in argumentation studies. However, he also pointed out that there are scholarly norms in the field that have tended to discourage argument evaluation in the past. The field itself is often called argumentation theory, and in the past there has been less of an emphasis on research that tests theory by applying it to detailed case studies. Perhaps also an awareness of the contextual nature of argument evaluation has intimidated argumentation scholars from directly confronting the problem of how to evaluate arguments. Certainly there are reasons for circumspection and care in approaching the subject of argument evaluation, because of its contextual nature. Legal argumentation, for example, has to be evaluated by standards, methods and procedures quite different from scientific argumentation of the kind that takes place within scientific research.

The examples of argumentation being evaluated by CAS in this chapter show definitively that the new formal and computational models of argumentation have finally begun to address the problem of argument evaluation. The CAS method of evaluation is based on argumentation schemes, tree structures that can be visualized using argument maps, and input from an audience determining which premises of an argument can be taken as accepted or rejected. With input from these devices, CAS automatically calculates whether the conclusion of any given argument represented in the model is acceptable or not. This model still has its limitations, and current research is ongoing at this time to improve its capability by applying the method to new examples and problem cases.

This chapter concludes that (1) it is generally a mistake, from the argumentation point of view, to trust experts, (2) even though it is often necessary to rely on expert opinion evidence, but that (3) we can provisionally accept conclusions drawn from expert opinion on a presumptive basis subject to retraction. The chapter showed how to evaluate an argument from expert opinion in a real case through a five-step procedure that proceeds by (1) identifying the parts of the argument, its premises and conclusion, using the argumentation scheme for argument from expert opinion (along with other schemes), (2) evaluating the argument by constructing an argument diagram that represents the mass of relevant evidence in the case, (3) taking the critical questions matching the scheme into account, (4) doing this by representing them as additional premises (assumptions and exceptions) of the scheme and (5) setting in place a system for showing the evidential relationships between the pro and con arguments preliminary to weighing the arguments both for and against the argument from expert opinion. It was shown that applying this procedure in a formal computational argumentation system is made possible by reconfiguring the critical questions by distinguishing three kinds of premises in the scheme called ordinary premises, assumptions and exceptions. Several examples were given showing how to carry out this general procedure, including the real example of the Getty kouros.

It was shown in this chapter how CAS applies this procedure because it uses a defeasible version of the scheme in its argument evaluation system based on acceptability of statements, burdens of proof, and proof standards (Gordon 2010, 145–156). For these reasons CAS fits the ESE (epistemology of scientific evidence) model (Walton and Zhang 2013). This model has been applied to the analysis and evaluation of expert testimony as evidence in law. It is specifically designed for the avoidance or minimization of error, and like CAS, it is acceptance-based rather than being based on the veristic view of Goldman. In a veristic epistemology, knowledge deductively implies truth. On this view one agent is more expert than another if its knowledge base contains more true propositions than that of the other. The ESE is a flexible epistemology for dealing with defeasible reasoning in a setting where knowledge is a set of commitments of the scientists in a domain of scientific knowledge that is subject to retraction as new evidence comes in. It is not a set of true beliefs, nor is it based exclusively on deductive or inductive reasoning (at least the kind represented by standard probability theory).

Mizrahi's argument goes wrong because he uses the single-premised version of the argument from expert opinion as his version of the form of the argument in general. This is unfortunate because it is precisely when this simple version of the scheme is used to represent argument from expert opinion that the other critical questions are not taken into account. The simple version has heuristic value because it shows how we often leap from the single premise that somebody is an expert to the conclusion that what this person says is true. But the simple version also illustrates precisely why leaping to a conclusion in this way without considering the questions of whether the person cited is a real expert, whether he or she is an expert in the appropriate field, and so forth. It is precisely by overlooking these critical questions, or even worse, ignoring them or shielding them off from consideration, that the *ad verecundiam* fallacy occurs. As shown in this chapter, argument from expert opinion in its single-premised form, is of no use for argument evaluation until the additional premises are taken into account. The single premise version of the scheme has initial explanatory value for teaching students about the simplest essentials of arguments from expert opinion, but to get anywhere we need to realize that additional premises are involved. This is shown by the model of argument from expert opinion in the CAS.

Freedman is open to the criticism of having engaged in a circular form of reasoning because he quoted many experts in his book to prove his claim that many experts are wrong. However this form of circular reasoning does not commit the fallacy of begging the question, because Freedman's conclusion is based on empirical evidence showing how often experts have been wrong, and he is able to interpret this evidence and draw conclusions from it in an informed manner. His arguments about errors in expert reasoning, and his findings about why arguments from expert opinion reasoning so often go wrong, take place at a meta-level where it is not only important but necessary for users of expert opinion evidence to become aware of the errors in their own reasoning and correct them, or at least be aware of the weaknesses of them. But he does not draw the conclusion that arguments from expert opinion are worthless, and ought to be entirely discounted. He went so far in an interview (Experts and Studies: Not Always Trustworthy, *Time*, June 29, 2010) to say that discarding expertise altogether "would be reckless and dangerous" and that the key to dealing with arguments from expert opinion is to learn to distinguish the better ones from the worse ones. It has been an objective of this chapter to find a systematic way to use argumentation tools to help accomplish this goal.

This chapter has illustrated some of the problems with evaluating argumentation in a particular case using a defeasible argumentation scheme such as the one for the argument from expert opinion. These arguments are typically used as heuristics to quickly derive a conclusion from a body of evidence as a basis for moving forward and collecting more evidence that may either support or defeat the hypothesis. One of the problems revealed was that CAS at its current state of development still does not have a method for updating a hypothesis when new evidence comes in. Another problem is that dealing with realistic cases most often involves a large mass of argumentation that would have to be structured in a very large argument diagram. Even so, we can see the potential is there for CAS, as well as the other computational systems of argumentation currently being developed, to deal with such larger cases. The next chapter will take a significant step in that direction.

## References


Dung, P.M. 1995. On the acceptability of arguments and its fundamental role in nonmonotonic reasoning, logic programming and n-person games. *Artificial Intelligence* 77(2): 321–357.

Freedman, D.H. 2010. *Wrong: Why experts keep failing us – And how to know when not to trust them*. New York: Little Brown and Company.

Goldman, A. 1999. *Knowledge in a social world*. Oxford: Clarendon.

Goldman, A. 2001. Experts: Which ones should you trust? *Philosophy and Phenomenological Research* LXIII(1): 85–110.

Gordon, T.F. 2010. The Carneades argumentation support system. In *Dialectics, dialogue and argumentation*, ed. C. Reed and C.W. Tindale. London: College Publications.

Gordon, T.F., and D. Walton. 2009. Proof burdens and standards. In *Argumentation and artificial intelligence*, ed. Iyad Rahwan and Guillermo Simari, 239–260. Berlin: Springer.

Grice, H.P. 1975. Logic and conversation. In *Syntax and semantics*, vol. 3, ed. P. Cole and J.L. Morgan, 43–58. New York: Academic.

Hahn, U., A. Harris, and M. Oaksford. 2013. Rational argument, rational inference. *Argument and Computation* 4(1): 21–35.

Hamblin, C.L. 1970. *Fallacies*. London: Methuen.

Haynes A.S., G.E. Derrick, S. Redman, W.D. Hall, J.A. Gillespie, et al. 2012. Identifying trustworthy experts: How do policymakers find and assess public health researchers worth consulting or collaborating with? *PLoS ONE* 7(3): e32665. doi:10.1371/journal.pone.0032665. Accessed 10 July 2013 at: http://www.plosone.org/article/info%3Adoi%2F10.1371%2Fjournal.pone.0032665.

Herz, N., and M. Waelkens. 1988. *Classical marble: Geochemistry, technology, trade*. Dordrecht: Kluwer Academic Publishers.

Li, H., and M. Sighal. 2007. Trust management in distributed systems. *Computer* 40(2): 45–53.

Margolis, S.T. 1989. Authenticating ancient marble sculpture. *Scientific American* 260(6): 104–114.

Mizrahi, M. 2013. Why arguments from expert opinion are weak arguments. *Informal Logic* 33(1): 57–79.

Modgil, S., and H. Prakken. 2014. The ASPIC+ framework for structured argumentation: A tutorial. *Argument and Computation* 5(1): 31–62.

Parsons, S., K. Atkinson, K. Haigh, K. Levitt, P. McBurney, J. Rowe, M.P. Singh, and E. Sklar. 2012. Argument schemes for reasoning about trust. In *Computational models of argument*, Frontiers in artificial intelligence and applications, vol. 245, 430–441. Amsterdam: IOS Press.

Pollock, J.L. 1995. *Cognitive carpentry*. Cambridge, MA: The MIT Press.

Prakken, H. 2005. A study of accrual of arguments, with applications to evidential reasoning. In *Proceedings of the tenth international conference on artificial intelligence and law, Bologna, 2005*, 85–94. New York: ACM Press.

Prakken, H. 2010. An abstract framework for argumentation with structured arguments. *Argument & Computation* 1(2): 93–124.

Prakken, H. 2011. An overview of formal models of argumentation and their application in philosophy. *Studies in Logic* 4(1): 65–86.

Prakken, H., and G. Sartor. 1997. Argument-based extended logic programming with defeasible priorities. *Journal of Applied Non-classical Logics* 7: 25–75.

Prakken, H., and G. Sartor. 2009. A logical analysis of burdens of proof. In *Legal evidence and proof: Statistics, stories, logic*, ed. H. Kaptein, H. Prakken, and B. Verheij, 223–253. Farnham: Ashgate.

Reed, C., and D. Walton. 2003. Diagramming, argumentation schemes and critical questions. In *Anyone who has a view: Theoretical contributions to the study of argumentation*, ed. F.H. van Eemeren, J.A. Blair, C.A. Willard, and A. Snoeck Henkemans, 195–211. Dordrecht: Kluwer.

Schiappa, E. 2002. Sophisticated modernism and the continuing importance of argument evaluation. In *Arguing communication and culture: Selected papers from the 12th NCA/AFA conference on argumentation*, ed. G.T. Goodnight, 51–58. Washington, DC: National Communication Association.

True, M. 1987. A Kouros at the Getty Museum. *The Burlington Magazine* 129(1006): 3–11.

Tversky, A., and D. Kahneman. 1982. Judgments of and by representativeness. In *Judgment under uncertainty: Heuristics and biases*, ed. D. Kahneman, P. Slovic, and A. Tversky. Cambridge: Cambridge University Press.

van Eemeren, F.H., and R. Grootendorst. 1992. *Argumentation, communication and fallacies*. Mahwah: Erlbaum.

Verheij, B. 2003. DefLog: On the logical interpretation of prima facie justified assumptions. *Journal of Logic and Computation* 13(3): 319–346.

Verheij, B. 2005. *Virtual arguments. On the design of argument assistants for lawyers and other arguers*. The Hague: TMC Asser Press.

Walton, D. 1989. *Informal logic*. Cambridge: Cambridge University Press.

Walton, D. 1997. *Appeal to expert opinion*. University Park: Penn State Press.

Walton, D. 2010. Why fallacies appear to be better arguments than they are. *Informal Logic* 30(2): 159–184.

Walton, D., and D. Godden. 2005. The nature and status of critical questions in argumentation schemes. In *The uses of argument: Proceedings of a conference at McMaster University 18–21 May, 2005*, ed. D. Hitchcock, 476–484, Hamilton, Ontario.

Walton, D., and T.F. Gordon. 2005. Critical questions in computational models of legal argument. In *Argumentation in artificial intelligence and law*, IAAIL workshop series, ed. P.E. Dunne and T.J.M. Bench-Capon, 103–111. Nijmegen: Wolf Legal Publishers.

Walton, D., and T.F. Gordon. 2011. Modeling critical questions as additional premises. In *Argument cultures: Proceedings of the 8th international OSSA conference*, ed. F. Zenker, 1–13. Windsor. Available at http://www.dougwalton.ca/papers%20in%20pdf/11OSSA.pdf.

Walton, D., and N. Zhang. 2013. The epistemology of scientific evidence. *Artificial Intelligence and Law* 21(2): 173–219.

Walton, D., C. Reed, and F. Macagno. 2008. *Argumentation schemes*. Cambridge: Cambridge University Press.

Wyner, A. 2012. Questions, arguments, and natural language semantics. In *Proceedings of the 12th workshop on Computational Models of Natural Argumentation (CMNA 2012)*, Montpellier, France, 16–20.

# Chapter 5
# Attribution of a Portrait to Leonardo da Vinci

**Abstract** In this chapter a case study is conducted to test the capability of the Carneades Argumentation System (CAS) to model the argumentation in a case where forensic evidence was collected in an investigation triggered by a conflict among art experts on the attribution of a portrait to Leonardo da Vinci. A claim that a portrait of a young woman in a Renaissance dress could be attributed to Leonardo was initially dismissed by art experts. Forensic investigations were carried out, and evidence was collected by art history experts and scientific experts. The expert opinions were initially in conflict, but new evidence shifted the burden of proof onto the side of the skeptics. This chapter presents an analysis of the structure of the interlocking argumentation in the case using argument mapping tools to track the accumulation of evidence pro and con.

In this chapter CAS (Gordon 2005; Gordon and Walton 2006; Gordon 2010) is used to model the argumentation in a case of conflict among art experts on the attribution of a portrait to Leonardo da Vinci. In this case an unsigned portrait of a young woman in a Renaissance dress sold for only $22,000 in 2007, but later investigations by experts turned up evidence it may have been painted by Leonardo. Forensic investigations were subsequently carried out, and evidence was collected by art history and forensic experts. The portrait was valued at $160 million in 2012, but if proved to the art world to be painted by Leonardo, it could be worth more than $600 million. The expert opinions were initially in conflict, but as the forensic evidence came in, new evidence shifted the burden of proof onto the side of the skeptics. This chapter presents an analysis of the structure of the interlocking argumentation in the case using argument diagrams to track the mass of evidence.

The way the actual dispute took place, and how the collection and marshaling of forensic evidence proceeded, is a very long and complicated story chronicled in several books and many articles about the subject of the disputed Leonardo portrait. It is important to realize that the analysis presented in this chapter is not an attempt to model all this data using argumentation tools. That would be a huge project, well beyond the scope of a single chapter. The purpose of this chapter is to take the data presented in parts one and two as the so-called "case", in which some key propositions in the investigation have been selected out as arguments to be modeled by the system. The secondary purpose is to put these propositions into an order so



D. Walton, *Argument Evaluation and Evidence*, Law, Governance and Technology Series 23, DOI 10.1007/978-3-319-19626-8_5

that they can be represented as a connected sequence of evidential argumentation that bears on the unsettled issue of whether the portrait can justifiably be attributed to Leonardo or not.

It is very important that attention be paid to the actual wording of what each expert said, for in the chapter each of these arguments will be modeled using the CAS argument mapping tool along with the argumentation schemes for argument from expert opinion. Argumentation schemes (Hastings 1963; Kienpointner 1992; Grennan 1997; Walton et al. 2008), as indicated in Chaps 1 and 2, are recognizable forms of argument that are generally defeasible but that can be used to create evidential support in favor of, or against a conclusion. Sections 5.1 and 5.2 outline the details of the case. Section 5.3 describes the two schemes for argument from expert opinion and abductive reasoning in more detail than given in Chaps 1, 2 and 3. Section 5.5 introduces the reader to more technical details of CAS. The remaining sections build six separate argument diagrams drawn to represent each of the arguments and examine them in order to see how each is linked to the next in a sequence. Section 5.6 displays a large argument diagram (Fig. 5.9) connecting the mass of evidence in the case. Sections 5.7, 5.8 and 5.9 discuss the problem of how to evaluate the argumentation in the case using this diagram, IBE, CAS, and the notion of burden of proof as defined in CAS. Section 5.10 presents the conclusions.

## 5.1 Case Outline

In this case a claim that a portrait of a young woman in a Renaissance dress could be attributed to Leonardo da Vinci was evaluated by experts. The portrait shows a side view of the head and shoulders of a young and attractive woman. She is facing to the left and the portrait shows details of her hair arrangement and her dress. She is shown against a dull yellow background and her hair and complexion is shown in a realistic coloring. She has a small headband and a netting arrangement drawing together the back of her hair, and thus the portrait exhibits a style that would be consistent with portraits of the aristocracy drawn by artists in the Italian Renaissance. A website dedicated to the portrait which shows a color picture of it gives an idea of the size of the portrait can be found at this website (as of August 18, 2014): https://sites.google.com/site/labellaprincipessacom/.

The claim that the portrait was a genuine Leonardo portrait was initially dismissed by art experts, but investigations were subsequently carried out and evidence was amassed on both sides of the issue. Gradually the body of evidence began to point towards acceptance of the hypothesis that the portrait was an authentic Leonardo, but controversy remained. The burden of proof rested heavily on the proponents of the hypothesis that the portrait was authentic, and there was much at stake, both financially and from the point of view of art history. Peter Silverman, an art collector, saw the portrait on sale in a New York gallery in 2007 and bought it for $22,000. It was done using colored chalks and ink on a calfskin material called vellum. The attribution to Leonardo remained controversial in the art world during the lengthy process of assessment of the forensic evidence by art experts. For one thing, the portrait was not signed. Although the vellum on which the portrait was painted was shown with more than 95 % probability by carbon dating to overlap Leonardo's life, skilled forgers will use original materials to make their copies and it is very common for collectors to spend millions of dollars on counterfeit works of art.

One expert claimed that the technique used in the portrait showed evidence of its being made by a left-handed artist. It is well known that Leonardo was a left-handed artist. However, another expert who disagreed noted that imitators of Leonardo's work had copied this characteristic in the past. Many art scholars have expressed skepticism about the attribution to Leonardo, some saying that it is a nineteenth-century German painting and others saying that it is a modern forgery.

The portrait was tested by another expert from Lumiere Technology in Paris, a company that offers in-depth technical analysis of paintings to authenticate masterpieces of fine art using a special high-resolution camera that can digitally scan under the surface of a painting. The founder of this company, an expert in such matters, had previously tested his technology on the Mona Lisa, and now applied it to this portrait of the woman in the Renaissance dress, sometimes called Portrait of a Young Fiancée or The Beautiful Princess. A partial fingerprint was found on the portrait, and it was consistent with fingerprints found on other paintings of Leonardo, but it was too poorly detailed to support a match. Technically, the portrait is not a "painting", but a drawing in mixed media.

Eventually, one expert tied the portrait to the Sforza family. Ludovico Sforza was a wealthy patron of Leonardo, and Leonardo lived in Milan from 1482 to 1499. The research of this expert found that Bianca, the illegitimate daughter of Ludovico, was likely the subject of the portrait. Another expert found, by using imaging technology, some unusual marks, indicating that someone had used a knife to cut along the left side of the vellum. As well he found three holes in the vellum on the same side. This evidence suggested that the portrait might have been originally made as a page in a book. At that point a book, a history of the Sforza family printed on vellum, was found in the Polish National Library. It was known that some copies of the book were printed on vellum and had added illumination. One such copy was presented to the husband of Bianca at her wedding. One sheet of vellum near the front of a copy of the hand-illuminated book found in the Polish National Library was missing. Further investigations showed that the stitch marks in the binding of this book matched the three holes in the portrait.[1]

The final findings of the examining of the stitch marks with holes in the portrait seemed to many to be a clincher that provided conclusive evidence to prove that the portrait was a genuine Leonardo. But despite the body of evidence that the extensive forensic investigations had amassed, there remain dissenting expert opinions.

[1] A NOVA program 'Mystery of a Masterpiece', aired by PBS on January 25, 2012, told the story of the case up to that date. A transcript can be found at www.pbs.org/wgbh/nova/tech/mystery-masterpiece.html, as of 08/09/2012.

## 5.2 What the Experts Said

When Silverman started to wonder whether Leonardo might have been the artist, he contacted Martin Kemp, Emeritus Research Professor in the History of Art at Oxford University, a specialist on Leonardo. Kemp was trained in Natural Sciences and Art History at Cambridge University and the Courtauld Institute, London. He was British Academy Wolfson Research Professor in 1993–1998. Kemp studied the details of the portrait carefully, examining the tiny marks made by the artist's brush, and he became convinced there was a chance for attribution to Leonardo. Other experts disagreed. David Eskerdjian, Professor of Art History at the University of Leicester, said that it did not compare with the quality of other paintings by Leonardo.

Silverman took the portrait to a lab in Paris to be tested by an expert, Pascal Cotte, inventor of special high-resolution camera that can take pictures to probe visually under the surface of the painting. Cotte, the founder of Lumiere Technologies, is an engineer who developed a tool that enables the in-depth study of fine art paintings to reveal the true pigments for viewing and analysis without touching or damaging the paintings. He compared characteristics of alterations in the portrait to those in a sketch universally agreed to have been made by Leonardo. He found the alterations made by the artist in both paintings strikingly similar.

Giammarco Cappuzo, an art specialist and friend of Silverman, pointed out that in order to prove that the portrait is a genuine Leonardo, one would have to prove to the skeptics that it is not a nineteenth-century forgery. The question was also raised whether the portrait could have been created by one of the other artists employed in his workshop. Cristina Geddo, an art historian and expert on Leonardo and his followers, examined the portrait. She noticed that the pen marks used to create shading around the face were in an unusual direction, suggesting an artist using his left hand. It is well known that Leonardo was left handed. Geddo stated that all of Leonardo's assistants worked with the right hand. This finding suggested that either the portrait was drawn by Leonardo, or it was drawn by a forger trying to copy his left handed style.

Pascal Cotte discovered a faint fingerprint at the top left corner of the portrait. It is known that Leonardo used his hands to spread paint, and that examples of his fingerprints can be found in his other paintings. Peter Paul Biro, a forensic art examiner, claimed that the partial fingerprint was comparable to a fingerprint found on St. Jerome in the Wilderness, a painting firmly attributed to Leonardo. But the match was not convincing enough to prove that the print on the Bianca portrait could definitely be attributed to him. Several forensic experts on fingerprint evidence found that the partial fingerprint was too poorly detailed to support the claim of the match. An analysis of these fingerprints was undertaken by the Institute of Criminology and Criminal Law in Lausanne, Switzerland. Professor Christoph Champaud, an expert in fingerprint identification, posted the image on a website and asked students and colleagues to analyze it. His opinion was that there was insufficient evidence to match this fingerprint with the other Leonardo fingerprints.

The characteristics of the fingerprint on the portrait could be matched with too many other non-Leonardo fingerprints to be of evidential value.

Sarah Simblet, a drawing instructor and professor at the Ruskin School of Fine Art in Oxford, was consulted by Kemp about the artistic techniques used in the portrait. She stated that the portrait was made by an exceptional draftsman and by someone who understood very well about the structure of the skull, facial bones and curvatures around the eyes in a human face. These characteristics both suggest that Leonardo could have been the artist. It is known that Leonardo dissected corpses and exposed bones, sinews and muscles in exceptional detail. She also showed that the portrait showed an unusual, experimental mix of materials put on the vellum. Such an unusual and experimental technique of painting was taken to point to Leonardo as the artist, since he was known to attempt such unusual methods. The fine painting techniques used in the portrait were consistent with the experimental painting techniques used by Leonardo, but this evidence was regarded as insufficient to prove attribution to him. At this point in the investigation, David Eskerdjian remarked that opinions were divided, and that others shared his reluctance to accept the hypothesis that the portrait was painted by Leonardo.

Martin Kemp then looked around to try to identify the person in the portrait. He narrowed down the candidates to Bianca, the illegitimate daughter of Ludovico Sforza. Historical evidence showed that she would have been about the right age to match the image of the girl in the portrait, but at that early point, there appeared to be no record of such a person, or listing of her in the Royal Inventory. Hence the history of the portrait remained in doubt.

At this point, Pascal Cotte opened up another line of investigation. He observed that there were three holes at the edge of the vellum, suggesting that these holes may have come from stitching of the kind used to bind a book. It had also previously been noticed that there was a knife cut along the edge of the portrait where the three holes were found. Such a knife cut could be explained by someone cutting out a single page of a book. These findings might explain why there are no accounts of the portrait, and why it was not listed among Leonardo's paintings. The line of investigation then took the direction of asking why Bianca's portrait would be put in a book. At this point, Kemp and Cotte argued that the portrait was a page in a book that celebrated the wedding of Bianca Sforza (Kemp and Cotte 2010). However, at that point, there was no evidence of the existence of such a book. So their hypothesis was still not strongly enough supported by the evidence to meet the burden of proof required to convince the art world that Leonardo painted the portrait.

The final stage in the collection of the evidence was the discovery of a 500-year-old book called the *Sforzada* that was found in the National Library of Poland, and that was printed on vellum. Historians agreed that the book was written in commemoration of the wedding of Bianca Sforza. Pascal Cotte used a special camera enabling him to photograph details of the pages of the book. He found that the missing page would have been at the front of the book, and that the three holes on the side of the portrait match the stitching there. He found that there were originally five stitches in the book. But Polish archivists said that when it was rebound centuries ago, it was believed that two stitches were added to the original three in order to strengthen the binding. Cotte found that the alignment between the three holes and the three stitch marks were perfect (or rather, close to high levels of probability).

## 5.3 Two Theoretical Instruments to Be Applied to the Case

This section describes two theoretical tools that will be applied from argumentation theory to the particulars of the case to be analyzed. The first tool is called an argumentation scheme. It is a defeasible form of argument that is evaluated in a given case by critical questions that are attached to each scheme. The critical questions probe into the weak points of the argument (Walton and Gordon 2011).

The most basic version of the argumentation scheme for argument from expert opinion given in (Walton et al. 2008, 310), is repeated here for the reader's convenience from Chap. 4, Sect. 4.4.

Major Premise: Source *E* is an expert in subject domain *S* containing proposition *A*.
Minor Premise: *E* asserts that proposition *A* is true (false).
Conclusion: *A* is true (false).

An argument from expert opinion should be evaluated by the asking of six basic critical questions, repeated here from Chap. 4, Sect. 4.4, but in a more usable format.

*Expertise Question*: How credible is *E* as an expert source?
*Field Question*: Is *E* an expert in the field *F* that *A* is in?
*Opinion Question*: What did *E* assert that implies *A*?
*Trustworthiness Question*: Is *E* personally reliable as a source?
*Consistency Question*: Is *A* consistent with what other experts assert?
*Backup Evidence Question*: Is *E*'s assertion based on evidence?

If a respondent asks any one of the six critical questions, the original argument defaults unless the question is answered adequately.

One form of argumentation that this case and other instances of scientific discovery are based on is abductive reasoning, or inference to the best explanation. An abductive inference (Josephson and Josephson 1994, 14) has the following form, where *H* is a variable representing a hypothesis and *D* is a variable representing a given set of data or (presumed) facts. This form is the argumentation scheme for abductive reasoning, first presented in Chap. 2, Sect. 2.4. It basically says that if *D* is a collection of data, hypothesis *H* explains *D*, and no other hypothesis can explain *D* as well as *H* does, then *H* is plausibly true. Josephson and Josephson (1994, 14) used six critical questions that can be applied to evaluate abductive reasoning in any given case.

1. How decisively does *H* surpass the alternative explanations?
2. How good is *H* by itself, independently of the alternatives?
3. How reliable are the data?

4. How much confidence is there that all plausible explanations have been considered?
5. Are there practical considerations, including the costs of being wrong?
6. How urgent is the need is to come to a conclusion at all before seeking further evidence?

The conclusion to be inferred using this scheme is selected as the best explanation of the data. However, abductive reasoning is taken to be defeasible, meaning that the conclusion may have to be withdrawn as new evidence is taken into account (Walton 2004).

The second tool is the framework of the investigation that the individual arguments in the case are situated within (Hamblin 1971). In argumentation theory, such a framework is called a type of dialogue, because it is viewed as a series of exchanges in which arguments are put forward by a proponent and then critically questioned by a respondent. There are several types of dialogue that have been studied, including persuasion dialogue, negotiation dialogue, deliberation, and information-seeking dialogue (Walton and Krabbe 1995). The particular type of dialogue that provides the framework in which the argumentation in this case is situated is called an inquiry.

At the opening stage of an inquiry dialogue, a particular statement has to be specified, so that the object of the inquiry as a whole is to prove or disprove this statement. In discovery dialogue there is no statement set at the beginning in such a manner that the goal of the whole dialogue is to prove or disprove this statement. The aim of the discovery dialogue is to try to find something, a hypothesis that might explain the facts of a case. Such a hypothesis cannot be set as something to be proved or disproved until the dialogue has found it. Thus burden of proof is different in these two types of dialogue. In inquiry dialogue, the burden of proof is set at the opening stage, governs the conduct of the argumentation through the whole argumentation stage, and then is used at the closing stage to determine when the argumentation stage should end, and whether the argumentation in it was successful or not in fulfilling the goal of the dialogue.

In discovery dialogue, what is set at the opening stage is some set of facts that need to be explained. As evidence comes in, hypotheses are formed, and it may be found that some explanations are better than others. One may then be shown to be the best explanation, the one supported by the most evidence, and least open to refutation by contrary evidence. Some anomaly or unexplained event is identified at the opening stage of a discovery dialogue, and then there is a shift to an argumentation stage where several competing explanations are evaluated. The evidence for one explanation is weighed against the evidence for a competing explanation, or a set of competing explanations (Josephson and Josephson 1994). In a successful discovery dialogue, sufficient evidence is brought forward to prove that one explanation is arguably better than the others. The standard of proof in inquiry dialogue tends to be set to a high level of support required to prove the hypothesis. Only if enough evidence has been put forward to satisfy the questioner, and remove

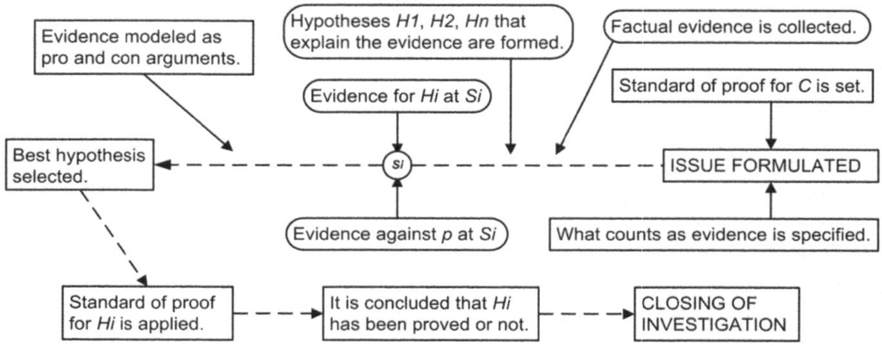


**Fig. 5.1** From the opening to the closing of the investigation

his doubts to a reasonable degree, can the argument be accepted as proved, at any given state $S_i$ of the investigation where new evidence comes in.

The inquiry model applies to the marshaling of evidence in the investigation of the portrait of the young woman as outlined by the sequence of argumentation in Fig. 5.1. As shown in Fig. 5.1, the investigation process begins with the formulation of a central claim at issue to be proved or disproved by the evidence that is brought to bear.

## 5.4 Evaluating Arguments Using the Carneades System

A problem with using critical questions to evaluate cases where expert opinion is used as a source of evidence is that we can no longer use an argument diagram to summarize, analyze or evaluate the basic evidence in a case and display its structure as a sequence of reasoning. The reason is that everything that appears in the text box on a standard argument diagram needs to be a statement, a proposition that is either true or false. It is harder to analyze the structure of questions, even though they are certainly very important as devices in both everyday and legal argumentation, for example in examining a witness. Using critical questions definitely takes us outside the realm of reasoning to the realm of argument, where claims are made and subjected to doubt by the asking of critical questions by an opponent.

As indicated in Chap. 4, Sect. 4.3, critical questions are modeled by CAS as additional premises corresponding to the critical questions of an argumentation scheme. CAS is a mathematical and computational model that defines mathematical properties of arguments that are used to identify, analyze and visualize real arguments. By applying argumentation schemes, CAS analyzes and evaluates the acceptability of arguments, based on proof standards, for example preponderance of the evidence. In CAS, critical questions matching an argument are reformulated as assumptions or exceptions (Walton and Gordon 2005; Gordon and Walton 2009).

Assumptions are assumed to be acceptable unless called into question. Exceptions are modeled as premises that are assumed to be not acceptable, but they can undercut an argument if found to be acceptable. Ordinary premises are assumed to be acceptable, but must be supported by further arguments if questioned. Whether or not the evidence is sufficient depends on the standard of proof, which in turn depends on the type of dialogue that is involved. During the closing stage, as shown along the bottom of Fig. 5.1, the standard of proof is applied to determine whether the proposition that was the subject of the inquiry can be said to have been proved or not.

CAS has developed through four versions. The first version (2006–2008) was implemented in the programming language Scheme. The second version was implemented in 2011, a desktop version with a graphical user interface called the Carneades Editor. The third version (Gordon 2011) was a web-based version of Carneades, developed in the IMPACT and MARKOS projects (2010–2015). A new version is planned but so far has not been implemented. In this book we are using and will use only a simplified style of presenting argument diagrams in the numerous examples of arguments that are analyzed using the CAS structure. We do not use some of the special features of the system, such as argument weights, that can be applied to argument evaluation, because we want keep things simple enough so that readers without specialize training can grasp the basic idea of how argument evaluation works in such a system without being overwhelmed by complexities.

An argument is defined in CAS as a directed graph consisting of text boxes and argument nodes connected by arrows (Freeman 1991). In a CAS argument diagram, the premises and conclusions of the argument are displayed in text boxes as leaves of a tree (Scheuer et al. 2010). A proposition in a text box can be accepted or rejected, or it can be neither accepted nor rejected. If it is accepted, the text box is colored green. If it is rejected, the text box is colored red. If it is neither accepted nor rejected the text box retains a white background. The arrows joining the text boxes represent arguments. The arguments themselves are represented as nodes. A convergent argument is represented as two separate arguments supporting the same conclusion. In a linked arguments configuration, the two or more premises each lead in to the same node. The type of argument, that is, its argumentation scheme, is displayed with the node. The ultimate proposition to be proved is displayed as the root of the tree. It may be helpful to look at how the visual user interface of CAS looks on a computer screen in the second version. This is shown in Fig. 5.2.

In Fig. 5.2, the ultimate conclusion to be proved, the proposition that the portrait is a genuine Leonardo, is shown at the left in a white box, indicating that it has not been accepted but only stated. On the right, we have three arguments supporting or attacking this conclusion. The argument at the top is a pro-argument, indicated by the plus symbol in its node. The argument just below it is a contra argument, indicated by the minus symbol in its node. The third argument, at the right, supports the top premise of the top argument, since it too is shown as a pro-argument.

All six propositions making up the premises of the three arguments just mentioned are shown in green boxes containing checkmarks. The checkmarks were added for color blind users. These notations show that all these propositions have

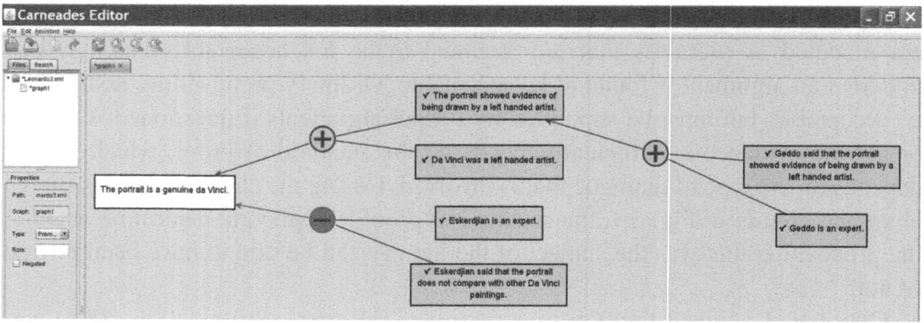


**Fig. 5.2** Screen shot of an example showing the CAS menu

been accepted. However, the conclusion, as noted above, is shown in a white box indicating that it is not accepted. The reason is that the standard of proof for all seven propositions (inserted into the part of the menu shown at the left) is that of beyond reasonable doubt. Even though the top argument supports the ultimate conclusion, and the argument at the right supports the premise of the top argument, the support is not enough to prove that the conclusion is true beyond a reasonable doubt. The reason is that the contra argument shown in the middle at the bottom of Fig. 5.2 raises doubt about the acceptability of the ultimate conclusion, and hence the conclusion is not drawn in a green box as being accepted.

Propositions are accepted or rejected by an audience (Tindale 1990; Bench-Capon et al. 2007) where the audience is assumed to have a priority ordering of values (Bench-Capon and Sartor 2003). The user inputs information into the argumentation tree indicating which propositions represented as leaves in the tree are accepted or rejected, or neither. CAS then automatically adjusts the colors of all the leaves of the tree to show how the new information has affected a particular argument, and how it changed as this particular argument changes the other arguments it is related to. In this manner, acceptance and rejection can be propagated (see Fig. 5.11) along the leaves of a tree so that any new argument can lead to either acceptance or rejection of the ultimate conclusion to be proved (Gordon 2010).

In this chapter our primary concern will not be the evaluation of the sequence of argumentation in the case of the portrait attributed to Leonardo. Our concern will be with the analysis of the structure of the sequence of argumentation making up the evidence in the case. From there, once the step has been taken to see how all the pieces of evidence in the case fit together into a large structure, and the step has been taken to determine whether there could be alternative interpretations of the argumentation in the case, then the step of running this sequence of argumentation through CAS in order to evaluate it can be taken. The procedure will be to break the lengthy sequence of argumentation down into manageable packages at a micro level, and then move to a macro level analysis where the arguments in each package are chained together representing a mass of evidence supporting the ultimate conclusion in the case as a whole.

Arguments can be chained together so that one argument can affect another, either by supporting it or undermining it. There are several ways to attack arguments using CAS. One is to present a counterargument showing that a premise of the original argument is untenable. A second way is to present a counterargument showing that the conclusion of the original argument is untenable. A third way is to undercut the original argument showing that it does not prove its conclusion. On the argument diagram this configuration is shown as one argument attacking another. That is, an arrow leads from one argument node to another. In this respect, a CAS argument diagram is different from the traditional argument diagrams we are generally used to in logic. Another important feature of CAS is that whether or not a proposition is acceptable, in light of the evidence for and against it represented on an argumentation graph, is a matter of burden of proof. Burden of proof is defined in CAS as resting on standard of proof. The four standards of proof (Gordon and Walton 2009) are set in increasing order of strictness, as indicated in Chap. 4, Sect. 4.3. The four standards can be specified more rigorously below.

- Scintilla of Evidence
  - There is at least one applicable argument
- Preponderance of Evidence
  - The scintilla of evidence standard is satisfied, and
  - the maximum weight assigned to an applicable pro argument is greater than the maximum weight of an applicable con argument.
- Clear and Convincing Evidence
  - The preponderance of evidence standard is satisfied,
  - the maximum weight of applicable pro arguments exceeds some threshold $\alpha$, and
  - the difference between the maximum weight of the applicable pro arguments and the maximum weight of the applicable con arguments exceeds some threshold $\beta$.
- Beyond Reasonable Doubt
  - The clear and convincing evidence standard is satisfied and
  - the maximum weight of the applicable con arguments is less than some threshold $\gamma$.

Notice once again that on this way of defining the standards of proof, the threshold $\gamma$ is left open, and is not given a fixed numerical value.

Burden of proof is determined by two components, one of them being the standard of proof. The other is the determination of which side the burden rests on at any given point in a dialogue, as the burden shifts back and forth. As noted above, in CAS, there are two sides who take turns putting forward arguments and responding by asking critical questions, or putting forward contra arguments. A dialogue is formally defined as an ordered 3-tuple $\langle O, A, C \rangle$ where $O$ is the opening stage, *A* is the argumentation stage, and *C* is the closing stage (Gordon and Walton 2009, 649). Dialogue rules of the kind described in Walton and Krabbe (1995) define what types of moves are allowed by the parties during the three stages. The initial situation poses the issue to be resolved at the opening stage, and the dialogue moves through the opening stage toward the closing stage.

In an inquiry dialogue, the ultimate proposition to be proved or disputed is formulated at the opening stage. Using different standards of proof, for example the standard of the preponderance of the evidence, a burden of proof is assigned to each proposition (Gordon and Walton 2009). The preponderance of the evidence standard means that in order to be proved, a proposition must have stronger pro arguments supporting it than the con arguments attacking it. However, there is not just one standard of proof used to define burden of proof in the system. Burden of proof is assigned in light of the type of argumentation that the participants are engaged in (Gordon et al. 2007). In an inquiry dialogue to prove that a painting of questionable provenance can be attributed to Leonardo, the burden of proof would have to be set very high. For example we might assign the burden of beyond reasonable doubt. There are several reasons for the appropriateness of this kind of assignment. One is that the art world (the audience) would be highly skeptical about such a claim. Another is the monetary value of any painting attributable to Leonardo. Another is the known fact that forgers will go to great lengths to create fakes.

## 5.5 Argument Diagrams of Each Argument

In this section the lengthy sequence of argumentation is broken down into a sequence of five subarguments and an argument diagram is drawn showing the structure of each of the subarguments. The first argument map, shown in Fig. 5.3, represents a conflict of opinions between two experts, Martin Kemp and David Eskerdjian. As is standard in argument mapping (Buckingham Shum et al. 1997) the propositions that function as premises or conclusions of the argument are displayed in text boxes as leaves of the tree. The arguments are shown as nodes connecting a set of premises to a conclusion. The argumentation scheme that a particular argument fits is shown in the node, where its name is displayed.

As shown in Fig. 5.3, Kemp became convinced after examining the details of the portrait that there was a chance for attribution to Leonardo. Eskerdjian disagreed, saying that the portrait did not compare with the quality of other Leonardo works. In the argument map shown in Fig. 5.3, the ultimate proposition at issue, the claim that the portrait of the young woman is a genuine Leonardo, is shown at the extreme left the tree structure as the root of the tree. To the right of this ultimate claim the opposed arguments on both sides are presented.

To the right of the node for that argument from expert opinion there is a con argument, as indicated by the minus sign in its argument node. This con argument represents the critical question for argument from expert opinion which asks whether the opinion of the expert cited is in accord with the opinions of other

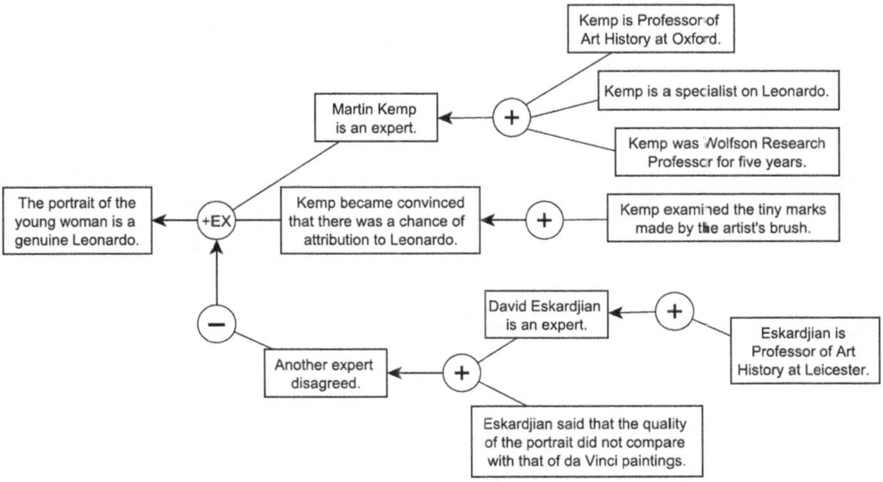


**Fig. 5.3** The first argument map

experts. This critical question functions as an exception, meaning that the original argument from expert opinion is defeated if evidence can be given to back up the claim that the original argument from expert opinion is not in accord with the opinions of some other experts.

In this case, as shown in Fig. 5.3, evidence is given from another expert who disagreed with Kemp. This expert presented a counterargument stating that the quality of the portrait does not compare with that of other Leonardo paintings. So here we have a case of an undercutter, where the second argument is a con argument that defeats the first argument because it is backed up by evidence to support its attack. At this point then, the argumentation is inconclusive. We have the word of one expert pitted against the word of another.

In the next part of the argument some new evidence is introduced, as shown in Fig. 5.4. A third expert, Cristina Geddo, an art historian and expert on Leonardo and his followers, presented an argument for attributing the portrait to Leonardo. She found pen marks around the face suggesting that the artist was left handed, and while it is known that Leonardo was left handed, it is also known that all of his assistants worked with the right hand (as noted above). This argument presents some evidence for the ultimate conclusion that the portrait can be attributed to Leonardo, but it is not conclusive by itself because it leaves open the possibility that a forger could have copied his left handed style. It remains possible that the portrait could have been painted by a nineteenth-century forger, because it is a known practice of forging to use original materials, for example vellum of a kind that would have been used in the Renaissance.

The next argument, shown in the argument map in Fig. 5.5, concerns fingerprint evidence. Once again, this part of the argument offers some evidence to support the

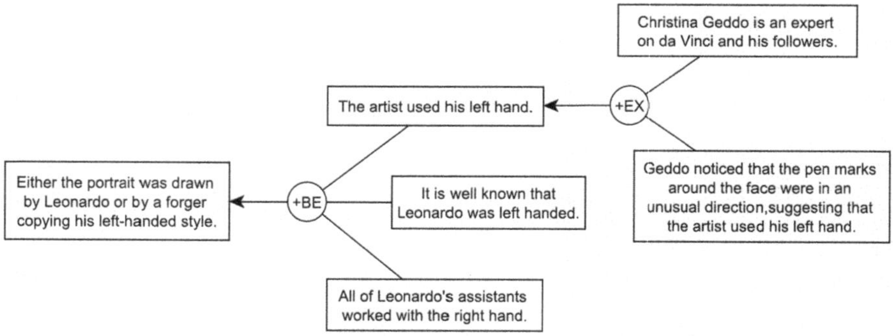


**Fig. 5.4** The second argument map

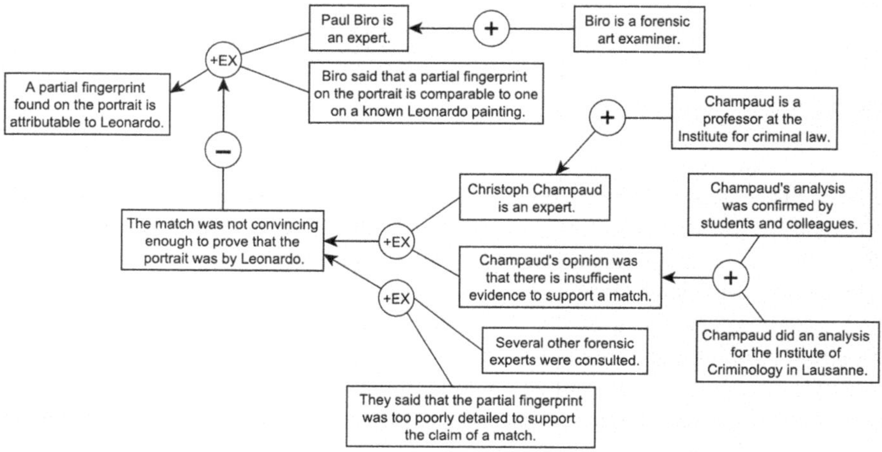


**Fig. 5.5** The third argument map

ultimate conclusion, but not enough to resolve the issue by meeting the burden of proof required to establish the conclusion that the portrait was painted by Leonardo. Here again we have a situation of the battle of the experts, comparable to the evidential situation shown in Fig. 5.3. We have an original argument by an expert attacked by a con argument offering evidence that other experts disagree with the claim made by the original expert. The argument map shown in Fig. 5.5 cites the expert opinion of Paul Biro, a forensic examiner, on the left of the argument map, as a pro argument supporting the ultimate claim that a fingerprint on the portrait is that of Leonardo. This third part of the argument only offers a small amount of evidence in support of the claim that the portrait is that of a genuine Leonardo. For the most part, the strength of the argument is counterbalanced by the opposing expert opinions offering evidence that the partial fingerprint is not a good enough match to offer much if any support to the ultimate conclusion.

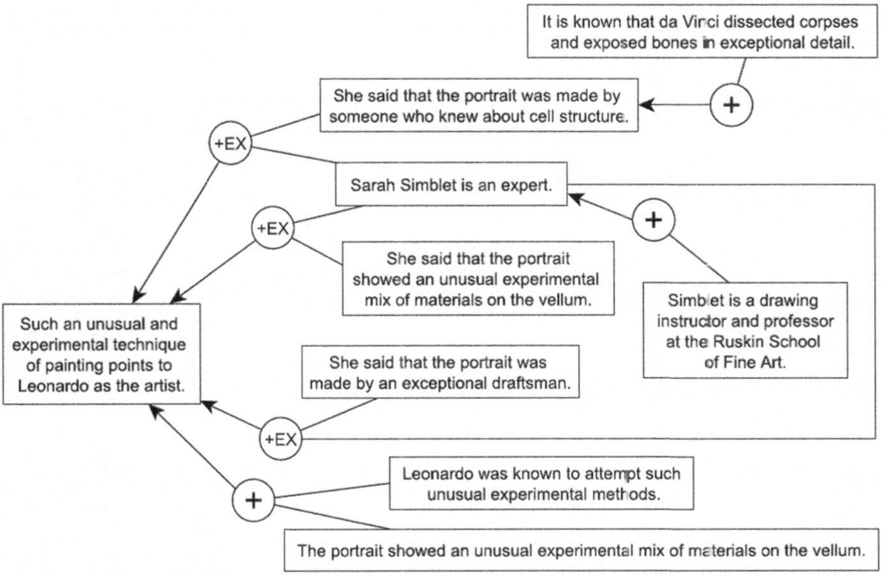


**Fig. 5.6** The fourth argument map

Next we go on to draw a map representing the structure of the expert opinion evidence given by Sarah Simblet, shown in Fig. 5.6. One premise, the statement 'Sarah Simblet is an expert' is shared by three arguments from expert opinion.

This part of the argument shows application of three arguments from expert opinion all provided by the same expert, Sarah Simblet. It seems like a strong argument.

The next stage in the sequence is the point where Cotte opened up another investigation using hypothetical reasoning before the book was discovered in the library. The three holes in the page suggested that they may have come from stitching of the kind used to bind a book.

Another observation was the knife cut along the edge of the portrait where the three holes were found. Such a cut could be explained by somebody cutting out a page of a book. Figure 5.7 shows three applications of the argumentation scheme for inference to the best explanation. This stage of the argument is conjectural, and uses inference to the best explanation to show how these observations could explain why there were no accounts of the Bianca portrait, and why it was not listed among Leonardo's paintings.

At this stage the conjecture was merely a hypothesis because there was no evidence of the existence of such a book. This conjectural evidence was not strong enough by itself to prove the ultimate conclusion. Figure 5.8 takes us to the final step of the argumentation concerning the finding of the book that originally contained the portrait and the evidence of the stitching and the holes in the portrait matching.

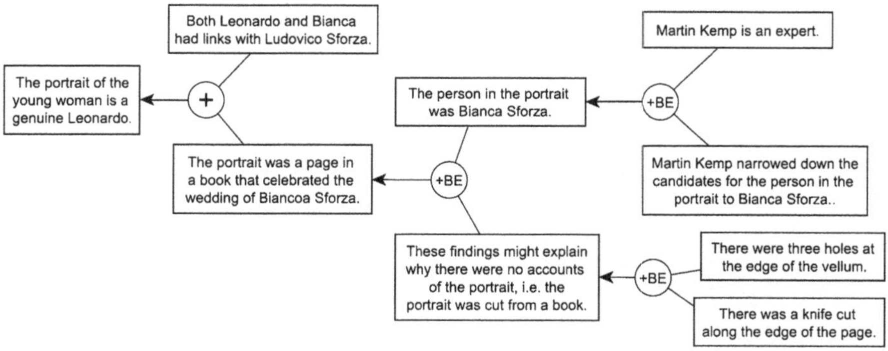


**Fig. 5.7** The fifth argument map

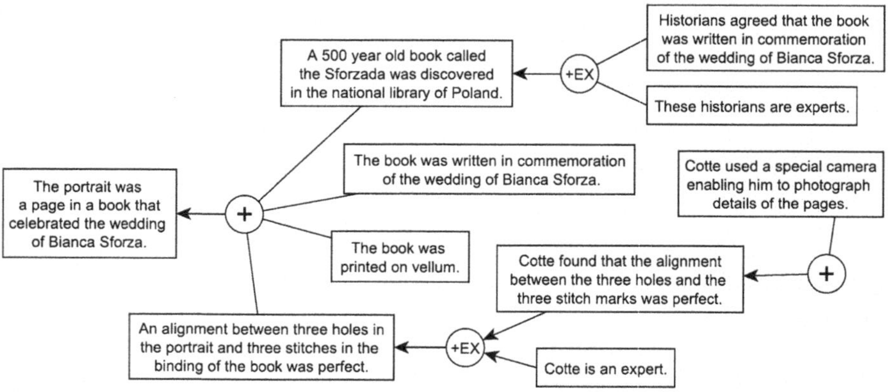


**Fig. 5.8** The sixth argument map

At the bottom right of Fig. 5.8 we have the expert testimony of Cotte claiming that he found a perfect alignment between the three holes in the portrait and three stitch marks in the binding of the book. This is a very strong argument from expert opinion, resting not only on Cotte's qualifications, but his use of a special camera to photograph the details of the pages in a very accurate manner. On the left at the bottom of Fig. 5.8 we see a corroborating argument from historians who agreed that the book was a commemoration of Bianca's wedding. In this case we have a pro argument from expert opinion, and another pro argument from expert opinion supporting a different premise of the original argument. But the main reason it is such a strong argument is the perfect match found between the three holes found in the vellum and the three corresponding stitches in the binding of the book. The match was found by Cotte to be so close that the likelihood of its being a coincidence would be very small.

## 5.6 Fitting the Argument Maps Together

The next task is to look at the five argument maps in order and see how each one is linked to the next one so that it is possible to get a picture of the whole sequence of argumentation. Looking at Fig. 5.3, we see that it is a classic case of the battle of the experts. Kemp stated his view that the portrait is a genuine Leonardo. Using the scheme for argument from expert opinion, since Kemp is an expert, some evidence has now been shifted to support the conclusion. But there is a counterargument, also based on argument from expert opinion. Eskerdjian is also an expert, and he disagrees. Both are qualified experts, but Eskerdjian also gave some evidence to support his argument from expert opinion by stating that in his opinion the quality of the portrait did not compare with that of other Leonardo works. Presenting this evidence makes his argument strong, strong enough to work as an undercutter that defeats the original argument from expert opinion from Kemp. At this point then, we can sum up the evidential situation by saying that an argument from expert opinion has been put forward from Kemp to prove the ultimate conclusion at issue, but it fails to prove this proposition because it is undercut by a countervailing argument from expert opinion.

Next let's deal with the third argument map in Fig. 5.5. It too is a battle of the experts, in this case, fingerprint experts. The expert evidence put forward by a forensic examiner supports the claim that a fingerprint found on the portrait is attributable to Leonardo, but this argument from expert opinion is undercut by the testimony of other experts who claim that the fingerprint was too poorly detailed to support the claim of a match. This counterargument is strong because it is based on the testimony of several other forensic experts who were consulted, and the finding of the original expert was confirmed by tests he ran on his students and colleagues. Thus evidence was given to back up this second argument from expert opinion, and therefore it defeats the original argument from expert opinion put forward by the forensic examiner Biro. This argument too is a battle of the experts, a stalemate that does not go any further. So it can drop out of consideration as a part of the argument that is significant for the evaluation.

Next let's deal with the argument map in Fig. 5.4. This map shows the argument from expert opinion put forward by Cristina Geddo, suggesting that the artist who painted the portrait worked with his left hand. As indicated just above, this argument by itself does not prove that the portrait is a genuine Leonardo, but it does carry some weight because it excludes the alternative explanation that the portrait could have been drawn by one of Leonardo's assistants. As indicated just above, this argument can be connected into the larger sequence of argumentation in the case by putting forward a counterargument that the portrait could have been drawn by a forger copying Leonardo's left-handed style, and then counterattacking this counterargument. Representing this argument on an argument map requires putting in an implicit counterattack and then refuting it. This is one reason for dropping it out of consideration as part of the argument taken into account when we turn to looking at the larger picture. Another reason is that once the final argument shown in

Fig. 5.8 is taken into account, this argument is less important in providing additional evidence to support the ultimate conclusion. For these reasons the argument in Fig. 5.4 will not be taken into account when we come to sum up the connected sequence of argumentation in one large argument map. But it could be added in later if desired.

Next we turn to Fig. 5.7. The argumentation shown in this figure supports the argument from expert opinion put forward by Kemp in Fig. 5.3. In Fig. 5.3 Kemp did not bring forward sufficient evidence to support his claim that the portrait is a genuine Leonardo. But now, the argumentation shown in Fig. 5.7 backs up that argument from expert opinion by presenting the evidence that Bianca Sforza was a likely candidate for the person in the portrait and that both Leonardo and Bianca had links to Ludovico Sforza. These arguments narrow down the scope of the investigation considerably. Also, Kemp presented evidence that the portrait was likely cut from a book. This would explain why there were no accounts of the portrait in the literature on Leonardo's works. It therefore serves as evidence to rebut the argument that the absence of accounts of the portrait suggests that it is a forgery. This new argument changed the focus of the investigation, but remains purely hypothetical so far, as a proof of the ultimate claim. It is a conjecture based on inference to the best explanation, but when seen in this way it can be evaluated as a strong abductive argument to move the investigation forward, backed by physical evidence confirmed by the experts who examined that physical evidence.

Next we return to the argument map in Fig. 5.8 in order to see how the arguments displayed in the first four figures fit into it. The first thing to notice is that one of the premises shown in Fig. 5.7, supporting the ultimate conclusion that the portrait of the young woman is a genuine Leonardo, is the same proposition as the ultimate conclusion of Fig. 5.8. This proposition states that the portrait was a page in a book that celebrated the wedding of Bianca Sforza. So we can now see how the argument map in Fig. 5.7 fits into the previous argument map shown in Fig. 5.6. And so we can combine these two argument maps together to make a larger argument map. It was already shown above how the argument map in Fig. 5.6 fits into the argument map in Fig. 5.3 by supporting Kemp's argument from expert opinion shown in Fig. 5.3. So now we can see how to connect Figs. 5.3, 5.7 and 5.8.

The argument map shown in Fig. 5.8 could be described as the clincher, because it presents strong physical evidence backed up by the technology employed by Cotte to analyze the portrait and the alignment between the three holes and the three stitch marks. The finding by Cotte that the alignment was perfect is very convincing evidence. These findings, shown at the bottom of the argument map in Fig. 5.8 propagate along the tree to the root proposition that the portrait was a page in a book that celebrated the wedding of Bianca Sforza. As suggested above, this very strong argument fits into the tree shown in Fig. 5.7 by supporting the premise that the portrait was from this book. By this means the part of the argument now composed jointly of the fifth and sixth argument maps is very strong. Once these two argumentation graphs are joined to the graph shown in the first argument map, the combined argument structure presents a very strong argument supporting the ultimate conclusion that the portrait is a genuine Leonardo. To sum up, we can produce a large argument map composed of the connected graphs composed of Figs. 5.3, 5.7 and 5.8 showing the whole sequence of argumentation supporting the ultimate conclusion.

Next we turn to Fig. 5.4, where a third argument from expert opinion was put forward by Cristina Geddo, an expert on Leonardo and his followers. She put forward the argument that the pen marks in the portrait suggested that the artist used his left hand, even though it is known that all of Leonardo's assistants worked with the right hand. This argument would give some evidence for the conclusion that the portrait is a genuine Leonardo, but it leaves open the possibility that anyone who was working left handed could have drawn the portrait. Therefore by itself it does not prove the ultimate conclusion that the portrait is a genuine Leonardo. Still, the argument is relevant, and does carry some weight in the case as a whole. The reason is that it excludes the alternative explanation that the portrait could have been drawn by one of Leonardo's assistants, because they are all known to have worked with their right hand only. Therefore the conclusion drawn in Fig. 5.4 is disjunctive. It states only that either the portrait was drawn by Leonardo or by a forger copying his left handed style. Figure 5.4 remains relevant, even after the evidence put forward shown in the argument map in Fig. 5.8. The reason is that even after the portrait was shown to be taken from the commemorative book on the wedding, the possibility still remains open that it could have been painted by one of Leonardo's assistants.

It is less straightforward to connect the argument tree shown in Fig. 5.4 into this larger argument map. Nevertheless, we can connect the argument shown in Fig. 5.4 to the large argument tree composed of Figs. 5.3, 5.7 and 5.8 by putting forward a counterargument stating that the portrait could have been drawn by a forger copying Leonardo's left handed style. This argument in turn can be counterattacked by pointing out that after it was shown that the portrait came from the commemorative book connected to Leonardo, as shown by the evidence presented in Fig. 5.8, it is less likely that it was painted by a forger copying his left handed style. The reason is that once we are given the evidence presented on the large argument map, if the Bianca portrait was painted by anyone else, it would have been by one of Leonardo's assistants. However, this possibility is ruled out by the evidence shown in the argument map in Fig. 5.4.

Once we have achieved some grasp of the larger picture by seeing how the argument maps in Figs. 5.3, 5.4, 5.5, 5.6, 5.7 and 5.8 can all be fitted together to compose one large argument map supporting the ultimate conclusion that the portrait is a genuine Leonardo, we can see how the evidence as a whole needs to be evaluated. The main argument put forward by Kemp overcomes counter arguments put forward by other experts only once it has been supported by the very strong argument shown in Fig. 5.8 proving that the portrait was originally a page in the commemorative book with links to Leonardo.

The next task is to look at the five argument maps in order and see how each one is linked to the next one so that it is possible to get a picture of the whole sequence of argumentation. Looking at Fig. 5.3, we see that it is a classic case of the battle of the experts. Kemp stated his view that the portrait is a genuine Leonardo. Using the scheme for argument from expert opinion, since Kemp is an expert, some evidence has now been shifted to support the conclusion. But there is a counterargument, also based on argument from expert opinion. Eskerdjian is also an expert, and he disagrees. Both are qualified experts, but Eskerdjian also gave some evidence to support his argument from expert opinion by stating that in his opinion the quality of the portrait did not compare with that of other Leonardo works. Presenting this evidence makes his argument strong, strong enough to work as an undercutter that defeats the original argument from expert opinion from Kemp. At this point then, we can sum up the evidential situation by saying that an argument from expert opinion has been put forward from Kemp to prove the ultimate conclusion at issue, but it fails to prove this proposition because it is undercut by a countervailing argument from expert opinion.

Next let's deal with the third argument map in Fig. 5.5. It too is a battle of the experts, in this case, fingerprint experts. The expert evidence put forward by a forensic examiner supports the claim that a fingerprint found on the portrait is attributable to Leonardo, but this argument from expert opinion is undercut by the testimony of other experts who claim that the fingerprint was too poorly detailed to support the claim of a match. This counterargument is strong because it is based on the testimony of several other forensic experts who were consulted, and the finding of the original expert was confirmed by tests he ran on his students and colleagues. Thus evidence was given to back up this second argument from expert opinion, and therefore it defeats the original argument from expert opinion put forward by the forensic examiner Biro. This argument too is a battle of the experts, a stalemate that does not take us any further. So it can drop out of consideration as a part of the argument that is centrally significant for the evaluation.

Next we turn to Fig. 5.7. The argumentation shown in this figure supports the argument from expert opinion put forward by Kemp in Fig. 5.3. In Fig. 5.3 Kemp did not bring forward sufficient evidence to support his claim that the portrait is a genuine Leonardo. But now, the argumentation shown in Fig. 5.7 backs up that argument from expert opinion by presenting the evidence that Bianca Sforza was a likely candidate for the person in the portrait and that both Leonardo and Bianca had links to Ludovico Sforza. These arguments narrow down the scope of the investigation considerably. Also Kemp presented evidence that the portrait was likely cut from a book. This would explain why there were no accounts of the portrait in the literature on Leonardo's works. It therefore serves as evidence to rebut the argument that the absence of accounts of the portrait suggests that it is a forgery. This new argument changes the focus of the investigation, but remains purely hypothetical. It is a conjecture based on inference to the best explanation, but it is backed by physical evidence confirmed by the experts.

Next we turn to the argument map in Fig. 5.8 in order to see how the arguments displayed in the first four argument maps fit into it. The first thing to notice is that one of the premises shown in Fig. 5.7, supporting the ultimate conclusion that the portrait of the young woman is genuine, is the same proposition as the ultimate conclusion of Fig. 5.8. So we can now see how the map in Fig. 5.8 fits into the map shown in Fig. 5.7.

And so we can combine these two argument maps together to make a larger argument map. It was already shown above how the argument map in Fig. 5.7 fits into the argument map in Fig. 5.3 by supporting Kemp's argument from expert opinion shown in Fig. 5.3. So now we can see how to connect Figs. 5.3, 5.7 and 5.8. A map that connects them is shown in Fig. 5.9. The large argument map in Fig. 5.9 composed of the connected graphs composed of Figs. 5.3, 5.7 and 5.8 shows the whole sequence of argumentation supporting the ultimate conclusion.

The argument map in Fig. 5.9 is close to being complete in representing the evidence of the case presented at the beginning of this chapter. The main reason it is incomplete is that it does not take into account the argumentation shown in Fig. 5.4 concerning the argument from expert opinion by Cristina Geddo. If we wanted to make it complete we could insert it into Fig. 5.9 by adding it as an additional argument that supports the ultimate conclusion of the argument in Fig. 5.9 by excluding the possibility that the portrait was painted by one of Leonardo's

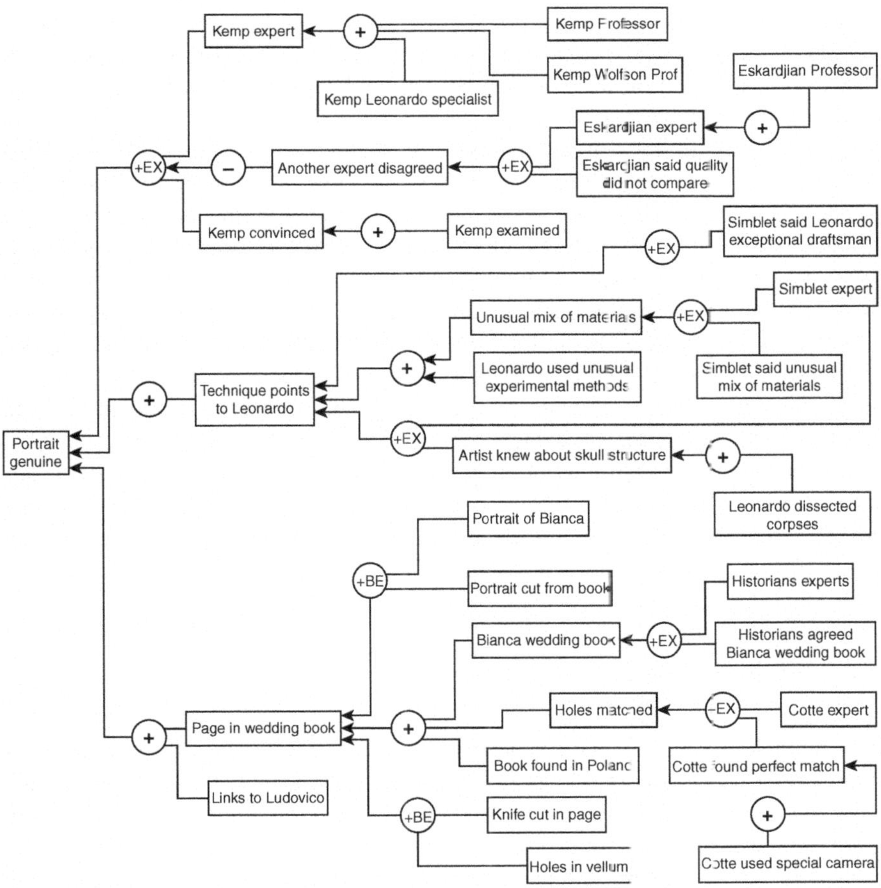


**Fig. 5.9** Large map connecting the mass of evidence in the case

assistants. We could do this by adding a counterargument to the ultimate conclusion that Leonardo painted the portrait, arguing that the portrait could have been painted by one of his assistants, and countering this argument with Geddo's argument from expert opinion. This argument is not shown in the large argument map in Fig. 5.9, because of the possibility of making the diagram too complicated, and because in the end that does not carry that much weight.

But how can we represent the entire sequence of argumentation in the case by using the argument diagram in Fig. 5.9 without taking into account the arguments shown in Figs. 5.4 and 5.5? Recall that we excluded the argument in Fig. 5.4 from the larger argument map in Fig. 5.9 for one reason, because it was susceptible to a counterargument that the portrait could have been drawn by a forger copying Leonardo's left handed style. We excluded Fig. 5.5 because the fingerprint argument in it was undercut by the testimony of other experts who claim that the fingerprint was too poorly detailed to support the claim of a match.

The formal model of burden of proof of Prakken and Sartor (2009) is an abstract argumentation formalism, and for this reason it can be used to model the exclusion of the arguments shown in Figs. 5.4 and 5.5 from the large argument maps shown in Figs. 5.9 and 5.11. The logical model of burden of proof of Prakken and Sartor (2009, 228) is based on the ASPIC+ system of Henry Prakken, which is in turn based on the abstract argumentation framework of Dung (1995). The theoretical basis for excluding these arguments finds its foundation in this way of modelling burden of proof. On this formal model, the proponent starts with an argument he wants to prove and then the opponent can defeat this argument by providing a counterargument. An abstract argumentation framework is defined as a pair (*Args*, *Def*), where *Args* is a set of arguments and $Def \subseteq Args \times Args$ is a binary relation of defeat. The idea is that each argument can be defeated by other arguments, as indicated in Chap. 1, Sect. 1.10. If the counterargument defeats the original argument, the original argument is knocked out of consideration, and a sequence of argumentation ends that point. If there is such a deadlock, the argument can then be excluded as providing any evidence to prove the conclusion at issue.

Recent research in artificial intelligence (van Gijzel and H. Prakken 2011) has shown that the structure of CAS is can be translated into that of ASPIC+. The two models appear to be converging toward a common conception of argumentation, and in this instance they can work together.

## 5.7 Stages of the Investigation

If we again look carefully at the way the evidence accumulated and was evaluated as shown in the large map in Fig. 5.9, we can see that the argumentation went through three main stages, the top stage, the middle stage and the bottom stage. At the top stage there were the five arguments from expert opinion. In the middle stage, there were two arguments from inference to the best explanation. At this middle stage all that was known is that there was a knife cut along the edge of the page, and three holes in the edge of the portrait, suggesting that the portrait was cut from a book. This was merely a plausible hypothesis, but it would explain why there were no accounts of the portrait known in the literature on Leonardo. At the bottom stage, a lot of new evidence came in once the 500 year old book was discovered in the National Library of Poland, and it was investigated by Cotte using his special camera. This sequence of argumentation in the buildup of evidence as a hypothesis is supported or refuted and is characteristic of how scientific investigations typically work. First the hypothesis is merely a conjecture based on weak evidence, for example argument from expert opinion, that is not enough by itself to prove the ultimate conclusion, but is enough to drive the investigation forward in an effort to collect more relevant evidence. The hypothesis works at this stage as an explanation of the facts that competes with other conjectures that could explain the same facts. As new evidence comes in, the competing explanations can be comparatively evaluated based on the arguments derived from that expanded body of evidence.

In Fig. 5.10 we see three competing explanations along the top of the argument map. The first explanation is that the portrait was painted by Leonardo. The second is that it was painted by a Leonardo follower. The third explanation is that it was painted by a modern forger, perhaps a nineteenth century artist. Each explanation is supported by pro and contra arguments, shown underneath the explanations. Shown here is an interesting relationship that indicates how explanations can be supported by arguments and also attacked or refuted by arguments. Which explanation is the best of the three? It depends on how well each of them can comparatively account for the evidence that supports or refutes it.

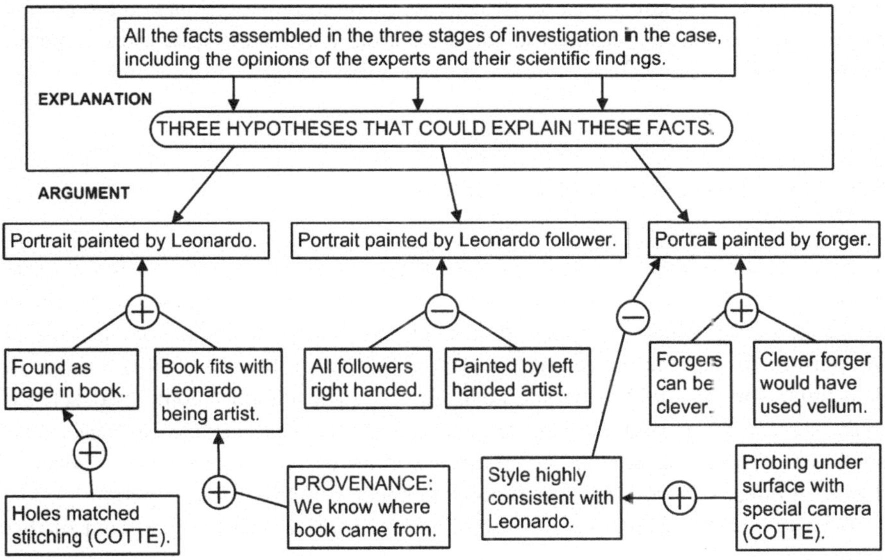


**Fig. 5.10** Three competing explanations of the facts

On the right is the argument that forgers can be clever and that a clever forger would have used vellum that came from the time and place of Leonardo. This is a very hard contra argument to overcome, because there are many known cases of extremely clever forgeries that have resisted detection for a long time, even when examined by highly knowledgeable experts. In the middle there is the explanation that the portrait was painted by a Leonardo follower. This might normally be hard to rule out, except for the evidence that not only was Leonardo left handed, but it is known that all his assistants who painted in his workshop were right handed artists. So there is strong evidence against this hypothesis, so strong that the center explanation does not compete very well with the one on the left and the one on the right. The explanation on the left is that the portrait was painted by Leonardo. This was a competing explanation from the beginning, because of the expert opinion of Kemp. And it was a reasonably strong explanation because the portrait has many of the characteristics of Leonardo as an artist. However it lacked enough strength as an explanation, by itself, to compete with the explanation that the portrait was painted by a modern forger. However, once the forensic evidence of the holes matching the stitching of the book came in, at the point where the book was discovered and examined by Cotte, suddenly this explanation became extremely powerful. The reason is that it was supported so well by the scientific evidence provided by Cotte showing that the holes in the portrait match the stitching of the book. Once this evidence came in, the hypothesis that the portrait was painted by Leonardo explained so much of the evidence so well that it overwhelmed the two competing explanations. It was now the so-called best explanation. By inference to the best explanation, the hypothesis that the portrait was painted by Leonardo became strong enough to convincingly match the burden of proof that would be required to satisfy leading experts in the world of fine art study.

## 5.8 The Three Tasks of Evaluation

To sort out the problem of evaluation we need to distinguish three different tasks of evaluation. The first is the task of judging how the audience, in the real world so to speak, would actually evaluate the acceptability of the ultimate conclusion that the portrait was a genuine Leonardo work. The first problem with this issue is to determine who the audience should be taken to be. The audience could be described as the art world. One needs to be careful here, however. There are two audiences that need to be distinguished, even though these audiences overlap. The first audience is the set of buyers of artworks. The second audience is the set of art experts.

It is proposed here that two factors could be used to make a judgment of this evaluation.

The first is the monetary value of the painting, and how that value changes over time as new evidence on whether the painting is a genuine Leonardo or not comes forward. The second is the acceptance of the painting as a genuine Leonardo or not by the experts.

The following list of leading experts who have agreed with attribution to Leonardo as of 06/09/2012 was given by the Wikipedia entry 'Portrait of a Young Fiancee'.[2]

- Martin Kemp, Emeritus Research Professor in the History of Art at Oxford University
- Carlo Pedretti, professor emeritus of art history and Armand Hammer Chair in Leonardo Studies at the University of California, Los Angeles
- Nicholas Turner, former curator at the British Museum and the J. Paul Getty Museum
- Alessandro Vezzosi, the director of the Museo Ideale Leonardo da Vinci in Vinci, Italy,
- Dr. Cristina Geddo, an expert on Leonardo and his followers
- Dr. Claudio Strinati of the Italian Ministry of Culture, and
- Mina Gregori, professor emerita at the University of Florence.

This is not to say that there is universal agreement in the fine art world that the portrait is a genuine Leonardo. It is only to say that there was a sufficient mass of evidence, and absence of counter-evidence, at this point to shift the burden of proof to the side of the skeptics. The change in market value of the portrait can also be taken as an indication of such a shift. Originally, the portrait was bought in 2007 for $22,000. In 2012, it was reported in many newspapers that its estimated value would be in excess of $160 million. These monetary figures can be used to give some rough indication of general acceptance of the claim that the portrait is a genuine Leonardo.

The second task is the one addressed by this chapter. It is the task of taking a particular description of the case and analyzing the argumentation specifically given in that case. We have to recognize that the issue of whether the portrait is a genuine Leonardo has been extensively investigated by forensic experts, and there is a mass of evidence that has been collected, analyzed by these experts, and communicated to other experts who are continually making judgments about whether the portrait is a genuine Leonardo or not. This body of evidence is continually changing, and is subject to change as time goes on and new evidence comes in, or as the given evidence is further discussed, analyzed and evaluated. No attempt has been made nor could it be made in this chapter to use all this evidence as a basis for evaluation of the issue of whether the portrait is genuine. What has been done, instead, is to designate a particular account, outlined in the first parts of the chapter, as the corpus to be analyzed.

The task is the one of taking this corpus as input into CAS and allowing the system to automatically generate the decision on whether the ultimate conclusion that the portrait is genuine can be proved or not, on the basis of the evidence

[2]http://en.wikipedia.org/wiki/Portrait_of_a_Young_Fianc%C3%A9e

put into CAS. This chapter has not attempted to carry out that task, but it is possible to do it, given that some agreement can be made on the input values for acceptance and rejection of the propositions in the argumentation tree used to make the calculation. To use CAS to evaluate the argument, we have to determine not only which propositions are accepted and which arguments are correctly applicable. We also have to set standards of proof for each of the propositions and each of the arguments. We want to set a high standard, because of the high degree of skepticism in the art world about any unsigned portrait not mentioned in the Leonardo literature describing his paintings. The standard of preponderance of the evidence would not be nearly high enough. Probably the beyond reasonable doubt standard would be the appropriate one to use.

All three of these tasks depend on what is taken to be the appropriate standard of proof for proving the ultimate conclusion, and for assigning burdens of proof both to this proposition and the component arguments in the argumentation tree leading to this ultimate conclusion. Any evaluation of an argument by some normative model depends not only on the structure of the argument identified using the model, but also on the input, the initial values assigned to premises and conclusions in the sequence of argumentation. In CAS, there are two types of input values, one for burdens of proof and one for representing whether the audience initially accepts or rejects the statements. In Sect. 5.4 it was shown how CAS defines burden of proof using four standards of proof set in increasing order of strictness. In defining standards for clear and convincing evidence and beyond reasonable doubt, the gamma threshold was left open and not given a fixed numerical value. The problem is that if we do assign numbers to all the propositions in the large argument map shown in Fig. 5.9 representing the mass of evidence in the case, there is a great risk of committing fallacies by assigning the numbers in an arbitrary way. Despite this difficulty, we can still apply the notions of burden of proof defined in CAS to the case in a way that throws light on how it should be evaluated. It is up to the argument analysts to set some value for gamma, depending on the context of dialogue of which the argument is part. In the Leonardo example described in case study, the context is that of a forensic investigation. According to the description of the case, there was considerable skepticism on the part of the audience, so that in order to convince this audience to reverse its initially skeptical opinion, it is necessary to set the gamma factor to a high level.

Given these limitations imposed by the specifics of the case, a highly realistic way to evaluate the case study argument analyzed in this chapter is to use the notion of reversal of burden of proof. At the second to last stage of the argumentation sequence, represented in the argument map of Fig. 5.5, the burden of proof was still on the proponents of the thesis to prove that the portrait was an authentic Leonardo, because there was no evidence of the existence of a book that might have contained the portrait. With the finding of the book, and the new evidence including the perfect match between the stitch marks in the book and holes in the portrait, the burden of proof was reversed. The pro evidence outweighs the con evidence to the extent that it would now be fair to say that the burden has reversed onto the critics who claim that the portrait is not a genuine work of Leonardo.

## 5.9 An Evaluation of the Evidence

The part of the argument map shown at the bottom of Fig. 5.9 (the part representing the evidence shown in Fig. 5.8) could be described as the clincher, because it presents strong physical evidence backed up by the technology employed by Cotte to analyze the portrait and the alignment between the three holes and the three stitch marks. The finding by Cotte that the alignment was perfect is very convincing evidence. These findings, shown at the bottom of the argument map in Fig. 5.9, propagate up the tree to the root proposition that the portrait was originally a page in a book that celebrated the wedding of Bianca Sforza. As suggested above, this strong argument fits into the tree shown in Fig. 5.6 by supporting the premise that the portrait was from this book. By this means the part of the argument now composed jointly of the fifth and the fourth argument maps is very strong. Once these two argumentation graphs are joined to the graph shown in the first argument map, the combined argument structure presents a very strong argument supporting the ultimate conclusion that the portrait is a genuine Leonardo.

How this propagation process works is shown in Fig. 5.11, a simplified model that can be used to illustrate to the reader in general how the argument should be evaluated in CAS. In the CAS diagramming tool, a text box is colored in green and a checkmark is inserted in it to show that the proposition has been accepted by the audience. To say it has been accepted by the audience means that it has an evidential value high enough to meet its required burden of proof. To represent this process in a simplified manner some of the text boxes in Fig. 5.11 have been darkened, indicating acceptance by the audience.

Notice that there are three arguments directly supporting the ultimate conclusion. As shown on the diagram in Fig. 5.11, the arguments most easily fall into three parts. The arguments in the middle are woven in together, and are based on arguments from the expert opinion of Simblet. This will be treated as the middle part. The bottom argument is based on the evidence of the book found in Poland, and on the expert opinion of Cotte about matching the portrait to the missing page in the book. This will be treated as the bottom part.

The top part represents the argument from the expert opinion of Kemp, and its attack by the counter argument of David Eskerdjian. Because all the premises of the second argument are accepted and the argument from expert opinion is correctly applicable, the argument from Kemp's expertise is refuted, even though all its premises are accepted. This tells us that Kemp's argument from expert opinion fails to carry enough weight to prove the ultimate conclusion because of the counterattack from the opposed argument from expert opinion by Eskerdjian.

The arguments from the expert opinion of Sarah Simblet are shown in the middle part of Fig. 5.11. Assuming that all the premises of the argument are accepted by the audience, and that in all three instances the argumentation scheme for argument from expert opinion correctly applies to the argument, the conclusion of this argument can be accepted, namely the proposition that such an unusual and

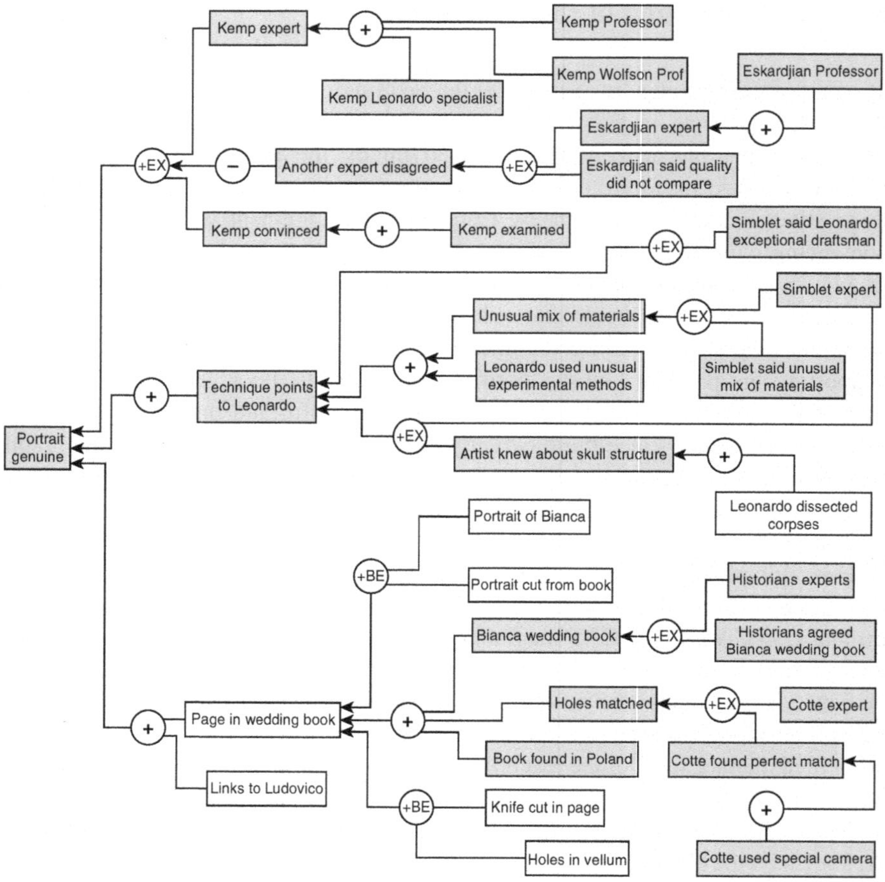


**Fig. 5.11** A first pass at evaluating the argumentation

experimental technique of painting points to Leonardo as the artist. All the premises are shown as darkened in this middle part of the argument, and let's say that all the arguments nodes leading to the ultimate conclusion carry enough weight to meet the preponderance of evidence standard.. What we have here then is the first successful pro argument supporting the ultimate conclusion that the portrait of the young woman is a genuine Leonardo.

When we come to the bottom part of Fig. 5.11 there is a problem posed by a limitation of CAS at its present state of development. Version 3 has not yet solved the problem of how to evaluate a hypothesis that has some evidence supporting it or attacking it, but then new evidence comes in that makes the hypothesis more plausible or less plausible, depending on what the evidence shows (so-called cumulative argumentation). At the earlier stage of the gathering of evidence shown in Fig. 5.7, there was evidence that the portrait had come from a book, indicated by the knife cuts on the page, and the holes in the vellum. But this evidence was still highly conjectural, and could not show that the portrait was a page in the wedding book of Bianca Sforza until later evidence was introduced. This later evidence is shown at the bottom right side of Fig. 5.11. It is the evidence by the historians agreeing that the book was the wedding book of Bianca Sforza, and by the expert evidence of Cotte, who found a perfect match.

So the problem now it is to figure out how we should treat the older evidence based on inference to the best explanation, in light of the new evidence from the findings of experts that not only confirm the old evidence but supersede it. How could the bottom part of the argumentation structure in Fig. 5.11 be reconfigured in a way that takes the new expert opinion evidence into account more adequately? The way we will solve this problem in the conclusions section is to work out a better representation of the evidence in the bottom part of Fig. 5.11. This model will indicate how the expert opinion evidence changes the evidential picture and supports the earlier conjectural evidence based on inference to the best explanation.

Let's review what has been achieved so far. This first attempt at evaluation shows that first there are three complex arguments leading to the ultimate conclusion. The first has strength, but is not strong enough to prove the ultimate conclusion to the appropriate standard. But there are two other arguments that provide support to the ultimate conclusion. One is the expert opinion argument from Sarah Simblet. The other is the large connected argument made up of the complex of connected arguments shown in the bottom part of Fig. 5.11. Once the bottom argument concerning the matching of the holes and the stitches is factored in, it strongly supports the conclusion that the portrait was a page in the wedding book, and this in turn strongly supports the ultimate conclusion when combined with another premise that is accepted. The two strong arguments offset the one that failed. But to see how the three parts of the argumentation can be fitted together in an evaluation of the whole body of evidence, more work is required.

## 5.10 Conclusions

The test case model using CAS in this chapter is of wider social interest as an investigation of how well state-of-the-art argumentation methods can be applied to modeling the aggregation of forensic evidence in controversial issues of fine art attribution. As Kemp and Cotte (2010, 9) noted, such investigations are based on "a plausible accumulation of evidence", rather than on absolute certainty. For this reason, it is reasonable to consider the utility of an argumentation approach that evaluates proof of the claim based on weighing the arguments supporting it against the arguments opposing it. This balance of considerations technique shows the way forward in the task of modeling evidential judgments of fine art attribution in the setting of a multi-staged social inquiry. To begin, let's have a short review.

Section 5.7 began this process by showing how the argument went through three main stages, and how the middle stage used inference to the best explanation to connect three sequences of argumentation to three hypotheses that could be used to explain the basic facts of the case. This analysis was used to build a model of the sequence beginning with the formulation of the ultimate issue and proceeding through the collection of evidence from which the best hypothesis was selected, to application of the burden of proof allowing the closure of the investigation. Section 5.9 showed how CAS models the whole sequence of argumentation as a tree structure with the ultimate conclusion at the right, and how as each piece of evidence was introduced, it propagates support for the final conclusion along the branches of the tree.

One of the limitations of Fig. 5.11, and also of Fig. 5.9 which it was based on, is the exclusion of the consideration of Figs. 5.4 and 5.5. It was argued that to simplify Fig. 5.9, Figs. 5.4 and 5.5 could be eliminated as parts of the evidential package because both were instances where the argument was attacked by a counterargument, and therefore the evidence provided by these two parts of the argument could be considered weak. Nevertheless, it is clear that Fig. 5.9 does not take all the relevant evidence found in the investigation into account. It would be nice to have a simplified overview of the sequence of argumentation that takes the arguments of Figs. 5.4 and 5.5 into account as well. Such an overview is provided by the argument map in Fig. 5.12.

The abstract argument framework, unlike CAS, represents each argument as a node in the tree, and does not represent the components of the argument, for example the premises and conclusion. This approach results in a simplified representation showing one argument attacking another, and another argument attacking the attacking argument, and so forth. Figure 5.12 is expressed in the style of an abstract argumentation framework, where each of the text boxes is taken to represent an argument. The only exception in Fig. 5.12 is the text box at the top which represents the ultimate conclusion, the statement that the portrait of the young woman is a genuine Leonardo. Also, in Fig. 5.12, supporting (pro) arguments are shown as well as attacking (con) arguments.

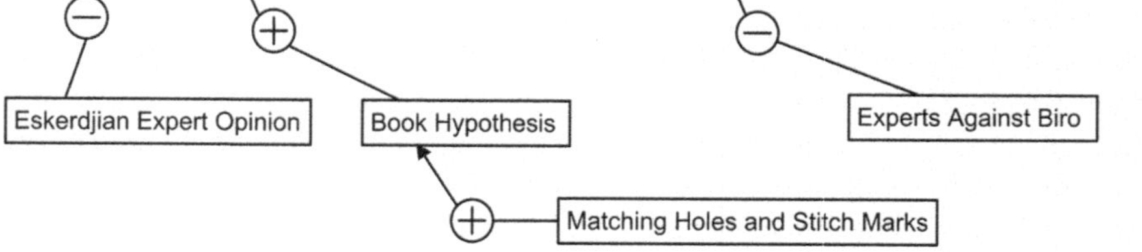


**Fig. 5.12** An overview of the evidence

Looking at Fig. 5.12, we see the original conjecture of Kemp, where he became convinced that there was a chance of attribution to Leonardo, shown as the Kemp Expert Opinion on the left. This node represents the argument shown in Fig. 5.3. The next argument to the right of that one shows the argument based on the expert opinion of Cristina Geddo, represented by the argument map of Fig. 5.4. This argument presents the evidence based on the portrait being drawn by a left handed artist. As noted in the discussion of Fig. 5.4, it is not a strong argument, because of the possibility of a forger copying Leonardo's left-handed style. But still, it does carry some evidential weight in the network of argumentation as a whole, and so in Fig. 5.12 it is represented as a pro argument supporting the ultimate conclusion. In the next argument to the right the fingerprint evidence of Biro is represented. As noted in the discussion of Fig. 5.12, it was a weak argument because it was attacked by the contrary expert opinion argument of Champaud. In Fig. 5.12, this argument is shown as having an attacking argument in which the other experts criticized the reliability of fingerprint evidence. The argument based on the expert opinion of Sarah Simblet is shown in the rightmost node at the top of Fig. 5.12. Finally, underneath the Kemp Expert Opinion Argument node, two pro arguments are shown, one supporting the other. The con argument is the contrary expert opinion of Eskerdjian. Figure 5.12 provides a summary of all the evidence in the case, so that the components missing in Fig. 5.11 can be taken into account. Still, Fig. 5.11 has proved useful for some significant points to be brought out.

Let's review Fig. 5.11 to see how the argumentation in that figure broke down into three stages. There is the top stage displaying the darkened boxes, which represents the original part of the argument where Kemp became convinced that there was a chance of attribution to Leonardo. Even though doubt was cast on Kemp's argument by the opposed argument from expert opinion of Eskerdjian, it still carried some weight. In the second part there were the four arguments from expert opinion of Simblet. All the arguments in this section were valid (acceptable as reasonable arguments) and have accepted premises. The so-called clincher argument provided by the forensic evidence of the stitches in the binding of the book appears to be the strongest. But the problem is that this argument, as displayed in Fig. 5.11, does not come together in the right way.

The solution to the problem posed in Sect. 5.9 of how to evaluate the argumentation represented in the bottom of Fig. 5.11 has to be tentative, given that CAS has not yet developed a method of evaluating cumulative argumentation. However, there is a need to revise Fig. 5.11 to represent what has taken place when the two instances of inference to the best explanation are added in with the evidence of the expert historians and the findings of Cotte. The solution can be shown by modifying Fig. 5.12 to represent the two additional items of abductive evidence as accepted. They support the argument node that directly supports the proposition that the portrait was originally a page in Bianca's wedding book. There was already the strong evidence represented in the middle section of the bottom part of the argumentation shown in Fig. 5.12, based on the expert testimony of Cotte and historians. The earlier evidence found by inference to the best explanation was weak at the earlier stage of the discovery process. Now of course it is strong, once it has been confirmed by the subsequent investigations once the book was found and the highly expert research of Cotte showed, to a high standard of proof, that the portrait came from the book, based on his finding of the perfect match between the holes in the vellum of the portrait and the stitching of the book.

This three-step sequence of development of the chain of argumentation is typical of how evidence fits together into a pattern of plausible reasoning in which there are three stages. First, there is a conjecture put forward that is interesting to investigate because it is not widely accepted, and perhaps even goes against the conventional climate of opinion. This stage represents the top part of Fig. 5.12. The hypothesis was put forward that the portrait was a work by Leonardo based on the expert opinion of Kemp, but it was challenged by the counter-argument of another expert. In the two middle arguments comprising the middle part of Fig. 5.12, new expert opinion evidence was put forward that corroborated the Kemp argument. The third stage is shown in the bottom part. Stronger evidence came in explaining the source of the portrait in the book found in Poland and the matching of the holes in the portrait and the stitching in the book. This new evidence was described as the clincher because it brought all three parts together into a coherent evidential picture so the evidence all fits together.

How it works can be seen when the argumentation shown in bottom part of Fig. 5.12 was modified to take the two last abductive arguments into account. This final step corroborates the argumentation in the middle part, and then evidence in the bottom two parts together moves upward, corroborating the argument shown in the top part. This mass of evidence now considerably outweighs the doubt expressed by the only counter-argument considered, the argument from the expert opinion of Eskardjian. Then the ultimate conclusion is proved.

When all three parts are joined, and the evidence has been updated, the result is that all the text boxes and argument nodes have been darkened, except the one node for argument from expert opinion shown at the top left of Fig. 5.12. At this point, some closure has been achieved. Closure does not mean that the investigation is now closed for all time, for a scientific investigation always has to be open to the possibility of new evidence, given the requirement of falsification. However, closure does mean that the ultimate conclusion can be accepted, on the basis that the evidence supporting it is strong enough to meet a burden of proof appropriate for the investigation. This case is not a legal trial, where a standard of proof such as preponderance of the evidence, clear and convincing evidence, or beyond reasonable doubt has been set. But still it can be said that a persuasive case has been made, persuasive enough to convince other experts to accept the ultimate conclusion (as indicated in Sect. 5.9).

It is concluded that the analysis of the evidential structure of the case shown visually in Fig. 5.12 provides a case study for testing proposed solutions to the problem of cumulative evidence. Once CAS and other comparable computational argumentation systems come forward with models of cumulative evidence, they can be tested by applying them to this case.

# References


Bench-Capon, T.J.M and G. Sartor. 2003. A model of legal reasoning with cases incorporating theories and values. *Artificial Intelligence* 150(1–2): 97–143.

Bench-Capon, T.J.M., S. Doutre, and P.E. Dunne. 2007. Audiences in argumentation frameworks. *Artificial Intelligence* 171(1): 42–71.

Buckingham Shum, S.J., A. MacLean, V.M.E. Bellotti, and N.V. Hammond. 1997. Graphical argumentation and design cognition. *Human-Computer Interaction* 12(3): 267–300.

Dung, P.M. 1995. On the acceptability of arguments and its fundamental role in nonmonotonic reasoning, logic programming and n-person games. *Artificial Intelligence* 77(2): 321–357.

Freeman, J.B. 1991. *Dialectics and the macrostructure of arguments*. Berlin: Foris.

Gordon, T.F. 2005. A computational model of argument for legal reasoning support systems. In *Argumentation in artificial intelligence and law*, IAAIL workshop series, ed. P.E. Dunne and T.J.M. Bench-Capon, 53–64. Nijmegen: Wolf Legal Publishers.

Gordon, T.F. 2010. The Carneades argumentation support system. In *Dialectics, dialogue and argumentation*, ed. C. Reed and C.W. Tindale. London: College Publications.

Gordon, T.F. 2011. Analyzing open source license compatibility issues with Carneades. In *Proceedings of the thirteenth international conference on artificial intelligence and law*, (ICAIL-2011: no editor given), 50–55. New York: ACM Press.

Gordon, T.F., and D. Walton. 2006. The Carneades argumentation framework. In *Computational models of argument: Proceedings of COMMA 2006*, ed. P.E. Dunne and T.J.M. Bench-Capon, 195–207. Amsterdam: IOS Press.

Gordon, T.F., and D. Walton. 2009. Proof burdens and standards. In *Argumentation and artificial intelligence*, ed. Iyad Rahwan and Guillermo Simari, 239–260. Berlin: Springer.

Gordon, T.F., H. Prakken, and D. Walton. 2007. The Carneades model of argument and burden of proof. *Artificial Intelligence* 171(10–15): 875–896.

Grennan, W. 1997. *Informal logic*. Montreal: McGill-Queen's University Press.

Hamblin, C.L. 1971. Mathematical models of dialogue. *Theoria* 37(2): 130–155.

Hastings, A.C. 1963. *A reformulation of the modes of reasoning in argumentation*. Ph.D. dissertation. Evanston: Northwestern University.

Josephson, J.R., and S.G. Josephson. 1994. *Abductive inference: Computation, philosophy, technology*. New York: Cambridge University Press.

Kemp, M., and P. Cotte. 2010. *La Bella Principessa*. London: Hodder and Stoughton.

Kienpointner, M. 1992. *Alltagslogik: Struktur und Funktion von Argumentationsmustern*. Stuttgart: Fromman-Holzboog.

Prakken, H., and G. Sartor. 2009. A logical analysis of burdens of proof. In *Legal evidence and proof: Statistics, stories, logic*, ed. H. Kaptein, H. Prakken, and B. Verheij, 223–253. Farnham: Ashgate.

Scheuer, O., F. Loll, N. Pinkwart, and B.M. McLaren. 2010. Computer-supported argumentation: A review of the state of the art. *Computer-Supported Collaborative Learning* 5(1): 43–102.

Tindale, C.W. 1990. Audiences and acceptable premises: Epistemic and logical conditions. In *Proceedings of the second international conference on argumentation*, ed. F. van Eemeren et al., 288–295. Amsterdam: SICSAT.

van Gijzel, B., and H. Prakken. 2011. *Relating carneades with abstract argumentation*. In *Proceedings of the 22nd International Joint Conference on Artificial Intelligence (IJCAI 2011)*, 1113–1119, Barcelona, Spain.

Walton, D. 2004. *Abductive reasoning*. Tuscaloosa: University of Alabama Press.

Walton, D., and T.F. Gordon. 2005. Critical questions in computational models of legal argument. In *Argumentation in artificial intelligence and law*, IAAIL workshop series, ed. P.E. Dunne and T.J.M. Bench-Capon, 103–111. Nijmegen: Wolf Legal Publishers.

Walton, D., and E.C.W. Krabbe. 1995. *Commitment in dialogue*. Albany: State University of New York Press.

Walton, D., and T.F. Gordon. 2011. Modeling Critical Questions as Additional Premises. In *Argument cultures: Proceedings of the 8th International OSSA* Conference, ed. F. Zenker, 1–13. Windsor, University of Windsor. Available at http://www.dougwalton.ca/papers%20in%20pdf/11OSSA.pdf.

Walton, D., C. Reed, and F. Macagno. 2008. *Argumentation schemes*. Cambridge: Cambridge University Press.

# Chapter 6
# Arguments from Correlation to Causation

**Abstract** The contested notion of cause is centrally important for evaluating evidential reasoning in law and science, especially in so many cases where a causal conclusion is drawn from statistical correlations. Three current examples of arguing from correlation to causation that are based on scientific reasoning and that are of broad public concern as health issues are described and evaluated in this chapter. The first one concerns the question of whether eating chocolate makes people smarter. The second one concerns a correlation between weather patterns in the southern Pacific and flu pandemics. The third one concerns the question of whether ingestion of copper causes Alzheimer's disease. This chapter shows how to improve the existing argumentation tools to enable us to judge whether a given instance is a reasonable argument or not and how to adjudicate cases where an allegation of drawing a hasty conclusion or even committing a fallacy is made.

This chapter argues that arguments from correlation to causation have to be studied at two levels. One is the inferential level of the argumentation scheme representing the structure of the argument as leading to a conclusion of a certain type based on premises of a certain type. The other is the dialectical level, which concerns the context of use of the argument. It will be shown that arguments from correlation to cause are initially scientific arguments used to collect evidence and draw conclusions in an investigation, but then they are also used both by scientists and non-scientists for all kinds of purposes. For example they may be used in medicine to give advice on treatment decisions or to set public policies.

In Sect. 6.1, three current examples of arguing from correlation to causation that are based on scientific reasoning and that are of broad public concern as health issues are described. The first one concerns the question about nutrition, the second one is about weather patterns and flu pandemics, and the third one is about whether ingestion of copper causes Alzheimer's disease. The chapter is built around analyzing the arguments from correlation to cause in these (and two other) examples. The main tool that has been used in the literature for this purpose is the argumentation scheme representing the form of argument from correlation to cause. In Sect. 6.2 some accounts are given of this argumentation scheme in informal logic textbooks, and the notions of correlation are defined for the purposes of this chapter. Needless to say, the notion of causation is highly controversial,



D. Walton, *Argument Evaluation and Evidence*, Law, Governance and Technology Series 23, DOI 10.1007/978-3-319-19626-8_6

so these definitions are provisional. It is also shown how CAS uses this scheme. In Sect. 6.3 nine conditions for drawing a scientific inference from causation to cause, called the Bradford Hill Criteria, are explained and summarized. Section 6.4 explains how heuristic devices are used in order to argue from correlation to cause in cases where the ultimate endpoint of a causal investigation may be difficult or impossible to measure. For example if a cancer treatment is shown to shrink tumors, the shrinking of the tumors may be taken as a surrogate marker to stand in for the ultimate endpoint, which is the extension of life. Section 6.5 compares how the argumentation in the three examples stands up to analysis, and ranges the arguments in an ordering of strength and weakness. Section 6.6 shows the need to examine arguments from correlation to cause a dialectical level that takes context into account, as shown by the examples in Sects. 6.7 and 6.8. Sections 6.7 and 6.8 present two more examples. One is the classic case of proving the causal link between smoking and lung cancer. The other is the currently controversial issue of the causal link between playing football and brain damage. Section 6.9 shows how to improve the current method of evaluating arguments from correlation to cause by reformulating the set of critical questions matching the argumentation scheme for argument from correlation to cause. Section 6.10 offers a solution to the problem of analyzing the *post hoc* fallacy.

## 6.1 Three Current Examples

The first of the three examples is called the chocolate example. Messerli (2012) conducted a statistical survey to support the hypothesis that chocolate consumption can improve cognitive function, and can even be effective in slowing down the reduction of cognitive performance that occurs with aging. He found there was a correlation between a country's level of chocolate consumption and cognitive function of the population. His starting point was the following assumption: "the total number of Nobel laureates per capita could serve as a surrogate endpoint reflecting the proportion with superior cognitive function and thereby give us some measure of the overall cognitive function of a given country" (Messerli 2012, 1562). One basis for the study was the list of countries ranked in order of Nobel laureates per capita found on Wikipedia, and another was a Swiss source that had data available on chocolate consumption in 23 countries.

It was found that there was a close significant linear correlation between chocolate consumption per capita and the number of Nobel laureates per ten million persons in these countries (Messerli 2012, 1563). Messerli added the qualification (1563) that even such a statistically strong correlation as this one does not prove causation, but he argued that it seems likely that "chocolate intake provides the abundant and fertile ground needed for the sprouting of Nobel laureates"(1563). He also considered the possibility of reverse causation, referring to the possibility that persons with superior cognitive function are more aware of health benefits of dark chocolate. But he decided to exclude this hypothesis (1563) because it seems unlikely that receiving the Nobel Prize "would in itself increase chocolate intake countrywide". He also had some theory-based biochemical basis to support his conclusion about the causal link: substances called flavonoids, present in cocoa, are known to improve blood flow in the brain, leading to improved cognitive performance in rats and humans.

The second example, called the birds example, can be described as follows. It was found by scientists that the four most recent human influenza pandemics, which took place in the years 1918, 1957, 1968, and 2009, occurred just after La Niña events that brought cool water to the surface in the South Pacific. La Niña is the cold counterpart to El Niño. The two events make up the weather variation that is called the El Niño southern oscillation. The correlation between these La Niña events and flu pandemics might suggest that there could be a causal link between them. But more likely it would suggest the conclusion that the two events happening one after the other in these four instances is merely a coincidence, and also the conclusion that to think otherwise would be an instance of the *post hoc* fallacy.

Nevertheless consideration of some other circumstances suggests that there could be three intervening variables connecting the two events. First, pandemics are caused by exposure to people of novel strains of a virus to which they have not developed immunity. Second, such a flu virus can be introduced to humans by animals, for example birds or pigs. Third, patterns of flight stopovers during bird migrations are affected by El Niño and La Niña events. And fourth, a change such as a La Niña event could easily cause birds to mingle together that do not otherwise mix. These intervening connections easily suggest how a virus causing a pandemic could be transmitted from birds to humans after a La Niña event.

Shaman and Lipsitch (2013) suggested that in light of this evidence a causal connection can be drawn: "We hypothesize that La Niña conditions bring divergent influenza subtypes together in some parts of the world and favor the reassortment of influenza through simultaneous multiple infection of individual hosts and the generation of novel pandemic strains". They tested this hypothesis by using evidence from influenza population genetics, virus prevalence in various host species, and avian migration patterns. They concluded (2013, 3690) that their findings indicate "a possible association between the emergence of pandemic influenza" during southern oscillation events such as La Niña. But they were careful to add that whether the association between the two events they found is causal or merely coincidental has not yet been established. They also added the conclusion that "the most plausible biological explanation" for the association between the four La Niña events and the four pandemic influenza events involves climate change shifts in bird migration patterns.

The third example is called the copper example. Many news media reports concern a study in the proceedings of the *National Academy of Sciences* that drew the conclusion that ingestion of copper can lead to plaque buildup in the brain causing Alzheimer's disease (Castellano et al. 2012). Alzheimer's disease is caused by the accumulation of a protein in the brain called amyloid beta. The study purported to show that the ingestion of copper has a cumulative effect of impairing the systems by which amyloid beta is removed from the brain. Copper is necessary for human health, and is found in meat, fruits and vegetables, as well as drinking water that often flows through copper pipes. Lead researcher Dr. Rashid Deane was reported in a University of Rochester Public Release as saying: "It is clear that, over time, copper's cumulative effect is to impair the systems by which amyloid beta is removed from the brain".[1] In the experiment conducted by Deane and his colleagues, copper-laced drinking water was given to mice for 3 months. Their theory is that the copper made its ways into the walls of capillaries that protect the brain from toxins, ultimately breaking down the blood brain barrier that prevents harmful substances from entering the brain. The resulting buildup of plaque was described as a "one-two punch" which both stimulates the production of amyloid beta and inhibits its clearance.[2] The research concluded that there is a causal connection between too much copper consumption and the creation of "logjams of the protein that the brain's waste disposal system cannot clear", the plaque buildup taken to be the cause of Alzheimer's disease.

An especially interesting aspect of this research finding is that other experts strongly disagreed with it. Christopher Exley, a professor of bioinorganic chemistry at Keele University, published a chapter (Exley et al. 2012) claiming that his team's research on brain tissues reached the opposite conclusion. Exley commented in a news interview on this research[3] by flatly disagreeing with its conclusion: "Research including our own shows the opposite, that copper prevents amyloid from forming the type of structures seen in the plaques". He based this claim on a chapter written by him and his colleagues in *Nature*. He said that according to everything his research group knows, based on their work with brain tissues, if anything, copper would be protective against Alzheimer's.

## 6.2 Current Versions of the Argumentation Scheme

Johnson and Blair (1983, 121) deal with fallacies such as the *post hoc* fallacy under the general category of arguments that make a causal claim. They define a more general kind of fallacy they call the fallacy of questionable cause, which has three identifying conditions. The first is that a causal claim appears in a proponent's argument. The second is that the proponent argues for the causal claim, but fails to provide adequate support for it. The third is that there are grounds for questioning

[1]James Gallagher, Copper Linked to Alzheimer's Disease, BBC News, Accessed August 21, 2013: http://www.bbc.co.uk/news/health-23755037.

[2]Mark Michaud, University of Rochester Public Release date Aug. 19, 2013. Copper Identified as Culprit in Alzheimer's Disease, Accessed Aug. 21, 2013. http://www.eurekalert.org/pub_releases/2013-08/uorm-cia081413.php.

[3]Deccan Chronicle (no author given). Copper linked to Alzheimer's? New Research Fuels Debate: http://www.deccanchronicle.com/130820/lifestyle-health-and-well-being/article/copper-linked-alzheimers-new-research-fuels-debate Accessed Wednesday, Aug 21, 2013.

the acceptability of the claim. This approach has two aspects that are especially interesting to note. One is that it links the failure of a causal argument with critical questions that express doubt about the acceptability of the causal claim, based on lack of supporting evidence. The other is it sees cases of fallacies of arguing to support a causal claim as being weak and questionable sorts of arguments that could in principle be supported by evidence, but where in fact insufficient evidence is given to support the claim. This approach suggests that what is objectionable about such arguments, when they are said to be fallacious, or logically defective, is not their inherent wrongness, but the overlooking of factors that do not address critical questions that can be raised.

Govier (2005, 343) also does not see arguing from correlation to cause as fallacious, and to emphasize the point, she renames the error as the fallacy of objectionable cause. She reconfigures the form of inference corresponding to this fallacy as an argument with three premises and a conclusion of the following form, where *A* and *B* represent events.

*A* occurred.
*B* occurred.
We can plausibly connect *A* to *B* in a causal relationship.
Therefore *A* caused *B*.

Her diagnosis of the problem with this kind of argument is that there is no basis given for ruling out alternative factors that might explain the connection between *A* and *B* as being something other than causal in nature.

Groarke and Tindale (2004, 305) reconfigure the *post hoc* fallacy by emphasizing that arguments from correlation to cause need to be evaluated in light of critical questions or counter-arguments that reveal how the argument might violate conditions for good causal reasoning. On their account, such critical questions and potential counterarguments can be built into additional premises that needed to be added to the simple argument from correlation and causation. They propose (2004, 303) the following scheme for general causal reasoning, where *X* and *Y* are causal variables for events of the kind that fit into a causal relation.

Premise 1: *X* is correlated with *Y*.
Premise 2: the correlation between *X* and *Y* is not due to chance.
Premise 3: the correlation between *X* and *Y* is not due to some mutual cause *Z*.
Premise 4: *Y* is not the cause of *X*.
Conclusion: *X* causes *Y*.

They also emphasize that the two events *X* and *Y* need to be regularly connected by showing that there is a general theory (normally based on the work of scientists) who have shown there is some deeper understanding of the chain of events connecting *X* and *Y*.

Pinto (1995) provided a useful summary of the textbook treatments of the *post hoc* fallacy stressing that a careful distinction needs to be drawn between particular events and types of events that figure in causal generalizations. Pinto (1995, 309) gave the example of a child bouncing a rubber ball against her bedroom wall when a hairline crack immediately appeared in the plaster of the wall in the exact spot where the ball struck. In this case, we have two particular events, the child's bouncing the rubber ball against her bedroom wall and the appearing of the crack in the plaster immediately afterwards. Statements about types of events frequently make up generalizations. For example, the statement that smoking causes lung cancer is a generalization that applies not just to one particular case where an individual person smoked and later developed lung cancer.

Next we need to define the notions of correlation and causation as they will be used in conjunction with argumentation schemes. A *correlation* between two (or more) events is an instance (or number of them) where both (or all) events occur. Correlation is a statistical notion, because the number of cases in which events occur can be counted, and these numbers can then be used as the basis for statistical calculations. Notice that on this definition a correlation can be between two events, or types of events or it can be among a sequence of events, or types of events. For example there could be a correlation between weather events in the South Pacific and flu pandemics. But there can also be a correlation among a sequence of events such as weather events in the South Pacific, bird migration patterns and flu pandemics.

Causation, as the term is used in this chapter is a practical notion, not a purely statistical notion. For the purposes of argumentation schemes, event *A* is said to cause another event *B* where the occurrence of *B* can be inferred as a normal outcome of the occurring of *A* based on the evidence in a case. On this definition, causation is a field-dependent notion. A *field* is a stable environment that can be presumed to be constant, but not completely identical, from one case to another. Causation, when defined in this way, is a defeasible evidential relation between events. The statement that *A* causes *B* means that *B* can be inferred from the evidence in a constellation of factors including *A*. A *cause* is defined as a set of conditions that are individually necessary for the occurrence of an event, and taken together are sufficient (*ceteris paribus*) for the occurrence of that event. Consider the event that a particular warehouse burned down, where there is evidence that just before the fire Bernie, a known arsonist, was seen leaving the location of the warehouse by a witness, who also noticed that Bernie was carrying a container that smelled like gasoline. In this case, the police formulate a hypothesis on which to base their investigations. This hypothesis is the statement that Bernie set the fire. The cause of the fire, according to this hypothesis, was Bernie's use of gasoline to start the fire. Such a case can be structured as an argument graph in formal argumentation systems, where the events are propositions and the causal inferences are argument nodes.

Schemes are now being incorporated into software systems that can be used for argument identification, analysis, diagramming, evaluation and construction (argument invention), for example CAS.[4] A user can also select argumentation schemes from a menu and use them to analyze and evaluate arguments, as well as to search through the database for new arguments to prove a claim. CAS is a mathematical model of argumentation (Gordon 2010) that has an Open Source

[4]The current version of the CAS editor can be downloaded from https://github.com/carneades.

argument mapping graphical user interface available at no cost to users. The current version of CAS is a web application with a three-tiered architecture consisting of a database, an applicable logic and a graphical user interface. The previous version of CAS, a desktop application called the Carneades Editor, is still available. The current version has a catalogue of argumentation schemes including such forms of argument as argument from expert opinion, argument from testimony, argument from analogy, argument from precedent, practical reasoning, and argument from correlation to cause.

CAS models critical questions by drawing a distinction between two kinds of premises in an argumentation scheme, assumptions and exceptions. The premises of the scheme that are explicitly stated are treated as assumptions, meaning that they are taken to hold unless they are challenged, but if they are challenged the arguer has to back up the premise with some evidence, or the argument fails. But there are other assumptions in addition to the ordinary stated ones. The kind of premise that represents an exception is taken to remain acceptable even when the question is posed. The current version of the scheme for argument from correlation to cause is given below.

**id:** correlation-to-cause
**strict:** false
**direction:** pro
**conclusion:** Event *E1* causes event *E2*.
**premises:**

- Events *E1* and *E2* are correlated.

**assumptions:**

- There exists a theory explaining how event *E1* causes event *E2*.

**exceptions:**

- Event *E3* causes events *E1* and *E2*.

The ordinary premise, the statement that *E1* and *E2* are correlated, is taken to hold, but if questioned, it is no longer accepted. The same criterion applies to the assumption that there exists a theory explaining how event *E1* causes event *E2*. But the exception is treated differently. Merely asking the question is not enough to make the premise no longer accepted. A specific event *E3* has to be cited in order for that to happen. In other words, we could say that with assumptions, the burden of proof is on the proponent of the argument whereas with exceptions the burden of proof is on the opponent.

The version of the scheme given in (Walton 1996, p. 142) is very simple. It has only one premise and one conclusion.

Premise: There is a positive correlation between *A* and *B*.
Conclusion: Therefore *A* causes *B*.

However, the same scheme can be more fully expressed as a form of argument with two premises.

Premise 1: If there is a positive correlation between *A* and *B* then *A* causes *B*.
Premise 2: There is a positive correlation between *A* and *B*.
Conclusion: Therefore *A* causes *B*.

This version of the scheme has the so-called DMP (defeasible *modus ponens*) format. This form of argument is treated in (Walton 1996) as defeasible and presumptive, meaning that commitment to the premise only gives a reason for commitment to the conclusion that may default when one of the appropriate critical questions is asked.

Matching the argument from correlation to cause is the following set of seven critical questions (Walton 1996, 142–143).

CQ1. Is there a positive correlation between *E1* and *E2*?
CQ2. Are there a significant number of instances of the positive correlation between *E1* and *E2*?
CQ3. Is there good evidence that the causal relationship goes from *E1* to *E2* and not just from *E2* to *E1*?
CQ4. Can it be ruled out that the correlation between *E1* and *E2* is accounted for by some third factor *E3* (a common cause) that causes both *E1* and *E2*?
CQ5. If there are intervening variables, can it be shown that the causal relationship between *E1* and *E2* is indirect (mediated through other causes)?
CQ6. If the correlation fails to hold outside a certain range of cases, then can the limits of the range be clearly indicated?
CQ7. Can it be shown that the increase or change in *E2* is not solely due to the way *E2* is defined, the way entities are classified as belonging to of *E2*, or changing standards, over time, in the way *E2* is defined or classified?

If the proponent puts forward an argument that fits the scheme for argument from correlation to cause, and the respondent accepts the premises of the argument, then she is also taken to accept the conclusion unless she can ask a critical question or provide a counter-argument.

As an example of critical question 3, we can consider this sort of case (Freedman 2010, 59). Many studies have shown that people who exercise more tend to be generally more healthy. The conclusion suggested is that exercise is a way to improve your health. But the question is which way the causal relationship goes. Is the exercise the cause of the good health, or is a person's good health a causal factor in making him or her more likely to exercise?

As an example of critical question 4, we can consider this sort of case (Freedman 2010, 57). On the grounds of the correlation between lack of sleep and obesity, it has been claimed that if someone starts getting more sleep they will lose weight. But there could be intermediate factors, rather than sleep levels, that produce, or are involved in the outcome of obesity. It may be that those who sleep less tend to be those who exercise less, eat less healthy foods, have a hormone disorder, or are depressed. It could be any of these other factors, or some combination of them that affects obesity. So it may be that once these other variables are taken into account, the connection between lack of sleep and obesity is merely incidental. Hence jumping to the conclusion that the lack of sleep is causing the obesity needs to be recognized as an instance of *post hoc* reasoning that is questionable at best.

Broadly speaking, what is common to these accounts of the argumentation scheme for argument from correlation to cause is that the scheme can be seen as taking a simple form with only one or two premises, or it can be seen as a more complex scheme that features a range of additional premises. There is variation on how many critical questions or additional premises there should be. The main theoretical difference among the various accounts of the scheme is whether these additional features are seen as critical questions or as additional premises. CAS deals with this difference in a systematic way by treating the critical questions as additional premises. On this way of managing the critical questions, you can see the scheme as having two additional kinds of premises, called assumptions and exceptions, in addition to the regular premises.

## 6.3 The Bradford Hill Criteria

The following nine conditions for drawing a scientific inference from causation to causality (Susser 1977; Doll 1992) are called the Bradford Hill Criteria (Hill 1965).

1. **Temporality**. The cause is supposed to precede the effect.
2. **Strength and Association**. The causal conclusion is derived by observations of a statistical correlation between a pair of events. The strength of the correlation can be measured numerically. The principle of measurement of the causal inference is that the stronger is the correlation between the two events, the stronger is the inference that the one causes the other.
3. **Dose-response Gradient**. There is expected to be a relationship between cause (the dose given, in a clinical case) and the effect (the reaction of the patient). The relationship may be expected to have minimal and maximum thresholds.
4. **Consistency**. The likelihood of the causal hypothesis holding is increased with its giving consistent results in a wider range of circumstances.
5. **Theoretical Possibility**. There should be a greater acceptance of an association between two events as causal when there is a theoretical scientific basis linking the two events.
6. **Specificity**. There can be multiple causes of a given event, and one suspected cause can be stronger than another if it better explains the occurrence of the event. Also a causal hypothesis can be strongest when there is no plausible competing explanation for the event.
7. **Evidence**. Research based on experiments, where other variables can be held stable to prevent them from interfering with results, will make a causal inference more plausible.

8. **Analogy**. A causal hypothesis that has been identified can be held more strongly when other supposed causes analogous to it have been identified and eliminated from the investigation.
9. **Coherence**. Coherence is defined as an alignment between the findings of scientific experiments in which variables are controlled, and independent everyday evidence based on common knowledge of events we are familiar with in our practical experiences.

Clearly there are a number of close similarities between the set of critical questions matching this scheme for argument from correlation cause and the Bradford Hill Criteria. Critical question 2 concerned the significance of the number of instances of the correlation, while Bradford Hill Criterion 2 takes this consideration further by stating the principle of measurement that when the correlation is stronger, the inference to the causal conclusion also becomes stronger. Bradford Hill Criterion 3 states another aspect relating to measurement of degree: when the cause is stronger the effect is expected to be stronger as well. Critical question 3, which concerns the directionality of the two events, relates to Bradford Hill Criterion 1, stating that the cause is supposed to precede the effect.

One factor that is suggested to be very important by the examples introduced above and analyzed below is the Bradford Criterion 5, which states that the causal inference is stronger when there is a theoretical scientific basis linking the two events. This particular factor was stressed in the scheme for argument from correlation to cause currently in the category of schemes in CAS (see above). Hence it is a recommendation that a critical question corresponding to this factor could be added to the list of seven critical questions of (Walton 1996), the leading list that occurs elsewhere in the literature including (Walton et al. 2008).

## 6.4 Surrogate Markers

Reasoning from cause to effect is typical in scientific investigations and clinical trials. For example in an investigation to determine whether a particular medication is effective for reducing heart attack or stroke, a clinical trial is carried out in which the effects of giving one group of patients the medication are compared with the effects of giving a placebo to another group of patients. The effect or so-called ultimate endpoint of such a causal investigation is the death of the patient by heart attack or stroke, for example. The causal factor being studied may be the taking of a particular medication. The purpose of the investigation is to delay the morbid outcome of shortening of life expectancy by heart attack or stroke.

Typically, however, there may be practical reasons why it is difficult or costly to measure the ultimate endpoint, and for this reason something called a surrogate marker is used to substitute for that endpoint. In clinical trials, a surrogate marker, sometimes also called a proxy measurement, is a measure of the effect of a certain treatment that is taken by inference to cause the ultimate clinical endpoint, but the inferential step from the cause to the endpoint is defeasible, and can be subject to critical questioning. For example, in clinical trials to study the causes of events such as heart failure and stroke, vascular disease is the most common cause (Cohn 2004). Vascular disease progresses through a mechanism that includes inflammation, plaque formation and thrombosis, and new technology makes it possible to track the progression of the sequence by using surrogate markers: "the availability of reliable markers for the disease might ultimately allow disease progression to replace endpoint events as a guide to the risk of disease and its responses to therapy" (Cohn 2004, 20). Such surrogate markers are used for practical reasons, to achieve results more rapidly and at less cost.

Surrogate markers are divided into two subtypes by Cohn (2004, 20), structural and functional surrogate markers. Cohn uses the diagnosis of cardiovascular disease as an example. Structural abnormalities of the arteries or the heart are considered to be structural surrogate markers of cardiovascular disease. Measurements of carotid artery wall thickness and left ventricular mass identify these two structural surrogate markers. They are taken to indicate cardiovascular disease of a kind that would be expected to worsen over the course of time. Functional surrogate markers are described as imperfect markers for the structure of cardiovascular disease. The presence of some of them may be expected to reduce the risk of the morbid event, "but with others it is less certain that the response of the surrogate is a prerequisite for the benefit on the disease process."(Cohn 2004, 20). Examples of functional surrogate markers for cardiovascular disease are blood pressure and arterial wall compliance or stiffness.

These descriptions of this example raise some questions about the inferential link that should properly be required between the surrogate marker and the endpoint. What is the nature of this inferential link? And how strong does it have to be in order for something to be considered a valid surrogate of an endpoint? Is it enough that there should be a correlation between the two events? Or should it be required that the surrogate marker causes the endpoint? And if the latter, how strong does the causal relationship need to be? Could it be merely a contributory cause, or is some stronger type of causal connection required? For example, there might be a correlation between high blood pressure and cardiovascular endpoints such as heart attack or stroke, but it might be questionable to say that either of these two indicators by themselves can be taken as surrogate markers of fatal cardiovascular events such as heart attack or stroke. High blood pressure might be a causal factor in heart attack and stroke, but that might not be a solid enough reason to treat it as a surrogate marker of these outcomes for purposes of clinical investigations.

It would appear that the connection between the two points in the sequence of reasoning must be stronger. But what requirements precisely should be used to define the criteria for a surrogate marker, and to determine how strong the inference needs to be to the final outcome in order for something to properly qualify as a surrogate marker? One such criterion might be that to properly justify some factor being used as a surrogate marker, the effect of carrying out the event taken to be the surrogate must cause the effect taken to be the endpoint. Another might be the sort of causal link whereby a significant increase in the presence of the surrogate marker is needed to increase the likelihood of the event taken to be the endpoint.

Consider the example where the endpoint is death from heart failure but the surrogate marker is increasing cholesterol levels. Increase in cholesterol level increases the likelihood of heart failure, but on the other hand there are many people who have normal cholesterol levels who go on to have heart failure, and also many who have high cholesterol levels who do not. So if a clinical trial shows that taking a particular drug has the outcome of reducing cholesterol, that is an interesting finding, but it does not show that taking this drug will prevent heart failure. On this basis, it would not be logically justified to treat high cholesterol as a surrogate marker of heart failure. There are cases where something was initially considered to be a surrogate marker for a potentially deadly endpoint, but where this hypothesis had to be retracted.

The drug bevacizumab, which goes by the trade name of Avastin, is an antibody that promotes shrinkage of cancerous tumors by slowing the growth of new blood vessels. Avastin was approved for treating several kinds of cancers by the FDA in 2004, and was approved for treatment of breast cancer in 2011. Although the drug did shrink cancer tumors, its approval by the FDA for the treatment of breast cancer was revoked on the grounds that there was no evidence that it extended life or quality-of-life (Couzin-Frankel and Ogale 2011). Moreover, there was evidence that it caused severe high blood pressure and hemorrhaging. In this case the surrogate marker was the shrinking of a cancer tumor, and the ultimate endpoint was extended life for the cancer patient. Here we have an instance of defeasible reasoning. Because Avastin was shown to shrink tumors, and tumor shrinkage was taken to be a surrogate marker of extension of life, it was concluded that Avastin would extend life. When further evidence came in showing that this surrogate marker did not connect up in the right way with the ultimate endpoint, the causal reasoning had to be retracted.

The Avastin example, and the other examples studied in the chapter, especially illustrating the dangers of the use of surrogate markers and drawing inferences from correlation to cause, show how important the critical questions are in analyzing and evaluating this type of argumentation. It would appear that is typical of statistical evidence used to argue from correlation to cause depends on the use of such surrogate markers. What is typically concealed, or at least not strongly enough emphasized in such cases is that the proper evaluation of the argument from correlation to cause depends crucially on an inference from a surrogate marker to the ultimate conclusion that is taken to be the endpoint of the inference. The structure of such a causal inference, as illustrated by the Avastin example, is shown in Fig. 6.1.

In this example the experimental action was the recommendation to take the drug Avastin as a treatment for cancer, based on the experimental finding that taking Avastin had been shown in the past to shrink tumors. But tumor shrinkage was taken as a surrogate marker for the intended effect of treatment which is to extend the patient's life. Further research showed, however, that the shrinking of the tumor in such cases did not have the desired effect of extending life.

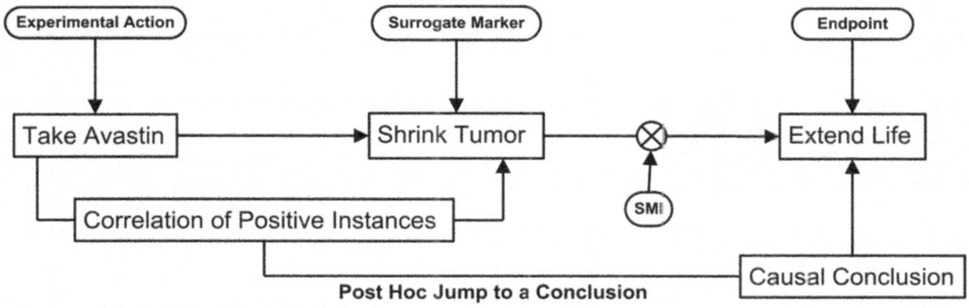


**Fig. 6.1** Structure of the inference from a surrogate marker to a causal conclusion

The implicit but questionable inference in such a case as shown in Fig. 6.1 is what is called the SMI, or surrogate marker inference, referring to the inference from the surrogate marker to the endpoint. Relating to the SMI, two critical questions concerning the use of surrogate markers, shown to be important in the examples studied in the chapter, need to be added to the existing set. The first question is whether the argument from correlation to cause as stated goes to the ultimate conclusion or whether instead it goes to a surrogate marker. The second question is to be asked when the surrogate marker has been identified. This question asks whether the inference from the surrogate marker to the conclusion is justified.

## 6.5 Comparison of Examples

The argumentation in the chocolate example relates to the critical questions from the list of (Walton 1996) in interesting ways. The first two critical questions are answered, because according to Mersserli's data, the statistical correlation between consumption of chocolate and Nobel Prize winners in countries where the Nobel Prize had been awarded were quite high. Pertaining to the third critical question, it was noted in the description of the chocolate example above that Messerli considered the possibility of reverse causation, but decided to exclude it. This consideration relates to the third critical question, which asks about the causal relationship going the other way.

Consideration of some of the other critical questions emerged during a discussion of the chocolate example with other scientists reported in the BBC News.[5] It was pointed out that Switzerland had the highest chocolate consumption per person and also the highest number of Nobel laureates of all the countries. However, Sweden appeared to be a counterexample to the causal relationship. Although it had a very high number of Nobel laureates, its people consume much less chocolate than the

[5]Charlotte Prichard, Does Chocolate Make You Clever?, *BBC News*, Nov. 19, 2012: http://www.bbc.co.uk/news/magazine-20356613.

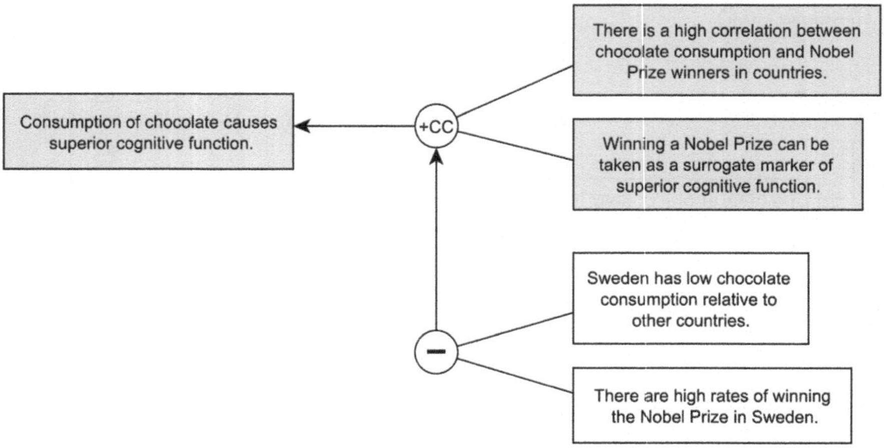


**Fig. 6.2** First stage of the chocolate argument

average of the other countries. Two explanations for this anomaly were offered by Mersserli. One was that since the Nobel Prize is evaluated in Sweden, "the Swedes might have a slightly patriotic bias". Let's break this sequence of argumentation down into two stages to see how CAS models its structure.

The pro argument shown at the top of Fig. 6.2 has two premises that are highly plausible. One is that there is a high correlation between chocolate consumption and Nobel Prize winners in countries. As noted above, Messerli found data that showed that this correlation was extremely high. The other is a proposition that winning a Nobel Prize can be taken as a surrogate marker of superior cognitive function. This too is a proposition that is highly plausible. Therefore in CAS the audience would accept these two propositions, and hence they are shown in Fig. 6.2 in green boxes. Assuming the top argument fits the scheme for argument from correlation to cause, the argument is defeasibly valid. On this basis, the conclusion that consumption of chocolate causes superior cognitive function is automatically calculated by CAS as accepted. Hence it is shown in a green box in Fig. 6.2.

However, now let's examine the con argument at the bottom of Fig. 6.2. This argument puts forward the counterexample of the case of Sweden, a country that has low chocolate consumption but high rates of winning the Nobel Prize. This argument would undercut the argument from correlation to cause if both its premises were to be accepted. What would happen in this instance?

If both premises in the lower argument were to be accepted, and it is accepted that the lower argument licenses the transfer of acceptance from its premises to its conclusion, the lower argument would function as an undercutter to the argument from correlation to cause shown above it in Fig. 6.2. What happens now? What happens is that the conclusion of the argument, the statement that consumption of chocolate causes superior cognitive function, is no longer accepted. This situation is shown in Fig. 6.3.

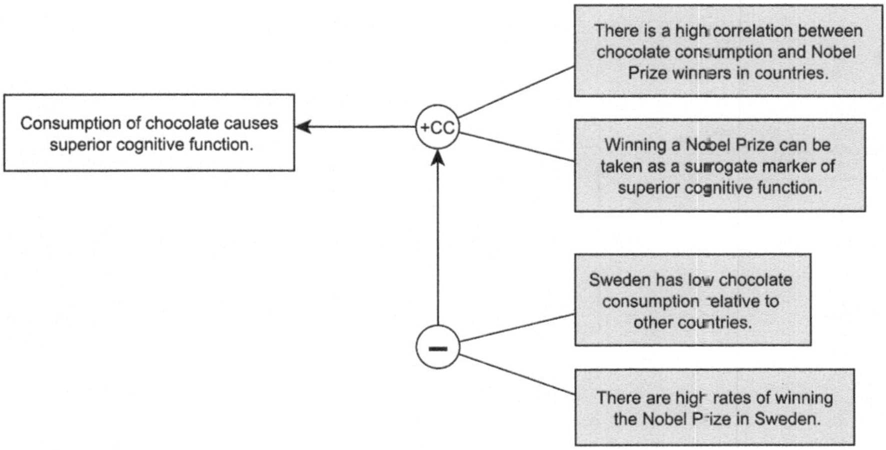


**Fig. 6.3** Second stage of the chocolate argument

The argument at the bottom cites the exception of the case of Sweden, and its node is shown in a gray box containing a minus sign. Assuming that both premises of this argument are plausible, the argument acts as an undercutting rebuttal of the previous pro argument. So represented, it attacks and defeats the previous argument. Hence on balance, the conclusion of the argument, the statement that consumption of chocolate causes superior cognitive function, is no longer taken by CAS to be accepted. Hence it is now shown in a white box.

In this instance the low chocolate consumption in Sweden is being used as a rebuttal to the argument from correlation to causation. The argument has two stages. Since the pro argument shown in Fig. 6.2 at the top has both premises accepted, and since it is a defeasibly valid argument, its conclusion is shown in a gray box. But once the rebutting argument at the bottom is put forward, as shown in Fig. 6.3, the conclusion at the left now appears in a white box, showing that it is no longer accepted.

Now let's look at Fig. 6.4, which shows the third stage of the chocolate argument. This argument has the same premises and conclusions as the one shown in Fig. 6.3, except that three new arguments have been added. The first argument has the premise that the Swedes might have a bias. This premise is shown as being supported by two further arguments. This statement is shown as a con argument attacking the con argument above it.

An exception in CAS is taken to be a premise that holds only if it is supported by backup evidence. In this instance the statement that the Swedes might have a bias is supported by the statement that the Nobel Prize is judged and financed in Sweden. This evidence is represented in Fig. 6.4 as two separate arguments. Therefore CAS evaluates the argument by ruling that the exception defeats the con argument. In this case what is displayed is another undercutting of a rebuttal. The undercutter defeats the Swedish argument counter-example rebuttal, which no longer proves that the ultimate conclusion is false. And for this reason the original argument displayed at

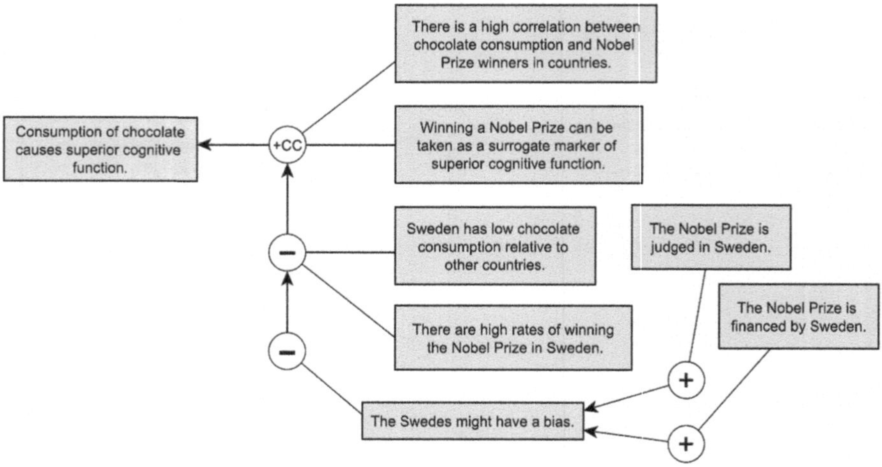


**Fig. 6.4** Third stage of the chocolate argument

the top of Fig. 6.4 is sufficient to warrant the acceptance of the ultimate conclusion that consumption of chocolate causes superior cognitive function, even though the premises of its undercutter are accepted.

There are two critical questions that should also be considered in evaluating this argument. First, there is the question of how we know whether the Nobel Prize winners are enthusiastic eaters of chocolate. Presumably, the basis for this assumption is that the Nobel Prize winners can be treated as a statistical sample that are comparable in regard to their chocolate eating habits with other people in their respective countries. This might not be so. For example, it might be true, as a matter of fact, that Nobel Prize winners eat less chocolate than other people in their countries. Still, it seems a reasonable statistical assumption that the Nobel Prize winners are on par with the others in their countries when it comes to eating chocolate. The second critical question is whether being a Nobel Prize winner can be taken as a surrogate marker for possessing the property of having a high cognitive function. However, I don't think the audience would question this assumption, because of the high regard we have for the award of the Nobel Prize, taken to be a prize that is only awarded to the brightest thinkers. This assumption could certainly be critically questioned, but it seems persuasive in the absence of evidence to the contrary.

Next, let's consider the birds example. At first sight, using the correlation between the four La Niña events and the four most recent flu pandemics to suggest the conclusion that there is a causal connection between these two events seems ridiculous. There are only four events involved, it is hard to see how there could be any causal connection between weather events in the Pacific and these four events. The best conclusion is that it is simply a coincidence. Once attention has been drawn to the three intervening variables connecting the two events however, the hypothesis that there is a causal connection between the two events becomes much more plausible. First we need to be aware that flu viruses of the kinds that caused the pandemics can be transmitted from birds or other animals to humans. Second, we need to see how these weather events influence patterns of flight stopovers during bird migrations, and how that could lead to birds mingling together that would not otherwise mix. Once these intervening causal variables are known, it becomes apparent that there could well be a sequence of events causally connecting weather events in the South Pacific with flu pandemics (answering CQ5).

Shaman and Lipsitch also supported their hypothesis that the La Niña conditions can favor the spreading of influenza by testing it using evidence from population genetics and bird migration patterns. So in addition to filling in the causal missing links between the two events, they also presented some theoretical backing connecting the two events and supporting their hypothesis. Note however that they were modest in describing their causal conjecture, expressing that their conclusion is based on argument to the best explanation. Their hypothesis was that the association between the La Niña events and the influenza events is the most plausible biological explanation of the correlation between the two sequences of events.

For these reasons, the argument from correlation to causation in the birds example can be evaluated as more plausible than the argument from correlation to causation in the chocolate example. The reason is that the argument in the a former example answers more critical questions, and is less open to some worrisome critical questions than the argument in the latter example.

The argument from correlation to causation in the copper example was also based on experimental results. Deane and his colleagues conducted an experiment on the results of feeding drinking water containing copper to mice for 3 months. They also offered a scientific theory joining the ingestion of copper with the kind of plaque buildup that leads to Alzheimer's disease. On this theory Alzheimer's disease is caused by the accumulation of amyloid beta in the brain. They offered a scientific theory explaining how copper can make its way into the walls of the capillaries that protect the brain from toxins, ultimately breaking down the blood brain barrier. They colorfully describe this procedure as a one-two punch that both stimulates the production of amyloid beta and prevents the brain from clearing it away.

If we were to stop the description of the argument from correlation to causation at this point, it would seem to be based on the right kind of scientific evidence, and right sort of explanation of the sequence of events linking the two variables. Hence we would probably evaluate the argument as being at least as plausible as those in the chocolate example and the birds example. But as we go on to examine additional evidence in the copper example in Sect. 6.6, we will need to recall that another expert strongly disagreed with the conclusion of Deane and his colleagues.

## 6.6 The Dialectical Context of an Argument

In the copper example we have a typical battle of the scientific experts, a common phenomenon in legal argumentation in trials (Walton and Zhang 2013). How should we proceed in a case where the conclusion claimed by one expert contradicts the conclusion put forward by another? There is another scheme that comes into play in such cases. The scheme for argument from expert opinion takes the following form (Walton et al. 2008, 310), as repeated from Sect. 5.3.

Major Premise: Source *E* is an expert in subject domain *S* containing proposition *A*.
Minor Premise: *E* asserts that proposition *A* is true (false).
Conclusion: *A* is true (false).

This scheme, like the scheme for argument from correlation to cause, can be formulated in a conditional form of a defeasible modus ponens argument (DMP). The conditional version can be formulated as follows (Reed and Walton 2003, 201).

Conditional Premise: If Source *E* is an expert in subject domain *S* containing proposition *A*, and *E* asserts that proposition *A* is true (false) then *A* is true (false).
Major Premise: Source *E* is an expert in subject domain *S* containing proposition *A*
Minor Premise: *E* asserts that proposition *A* is true (false).
Conclusion: *A* is true (false).

There are six basic critical questions (Walton et al. 2008, 310) matching this scheme, repeated from Sect. 5.3 for the reader's convenience.

*Expertise Question*: How credible is *E* as an expert source?
*Field Question*: Is *E* an expert in the field *F* that *A* is in?
*Opinion Question*: What did *E* assert that implies *A*?
*Trustworthiness Question*: Is *E* personally reliable as a source?
*Consistency Question*: Is *A* consistent with what other experts assert?
*Backup Evidence Question*: Is *E*'s assertion based on evidence?

The consistency question is the one on point in the copper example. This critical question is treated as an exception in CAS. In order to defeat the argument from expert opinion, a critic needs to cite the opinion of an opposed expert.

The structure of this situation can also be modeled as a rebuttal as shown in Fig. 6.5. The problem is how to deal with this kind of case. The argument at the top of Fig. 6.5 is a pro argument from expert opinion supporting the conclusion that proposition *A* should be accepted. The argument at the bottom is a con argument from expert opinion supporting the conclusion that *A* should not be accepted. Just considering the top argument as having premises that are accepted, as shown in Fig. 6.5, the conclusion is also automatically accepted by the system.

But once we consider both arguments as having accepted premises, as shown in Fig. 6.6, the conclusion that *A* is true is no longer accepted. Unless we know that the one argument is stronger than the other, or unless further arguments can be brought in on one side or the other to break the deadlock, the solution is to suspend judgment. The proper conclusion to draw is that research on the question of whether the argument from correlation to cause in the copper example put forward by Deane as a hypothesis is in dispute. Since Deane admits himself that it is only a provisional hypothesis which needs to be subject to further testing and investigation, this hypothesis of a deadlock seems to be the right solution in this instance.

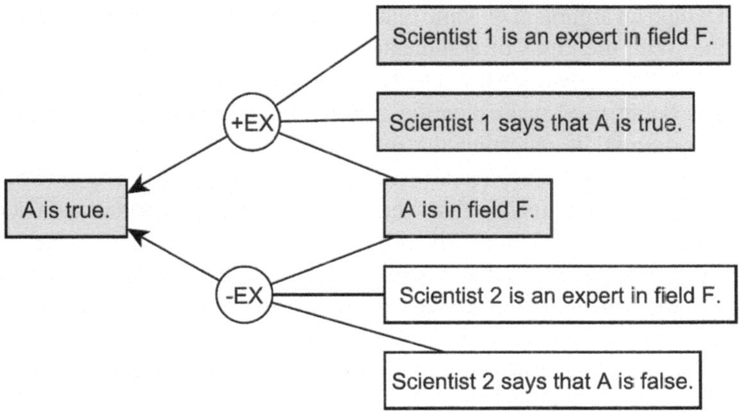


**Fig. 6.5** Battle of the experts stage 1

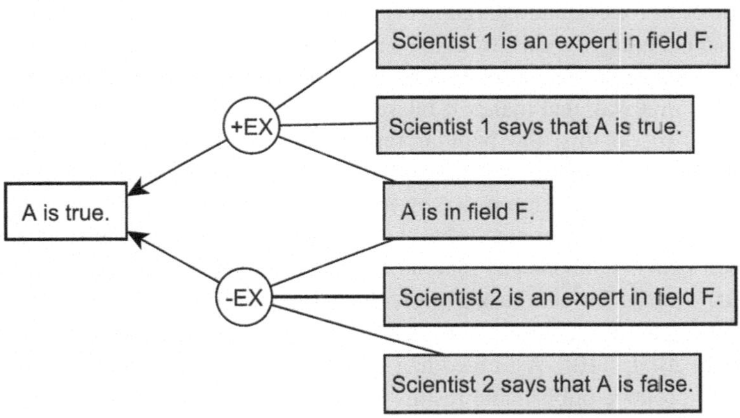


**Fig. 6.6** Battle of the experts stage 2

But there is another aspect of this kind of situation to be considered. How is a physician supposed to advise his or her patient on the question of whether ingestion of copper should be avoided in order to prevent or treat Alzheimer's disease? Or how is a person to proceed who has Alzheimer's disease and is worried about it to change his or her diet in light of the scientific knowledge about causation of Alzheimer's disease by ingestion of food or water containing copper? Such a person cannot normally go out and test the scientific evidence. The best he or she can do is to examine the scientific literature, collect the findings supported by the experts, and judge what conclusion on the subject is best to move ahead with.

To deal with the problem of the battle of the experts the argumentation approach needs to take into account the transmission of scientific expertise to those outside the particular field in which a scientific claim lies (Walton and Zhang 2013). As well as the argumentation scheme, the argumentation approach takes into account the setting in which an argument or some related speech act was put forward in a context of dialogue. With the kinds of arguments being considered here, it is important to differentiate between two such contexts of argument use. In the first setting, the argument is being used in a scientific context where a research paper published in a science journal is reporting the results of a correlation based on statistical findings and possibly experimental evidence, and conclusions are drawn. In the second setting, the conclusions that were drawn are being reported as a scientific finding that is of interest to those who might wish to apply it to solve some problem, normally a problem about what to do. For example, typically such scientific findings are used by physicians to give advice to patients on what course of action to take. But scientific findings that are especially interesting to a large number of people will be reported in the popular media, and described in a manner that their readers will be able to understand, and will find interesting.

For this reason, for those of us interested in studying examples of arguments of this sort, and even studying biases and logical shortcomings in them, and trying to find some basis for evaluating arguments from correlation and causation as strong or weak, understanding the shift from the one setting to the other is of vital importance.

There is pressure on those who report in the popular news media to present information in a way that makes it interesting and exciting by creating a favorable impression. To do this, the popular report may ignore important qualifications expressed by the scientific researcher, for example mention of side effects, or limitations on the conclusion posed by the need for further scientific investigations. However, it has also been noted that there is pressure on the scientists themselves to get their papers published by making their findings appear exciting. For example, scientific journals have a strong preference for publishing positive findings, as opposed to negative findings to the effect that an expected result did not occur (Freedman 2010, 110). As Freedman (2010, 11) reported, there is an intense pressure to produce publishable results that are positive and exciting, while at the same time there is a principle that the more novel and exciting an idea is, the less likely it is to be right (Ioannidis 2005). Hence there are good reasons to accept the proposition that the biases and other shortcomings of scientific arguments from correlation and causation in such matters as nutrition and health are not exclusively due to misreporting of scientific research by the media.

## 6.7 Contesting the Causal Link Between Smoking and Lung Cancer

The kinds of examples studied so far are instances of the traditional *post hoc* fallacy, where a premature leap is made from a correlation based on scientific evidence that has been collected to a causal conclusion. But there are also interesting cases of the opposite problem to be found. In these cases, the scientific evidence supporting the existence of a causal link between two events is played down by denying or minimizing it using opposed scientific evidence. Instead of arguments supporting the causal link between *A* and *B*, there are counterarguments attacking the hypothesis of a causal link between *A* and *B*. The most famous case of this sort is the campaign of the tobacco industry to argue against the hypothesis of a causal link between smoking and lung cancer (and other causes of premature morbidity).

By the 1960s there was a growing body of scientific evidence showing a causal link between tobacco and harm from cancer, and there was an especially strong causal link established by many scientific studies between smoking and dying from lung cancer. An organization called the Council for Tobacco Research, funded by the tobacco industry, supported scientific research purporting to show that the link between cancer and cigarettes was "merely statistical". The opposed scientific evidence funded and presented by this organization claim to show that it would be premature to accept the causal theory linking smoking and cancer (Proctor 1995, 1060). Nowadays this tobacco industry research is ridiculed as biased science of the kind promoted by public relations firms. But at the time it exerted a powerful influence on public opinion concerning the effects of smoking on cancer.

During this period there was a great public debate marshaling scientific findings on both sides. Tobacco industry-supported research argued that there might be a genetic explanation showing a personality type that leads people to smoke and at the same time predisposes them towards lung cancer (Proctor 1995, 107). This argument corresponds to the critical question of argument from correlation to cause asking whether there might be a common cause linking the two events that are supposed to be causally connected. Asking this critical question is a way of casting doubt on the hypothesis, in this instance, that smoking causes lung cancer. Instead, it is suggested that there is some third variable causing both the smoking and lung cancer.

The asking of this critical question in this case can also be modeled as a counter-argument. The counter-argument can be expressed as follows.

- Scientific evidence shows that people who smoke and develop lung cancer are predisposed to both smoke and get this disease by reason of their heredity.
- Therefore there is a better explanation of the statistical correlation between smoking and lung cancer than the causal link theory.
- This better explanation is the genetic explanation that there is a common cause linking smoking and lung cancer.
- This genetic explanation is supported by scientific research.
- Therefore it is doubtful that smoking causes lung cancer.

This counterargument can be modeled using the argumentation scheme for inference to the best explanation. In Fig. 6.7, the conclusion, the statement that smoking causes lung cancer, is shown at the left. The argument from correlation to cause is shown at the top, indicated by the +CC notation in the argument node. The plus sign indicates it is a pro-argument. This argument is shown as being attacked by a counterargument that has the form of inference to the best explanation, indicated by the notation -IB in the argument node. The minus sign indicates it is a con argument.

What is illustrated in Fig. 6.7 is an argument from correlation to cause being put into question by an undercutter that performs the role of posing a critical question

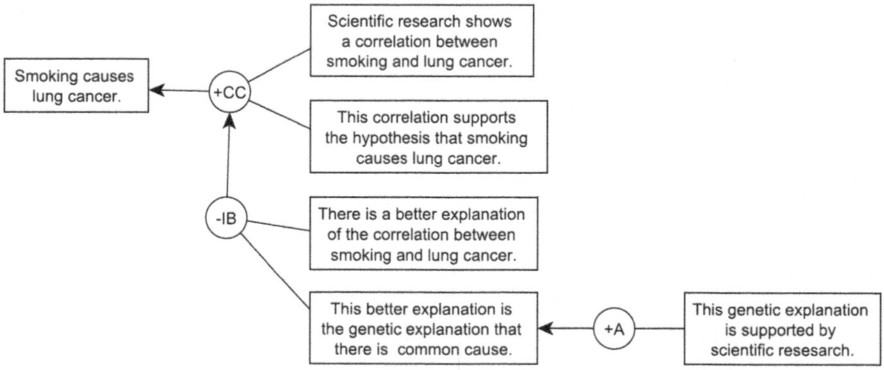


**Fig. 6.7** Counter-argument to the causal lung cancer argument

that casts the original argument into doubt. Moreover, the undercutting argument is successful because one of its premises is backed up by supporting evidence, expressed in the statement that the genetic explanation is supported by scientific research.

What is especially interesting to note in this case is that the argument is not purely a scientific one. Is this a use of scientific evidence for the purpose of public relations? As Proctor (1995, 107) explained, there is a legal and public relations value of such studies.

> If differential cancer susceptibilities could ever be established, one could plausibly argue that people who come down with the disease have a least partly their own heredity to blame. Perhaps many of those who smoke are invulnerable, after all, only about one in five smokers ever gets lung cancer - why doesn't everyone?

In this case then we can see that the mounting evidence of the link between smoking and lung cancer based on argument from correlation to cause became stronger and stronger, threatening the interests of the tobacco companies. They fought back by funding their own scientific research that not only critically questioned the argument from correlation to cause, but actually counterattacked it by financing their own scientific studies, and using these to mount counterarguments.

## 6.8 Contesting the Causal Link Between Football and Brain Damage

The following case concerned the scientific question of whether playing football causes brain damage. A *Frontline* program first aired in 2013, *League of Denial: The NFL's Concussion Crisis*, chaired by Mark Fainaru-Wada and Steve Fainaru, chronicled the story of how this causal connection first came to be suspected by clinical investigators, and how it played out in the subsequent inquiry. At that time both men were employees of the entertainment and sports programming network

(ESPN), a media empire operating seven 24-h sports channels, a website with more than 37 million visitors every month, and a radio network of more than 400 stations. The huge fan base for professional football in the USA made the NFL an extremely rich and powerful organization. In the same year that the *Frontline* program appeared, a book was published (Fainaru-Wada and Fainaru 2013) that gave a detailed and carefully documented account of the events and scientific investigations making up the story.

The best place to begin is with Mike Webster. "Iron Mike" was a famous football player for the Pittsburgh Steelers when they won four Super Bowls in the 1970s. He was famous for his aggressive style of play and his ability to take extreme punishment, take the blows and absorb the pain, when colliding with other players. After he retired, his health deteriorated through states of depression and into progressively serious dementia. Webster's family told how his life spiraled out of control. He was unable to remember things, unable to get his thoughts together, he was an angry and confused man who threatened to commit suicide, and in the end wound up living in his truck, separated from his family (Fainaru-Wada and Fainaru 2013, 3). Eventually he decided to sue the NFL, arguing that his injuries were caused by playing football. When the NFL's physicians eventually agreed with Webster's doctors that his injuries were due to football, they agreed to pay him a monthly check.

When Webster died at the age of 50 in 2002, Pittsburgh Medical Examiner, Dr. Bennet Omalu performed the autopsy. When he first examined Webster's brain, it appeared to be in a normal condition. Fortunately however, he made the decision to preserve the brain, and after further investigations found that it was filled with the protein characteristic of CTE (chronic traumatic encephalopathy). CTE is a progressive degenerative disease found in individuals with a history of multiple concussions or other forms of serious head injury. It can be definitively diagnosed only by pathological examination of the brain (after death).

What is interesting from our point of view in this book is the opposition to Dr. Omalu's findings and how it was strongly backed by scientific and medical experts. When Dr. Omalu published his findings, the NFL tried to have the journal retract his article. The journal refused, but the NFL continued to attack Dr. Omalu's research and his credentials. The NFL published its own medical articles claiming that football is safe and denying the connection between brain injuries and football. Next, the NFL founded a Mild Traumatic Brain Injury Committee in the 1990s chaired by a medical doctor. This powerful and well-financed committee continued to advocate the position that there was no causal connection between football and brain injuries. The committee was chaired by several successive leaders, and was at a later stage chaired by a neurologist who went so far as to make the claim that the findings of Dr. Omalu were wrong.

The next stage in the evolution of the case was that Boston University formed a research team to look at the impact of football injuries on the brain. They recruited Dr. Anne McKee, a pathologist specializing in studying Alzheimer's disease. She started to collect the brains of former football players and study them. She found evidence of CTE in almost all of the brain she studied. When the researchers made this discovery, they thought the NFL executives would support their findings and try to make football safer. Instead what happened is that the NFL used its scientific and media power to attack the research. The NFL had co-opted an influential medical journal to publish a series of papers that denied concussions were due to football. Several of these papers were rejected by peer reviewers and later even disavowed by some of their own authors (Fainaru-Wada and Fainaru 2013, 6).

Gradually a number of cases came to be publicized (Fainaru-Wada and Fainaru 2013, 7). One well-known NFL player killed himself by drinking antifreeze. Two players fired handguns into their chests, and a famous linebacker shot himself in the guest room of his beach house. These football players were public figures who were well known to be good citizens and widely admired people, in contrast with their degeneration into almost unrecognizable states. Eventually, nearly 6,000 retired players and their families sued the NFL for negligence and fraud, arguing that the NFL had propagated its own industry funded and falsified research in order to conceal the causal link between football and brain damage.

After Boston University researchers had published their findings, congressional hearings compared the NFL to the tobacco industry's marshaling of scientific evidence for so many years supporting the claim that there was no causal link between smoking and lung cancer. To broadly summarize the sequence of events in the case, the NFL had spent over 20 years marshaling a series of their own scientific studies designed to systematically attack the causal connection between football and brain damage. A neurosurgeon connected to the NFL claimed that children were more likely to sustain brain injuries from riding a bike or falling down (Fainaru-Wada and Fainaru 2013, 7). Just as in the case of the tobacco industry the NFL had supported their arguments by funding their own opposed expert scientific findings.

In the smoking and football examples, it is more than just a case of critically questioning an expert opinion by posing the critical question that other experts do not agree with a claim made by a particular expert. In these cases, there is a systematic disagreement between the two sides, each representing a group of scientific experts. The opinions of each group may be internally consistent, but as a whole constellation of expert opinions, they each disagree with each other. Not only that, we can see that the arguments put forward by the second group of experts have been specifically designed to attack the arguments put forward by the first group of experts.

In these kinds of cases, there is a large mass of evidence on both sides. To analyze such a case using argumentation methods, you have to collect the arguments on the one side, and show how they are connected to the arguments on the other side. An examination has to be made of how each argument either supports or attacks other arguments put forward by the other side, and you also have to collect and examine all the evidence that has been put forward by experts that both sides agree to. Examining either of these cases in detail is a project beyond the resources of this book. Analyzing them using argumentation methods of the kind described and illustrated in the book can be a project for future research. But both cases are especially interesting for the purposes of studying argument from correlation to causation because both illustrate the problem of biased scientific evidence employed for public relations purposes to promote the interests of the group with something to gain. This kind of strategy uses argument from expert opinion to attack a prior argument from correlation to cause.

## 6.9 Reformulating the Critical Questions

A recommendation for modifying the set of critical questions matching this scheme for argument from correlation to cause concerns Bradford Criterion 5, which states that the causal inference is stronger when there is a theoretical scientific basis linking the two events. This particular factor was stressed in CAS. It is proposed that the following critical question be added to the existing list of seven: is there a theoretical scientific basis linking the two events *E1* and *E2*? There are also some other critical questions to be considered.

The structure of the inference from a surrogate marker to a causal conclusion shown in Fig. 6.5 suggests other critical questions. The first is whether the argument from correlation to cause as stated goes to the ultimate conclusion or whether instead it goes to a surrogate marker. The second question is to be asked when the surrogate marker has been identified. The third question asks whether the inference from the surrogate marker to the conclusion is justified. It could be argued that consideration of the SMI is already included in the existing critical question 7, and so the three new critical questions could be seen as subquestions of the old critical question 7. However because of the importance of the SMI, as demonstrated in the examples treated in this chapter, it is concluded that these new questions should be added to the existing set.

Adding these three new critical questions suggests revising the set of critical questions matching the scheme for argument from correlation to causation as follows.

CQ1. Is there a positive correlation between *E1* and *E2*?
CQ2. Are there a significant number of instances of the positive correlation between *E1* and *E2*?
CQ3. Is there good evidence that the causal relationship goes from *E1* to *E2* and not just from *E2* to *E1*?
CQ4. Can it be ruled out that the correlation between *E1* and *E2* is accounted for by some third factor *E3* (a common cause) that causes both *E1* and *E2*?
CQ5. If there are intervening variables, can it be shown that the causal relationship between *E1* and *E2* is indirect (mediated through other causes)?
CQ6. If the correlation fails to hold outside a certain range of cases, then can the limits of the range be clearly indicated?
CQ7. Can it be shown that the increase or change in *E2* is not solely due to the way *E2* is defined, the way entities are classified as belonging to *E2*, or changing standards, over time, in the way *E2* is defined or classified?
CQ8. Is there a theoretical scientific basis linking the two events *E1* and *E2*?
CQ9. Does the argument from correlation to cause as stated go to the ultimate conclusion or to a surrogate marker?

CQ10. If a surrogate marker has been identified, is the inference from the surrogate marker to the conclusion justified?

As each critical question is asked, and replied to appropriately by the arguer, the argument from correlation to cause is strengthened. As suggested by the three textbook accounts of Johnson and Blair (1983), Govier (2005) and Groarke and Tindale (2004), the supporting evidence gained by answering the questions appropriately makes the argument less weak and less open to the *post hoc* objection. The approach suggested by this chapter is that arguments from correlation to cause should be judged on a dialectical continuum, so that as more and more critical questions concerning the hypothesis that there is a causal relation between the two events are answered appropriately, support for the hypothesis becomes stronger and stronger. As the pro evidence outweighs the con evidence and answers critical questions, the strength of the argument from correlation to causation increases. Alternatively, it can decrease as critical questions are not answered, or as counter-arguments are brought against the argument.

More precise details of how this dialectical evaluation procedure works can be shown by explaining how CAS manages the burden of proof between the arguer and the critical questioner in a dialogue sequence (Walton and Gordon 2011). Argument from correlation to causation is evaluated by using a set of critical questions matching the scheme in a dialectical procedure where a burden of proof is shifted back and forth between the proponent and the questioner. The problem with modeling this procedure using an argument diagram of the kind shown in Figs. 6.2, 6.3 and 6.4 is that some critical questions shift the initiative back to the proponent, while others only do so when evidence to back up the question is given. In CAS, the former types of critical questions are treated as assumptions while the latter one are treated as exceptions. The ordinary premises of a scheme are taken to hold in CAS, but if questioned they are taken to be no longer accepted until they are supported by some evidence. But there are two additional kinds of premises that have been designed to model the two different kinds of critical questions. Assumptions, like the ordinary premises, only need to be backed up if they have been questioned, while exceptions are assumed not to hold until evidence is given showing that they do.

It should be noted that the list of ten critical questions can be used to guide a causal inquiry as well as to evaluate arguments from correlation to causation. A causal inquiry might typically start from a correlation between two events or types of events that is puzzling because there is yet no explanation of the connection, if any, between the events. The list of critical questions can aid an investigation to move forward by searching for experimental evidence or other kinds of evidence that might link the two events together. This can be done either by finding intervening events that connect them, or by bringing a scientific theory to bear on experimental evidence that shows a much more convincing kind of connection than one that can be established by statistical evidence of correlation alone. Next, the causal inquiry might move to a stage where a scientific explanation is offered that reveals the underlying connection, a physical, chemical or biochemical connection for example, between the two events. At the next step, inference to the best explanation can be applied to the evidence in the case, and alternative explanations to the most plausible one may be rejected, again based on the evidence known at that point as the inquiry proceeds. To fill out this suggestion, more needs to be known about the opening and closing stages of such an inquiry, and how the evidential reasoning in the stage between them moves forward to the stage of proof or disproof of the hypothesis. Such a model of evidential reasoning in an inquiry is outlined in Chap. 7.

## 6.10 The *Post Hoc* Fallacy

The problem posed by arguing from correlation to causation is that it has traditionally been associated in logic with the fallacy of *post hoc ergo propter hoc*, but is often a reasonable form of argument, under the right conditions. It is not only one of the most prominent forms of argument in medicine and other applied sciences, but it is also a kind of reasoning we constantly depend on in everyday life, as the examples given in Sect. 6.1 suggest. The problem is generally that, as shown in this chapter, there is a continuum of instances of this type of argument from the very weak, to the basically reasonable but questionable, to the fallacious. We have limited the scope of this chapter to five main examples, but there are other examples at both ends of the continuum that could be studied in future research. Let's consider just one example at the weak end and one at the strong end. According to a BBC News Report[6] a study by Barclays Capital linked skyscrapers with impending financial crashes, citing the building of the Empire state building just before the Great Depression and the building of the Burj Khalifa just before the large recession in Dubai. Although an impressive set of examples of correlations between these two events was cited in the report, there appears to be no other evidence to suggest that the building of skyscrapers causes financial crashes. As an example at the strong end, consider the correlation between smoking and lung cancer. At one time in history the existence of a causal link of this nature was strongly denied, especially by tobacco company research, as shown in Sect. 6.8, but now the evidence makes this argument convincingly strong.

Also there is a variation of context in examples that needs to be taken into account. A very weak argument from correlation to causation might well be reasonable as a form of argument used to suggest a hypothesis at a very early discovery stage of an investigation. However the very same argument used at a later stage of the investigation, could well be inadequately supported, or even fallacious, if it pressed too strongly for a causal conclusion while overlooking critical questions that need to be asked at that point. The dialectical complexity of the situation is compounded when authors of a research report make a claim for a causal conclusion based on experimental or statistical findings about correlation between the two events in question, and this conclusion is accepted and advocated by parties external to the scientific research. The typical kind of example studied above has two stages.

[6]http://www.bbc.co.uk/news/business-16494013.

The first is that of a scientific paper arguing from correlation and causation as the basis for inferring a causal conclusion. The second is that of a news report in the media or other public source of information, or other academic journals, reporting the causal conclusion and describing the evidence that led the scientific investigators to it, based on a correlation. Both instances can be classified as cases of arguing from a correlation to a causal conclusion, but the standards of proof and the methods of argumentation used in each instance are different.

Some traditional logical fallacies have been associated with heuristics, or fast and frugal rules of thumb that are commonly used, and also are very useful means of quickly jumping to a tentative conclusion that may later need to be retracted or revised as more calculative methods are brought into play (Walton and Gordon 2009). The examples studied in this chapter show that argument from correlation to causation fits this category very well. At the first stage of the typical sequence of argumentation of this sort, a surprising correlation is found. The question at this stage is whether it is merely a coincidence or whether there may be some causal connection between the two events at issue. The conjecture of a possible causal connection between the two events at this point should be treated as a very weak argument that may be presumptively acceptable as a means to move forward towards further collection of evidence, but that should be seen as inherently open to critical questioning. At the next points in the sequence, some further evidence connecting the two events may be found. For example, there may be other events intervening between the two events that connect them together as a longer sequence. Or there may be some scientific evidence, or a scientific theory, that tends to confirm the connection between the two events, creating a more plausible hypothesis that they are causally connected.

Given this procedure of evaluation, Fig. 6.1 can be used to illustrate how the *post hoc* fallacy can be explained. As shown along the bottom of Fig. 6.1, there is a tendency to jump from a correlation to a causal conclusion. This kind of inferential jump is extremely common in everyday reasoning, as well as in scientific reasoning such as medical reasoning. It is hard to resist it, and easy to take advantage of it. As soon as we see a correlation between two events, or even one event happening after another one, using the causal heuristic we jump to the conclusion that the one event might cause the other. Depending on how strong we take the argument from correlation to cause to be, succumbing to the heuristic to accept the conclusion that the one event causes the other can be a good guess, unfounded speculation, or even a fallacious argument. The fallacy, or the error of *post hoc* reasoning, essentially occurs when the arguer jumps ahead on the basis of a correlation to conclude that a causal connection exists, without taking the critical questions into account. In the example shown in Fig. 6.1, such a presumptive leap to a causal conclusion would not be justified unless it is taken into account to what extent the SMI can be justified. So the kind of reasoning shown in Fig. 6.1 can be generalized to offer a theoretical explanation of how the *post hoc* fallacy works, an explanation that confirms and extends the approach to arguments from correlation to cause taken by Johnson and Blair (1983), Govier (2005) and Groarke and Tindale (2004). An argument from correlation to cause can be weak, but that can be tentatively accepted if it was only put forward as a hypothesis not yet fully tested. But if questioned, the questioning and answering procedure must fulfill the requirements of burden of proof appropriate for the discussion.

If the arguer persists too aggressively or thoughtlessly by overlooking appropriate critical questions, or even by trying to prevent the questioner from asking them, or evading the burden of answering them, then this is a kind of case where an accusation of committing the *post hoc* fallacy can be brought into play. The smoking and the football examples have shown that the *post hoc* fallacy does not consist exclusively in the error of using a heuristic to jump too quickly to conclude that a causal connection exists based on a correlation. In some cases, the fallacy consists of a strategic maneuver designed to forestall the drawing of a reasonable inference from correlation to causation by means of employing a systematic tactic of attempting to prevent critical questions from being asked. Some significant similarities between the tactics used in the football case and the smoking case were noted by Fainaru-Wada and Fainaru (2013, 280). In both cases powerful companies had used their power and vast financial resources to discredit scientists they disagreed with. They tried to downplay work of scientists who had opposed expert opinions. They used inappropriate kinds of critical questions to attack these opposed expert opinion arguments. They put forward expert opinion arguments of their own based on scientific research that served their interests and that they had financially supported.

These cases show evidence of systematic public relations campaigns, supported by the use of scientific evidence, to try to shift the burden of proof back to the side who has claimed that a causal conclusion can be inferred from a correlation. The variant of the *post hoc* fallacy illustrated by these examples does not represent the error of jumping too quickly to a conclusion. It is just the opposite. It represents a strategy of pushing back too hard against a well-supported argument from correlation to cause by using all kinds dubious tactics to try to persuade the audience (the public) without giving the argument a fair hearing. For the purposes of this chapter, these cases are merely examples of a certain kind of argumentation strategy used to rebut arguments from correlation to causation. However, from a point of view of argumentation logic, they represent patterns of argument that we need to be aware of, and that we need to study further.

## References


Castellano, J.M., R. Deane, A.J. Gottesdiener, P.B. Verghese, F.R. Stewart, T. West, A.C. Paoletti, T.R. Kasper, R.B. DeMattos, B.V. Zlokovic, and D.M. Holtzman. 2012. Low-density lipoprotein receptor overexpression enhances the rate of brain-to-blood Aß clearance in a mouse model of ß-amyloidosis. *Proceedings of the National Academy of Sciences U S A* 109(38): 15502–15507.

Cohn, J. 2004. Markers of malign across the cardiovascular continuum: Interpretation and application: Introduction to surrogate markers. *Circulation* 109: IV-20-IV-21(109[suppl. IV]: 20–21.) http://circ.ahajournals.org/content/109/25_suppl_1/IV-20.full. Accessed 14 Aug 2013.

Couzin-Frankel, J., and Y. Ogale. 2011. Once on "fast track", Avastin now derailed. *Science* 333(6039): 143–144. doi:10.1126/science.333.6039.143.

Doll, R. 1992. Sir Austin Bradford Hill and the progress of medical science. *British Medical Journal* 305(6868): 1521–1526.

Exley, C., E. House, A. Polwart, and M.M. Esiri. 2012. Brain burdens of aluminum, iron, and copper, and their relationships with amyloid-β pathology in 60 human brains. *Journal of Alzheimer's Disease* 31(4): 725–730.

Fainaru-Wada, M., and S. Fainaru. 2013. *League of denial*. New York: Random House.

Freedman, D.H. 2010. *Wrong: Why experts keep failing us – And how to know when not to trust them*. New York: Little Brown and Company.

Gordon, T.F. 2010. The Carneades argumentation support system. In *Dialectics, dialogue and argumentation*, ed. C. Reed and C.W. Tindale. London: College Publications.

Govier, T. 2005. *A practical study of argument*, 6th ed. Belmont: Wadsworth.

Groarke, L.A., and C.W. Tindale. 2004. *Good reasoning matters!* 3rd ed. Oxford: Oxford University Press.

Hill, B.A. 1965. The environment and disease: Association or causation? *Proceedings of the Royal Society of Medicine* 58(5): 295–300.

Ioannidis, J.P.A. 2005. Why most published research findings are false. *PLoS Med* 2(8): e124. Published online 2005 August 30. doi: 10.1371/journal.pmed.0020124. PMCID: PMC1182327.

Johnson, R.H., and J.A. Blair. 1983. *Logical self-defense*, 2nd ed. Toronto: McGraw-Hill Ryerson.

Messerli, F. 2012. Chocolate consumption, cognitive function and nobel laureates. *New England Journal of Medicine* 367(16): 1562–1564.

Pinto, R. 1995. Post hoc ergo propter hoc. In *Fallacies: Classical and contemporary readings*, ed. H.V. Hansen and R.C. Pinto, 302–311. University Park: Penn State Press.

Proctor, R.N. 1995. *Cancer wars*. New York: Basic Books.

Reed, C., and D. Walton. 2003. Diagramming, argumentation schemes and critical questions. In *Anyone who has a view: Theoretical contributions to the study of argumentation*, ed. F.H. van Eemeren, J.A. Blair, C.A. Willard, and A. Snoeck Henkemans, 195–211. Dordrecht: Kluwer.

Shaman, J., and M. Lipsitch. 2013. The ENSO-pandemic influenza connection: Coincident or causal? *Proceedings of the National Academy of Sciences* 110(Suppl. 1): 3689–3691.

Susser, M. 1977. Judgement and causal inference: Criteria in epidemiologic studies. *American Journal of Epidemiology* 105(1): 1–15.

Walton, D. 1996. *Argumentation schemes for presumptive reasoning*. Mahwah: Lawrence Erlbaum Publishers.

Walton, D., and T.F. Gordon. 2009. Jumping to a conclusion: Fallacies and standards of proof. *Informal Logic* 29(2): 215–243.

Walton, D., and T.F. Gordon. 2011. Modeling critical questions as additional premises. In *Argument cultures: Proceedings of the 8th International OSSA* Conference, ed. F. Zenker, 1–13. Windsor, University of Windsor. Available at http://www.dougwalton.ca/papers%20in%20pdf/11OSSA.pdf.

Walton, D., and N. Zhang. 2013. The epistemology of scientific evidence. *Artificial Intelligence and Law* 21(2): 173–219.

Walton, D., C. Reed, and F. Macagno. 2008. *Argumentation schemes*. Cambridge: Cambridge University Press.

# Chapter 7
# Knowledge and Inquiry

**Abstract** Scientific reasoning of the kind used to collect evidence and bring it to bear on a scientific hypothesis, has to be seen as defeasible according to the previous six chapters of this book. This is shown by the cases where expert scientific opinions have disagreed. It is also shown by the reality that scientific opinions sometimes have to be retracted as new evidence comes in and scientific research moves forward. For these reasons, to have a concept of knowledge that is adequate for argumentation studies of the kind pursued in the first six chapters of this book, it is necessary for this concept to include defeasible knowledge, and to include standards of proof as much more important for reasoning about knowledge and lack of knowledge than they have traditionally been held to be. This chapter presents an evidence-based model of inquiry, and defends a fallibilistic view of knowledge. In the model, knowledge is established in a multiagent inquiry in which agents take part in building explanations of the facts comprising the evidence that are subject to critical questioning and counter-arguments.

This chapter advocates a viewpoint of bounded procedural rationality to build a model representing the structure of the process whereby reasoning is used to justify the claim that a proposition should have the status of knowledge. Two important elements of the model are the requirements that the process uses evidence both for and against the claim and that it is based on defeasible reasoning. The model is primarily meant to represent scientific knowledge as a body of accepted propositions, but subject to some reservations, it may also be used to represent the reasoning used in knowledge claims in everyday conversational discourse. The model is implemented in CAS, a system that supports defeasible argumentation schemes that can be used in an open knowledge base. In the model, a proposition can be classified as knowledge if and only if (1) it has been proved in an investigative procedure called an inquiry, (2) to the proof standard appropriate for the inquiry (3) based on the evidence marshaled during the inquiry, and (4) using the kind of evidence that is admissible in the inquiry.

The chapter begins in Sect. 7.1 by describing the philosophical conflict between two opposed views of knowledge. The one view, currently the dominant view in epistemology, is shown to be characterized by four defining principles stating that (1) knowledge bases contain only truths, (2) knowledge bases are consistent, (3)


D. Walton, *Argument Evaluation and Evidence*, Law, Governance and Technology Series 23, DOI 10.1007/978-3-319-19626-8_7

knowledge bases are closed under deductive implication, and (4) knowledge bases contain the assumption that if a proposition is known, then it is known that it is known. The other view, a fallibilistic view attributed to Peirce and Popper, holds that a proposition can be established as knowledge during the course of an inquiry, but later rejected as knowledge once new evidence has falsified it. The two views of knowledge are shown to be incompatible. The skeptical roots of this fallibilistic view of knowledge are shown to be traceable back to the ancient skepticism of Arcesilaus and Carneades. In Sect. 7.2, an evidence-based model of inquiry that has five defining characteristics is applied to a standard example of reasoning about knowledge using the CAS. This model is shown in Sect. 7.3 to be based on a procedural view of inquiry in which evidence can support or defeat claims to knowledge. The argumentation structure of this procedure is modeled in Sect. 7.4 by an extension of CAS as a sequence of moves in a collaborative group inquiry in which parties take turns making assertions and putting forward evidence to support them. It is shown in Sect. 7.5 how this model of evaluating evidence in an inquiry is based on a defeasible logic using forms of argumentation that admit of exceptions. It is the contention of Sects 7.6 and 7.7 that reasoning from absence of knowledge, or lack of evidence, is as important to inquiry as positive reasoning from evidence to knowledge. The philosophical conflict between the two views of reasoning about knowledge is revisited in Sect. 7.8, where the main objections and replies on both sides are discussed. Section 7.9 gives a summary of the characteristics of fallibilistic knowledge-based inquiry. The conclusions of the chapter are presented in Sect. 7.10.

## 7.1 Two Opposed Views of Reasoning About Knowledge

According to the justified true belief analysis, to qualify as knowledge, a proposition[1] *p* must meet the following three requirements: (1) *p* is true, (2) the agent who claims to know that *p* is true believes that *p*, and (3) the agent is justified in believing that *p*. Surprisingly, (1), the veracity condition, has not generated any significant degree of discussion (Steup 2010). Perhaps the most familiar philosophical definition of knowledge is captured by Zagzebski's (1999, 93) phrase that knowledge is "true belief plus something else." On this type of account, propositional knowledge is explained as some form of "good true belief" (Zagzebski 1999, 99). The justification condition has been explained in a variety of ways, including evidentialist accounts, causal accounts, and reliabilist accounts (to mention a few).

Accounts of knowledge as true-belief-plus have also been adopted by many theorists working within an epistemological approach to argumentation (Lumer 2005a, 190, b, 215). Indeed, Lumer (2005a, 192) has gone so far as to claim that theories which use the term 'knowledge' in a sense different than that adopted within

[1]In this paper, the terms 'proposition' and 'statement' are used interchangeably.

normative epistemology – which, Lumer claims, relates knowledge and justified belief to objective truth conditions (e.g., by identifying knowledge with the current stock of expert opinions) – do not count as epistemological approaches.

Bonjour (2010) distinguished between two conceptions of knowledge. According to the Cartesian conception, knowledge requires conclusive justification, meaning a kind of justification that guarantees the truth of the claim being considered. According to his so-called fallible (better called fallibilistic) conception, knowledge only requires a degree of justification short of conclusive justification. On the fallibilistic conception, a proposition can be considered to be knowledge if the justification for it is fairly strong, even if the justification does not guarantee it. Bonjour rejects the fallible conception for two reasons. The first one is that he claims there is no satisfactory way to specify the level of justification required for fallible knowledge. Second, he claims that knowledge is the "supremely valuable cognitive state" representing full cognitive success, and therefore no level of justification that is less than fully conclusive should be sufficient to prove that a proposition can be classified as knowledge (Bonjour 2010, 58).

Hannon (2014, 1126) responded to Bonjour's attack on fallibilism by extending Bonjour's objections to fallible knowledge to questions on how to reasonably derive evidence from expert opinions. One of these questions is how to model expertise. Presumably we reasonably accept someone as an expert because we assume that this agent has knowledge in a domain of expertise. But if we model such knowledge as infallible, that would imply that this expert could never be wrong, could never make any mistakes, and indeed could not even improve by correcting her mistakes. The investigations of arguments from expert opinion in Chaps. 4 and 5 abundantly revealed that treating expert knowledge as infallible in the way advocated by Bonjour would simply not enable us to deal with arguments from expert opinion in a reasonable and useful manner. For this reason and others Hannon, joining a growing group of fallibilist philosophers in epistemology (Conee and Feldman 2004), has advocated the adoption of a fallibilist theory of knowledge. The problem arises, for example, in cases where the opinion of one expert contradicts the opinion of another expert. There are many reasons that can be found in the previous chapter for moving to a fallibilist conception of knowledge, but there are also many problems for fallibilists to solve. This chapter will address some of them by showing how CAS can provide a model of evidential reasoning in which evidence-based arguments can qualify as fallible knowledge by meeting an appropriate standard of proof set in place at the opening stage if the inquiry. What will be provided is a new kind of defeasible logic that enables the user to deal reasonably with fallible arguments such as the argument from expert opinion.

Classical logic has a model-based semantics established on a notion of truth in which truth is a relation between a proposition and an external reality that provides a criterion for telling whether a proposition is true or false. This feature can be seen in classical deductive logic in which the propositions take on the truth values true and false. It has proved to be a useful model to represent mathematical reasoning. Epistemic reasoning has traditionally accepted this model, which is based on four key assumptions about how knowledge relates to truth and logical reasoning. The general assumption has been that knowledge can be modeled in formal systems of modal logic, following four assumptions. The relation $\rightarrow$ represents the material conditional used in classical deductive logic. Rescher (2003, 10–11) takes these four principles, along with some others, to represent defining characteristics of knowledge. He wrote (2003, 10) that although "some writers see the linkage between truth and knowledge as a merely contingent one", this view in not tenable. For the purposes of this chapter, these four principles are taken as axioms representing the currently dominant view in epistemology.

1. veracity: $Kp \rightarrow p$ knowledge bases contain only truths; if $p$ is known then $p$ is true
2. consistency: $\sim(Kp \mathbin{\&} K{\sim}p)$ knowledge bases are consistent; if $p$ is known then it is not the case that not-$p$ is known
3. deductive closure: $K(p \rightarrow q) \rightarrow (Kp \rightarrow Kq)$ knowledge bases are closed under deductive implication; knowledge includes all of the logical consequences of any proposition known
4. iteration: $Kp \rightarrow KKp$ the contents of knowledge bases are transparent; if $p$ is known, then it is known that $p$ is known

In his survey of the logic of knowledge, Rescher (2005, 4) wrote that the veracity assumption obtains as a general principle for systems of epistemic logic. He formulated this principle as saying 'If $K_x p$ then $p$', where $x$ is an intelligent knower. This 'if-then' is taken to represent a deductive connection. It could be strict implication based on the modal necessity operator, but here we take it to represent the material conditional of classical deductive logic.

Cooke (2006, 1) defined Peirce's way of viewing fallibilism by linking it to iterated knowledge claims and by contrasting it with the view of knowledge held in traditional epistemology. According to traditional epistemologists, in order to know, an inquiring agent must be in an epistemic position to know that he knows. In contrast, the doctrine of fallibilism does not allow an inquirer to judge that he possesses the truth concerning the matter inquired into. He not only denies the iterated axiom that if $A$ is known to be true then $A$ is known to be known to be true. He even denies that the agent can be in an epistemic position to know that he knows that $A$ is true. Thus the iteration fails, following the view of the Peircean fallibilist.

Walton (2005) calls any theory of knowledge meeting these four criteria an *idealized* model of knowledge, and argues that any such idealized model is unsuitable for pragmatic purposes of modeling knowledge based on defeasible epistemic reasoning of the kind found in scientific discovery and investigation. Walton argues that in such cases, knowledge bases are not consistent, transparent, or closed under deductive implication. The reason is that scientific knowledge, even if based on confirmation that meets a high standard of proof, needs to always be open to continued testing, and hence needs to be seen as defeasible. Walton (2005) proposed a pragmatic conception of knowledge which is built upon two common-sense platitudes that capture our everyday epistemic situation in the world: (1) a knowledge-base can be incomplete, and (2) a knowledge-base can be fallible. A knowledge base can be incomplete in the sense that there can be many true claims which are not included in the knowledge base. Further, "[o]n this [pragmatic] model, knowledge is defeasible, meaning that a proposition now known may later be refuted (defeated as knowledge)" (Walton 2005, 59–60), thus allowing for retraction in the process of inquiry, investigation, and discovery.

On the Peircean view, the real aim of an inquiry of the kind that takes place in a finite amount of time and resources for collecting evidence is not that of actually reaching the truth, and knowing that it has been reached, but only that of a firm settling of opinion. Peirce (1984, 354) wrote that the "only legitimate aim of reasoning is to ascertain what decision would be agreed upon if the question were sufficiently ventilated". Taking the view that truth is the result of inquiry would "block the path of inquiry because our minds would be closed, and hence, we would never be motivated enough to inquire" (Peirce 1931, 6.3). Clearly acceptance of the veracity axiom is not consistent with Peirce's view of the inquiry. In addition, he warned us not to infer from the premise that we can be substantially certain about many things to the conclusion that we "perfectly know when we know" (Misak 1987, 260). It is a corollary that the iteration axiom does not work in the Peircean inquiry either. Maintaining the veracity condition is at odds with the important role that defeasible reasoning plays in the process of evaluating claims to knowledge in an inquiry.

These are strongly opposed views. The veracity principle is so widely accepted in epistemology that epistemologists feel that it would be unthinkable to reject it. Rescher (2003, 10) considers that holding that the linkage between knowledge and truth is merely contingent "inflicts violence on the concept of knowledge as it actually operates in discourse". His reason is that the locution 'an agent knows that proposition *p* but *p* is not true' is "senseless". He gives two arguments to back up this contention.

The first argument is based on the premise that a person cannot be said to know that something is the case when this person is not prepared to accept it. The conclusion he holds to follow from this premise is that a claim that a person knows that proposition *p* is only tenable when that person holds *p* to be the case. Note however that given that the premise of this argument is true, it does not follow that proposition *p* has to be true. It only follows that the person holds *p* to be true. In other words, what follows is not truth but acceptance: if a person says that he knows that a proposition is the case, it follows that he must be taken to accept this proposition. What does not follow is that the proposition itself must actually be true.

The second argument is that a person cannot properly be said to know that a proposition is true unless he is prepared to accept the proposition, as a true premise in his thinking and a suitable basis for his actions. But as with the first argument, the conclusion of this argument is that knowledge implies acceptance. The argument does not prove the veracity principle that knowledge implies truth.

Both these arguments can be seen to be open to doubt, based on the defeasible model of reasoning in an inquiry presented in the rest of the chapter. It is an acceptance-based model, and does not require any of the four principles of reasoning about knowledge. In this fallibilistic model, because of the principle of falsification of scientific knowledge, disputed cases may need to become the subject of further inquiry. In defeasible epistemic reasoning, there is no guarantee that a conclusion drawn is actually true, with reference to some standard of truth that is a relation between a proposition and an external reality. In defeasible reasoning, the conclusion can be taken to be proved to be true based on the evidence that has been collected so far, but when new evidence is collected that same proposition may turn out later to be proved to be false, as much as this outcome is meant to be avoided in a careful investigation.

The problem is that we can have lots of evidence in favor of a proposition and no evidence against it, so that on balance, the proposition can rightly be said to be known to be true, but later on, as more evidence comes in, we might find that this proposition is false. It is important for scientific knowledge that it be represented as open to defeat in this kind of situation as new evidence comes in. This defeasibility requirement, however, is inconsistent with the traditional definition of knowledge as justified true belief. This requirement is not consistent with the notion that sometimes propositions rightly accepted as scientific knowledge later on turn out to be disqualified or rejected as knowledge, once new experimental findings come in, or a new theory comes in that offers a better explanation than the previous one.

The historical motivation of the defeasible knowledge approach is to be found in the variant of Academic skepticism developed by Arcesilaus, Carneades, Philo of Larissa and Cicero. As reported by Cicero, the Greek skeptic Arcesilaus adopted the view, appropriated from the Socratic dialogues, that nothing can be apprehended with certainty by the senses or the mind. He concluded that "truth is submerged in the depths" (Thorsrud 2002, 6). From these premises, Arcesilaus also drew the conclusion that knowledge is not possible. From his premises and conclusions, we can take it that Arcesilaus assumed, as an implicit premise, that truth is a requirement of genuine knowledge. So reconstructed, his argument runs as follows: we cannot have truth (or be sure we have it); knowledge requires truth; therefore we cannot have knowledge. His conclusion is the classical one of the skeptic. But one can be a fallibilist without being a skeptic, for there is another route open to the fallibilist. He can concede that while truth cannot be known, at least with certainty beyond all doubt, knowledge of a fallible sort can be obtained through a process of collecting and testing evidence in a systematic inquiry, even though the knowledge obtained as the outcome of this procedure cannot be verified at the end of it (beyond further questioning) as a true proposition.

This view that Cicero attributes to the Academic skeptics suggests an approach to epistemology that does not require the axiom of veracity. According to this epistemology, an open-minded rational agent who is in search of the truth can be motivated and directed by this concern, even though he is skeptical about arriving at the end of the search with knowledge of the truth that cannot later be disputed or doubted. Truth is very important in such an inquiry, because regard for the truth is an ideal that motivates the inquiry. But one can argue that this view is consistent with the view that there are difficulties and human limitations concerning the acquisition of a kind of knowledge that implies the truth.

Peirce held a form of fallibilism that held that all our knowledge is fallible, subject perhaps to only one exception: "No; but there is nothing at all in our knowledge which we have any warrant at all for regarding as absolute in any particular.... If I must make any exception, let it be that the assertion that every assertion but this is fallible, is the only one that is absolutely infallible" (Peirce 1931, 2.75). Peirce wrote that many things are "substantially certain" (Peirce 1931, 1.152), but that this is different from the kind of absolute certainty that implies truth. On his view truth is an aim of inquiry but it can only be reached during the procedure of an inquiry after an infinite process of evidence and argumentation that would take an infinite time. He concluded that knowledge needs to be seen as an approximation to the truth that has survived the testing inquiry that has examined all plausible views, and selected the one that is most likely to be true. On this view there is an asymmetry, in that while knowledge can be falsified by testing, it can never be verified in the sense that it can be proved to be true beyond doubt.

The distinction between verifiability and falsifiability is central to Popper's philosophy of science and an important aspect of how Popper defined scientific knowledge. On his view, to be correctly considered scientific knowledge, a theory must be falsifiable. However, note that it does not have to be verifiable, at any rate meaning that it has to be true beyond any possibility of doubt. According to Popper's philosophy of critical rationalism, human knowledge is based on reasoning of a kind that is conjectural. He held that scientific hypotheses are falsifiable, but not verifiable, in the sense that positive outcomes in experimental testing can give evidence to support a hypothesis, but do not imply the conclusion that the hypothesis is true, or known to be true. For Popper, the search for truth is one of the strongest motives for scientific discovery. Like Peirce, he held that a scientific investigation can measurably come closer to truth (verisimilitude) with respect to the amount of truth and falsity it implies. He claimed that verisimilitude is measurable, and contended that it was an aspect of his philosophy of science that scientific knowledge is objective, in the sense that it is (1) based on an evidential procedure that moves toward truth as its goal and (2) is independent of the knowing subject.

The fallibilist approach to reasoning about knowledge is strongly opposed to the generally dominant approach in epistemology that views knowledge as justified true belief. On the fallibilist view, all that is necessary for a proposition to be accepted as knowledge is for the inquiry procedure to prove the proposition, based on the arguments for and against it that are produced and evaluated during the procedure itself.

## 7.2 Evidence and Knowledge

What is evidence, and how is it related to knowledge? Evidence is made up of a set of evidential data or items of evidence and of inferences reasonably drawn from them. One part of evidence is the perception of the data through the senses, or sensors (in the case of an automated agent or a device with memory, like a black box data recorder). The other is the drawing of conclusions from the perception of such data, based on inference. If I see something that looks like a red car in the parking lot, my perception of the red car is data, and from this data I can draw a reasonable inference to the conclusion that there is a red car in the parking lot. If I say later that there was a red car in the parking lot, this conclusion can also be accepted as evidence, but in such an instance it depends on my memory. If I tell somebody else later that I saw a red car in the parking lot, they can also draw the inference to the conclusion that there was a red car in the parking lot, based on testimonial (witness) evidence.

Knowledge is based on evidence. Indeed, being evidence-based is a requirement of knowledge, in the sense of the term meant here. This meaning of the term comprises evidence in many different disciplines, including ones in science and law, like archaeology, forensic evidence, medicine and authentication of works of art and other artifacts.

In general the relationship between knowledge and evidence has five components. The first component is the ultimate conclusion to be proved, the proposition that is claimed to have the status of knowledge. The second is the body of data that is being put forward as the basis for drawing inferences from the data. The third is the marshaling, or collecting together of the data and conclusion drawn from them that are relevant to support the claim that this proposition can be classified as knowledge. This is the body (or mass) of evidence. The fourth is the chain of reasoning that provides the argumentation, or justification as it might equivalently be called, proving the ultimate proposition from the mass of evidence. The fifth is the standard of proof that this chain of reasoning has to meet in order to prove the ultimate conclusion. Evidence comes to be knowledge through a dialogue procedure called an inquiry which can be modeled as a dialogue system.

A basic proposition is taken in current epistemology to be one like 'I see a red patch now' that is not justified as knowledge by some other proposition that functions as evidence supporting it. A basic proposition, in other words, is taken to be knowledge because it is immediately evident, rather than requiring some other evidence to back it up. The possibility of there being basic propositions seems to go against the fallibilistic view that all knowledge is based on evidence collected in an inquiry and supported by reasoning from the evidence that backs up the claim to knowledge. For it would appear that in the case of a basic proposition, something can be taken as knowledge even if no additional evidential basis supported by rational argumentation is needed to back it up.

A reply to this objection can be given by considering Pollock's (1995) theory of defeasible reasoning, as outlined in Chap. 1, Sect. 1.6. The structure of Pollock's argument is displayed in the CAS argument map (Gordon and Walton 2009) shown in Fig. 7.1.

The conclusion, the statement that the object is red, is shown in the text box at the left. The two text boxes on the right at the top represent premises that support the conclusion. The node in the middle containing the + indicates an argument leading from these two premises to the conclusion. The argument joining these two premises to the conclusion is pro, indicating that these two premises support the conclusion. They are premises that behave like assumptions, meaning that they are

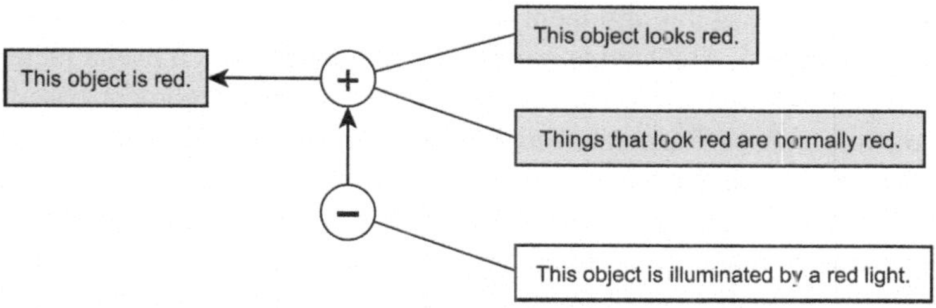


**Fig. 7.1** Pollock's red light example in the CAS model

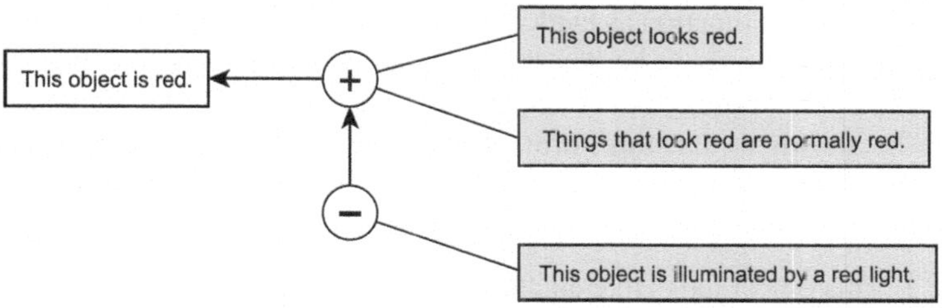


**Fig. 7.2** The red light example shown as an argument undercut by an exception

taken to hold. However, there is a third premise that appears in the text box with no fill. The con argument joining this premise to the argument node above it indicates that the con argument is classified in CAS as an undercutter. An undercutter is a type of argument that attacks a prior argument, and that can defeat the prior argument.

Why is this argument defeasible on Pollock's theory? The reason is that there is a counter-argument that can undercut the original argument by attacking the connection between the claim and the reason. If the premise of the counter-argument is accepted, and if the argument fits the argumentation scheme leading from its premise or premises to the conclusion the conclusion must be tentatively accepted as well.

This type of evidential situation is shown in Fig. 7.2, where the exception, the statement that the object is illuminated by red light, has now been accepted. Once it has been accepted, even though the argument retains the support given to it by the two previous premises, it now defaults once the exception has been activated. Then the argument, indicated by the round circle containing the plus mark, no longer has the support needed to prove the conclusion. The conclusion is now undercut by the exception.

According to Pollock's theory (1995, 41) the second argument is an undercutting defeater but not a rebutting defeater of the first one, because the second one is based on a defeasible generalization, namely the proposition that red objects look red in red light too. The object may still be red, for all we know, despite the second argument above. What is shown is that there is an argument needed to support the claim to knowledge.

The precise nature of this argument has even been defined by Pollock's defeasible perception rule (1995, 41): having a percept with content $\varphi$ is a prima facie reason to believe $\varphi$. Moreover, the undercutting defeater for any argument based on the perception rule can be formulated as follows (Bex et al. 2003, 38): 'the present circumstances are such that having a percept with content $\varphi$ is not a reliable indicator of $\varphi'$ undercuts the original argument. This rule has a function similar to that of a critical question matching an argumentation scheme. It leaves open a possibility that can be subject to doubt, and if questioned in response to an argument that fits the scheme, it can shift a burden of proof onto the proponent of the argument to respond to the doubt or give up the argument as a knowledge claim.

What has been shown is that so-called basic propositions are based on argumentation needed to function as evidence supporting the claim to knowledge made. Such an argument needs to be based on Pollock's defeasible perception rule, the generalization or warrant on which the inference to the claim depends. What can also be shown is that this form of argument is quite common in everyday conversational argumentation. An interesting legal example (Prakken 2003, 858) shows that it is common in legal argumentation as well.

Premise 1: This object looks like an affidavit.
Premise 2: If something looks like an affidavit, then it is an affidavit.
Conclusion: This object is an affidavit.

This argument is defeasible, for on a more detailed reading of the document, it might be found that it is not a real affidavit, but merely a forgery. Under the right conditions however, it may be justifiable to go ahead on the reasonable assumption that the document is an affidavit without verifying that by having experts check it. It can be tentatively assumed it is an affidavit, because based on appearances and what else we know about the document, we can accept it given that there is no reason to doubt its genuineness.

In (Walton 2006) an argumentation scheme for this kind of defeasible argument has been formulated, called the scheme for argument from appearance.

It appears that this object could be classified under verbal category *C*.
Therefore this object can be classified under verbal category *C*.

As shown by Pollock, and supported by ancient skeptical objections as well, this form of argument is best seen as defeasible rather than as conclusive. It is best evaluated on a balance of considerations, and should be seen as subject to skeptical doubt. According to the account given in (Walton 2005) the scheme has the following matching critical questions attached to it.

$CQ_1$: Could the appearance of its looking like it could be classified under *C* be misleading for some reason?

$CQ_2$: Although it may look like it can be classified under *C*, could there be grounds for indicating that it might be more justifiable to classify it under another category *D*?

If either of these questions is asked in a given case, the original claim to knowledge needs to be suspended temporarily until the claimant to knowledge offers a satisfactory answer. Thus even the most simple and straightforward claim to direct knowledge, like 'I see a red patch now', once analyzed carefully in the Pollock manner, needs to be seen as a defeasible argument that does at least partly rest on external evidence that may need to be marshalled to support it.

## 7.3 The Procedural View of Inquiry

In this section, a new procedural view of inquiry is outlined that enables a clear formulation of the view that the idea of evidence supporting knowledge being defeasible makes sense. On this model, a proposition is classified as knowledge if it is accepted as supported strongly enough by the evidence to meet an appropriate standard of proof. In the model, a proposition *p* does not have to be true to be included in knowledge. Even though the external truth condition is dropped however, there are still links with external reality. The acquisition of knowledge is seen as part of a procedure in which evidence is collected, tested, and measured against standards of proof.

The model thus supports a theory of knowledge that could be classified as pragmatic, in that it varies with the standards of proof appropriate for kinds of inquiry in a field of knowledge and with criteria for it to be considered to be evidence. According to the CAS model, a group of interacting agents is collecting data as part of a search for the truth of a matter they are collaboratively investigating. As they go along during the search process, they verify or falsify hypotheses by testing them against the data they have collected so far, at the same time as they are engaged in the process of collecting new data. As the search for knowledge continues, some hypotheses become better supported by the evidence, but at the same time, some of the hypotheses previously accepted have to be given up, because they are falsified by the new data that are streaming in. Depending on the type of investigation, for example it might be a scientific investigation or a legal inquiry, there will be an established proof standard that enables the investigation to determine whether a proposition can be accepted as proved or not (McBurney and Parsons 2001).

Such a pragmatic model of epistemic rationality is procedural, meaning that whether a proposition is accepted as knowledge at any given point depends on the standard of proof and the data that has been collected to that point. A proposition rightly said to be known to be true at a given point in the investigation could later on turn out to be proved to be false. Or at a particular point, the set of data collected at that point could justify two hypotheses, one of which is not consistent with the other. In this model, a particular proposition might rightly be classified as knowledge at one point in the investigation, whereas at a later point, the same proposition might turn out to be no longer classified as knowledge. In general, whether the proposition is rightly said to be knowledge or not depends on its rational acceptance, given the evidence then for it, as balanced against the evidence then against it, at that point in the investigation. In this pragmatic model, knowledge is not defined as justified true belief, or even as any kind of belief. It is based on the evidence collected at a given point in the investigation, on the kinds of arguments that can properly be used to justify a claim in that type of investigation, and on the standard of proof set for knowledge in that type of investigation. On this model, the strict barrier between discovery and verification of knowledge characteristic of older ways of thinking in analytical philosophy is no longer absolute.

Popper's theory of knowledge is procedural, in that he holds that scientific knowledge advances toward the truth by improving tentative theories through a process of error reduction achieved by criticism and testing. This procedure of conjecture and refutation begins with the formulation of a problem $P_1$ and proceeds from there to a theory TT that is the conjectured solution to the problem. The next stage is that of error elimination (EE) that consists, in Popper's words of a "severe critical examination of our conjecture", or of several competing conjectures, if we have them, and a critical discussion that comparatively evaluates the competing conjectures (Popper 1972, 164). Finally, $P_2$ is the problem situation as it emerges from the process of testing the first hypothesis. According to Popper (1972, 164), the whole procedure takes this form: $P_1 \rightarrow TT \rightarrow EE \rightarrow P_2$. This procedure repeats itself through successive refinements of the problem $P_1, P_2, \ldots, P_n$ so that progress can be gained in the movement towards finding the truth of the matter being discussed. On this approach, it is not a requirement for a proposition to be part of scientific knowledge that it be true. It is only required that it be accepted as true based on the evidence provided by testing and criticism, so that the procedure of scientific inquiry of which it is part is moving toward the truth. Popper (1963, 312) saw this procedure as a slow, steady and continuous movement of trial and error that proceeds by successive degrees of improvement. Although he accepted the idea that the task of science is to search for truth, he conceded that on his view of the scientific method we may never get to a hypothesis that is true, or know that it is true when we get it (1963, 229). He accepted a variant of an old view that our knowledge is fallible.

This way of viewing the issue turns it into a problem of formulating conditions for the closure of the inquiry procedure in which the collection and processing of evidence should take place. At the opening stage, an appropriate proof standard for that type of inquiry needs to be set, and then a proposition can be said to be proved as acceptable by the investigation when the pro evidence supporting the proposition minus the contra evidence, is sufficient to meet that standard. If the evidence supporting the ultimate proposition is strong enough so that the inquiry has reached its standard of proof at that point, then that proposition can be taken as known to be true based on the evidence for and against it that has been assembled and evaluated during the procedure. The degree of corroboration of a scientific theory, according to Popper (1972, 18), is determined by the critical discussion of the theory that has taken place, the degree of testability of the theory, the severity of the tests it has undergone, and the way it has stood up to these tests.

## 7.4 The Carneades Model of Inquiry

A dialogue system is a model of a sequence of exchanges in which two parties (or more) take turns making moves in an orderly manner engaging in speech activities like questioning, argumentation and explanation in a rule-governed environment, in an orderly way as a transaction between the two parties. Formal dialogues are abstract normative structures that may be used to model argumentation in real dialogues, for example parliamentary debates, or scientific investigations. On the CAS model, a formal dialogue is defined as an ordered 3-tuple $<O, A, C>$ where $O$ is the opening stage, $A$ is the argumentation stage, and $C$ is the closing stage (Gordon and Walton 2009, 244). Dialogue rules (protocols) define what types of moves are allowed and how each type of move can or must be responded to. Commitment rules determine when and how insertions and retractions take place (Walton and Krabbe 1995). Each party has an individual goal and the dialogue itself has a collective goal. The seven basic types of dialogue are persuasion dialogue, discovery, inquiry, negotiation dialogue, information-seeking dialogue, deliberation, and eristic dialogue (Walton and Krabbe 1995). In an inquiry dialogue, the collective goal is to prove a designated statement, or if it cannot be proved by the evidence collected, to prove that it cannot be proved. The best argument standard is typical for deliberation dialogue, whereas a higher standard like reasonable doubt is typical for inquiry dialogue. During the closing stage it is determined, according to the standard of proof set at the opening stage, which party has won or lost the dialogue.

The goal of the inquiry type of dialogue is to prove that a statement designated at the opening stage as the ultimate claim is true or false, or if neither of these findings can be proved, to prove that there is insufficient evidence to prove that it is true or false (Walton 1998, chapter 3). To say a dialogue is *cumulative* means that once a statement has been accepted as true at any point in the argumentation stage of the inquiry, that statement must remain true at every succeeding point in the inquiry through the argumentation stage and to the closing stage. The cumulative argumentation in an inquiry is modeled by the (Kripke 1965) semantics for intuitionistic logic. This model has a tree structure, where the nodes are taken to represent evidential situations at a given point in an investigation in which more evidence comes to be verified. It can never happen, however, that a proposition is falsified and has to be retracted. For this reason, modeling inquiry as strictly cumulative is often called foundationalism, a view not compatible with retraction of an evidence-based commitment when it has been falsified by new evidence.

To build a more realistic model of inquiry Black and Hunter (2007) built a formal dialogue system for use in medical domains where retraction is necessary because the database is typically incomplete, inconsistent, and has conditions of uncertainty. These conditions obtain in cases where many different health care professionals cooperate by sharing specialized knowledge in order to provide care for a patient. Black and Hunter (2007, 2) explore inquiry dialogues in which strict cumulativeness is not required. This type of system has to have rules for the retraction of commitments (Walton and Krabbe 1995).

The argumentation stage *A* of a dialogue is made up of a sequence of moves, where each move *M* is an ordered pair <*SpA*, *Con*>, where *A* is the content of the move and *SpA* is a speech act representing the type of move whereby *A* was put forward in *D*. For example there is a speech act for making a claim, or assertion as it can equivalently be called. The speaker can say 'I assert proposition *A*', and the commitment rule for assertions requires that proposition *A* be inserted into the speaker's commitment set. Generally there is a rule regarding burden of proof such that whenever a speaker puts forward a speech act of this sort, and the hearer challenges it, requiring the speaker to back up his claim with some evidence, the speaker must either provide the appropriate evidence or give up his claim. It is a problem in formal dialogue systems that this rule does not always apply to all assertions. Sometimes a participant may assert a statement hypothetically as a hypothesis, even though he can't presently prove it. However, if the speaker makes a move claiming that he knows proposition *A*, then he not only has to give evidence to back up this claim, but the evidence has to meet a standard of proof that is high enough to sustain a claim to knowledge. In dialogue systems, there is a way to distinguish between knowledge claims, and weaker kinds of claims that require less strong supporting arguments to back them up when they are challenged.

In an adequate model of this sort, knowledge should be defeasible in a way that allows for external evidence from reality to have some role in the procedure, and attainment of truth is not necessary for the procedure to decide whether a proposition is knowledge or not. Instead, what determines whether a proposition is knowledge is the weighing of the evidence for and against it, based on the collection of evidence that has been marshaled during the procedure. For the proposition to be knowledge, the evidence for it has to be stronger than the evidence against it, to a degree stipulated at the opening stage of the inquiry. This degree of strength that is required is called the standard of proof. The standard of proof needs to be high, in order to avoid the practical possibility of a later need to retract the proposition that was claimed to be known to be true.

In this model of defeasible knowledge, the product of the procedure can be called knowledge, and in the CAS model, the criteria used to judge something as knowledge are linked to the procedure that generates the knowledge as its end state. However, this model does not merely represent a "consensus-based approach", for several reasons. First, the reasoning has to be based on external evidence, so that claim to knowledge can be tested by using this external evidence. Such evidence can come in, for example, by observation, or by testing of a hypothesis. Second, if a proposition *p* is known to be true, it follows by defeasible logic that it must be accepted as true, unless it can be shown by additional evidence that it is false. In other words, through the argumentation scheme for the argument from ignorance, a proposition can be concluded to be known to be true provided it has not been proved to be false, subject to the additional assumption that the knowledge base is complete enough to warrant this inference. If the knowledge base is complete enough for the argument from ignorance to meet its standard of proof and go through as an acceptable defeasible argument, the appropriate conclusion can be drawn. The

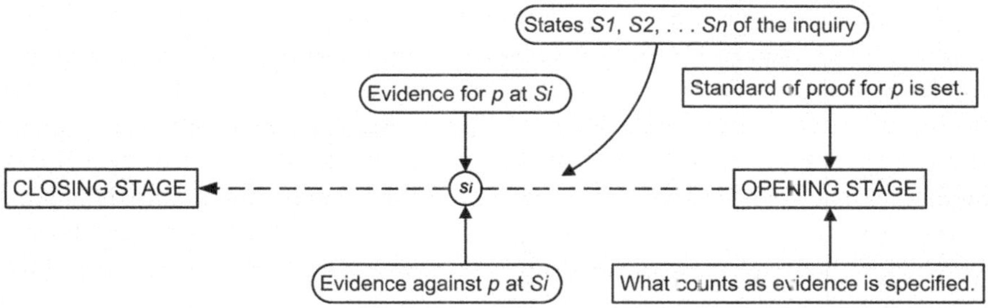


**Fig. 7.3** Procedure for evaluating a defeasible knowledge claim

inferential procedure that takes us from the evidence pro and contra to a knowledge claim for a proposition *p* to the conclusion that *p* is knowledge (or not) is shown in Fig. 7.3.

As shown in Fig. 7.3, as new evidence comes in, a claim to knowledge should be subject to testing by marshalling evidence both for and against it. As this process is underway, what is knowledge at a given point must yield to new knowledge, as the old knowledge is undercut or defeated by new evidence This part represents the progress of defeasible knowledge underneath shown by the dotted arrow in Fig. 7.3. As the process of accumulating knowledge is underway, objections and refutations will lead us to reject propositions that we formerly classified as knowledge. They really were knowledge at that time, but now they no longer are. The need for us to reject propositions that are shown to be false by the evidence that is coming in, based on rational argumentation standards appropriate for the inquiry, is required by the goal of the process itself, which is that of obtaining the truth, or at least coming as close to it as we can get, as well as avoiding falsehood, fallacies, dismissal of evidence, other faults of rational inquiry.

It can be argued that this pragmatic model of knowledge is more useful than the prevailing epistemological one, because it arguably shows better how the external standard should be applied to reality in an inquiry (McBurney and Parsons 2001).

It is not possible to set a single standard of proof for every scientific investigation. There is also the question of the conditions under which an inquiry should be reopened. From a fallibilist point of view, it is unrealistic to set a standard of beyond all doubt, and it is necessary even if one wants to set a very high standard, like that of beyond reasonable doubt, to leave open the possibility that the inquiry can be reopened for further scientific investigation bringing in new evidence. This assumption is based on the defeasibility of scientific knowledge, which is in turn based on falsifiability as a criterion of genuine scientific knowledge.

When Hannon (2014, 1127) tries to diagnose how Bonjour's representation of knowledge as infallible goes wrong, he suggests that this position demands too much precision, but adds that the difficult question to determine what the required nonconclusive level of justification should be in order to prove something is one to which he can provide no "pithy" answer. One of Bonjour's objections to the fallible conception of knowledge, the reader will recall, is that there is no apparent way to determine what the required level of justification should be for knowledge. Conee and Feldman (2004, 296) responded to this question by arguing that legal standards of proof can be adapted to other contexts as well. On their view, the beyond reasonable doubt standard used in criminal law can be applied to cases of everyday conversational argumentation outside the legal context by applying a comparable standard they call having strong reasons in support of a claim. However, on their version of fallibilism, the measure of this standard of proof should leave open exactly how strong an arguer's supporting evidence must be in order to qualify as sufficient for acceptance of her claim.

The procedure outlined in the model represented in Fig. 7.3 aims towards the truth by avoiding the errors revealed during the argumentation brought in by the evidence applied to the proposition claimed to be knowledge during the procedure. In an inquiry to assess knowledge, the goal is to prove that some designated proposition is true or false, or otherwise to determine that it cannot be proved to be true or false based on all the evidence that has been collected. The assumption is that enough evidence has been collected so that this conclusion can be established as meeting an appropriate standard of proof. The following four standards of proof used in CAS (Gordon and Walton 2009) can be used to give the reader an idea how appropriate proof standards can be set in the kind of argumentation procedure outlined in Fig. 7.1.

- Scintilla of Evidence (SE) is met if there is at least one applicable argument for a claim.
- Preponderance of the Evidence (PE) is met if SE is satisfied and the maximum weight assigned to an applicable *pro* argument (for the claim) is greater than the maximum weight of an applicable *con* argument (against the claim).
- Clear and Convincing Evidence (CCE), is met if PE is satisfied, the maximum weight of applicable *pro* arguments exceeds some threshold $\alpha$, and the difference between the maximum weight of the applicable *pro* arguments and the maximum weight of the applicable *con* arguments exceeds some threshold $\beta$.
- Beyond Reasonable Doubt (BRD) is met if CCE is satisfied and the maximum weight of the applicable con arguments is less than some threshold $\gamma$.

When I say that I know something, or say that it is knowledge, it should mean that I have strong enough evidence to support and to meet a standard of proof justifying my including it under the category of knowledge. To say that something is knowledge, it is important that the proposition claimed as knowledge be based on evidence of a kind that reaches a level where the proposition passes beyond the level of being accepted as true because it is based on evidence. Only when it is proved by a certain kind of evidence, that is sufficient for the discipline, or more generally the context in which the proposition was claimed, can something be properly said to be knowledge.

The standard has to be high enough in a scientific inquiry to minimize the possibility that the proposition accepted as true will later have to be retracted. On the model, however, since epistemic reasoning that results in knowledge is inherently defeasible, the possibility of retraction can never be excluded entirely. Even once the procedure is closed off, and the conclusion is accepted, there is always the possibility that it can be re-opened, should new evidence come to light.

The CAS model of inquiry makes sense of the defeasible notion of evidence-based knowledge that does not require the four epistemic reasoning principles set out in Sect. 7.1 as parts of the method for proving a proposition to be an item of knowledge.

## 7.5 Defeasible Logic

In the model, the statement '*p* is known to be true' does not deductively imply the statement '*p* is true'. But a comparable inference holds: '*p* is known to be true' defeasibly implies the statement '*p* is true'. To say that *p* defeasibly implies *q* is taken to mean that all else being equal, subject to exceptions, if *p* is true, then *q* is true. This defeasible relationship between knowledge and truth does imply a link with external reality. Hence the model does not entirely forsake external standards. Truth is not guaranteed to be produced by the procedure outlined in the model, but defeasible support for what should be classified as knowledge, based on the evidence, can be. The reason is that the arguments based on evidence that are used to support and attack a claim to knowledge are based on external reality. For example, they can be based on the scheme for argument from appearances. This form of argument, as shown in Sect. 7.4, is defeasible, but it is also based on reality as we know it, through our perception of it.

Defeasible logic (Nute 1994) is a rule-based non-monotonic formal system that models reasoning used to derive plausible conclusions from partial and sometimes conflicting information. A conclusion derived in such a system is only tentatively accepted, subject to new information that comes in later, requiring its retraction (Simari and Loui 1992). The basic units of the system are facts and rules. There are two kinds of rules, strict rules and defeasible rules. Facts are indisputable statements that are accepted as true within the confines of a discussion. Statements are denoted by letters, *A*, *B*, *C*, …., and so forth, using subscripts if we run out of letters. Strict rules are rules in the classical sense: whenever the premises are indisputable (e.g., facts) then so is the conclusion, e.g. 'Penguins are birds'. A strict rule has the form of a conditional, $A_1, A_2, A_n, \ldots, \rightarrow B$, where it is not possible for all the $A_i$ to be true and the *B* false. Defeasible rules are rules that can be defeated by contrary evidence, e.g. 'Birds fly'. A defeasible rule has the form of a conditional, $A_1, A_2, A_n, \ldots, \Rightarrow B$, where each of the $A_i$ is called a prerequisite, all the $A_i$ together are called the antecedent, and *B* is called the consequent. One source of defeat for the defeasible conditional is that it is open to exceptions, e.g. 'This bird is a penguin'. One rule can conflict with another. A priority relation defined over the set of rules that determines the relative strength of any two conflicting rules.

One purpose of defeasible logic is to resolve a conflict of opinions, but it can also be used to model epistemic reasoning where a knowledge base is incomplete, and hence where we have to reason on the basis of what is not known, as well as on the basis of what is known. In cases where there is some support for concluding *A* but also support for concluding ~*A*, defeasible logic determines which conclusion is drawn by using a priority relation. For example priority can be given to what is better known. If the support for *A* has priority over the support for ~*A*, the conclusion to accept *A* is drawn. Defeasible logic can also be used with temporal reasoning (Riveret et al. 2006). For example, a proposition known at one time may not be known at another time. A definite conclusion is a conclusion that cannot ever be retracted, even if new information comes in. A defeasible conclusion is only a tentative conclusion and might have to be retracted if new information comes in. In addition, defeasible logic is able to tell whether a conclusion is or is not provable.

It is possible to have four types of conclusions (Governatori 2008):

- Positive definite conclusions: meaning that the conclusion is provable using only facts and strict rules;
- Negative definite conclusions: meaning that it is not possible to prove the conclusion using only facts and strict rules;
- Positive defeasible conclusions: meaning that the conclusions can be defeasibly proved;
- Negative defeasible conclusions: meaning that one can show that the conclusion is not even defeasibly provable.

A defeasible conclusion *A* can be accepted if there is a rule whose conclusion is *A*, whose prerequisites are facts, and any stronger rule whose conclusion is ~*A* has prerequisites that fail to be derived.

The reasoning process can be explained in terms of argumentation. To prove a conclusion you have to carry out three steps (Governatori 2008).

1. Give an argument for the conclusion to be proved.
2. Consider all possible counter-arguments for the conclusion.
3. Defeat these counter-arguments by either showing that some premises in each of them do not hold, or defeat each of them by producing a counter-argument with a stronger argument supporting its conclusion.

Defeasible logic is most useful where there is a procedure that has the goal of proving or disproving some claim at issue that moves forward by bringing forward the pro and contra arguments with respect to the claim. A conclusion is proved as the outcome if there is an argument supporting it and all the arguments against it are defeated.

An important component of defeasible logic is the notion of a defeater (rebuttal) of an argument. A defeater might be thought to be a rule and a set of facts that proves a conclusion that is the opposite of the original argument. But this definition seems too simple, suggesting the following more complex definition. On this definition, a defeater is a counter-argument of three types directed to a prior argument that has already been put forward. It can be a counter-argument that shows that one of the prerequisites (premises) of the original argument does not hold. It can be a stronger argument that proves the opposite conclusion of the original argument. Or it can be an argument that challenges the inference from the premises to the conclusion.

Simari and Loui (1992), Verheij (1999, 115), and Walton (2002, 43) have put forward the proposal that many common argumentation schemes fit under a defeasible form of the deductive form of *modus ponens* that we are familiar with in deductive logic. The normal *modus ponens* form of argument is based on the material conditional binary constant $\rightarrow$ sometimes called strict implication. The variables $p$, $q$, $r$, ..., stand for propositions (statements).

Major Premise: $p \rightarrow q$
Minor Premise: $p$
Conclusion: $q$

This form of argument can be called strict *modus ponens* (SMP). In contrast, there is also a defeasible *modus ponens* having the following form, where the symbol => is a binary constant representing the defeasible conditional.

Major Premise: $p => q$
Minor Premise: $p$
Conclusion: $q$

This form of argument is called defeasible *modus ponens* (DMP) in (Walton 2002, 43).[2] To cite an example, the following argument arguably fits the form of DMP: if something is a bird and generally, but subject to exceptions, it flies; Tweety is a bird; therefore Tweety flies. This argument is the canonical example of defeasible reasoning used in computer science. Suppose we find out that Tweety has a broken wing that prevents him from flying, or that Tweety is a penguin, a type of bird that does not fly. If we find out that in the given case one of these characteristics fits Tweety, the original DMP argument defaults. The argument is best not seen as one that is deductively valid, and that still holds even if new information comes in showing that the argument no longer applies to the particular case in the way anticipated. Instead, it is better seen as an argument that holds only tentatively during an investigation, but that can fail to hold any longer if new evidence comes in that cites an exception to the rule specified in the major premise.

The current trend in applications of defeasible logic in artificial intelligence is to sanction a defeasible form of *modus ponens*, but not to sanction any form of *modus tollens* (Caminada 2008, 111). Examples of two systems of defeasible logic that follow this pattern are (Prakken and Sartor 1997) and (Reiter 1980). Caminada (2008) draws a distinction between epistemic reasoning, which is supposed to be based on an objective reality that can support a claim to knowledge, and other kinds of reasoning where contradictions represent soft conflicts that can be dealt with by prioritizing defeasible rules. On Caminada's view, *modus tollens* applies to defeasible epistemic reasoning, because it is characterized by hard conflicts. If the second proposition is inferred defeasibly from the first proposition and the second proposition exhibits a hard conflict so that it cannot be the case, it follows that the

[2]Verheij (1999, 115, 5) called this second form of inference *modus non excipiens*, arguing that it needs to be applied in cases where a general rule admits of exceptions.

first proposition cannot be the case either. However, the same inference principle does not work for soft conflicts, for example in legal and ethical reasoning, where dilemmas and conflicts of rulings can occur.

## 7.6 Reasoning from Absence of Knowledge

It is clear that defeasible logic is closely related to argumentation schemes of the kind that represent reasoning from knowledge and perception. Two motivating examples given by Nute (2001, 89) make some significant connections with such forms of epistemic reasoning. The first example [quoted below] is a typical case of the lack of knowledge argument, or argument from ignorance, as it is more often known.

> The absence of information can sometimes be a positive reason for believing something. Is there any milk in the refrigerator? We look and we do not see any milk. The failure to find evidence of milk in this case is a good reason to believe that there is no milk in the refrigerator.

The second example [quoted below] is a typical case of argument from appearance.

> For another example, I believe that there is a cat in front of me. I believe this because there appears to be a cat in front of me. That seems to be ample evidence. Of course, we can think of situations where I would be wrong. I might be hallucinating, or there might be a hologram of a cat, or there might be a mirror and the cat I think I see in front of me is actually behind me. But I have no reason to believe that I am hallucinating, and there is no evidence of a holographic projector or of a mirror. The absence of evidence that my perceptual circumstances are abnormal provides part of the justification for my belief that there is a cat in front of me.

This example is suggestive, not only in relation to traditional epistemological issues arising from skepticism, but also because part of the structure of the chain of argumentation is an instance of reasoning from absence of knowledge (RAK). In the field of argumentation studies, RAK is represented by the so-called argument from ignorance, traditionally taken to be a fallacious form of reasoning. However, recent studies have shown that non-fallacious uses of it are very common.

Indeed, this form of reasoning, called the closed world assumption (Bondarenko et al. 1993), means that all the information that there is to know or find is listed in the collection of information one already has. The closed world assumption is met if all the positive information in a database is listed, and therefore negative information is represented by default (Reiter 1980, 69). Reiter (1987, 150) offers the example of a database for an airline flight schedule. It would be too much information to include in such a database to list all flights and also all city pairs they do not connect. The closed world assumption tells us that if a positive flight connection between a pair of cities is not listed, the conclusion can be drawn that there is no flight connecting these two cities. This form of argument used in this sequence of knowledge-based reasoning implies that failure to find a proof has sanctioned an inference (Kakas and Toni 1999; Toni 2008). Such a use of the closed world assumption seems to make it equivalent to argument from ignorance, but before going further let's define argument from ignorance.

The argumentation scheme for argument from ignorance has two premises in which knowledge, or the absence of it, plays a reason-giving role (Walton 1996, 254).

*Lack of Knowledge Premise*: Proposition A is not known to be true (false).
*Conditional Premise*: If A were true (false), then A would be known to be true (false).
*Conclusion*: Therefore A is false (true).

The scheme for argument from ignorance looks to be the same form of reasoning as RAK, which in turn is the same kind of default reasoning expressed by the closed world assumption. The last sentence of Nute's example of an argument from appearance is case in point.

The conditions under which RAK is most typically fallacious can be formulated by distinguishing between two forms of reasoning. The fallacious reasoning takes the form $\sim Kp \Rightarrow \sim p$. Here there is a leap from the absence of knowledge to falsity without taking the conditional premise into account. The nonfallacious instances of this kind of reasoning take a different form:

$(\sim Kp \;\&\; (p \Rightarrow Kp)) \Rightarrow \sim p$. Once the depth of search is taken into account by the conditional premise, the inference now clearly has a *modus tollens* form.

Whether the conditional premise holds in a given case depends on how complete the knowledge base is in that case. For example, suppose the question asked is whether Guyana is a major rubber producer in South America, and the knowledge base we have about rubber producers in South America contains a lot of knowledge about this subject. If Guyana were a major producer, that knowledge would almost certainly be contained in the knowledge base. Suppose we look through the knowledge base, and the proposition 'Guyana is a major rubber producer' is not known to be true. We could then conclude, on the basis of an argument from ignorance, that Guyana is not a major rubber producer. Thus argument from ignorance, or argument from absence of evidence as it might less prejudicially be called, is often reasonable even though we must be careful to realize that it needs to depend on what is known as well as what is not known.

Since RAK has the *modus tollens* form, this takes us back to the issue of whether *modus tollens* should be taken to hold for epistemic reasoning. This sequence of reasoning has the following *modus tollens* form: if $p$ then $q$; $\sim q$; therefore $\sim p$. This example seems to be convincing (Caminada 2004, 87), but other authors do not accept defeasible contraposition for *modus tollens*. Brewka (1989) offers this counterexample: men usually do not have beards, but this does not mean that if someone does have a beard, it's usually not a man. In this example, we have the statement that if a person is a man then he usually does not have a beard. The contraposition of the sentence will be the statement that if a person does have a beard then usually that person is not a man. If we had the statement that this person has a beard, and we accept the contraposition of defeasible rules, we can derive the statement that this person is not a man. This conclusion seems wrong. Hence we have to realize that defeasible rules are different from strict rules based on deductive logic. In the case of a strict rule, we know that whenever the antecedent holds the consequent also holds. Therefore we know that when the consequent does not hold we can be sure that the antecedent does not hold either. Defeasible rules are quite different. A defeasible rule only says that if you know that the antecedent holds you have some inclination to believe that the consequent holds. Hence, as Brewka's example shows, the relationship between the negated consequent and the negated antecedent could be very different.

*Modus tollens* is closely related to contraposition. Contraposition for defeasible implication is the rule of inference '$(p => q) \Leftrightarrow (\sim q => \sim p)$', where $\Leftrightarrow$ stands for mutual defeasible implication, $(p => q)$ & $(q => p)$. Mutual defeasible implication is a form of equivalence for defeasible reasoning, enabling us to replace a formula wherever it occurs with a defeasibly equivalent formula. Defeasible *modus tollens* is the inference from premises $p => q$ and $\sim q$ to the conclusion $\sim p$. If we assume that defeasible *modus ponens* holds, and as well that defeasible contraposition holds, defeasible *modus tollens* follows. *Modus ponens* is this form of inference:

$p => q$
$p$
Therefore $q$

By contraposition we can replace the first premise with $\sim q => \sim p$. Then by double negation $(p \Leftrightarrow \sim\sim p)$, which we assume holds, we can change the second premise to $\sim\sim p$, and we can change the conclusion to $\sim\sim q$. The resulting inference looks like this.

$\sim q => \sim p$
$\sim\sim p$
Therefore $\sim\sim q$

This inference is clearly a species of defeasible *modus tollens*. In other words, if double negation, defeasible *modus ponens* and defeasible contraposition hold, so does defeasible *modus tollens*.

In the next section, we will show that there are some distinctions to be made between the closed world assumption and argument from ignorance. To sum up what we have seen so far, ignorance (lack of knowledge) is as important as knowledge for understanding epistemic reasoning, and the various forms of reasoning used in transitions from ignorance to knowledge need to be understood and modeled in any practically realistic theory of knowledge. Although the models of inquiry of Peirce and Popper postulate that verisimilitude is an important property of the successful marshaling of evidence in this kind of procedure, it needs to be pointed out that the property of moving away from ignorance is equally important in judging the success of the inquiry as a whole. Especially as stressed by Popper, inquiry moves forward through a process of rational criticism that reveals errors and fallacies in arguments and hypotheses that were previously accepted, but are now revealed as simplistic theories or even superstitions based on ignorance. In addition to moving toward the truth, a successful inquiry also moves away from falsehood and error.

## 7.7 Defeasible Knowledge, Evidence and Lack of Evidence

A perennial problem for the theory of defeasible knowledge concerns statements made in everyday conversational argumentation where somebody says 'I know this proposition is true' as opposed to saying 'I think it is true'. because it is so obvious that there can be no doubt about it. For example, if I look at my two hands in front of me and say "I see two hands in front of my face", I can say I know that there are two hands in front of my face, because I am confident that no amount of new evidence is ever going to make this proposition false. When I see that this proposition is true, it can be taken to mean that I am so confident that it is true that there can be no doubt about it, and therefore I know it is true. The fact is immediately evident. So it needs no evidence, of the kind required by the new model of defeasible knowledge, to justify it.

The speaker in Nute's example says that he believes there is a cat in front of him, and the reason he gives for this belief is that he believes there appears to be a cat in front of him. But when we come to examine how his beliefs can be justified, and we analyze it carefully, it can be seen to be based on an implicit premise. He needs to base his view on evidence, if he were to be challenged to support by someone who is skeptical. As we will show below using the new defeasible model of knowledge, although the speaker does not say so explicitly, this belief is also based on lack of knowledge. As noted in the earlier discussion of the example in Sect. 7.2 it can be well represented as an instance of the argument from ignorance, or reasoning from absence of knowledge (RAK).

The first part of the argumentation in Nute's example is represented using the CAS model in Fig. 7.4. On the left there is a conclusion that there is a cat in front of me. In the box at the top is the evidence. This evidence is the proposition that there appears to be a cat in front of me. This argument is an instance of the scheme called argument from appearance. As noted in Sect. 7.2, Pollock saw this kind of reasoning as based on his defeasible perception rule. It is represented in the argument node as +AP, the argumentation scheme for argument from perception.

The two premises shown in the white boxes in Fig. 7.4 are modeled in CAS as exceptions. An exception represents a kind of critical question that defeats the given argument if and only if there is evidence to back it up. For example if there were evidence that I might be hallucinating, that would undercut the argument from the premise that there appears to be a cat in front of me to the conclusion that there is a cat in front of me.

Similarly if there is evidence that I might be seeing a hologram, that would undercut the argument that there appears to be a cat in front of me to the conclusion that there is a cat in front of me. But since at the present state, neither of the

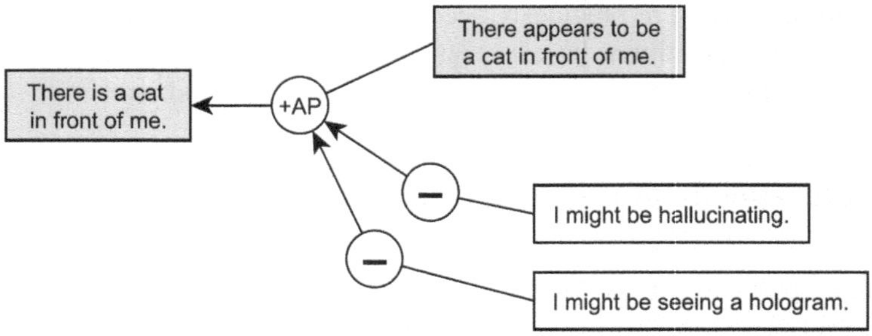


**Fig. 7.4** First step in the CAS model of the cat example

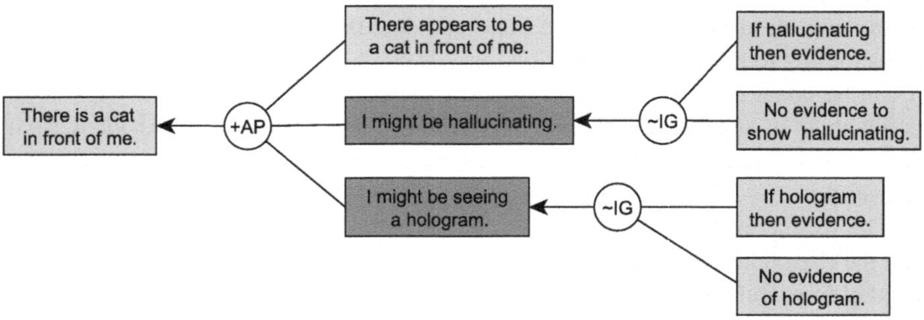


**Fig. 7.5** Second step in the CAS model of the cat example

exceptions obtains, and the since the premise of the argument from perception holds, so does the conclusion that there is a cat in front of me.

Next, look at the text boxes on the right side of Fig. 7.5. Each of the two arguments displayed on the right is an RAK argument, fitting the argumentation scheme for the argument from ignorance, as shown by the +IG notation in the nodes. Each of these two arguments is grey inside the text boxes representing their premises. This means that these premises have been accepted. Also, the circles representing each of these two arguments are shown with a grey background, showing that they fit the scheme for argument from lack of evidence (argument from ignorance). Also, each scheme name has a plus sign in from of it. This indicates that each of the arguments is a pro argument that supports the conclusion that it leads to. Also, each of the two statements ‘I might be hallucinating’ and I might be seeing a hologram’ is shown in a darker than normal grey box. This indicates that both statements have been rejected. If either statement had been accepted, the conclusion shown at the right would not be accepted. It would be shown in a white box. But now that both exceptions have been excluded, the ultimate conclusion is shown as accepted, just as in Fig. 7.4

What is shown by Fig. 7.5 is that the evidence standing behind two exceptions would defeat the original defeasible argument. So what is shown is that the absence of the evidence required to defeat the original argument is actually a reason that shows why it is not defeated. And these evidential conditions show that I am justified in believing that there is a cat in front of me. Given the strength of the original argument from appearances, taken along with the absence of any reason to doubt the veracity of these appearances, I am justified, on balance, in saying that I know there is a cat in front of me. Even though this knowledge claim is defeasible, the evidence displayed in Fig. 7.4, along with the absence of evidence included in Fig. 7.5 as part of the evidential situation, justifies the claim that there is a cat in front of me so strongly that I can justifiably say that I know there is a cat in front of me.

When using CAS to represent an argument, standards of proof have to be inserted for all the propositions that function as premises and conclusions in the argument. In order to reduce the complexities of modeling the example, standards of proof have not been inserted. All that has been represented in the diagram is the structure of the argumentation, and whether each proposition that is a premise or conclusion is accepted or rejected. When using the CAS graphical user interface, the user has to insert a standard of proof, like the preponderance of evidence standard for example, meaning that the evidence pro the claim has to be stronger than the evidence contra the claim. The user is also asked to indicate whether each of the premises in the chain of argumentation has been accepted, rejected, questioned or stated. Ordinary premises, for example are stated, and therefore initially appear in a box containing no color fill or mark. But once such a premise has been accepted, a checkmark appears in the box containing it. All this information is inserted by the user into the CAS menu. Once the status of all the premises and conclusions in the chain of argumentation leading to the ultimate conclusion has been indicated, CAS automatically indicates the status of the ultimate conclusion, depending of course on what the standard of proof is.

Finally in this section there needs to be a more carefully drawn distinction made between the argument from ignorance and the closed world assumption. It can be observed that the closed world assumption does not work well in knowledge bases that include sentences from classical logic. Consider a knowledge base that contains the disjunction {*A* v *B*}. Since neither *A* nor *B* can be derived from {*A* v *B*}, using the closed world assumption it is possible to derive both the negation of *A* and the negation of *B*. From that, using the rule of disjunctive syllogism in classical logic, both *A* and *B* can be derived, making the database inconsistent. This result shows that using classical logic along with the closed world assumption is problematic in a formal system of knowledge inquiry. This result suggests that a careful distinction needs to be drawn between how RAK and the closed world assumption are applied when modeling the structure of inquiry. As a hypothesis we propose here that one way to deal with the problem would be to only apply the closed world assumption at the closing stage of the inquiry, and only apply RAK during the argumentation stage. Typically the argument from ignorance works as a device for shifting burden of proof from one side to the other during this sequence of speech acts in the argumentation stage when one party makes an assertion the other party requests that the other party give some evidence to support her assertion. This sort of argumentation exchange is typically the kind of case in which the argument from ignorance poses a problem. On the other hand, the closed world assumption is a vitally important device for marking the point when the argumentation stage should be closed off so that the arguments on both sides can be evaluated to determine which side meets that standard of proof.

## 7.8 Objections and Replies

In this section we revisit the conflict between the two views of reasoning about knowledge described in Sect. 7.1. We need to better understand how either trying to maintain or refute this view makes for a philosophical difficulty, and puts us at odds with ordinary language. We often refer to the contents of the various scientific disciplines as being knowledge of the kind that we possess. However, it seems that these sets of propositions are not really knowledge at all, in the sense required by the four epistemological principles stated in Sect. 7.1. The reason is that we cannot *know* that the propositions established in the various scientific disciplines are true, at least if we mean by 'know' that we can prove them by such a high standard of proof that there remains no possibility at all, even a logical possibility, that they will be retracted and withdrawn as knowledge at some time in the future. This view has the unfortunate consequence that scientific knowledge is not defeasible, and that is, as we have seen, in conflict with even a weak form of fallibilism. This view represents one horn of a dilemma. The other horn is to take the fallibility approach and embrace the claim that these sets of propositions current in the various scientific disciplines legitimately qualify as being knowledge in a different sense of the word. This fallibilistic view also has a consequence that does not square very well with ways we commonly speak about knowledge. Suppose we have a proposition that is presently accepted as part of established scientific knowledge, but new scientific results show that there is evidence against it, leading the scientists in the field to reject it. On the CAS model of the inquiry, we can describe the situation by saying that this proposition was formerly knowledge, but is no longer knowledge. To many, it would appear that this way of speaking is not right. They would say that it is much more natural to describe the situation by saying that we thought this proposition was knowledge, but then we found out it wasn't really knowledge after all.

Although there are the beginnings of a shift away from the traditional epistemological view of knowledge represented by the four principles stated in Sect. 7.1 towards some form of fallibilism, neither view is philosophically unproblematic. The conflict between the two views is one of those perennial philosophical problems that will most likely always be with us. So far, the position represented by the four principles is the most widely accepted view in current epistemology. However, the fallibilistic view is a very old one, and can claim two well-known recent philosophers as supporters, Peirce and Popper.

Knowledge statements in everyday language assertions are often ambiguous. A knowledge statement could mean that I am claiming that a proposition is scientific knowledge, or it could mean merely that I am saying I am personally very confident about its being true, independently of whether I have good evidence that it can be taken as scientific knowledge. Another tricky aspect is the shift between the abstract noun knowledge and the verb 'know', where the latter may have a much stronger suggestion of personal conviction or belief. The CAS model of the inquiry postulates an orderly procedure in which a knowledge claim is evaluated by evidence that is collected and tested. But in philosophical discussions of its applicability, we always seem to come back to the same old problem of how it fits with the ways we ordinarily speak about knowledge. What happens, for example in the history of science where something was taken as knowledge at one point, but later a new theory was developed or some new finding was introduced that defeated this claim to knowledge? From the defeasible knowledge inquiry viewpoint, it was really knowledge at the earlier point, even though it was subsequently defeated so that at the next point some other proposition that was inconsistent with the first one now came to be taken as knowledge. This view seems paradoxical to some. How can it really have been knowledge before a given point if it was defeated after that point? Surely it is more natural to say that it wasn't really knowledge after all. It only seemed to be knowledge at that time, but at the later time it can no longer be said to be knowledge.

On this objection there is an alternative description of the situation which is better and removes the inconsistency between saying that something both is and is not knowledge. On this alternative description, we were justified in saying that the proposition in question was knowledge at the earlier point, but that doesn't mean that it really was knowledge. It only means that we were justified in believing it to be knowledge at that point, even though later on it turned out that it was not really knowledge after all. On this alternative view, a proposition may be justifiably believed to be knowledge at a particular point as an investigation proceeds, but the claim that this proposition is knowledge may subsequently be defeated when the proposition is falsified by new evidence. According to this theory, the proper description of the situation is that this proposition was not knowledge at the earlier point in the investigation, even though it was justifiably believed to be knowledge at that point, based on the evidence available at the time.

The CAS model of the inquiry embraces the assumption that knowledge really is defeasible. It is not only saying that claims to knowledge are defeasible, or that what we are justified in believing to be knowledge is defeasible. It rejects the assumption that knowledge always implies truth, because that would take with it the consequence that anything proven false could never have really been knowledge at some earlier point in an investigation, even though we were previously justified in accepting it as knowledge. The CAS model of the inquiry adopts the view that what is or is not knowledge can change over time. In particular, it allows that something that was knowledge at an earlier time can cease to be knowledge at a later time. The competing approach does not allow for this possibility. Once something is knowledge, it must always remain knowledge forever, during an infinite inquiry, as Peirce showed.

One possibility is that the two approaches model different kinds of knowledge. For example the truth-implying notion of knowledge may best model mathematical epistemic reasoning, whereas the defeasible knowledge approach best models epistemic reasoning in the experimental sciences. However, Peirce even extended fallibilism to mathematical knowledge. He asked if you would bet your life against a penny on the truth of some observational or mathematical statement that you do not in fact doubt. We may be hesitant about observational statements in this regard, but there are reasons for extending this hesitancy to mathematical statements as well. Even the greatest mathematicians, he observed, are susceptible to making a small arithmetical mistake because of a little lapse of attention. He concluded that no rational person would make these kinds of bets on the truth of mathematical statements because "you could not go on making very many millions of such bets before you would lose!" (Peirce 1931, 1.150).

Some might think that the fallibilistic view of reasoning about knowledge advocated in this chapter implies a pernicious relativism that allows us to say that we can be taken to know all kinds of propositions that are not true. In reply to this objection, it needs to be stated that the inquiry procedure is evidence-based and requires the principle of the falsifiability of knowledge claims. On this model, if a proposition is found to be false, based on sufficient evidence to meet the appropriate standard of proof to support this finding, it has to be retracted. To make this view explicit, some clarification of its logical implications are helpful.

If we find out that a proposition is false, then we cannot say that it is known to be true. Indeed, if we find out if it is false, by means of some evidence, but before that we had thought it was true, then we have to give up the assumption that it is known to be true. Essentially, this statement represents the principle of falsifiability of scientific knowledge proposed by Popper (1963). But it does not follow from this principle of falsifiability that if a proposition is known to be true, then it is true. Even though a proposition is known to be true, it doesn't follow necessarily that it is true. In fact, in order for the principle of falsifiability to be tenable, the notion that knowledge implies truth has to be given up. For even though a proposition is part of scientific knowledge, according to the principle of falsifiability, all genuine scientific knowledge must be falsifiable. That is, the reasoning on which it rests must be defeasible.

Consider once again Pollock's example of seeing a red light. Or for that matter, take any statement of commonsense knowledge like G.E. Moore's example, 'I see a hand in front of my face'. I may be very confident that I am seeing a red light, or that I am seeing a hand in front of my face, so that I am entitled to claim in everyday conversational discourse that I know I see a red light, or that I know I see a hand in front of my face. It depends on what the appropriate standard of proof is for the situation in which I am seeing a red light or seeing hand in front of my face, and what the consequences of being wrong might be. But as Pollock noted, if the room is illuminated by red light, since everything looks red when illuminated by red light, the light I am seeing may not be red. For all the various reasons advanced by skeptics since ancient times, as indicated in Sect. 7.1, even though I might be very confident that I am seeing a hand in front of my face, so much so that I can even say that I know I see a hand there, it does not follow by deductive necessity that the light is red, or that the hand is there. The reason is that, although it may seem very unlikely, the possibility is there that I am mistaken.

As shown in Sect. 7.1, Rescher, outlining the traditional epistemological view of knowledge, wrote that holding that the linkage between knowledge and truth is merely contingent does violence to the way we use the term 'knowledge' in everyday discourse. When you make a knowledge claim, you are claiming that a particular proposition is true. If I say that I know this particular proposition is true, it follows that I am claiming that the proposition is true. But as shown in Sect. 7.1, this observation does not show that knowledge deductively implies truth. It does not mean that if you know a proposition, it has to be true. It does not follow that the proposition has to be true. It only follows that the person holds it to be true. On the CAS model, what follows is not truth but acceptance: if a person says that he knows that a proposition is the case, it follows that he must be taken to accept this proposition. What does not follow is that the proposition itself must actually be true, in a sense that it can never be rejected as false once the inquiry has proceeded further.

## 7.9 The Fallibilistic Conception of Defeasible Knowledge

Hannon (2014) proposed that the central purpose of knowledge is to "flag reliable informants", and that this purpose can be achieved by a level of justification that is less than fully conclusive. Hannon (2014, 1128) proposes what he calls a reliable informant standard for knowledge. According to this standard, the level of justification needed for knowledge is that which puts an agent possessing knowledge in a "strong enough position" to fittingly serve as a reliable source of information for a community of knowers that has "diverse projects, purposes and interests". On this fallibilistic theory (Hannon, 2014, 1129), for this purpose we have a need to identify individuals who are reliable as sources from which knowledge can be extracted (and used), the concept of knowledge derives from "our need to identify reliable informants". This theory assumes that we all need reliable information to guide our actions, and for this purpose we need a shared pool of information that can be transferred between us so that it can become accessible as shared knowledge of the kind required. Therefore, there is a practical need to identify informants who have knowledge, and to access the quality of what they claim to be knowledge. The case studies of arguments from expert opinion carried out in Chaps. 4 and 5 of this book show the necessity of adopting such a fallibilistic conception of knowledge if we are to move ahead with the project of combining the concepts of argument, explanation, evidence and knowledge into a theoretically and practically viable argumentation model.

This disagreement between Bonjour and Hannon, as noted in Sect. 7.1, turns on the meanings of the term 'conclusive' and 'justification' as these terms are used in traditional epistemology and philosophy. In this book we have used different terms. First let's consider the term 'conclusive'. Stemming from the field of artificial intelligence, as shown in this chapter above, a distinction has been drawn between monotonic reasoning, associated with deductive logic, and nonmonotonic reasoning, of the kind associated with defeasible logic. A deductive inference can be accepted as a conclusive proof of its conclusion, provided its premises are not subject to challenge or critical questioning. You can only attack such a conclusive argument by attacking the conclusion or attacking one of its premises. The defeasible inference can be attacked in the above two ways, but also by attacking the inferential link joining the premises to the conclusion. For example, it can be attacked by arguing that there is an exception to the rule on which one of the premises is based. This form of attack is what Pollock called an undercutter.

Next let's consider the term 'justification'. In the framework of this book, the term 'justification' simply refers to a pro argument used to support the claim at issue, as opposed to a con argument used to attack the claim. Moreover, according to the evidence-based theory of argumentation advocated in this book, 'justification' could also refer to a pro-argument based on evidence used to support a claim. In this book it has been shown that there is at least one formal and computational model developed in artificial intelligence, namely CAS, that can not only bring these concepts together in a defeasible logic framework, but can also apply the framework to the problem of analyzing and evaluating arguments from expert opinion. Of course, it can also be applied to modeling all kinds of other arguments as well, as shown in the book.

By linking knowledge to an orderly process of inquiry, and by recognizing the role that evidence plays in that process, the model represents knowledge as defeasible. The main characteristics of the new model of defeasible knowledge can be summarized as follows.

1. Knowledge is the result of a process of inquiry in which existing knowledge can continue to be tested, and is subject to retraction. Knowledge must not only be undefeated at present, but must be able to answer new objections, and to survive testing as new evidence comes in.
2. Knowledge bases can be incomplete and even inconsistent during the procedure where a claim to knowledge is being investigated, but it should be a requirement of knowledge of the kind accepted at the final stage in the defeasible model that the knowledge be consistent.
3. The reasoning on which knowledge is based is defeasible rather than deductively valid. As such, (a) certainty beyond all doubt is an inappropriate standard for knowledge, and (b) knowledge claims must be retractable under the right sorts of circumstances.
4. Because the correction that comes in from the evidence supporting the pro and contra arguments is based on perception of an external reality, there is no need to require an external standard of truth for a proposition to be accepted (or rejected) as knowledge.
5. The veracity condition $\mathrm{K}p \rightarrow p$ is replaced with the weaker assumption $\mathrm{K}p \Rightarrow p$.
6. Knowledge bases are not closed under deductive implication. Nor are they closed under defeasible implication. The assumption $\mathrm{K}(p \Rightarrow q) \Rightarrow [\mathrm{K}p \Rightarrow \mathrm{K}q]$ fails to hold.
7. Iteration for defeasible implication $\mathrm{K}p \Rightarrow \mathrm{KK}p$ fails to hold.

8. Whether or not a proposition is rightly classified as knowledge or not depends on evidence of the right kind appropriate for the investigation, and the standard of proof set for the investigation.

The model maintains some but not all of the elements of a justified true belief analysis. It maintains the element of justification, but models justification using defeasible logic. Defeasible logic admits both of strict deductive implication and defeasible implication, but on this model it structures the process of evaluation of knowledge claims using defeasible implication. However, it does not entirely exclude the use of deductive implication in some instances.

## 7.10 Conclusions

It is concluded that, as opposed to the way of defining knowledge as a species of true belief, the model provides a coherent and defensible model of knowledge as a set of propositions based defeasibly on evidence and supported to a specified standard of proof. The specified standard can be set sufficiently high to distinguish between propositions that can rightly be said to be knowledge versus propositions that can be reasonably accepted as based on evidence, but where the evidence is not so strong that we should call the proposition knowledge. An important implication of the new model is that it puts much more of an emphasis on the notion of evidence than one finds in traditional theories of knowledge in philosophy. Evidence, on this model, is based on logical reasoning and on appearances (perceptions) that fit in with other appearances in a consistent manner, that can be tested, and that give reasons to support or refute a claim.

According to the requirements of the model, a proposition may rightly be said to be classifiable as scientific knowledge if it is supported by evidence of the kind used in a particular scientific discipline to the standard of proof appropriate for what counts as knowledge and what does not. A leading feature of the model is that it does not require that for a proposition to be included in knowledge, it must be true. However, it does require that in order to be classified as knowledge, a proposition must be based on input that comes from an external reality as evidential data. It is presumed that this evidential data comes from external reality and that the knowledge resting on it is falsifiable. Hence on this new view, even though knowledge does not require an external criterion of truth, it is subject to support and refutation by evidence that can be tested and that comes from external reality. The model allows that knowledge claims that were formerly accepted can be defeated as new evidence comes to light. It is implied by the model that a standard of proving beyond doubt is not appropriate for claims to knowledge. The model is a doubly dynamic one whereby knowledge is not only continually being added to, but is subject to retraction. In the model, known propositions, even properly proved ones, can be retracted as new evidence is acquired.

The model of how knowledge is processed in an inquiry has been made as simple as possible in order to illustrate its central features, but further research would be useful to extend it. It has mainly been applied to representing scientific knowledge, but it also applies to modeling how a detective conducts an inquiry using everyday conversational reasoning. The paradigm examples are the Study in Scarlet case presented in Chap. 1 and the forensic evidence brought together in the Leonardo da Vinci case studied in Chap. 5.

The model departs most notably from the justified true belief analysis in its rejection of the external truth requirement. The model does not require that there is an agent who believes that the proposition in question is true. Indeed, the model, at least in the simplest form outlined here, does not require either the notion of the agent or the notion of belief, although it represents inquiry as a collaborative procedure undertaken by a group. The model requires weighing of evidence within a procedure in which a knowledge claim can be either accepted or rejected.

This chapter showed how knowledge needs to be redefined as being the outcome of a procedure of rational inquiry that leads to defeasible knowledge of the kind that is indefinitely open to falsification by new evidence that comes in through scientific investigations and the continuing advance of knowledge. This chapter has presented a model of scientific knowledge from the internal point of view of the scientific investigators themselves as they work together to produce results that can be proved by the standards appropriate for a field and thereby find new knowledge. But it needs to be recognized that scientists have an obligation not only to carry out this research by the standards they set for themselves, but also to make the findings of it available for those, including other scientists, who can make use of them in their investigations and deliberations.

The first six chapters of this book have been mainly concerned with an external point of view of a wider audience, including other scientists and those of us who depend on scientific research to make evidence-based decisions on political policies and personal conduct. From this external point of view, the problem is how to in interpret findings based on scientific research, and weigh them against other evidence, including the findings of scientific research efforts that have apparently come to a different conclusion. The first six chapters build on AI systems to show how this kind of argumentation can be identified, analyzed and evaluated. But this whole enterprise would not be possible without adopting the view of knowledge that accommodates the possibility that knowledge can be revised, so that a proposition that really is known to be true can later on be found to be false or unacceptable, and therefore replaced by new knowledge. This evidential theory of knowledge-based reasoning, in which a knowledge base is continually updated, provides the theoretical framework that enables the problems posed in the first six chapters of the book to be solved.

# References


Bex, F., H. Prakken, C. Reed, and D. Walton. 2003. Towards a formal account of reasoning about evidence: Argument schemes and generalizations. *Artificial Intelligence and Law* 11(2–3): 125–165.

Black, E., and A. Hunter. 2007. A generative inquiry dialogue system, In *Sixth international joint conference on autonomous agents and multi-agent systems*, ed. M. Huhns and O. Shehory, 1010–1017.

Bondarenko, A., F. Toni. and R.A. Kowalski. 1993. An assumption-based framework for non-monotonic reasoning, In *2nd international workshop on logic programming and non-monotonic reasoning*, ed. L.M. Pereira and A. Nerode, 171–189.

Bonjour, L. 2010. The myth of knowledge. *Philosophical Perspectives* 24(1): 57–83.

Brewka, G. 1989. *Nonmonotonic reasoning: From theoretical foundations towards efficient computation*. PhD thesis, University of Hamburg.

Caminada, M. 2004. *For the sake of argument: Explorations into argument-based reasoning*. PhD thesis, Free University of Amsterdam. http://icr.uni.lu/~martinc/publications/thesis.pdf.

Caminada, M. 2008. On the issue of contraposition of defeasible rules. In *Computational models of argument: Proceedings of COMMA 2008*, ed. P. Besnard, S. Doutre, and A. Hunter, 109–115. Amsterdam: Ios Press.

Conee, E., and R. Feldman. 2004. *Evidentialism: Essays in epistemology*. Oxford: Oxford University Press.

Cooke, E. 2006. *Peirce's pragmatic theory of inquiry: Fallibilism and indeterminacy*. London: Continuum.

Gordon, T.F., and D. Walton. 2009. Proof burdens and standards. In *Argumentation and artificial intelligence*, ed. Iyad Rahwan and Guillermo Simari, 239–260. Berlin: Springer.

Governatori, G. 2008. *Defeasible logic*, http://defeasible.org.

Hannon, M. 2014. Fallibilism and the value of knowledge. *Synthese* 191(6): 1119–1146.

Kakas, A., and F. Toni. 1999. Computing argumentation in logic programming. *Journal of Logic and Computation* 9(4): 515–562.

Kripke, S. 1965. Semantical analysis of intuitionistic logic I. In *Formal systems and recursive functions*, ed. J.N. Crossley and Dummet Michael, 92–113. Amsterdam: North-Holland.

Lumer, C. 2005a. Introduction: The epistemological approach to argumentation – A map. *Informal Logic* 25(3): 189–212.

Lumer, C. 2005b. The epistemological theory of argument: How and why? *Informal Logic* 25(3): 213–243.

McBurney, P., and S. Parsons. 2001. Representing epistemic uncertainty by means of dialectical argumentation. *Annals of Mathematics and Artificial Intelligence* 32(1–4): 125–169.

Misak, C. 1987. Peirce, Levi and the aims of inquiry. *Philosophy of Science* 54(2): 256–265.

Nute, D. 1994. Defeasible logic. In *Handbook of logic in artificial intelligence and logic programming*, Nonmonotonic reasoning and uncertain reasoning, vol. 3, 353–395. Oxford: Oxford University Press.

Nute, D. 2001. Defeasible logic: Theory, implementation, and applications. In *Proceedings of INAP 2001, 14th international conference on applications of prolog*, 87–114. Tokyo: IF Computer Japan.

Peirce, C.S. 1931. *Collected papers*, ed. C. Hartshorne and P. Weiss, Cambridge: Harvard University Press.

Peirce, C.S. 1984. *Writings of Charles S. Peirce*, vol. 2, ed. E. C. Moore, Bloomington: Indiana University Press.

Pollock, J.L. 1995. *Cognitive carpentry*. Cambridge, MA: The MIT Press.

Popper, K. 1963. *Conjectures and refutations: The growth of scientific knowledge*. London: Routledge.

Popper, K. 1972. *Objective knowledge: An evolutionary approach*. Oxford: Oxford University Press.

Prakken, H. 2003. Logical dialectics: The missing link between deductivism and pragma-dialectics. In *Proceedings of the fifth conference of the international society for the study of argumentation*, ed. Frans H. van Eemeren et al., 857–860. Amsterdam: SicSat.
Prakken, H., and G. Sartor. 1997. Argument-based extended logic programming with defeasible priorities. *Journal of Applied Non-classical Logics* 7(1–2): 25–75.
Reiter, R. 1980. A logic for default reasoning. *Artificial Intelligence* 13(1–2): 81–132.
Reiter, R. 1987. Nonmonotonic reasoning. *Annual Review of Computer Science* 2: 147–186.
Rescher, N. 2003. *Epistemology: An introduction to the theory of knowledge*. Albany: Sate University of New York Press.
Rescher, N. 2005. *Epistemic logic: A survey of the logic of knowledge*. Pittsburgh: University of Pittsburgh Press.
Riveret, R., G. Governatori, and A. Rotolo. 2006. Argumentation semantics for temporal defeasible logic. In *Third European starting AI researcher symposium (STAIRS 2006) Riva del Garda*, Frontiers in artificial intelligence and applications, vol. 42, ed. L. Penserini, P. Peppas, and A. Perini, 267–268. Amsterdam: Ios Press.
Simari, G., and R. Loui. 1992. A mathematical treatment of defeasible reasoning and its implementation. *Artificial Intelligence* 2(3): 125–157.
Steup, M. 2010. The analysis of knowledge. *Stanford encyclopedia of philosophy*.http://plato.stanford.edu/entries/knowledge-analysis/. Accessed 18 Oct 2010.
Thorsrud, H. 2002. Cicero on his academic predecessors: The fallibilism of Arcesilaus and Carneades. *Journal of the History of Philosophy* 40(1): 1–18.
Toni, F. 2008. Assumption-based argumentation for epistemic and practical reasoning. In *Computable models of the law: Languages, dialogues, games, ontologies*, ed. G. Sartor et al., 185–202. Berlin: Springer.
Verheij, B. 1999. Logic, context and valid inference. In *Legal knowledge based systems. JURIX 1999*, ed. H.J. van den Herik et al., 109–121. Nijmegen: Gerard Noodt Instituut.
Walton, D. 1996. *Argumentation schemes for presumptive reasoning*. Mahwah: Lawrence Erlbaum Publishers.
Walton, D. 1998. *The new dialectic: Conversational contexts of argument*. Toronto: University of Toronto Press.
Walton, D. 2002. Are some *Modus Ponens* arguments deductively invalid? *Informal Logic* 22(1): 19–46.
Walton, D. 2005. Pragmatic and idealized models of knowledge and ignorance. *American Philosophical Quarterly* 42(1): 59–69.
Walton, D. 2006. *Character evidence: An abductive theory*. Dordrecht: Springer.
Walton, D., and E.C.W. Krabbe. 1995. *Commitment in dialogue*. Albany: State University of New York Press.
Zagzebski, L. 1999. What is knowledge? In *The Blackwell guide to epistemology*, ed. J. Greco and E. Sosa, 92–116. Oxford: Blackwell.

# Chapter 8
# Evidence and Argument Evaluation

**Abstract** This chapter confronts the central problem in the current state of argumentation studies, that of clarifying the relationship between argument and evidence. This problem was posed in Chaps. 5 and 6, where the notions of argument and evidence were notably prominent in the use of forensic evidence in the case of the Leonardo Da Vinci portrait and also in the examples of evaluating scientific arguments from correlation to causation. It remains open to be seen how evidence is related to argument generally, as part of the project of argument evaluation. Because this is such a pervasive issue of high generality, it has been reserved for the last chapter. The solution proposed is to fit six argumentation schemes for epistemic defeasible reasoning into a cluster of schemes enabling the basic evidence in a case to generate indirect evidence by using other schemes. This division helps to explain an ambiguity in the use of the term 'evidence'. Used in a broader sense, 'evidence' can include any argument presented to support or attack a claim. In a narrower sense, 'evidence' refers to particular kinds of arguments, such as those based on observations, factual findings, statistics, experimental tests or other scientific findings.

The first seven chapters of this book have illustrated how formal argumentation systems such as CAS, ASPIC+ and DefLog have the capability for evaluating argumentation, as shown by the processing of many examples representing a wide range of cases. This chapter re-examines five of these original examples and introduces and analyzes three new examples to show how such argumentation systems need to be extended in certain directions so that their capabilities for argument evaluation can be improved. The primary problems are to see how evidence can be modelled as part of the argumentation in cases of the kind that have been studied in the previous chapter, and how evidence can be identified in a sequence of argumentation.

Section 8.1 compares the Bayesian probabilistic theory of evidence with computational argumentation systems that model evidential reasoning using defeasible argumentation schemes, forms of evidential reasoning such as argument from perception and inference to the best explanation. Section 8.1 also formally defines



D. Walton, *Argument Evaluation and Evidence*, Law, Governance and Technology Series 23, DOI 10.1007/978-3-319-19626-8_8

the term 'argument', as a preliminary to the central goal of this chapter, which is to clarify the relationship between argument and evidence. Section 8.2 presents a general summary of how CAS works as a methodical procedure for evaluating arguments and evidence.

Section 8.4 re-examines the chocolate example and a new example to see how some parts of the argumentation in the example can be identified as evidence. Section 8.5 uses a new example to show how the argumentation in it can be reconfigured to bring out some lessons on how to model evidence in argument diagrams. Section 8.6 re-examines the Study in Scarlet example to show more precisely how it illustrates the use of observational evidence and evidence deriving from common knowledge. Section 8.7 reviews all the previous examples and briefly poses the main problems in how to model evidential reasoning in them. Section 8.8 explains how the current formal and computational models of reasoning about evidence use logical systems for defeasible argumentation that have a knowledge base. An example is given to show how a knowledge base can be useful for identifying what constitutes the evidence in a case. Section 8.9 is shows how rule-based systems have rules that are comparable to some of the argumentation schemes shown to be important in the example used in previous chapters of the book. Section 8.9 also shows how knowledge-based systems can be used to search for evidence in a knowledge base to construct a sequence of argumentation to support an ultimate conclusion. It is argued that certain argumentation schemes, such as argument from perception and argument from expert opinion, can be used to identify particular kinds of evidence. Section 8.10 summarizes the general solution to the problem of providing means to determine where careful lines of demarcation between argument and evidence can be drawn.

## 8.1 Probability and Evidence

As Prakken (2004) pointed out, there have been two main approaches to building formal models of reasoning about evidence. One is the use of probabilistic networks based on the standard theory of probability. This approach uses probability assignments to propositions along with Bayesian rules of inference to make calculations of conditional probability (Hahn and Oaksford 2006). This Bayesian approach has long seemed attractive because almost all evidential reasoning is concerned with uncertainty (Vreeswik 2003, 289). One problem with it is that it requires numbers as input to the propositions that make up the premises and conclusions, and the inferences drawn from them by evidential reasoning. Consider the Study in Scarlet case as an example. How could we assign probability values to the propositions listed as items of the basic evidence in the case? There seems to be no way to carry out such an assignment of probability values in a non-arbitrary way. But if these values are assigned arbitrarily, the probability of the ultimate conclusion in the case might be calculated with an inappropriate precision that conceals fallacious reasoning.

Evaluating evidence using the Bayesian formula for calculating updating of evidence rests on the way in which conjunction is defined in the system. Conjunctive probability represents the probability of two events occurring together. Assuming that the two events are independent of each other, the conjunction of the two of them is always less than or equal to the probability of either one occurring alone. But it has been shown by Tversky and Kahneman (1982) that this way of calculating probability values of evidence leads to an outcome called the conjunction fallacy. Consider the case of Linda, a 31-year-old outspoken and very bright bank teller who majored in philosophy. As a student she was concerned with issues of social justice, and she participated in antinuclear demonstrations. Against this factual background, Tversky and Kahneman queried a group of respondents by asking them which of two propositions is more probable: (1) Linda is a bank teller, or (2) Linda is a bank teller and is active in the feminist movement. The majority of respondents tested chose option 2. But according to the Bayesian rules for calculating probabilities, the probability of both propositions being true at once (their conjunction) is less than the probability of either one taken individually. This kind of evaluation would make (2) less probable than (1), because it is more specific (claims more). This outcome seems to pose a serious problem for using the Bayesian rules to evaluate evidential reasoning, because in some real cases the evidential value of the conjunction will be lower than the evidential value of either conjunct taken individually, whereas in other real cases, the value will be higher (Prakken 2005). The conjunction fallacy has been much discussed in the cognitive science literature, but the solutions proposed have not been widely accepted.

Another problem is that the Bayesian approach, by combining all the evidential knowledge in a case into probability distributions, may blur the distinction between directly relevant and ancillary evidence (Prakken 2004, 35). This difficulty is quite a serious problem from the point of view of the argumentation theory of evidence advocated in this chapter, because it is vitally important, according to this theory, to distinguish between basic evidence and indirect evidence. The reason for this difficulty may be that at least in cases of legal evidence, there is an exchange of arguments and counterarguments by opposing sides that forms the evidential basis for evaluating the argumentation. In such cases, the argumentation model applies naturally to evidential reasoning, because this model works by building a tree structure to represent the exchange of arguments and counterarguments by the opposing sides, and then determines support for the ultimate conclusion by propagating acceptance through the tree.

The application of the Bayesian rules as a method of evaluating evidence is closely associated with interpreting probability using what is called subjective probability, taken to quantify the measure of a subject's personal belief. But it is a serious problem that one agent cannot know the personal beliefs of another. This difficulty is traditionally called the problem of other minds in philosophy. The argumentation approach avoids this problem by adopting commitment in dialogue (Walton and Krabbe 1995) as the central factor that determines acceptance. The CAS method of evaluating argumentation follows this approach by using acceptance rather than personal belief as the key determinant for evaluating arguments.

The other problem with the subjective probability approach, once again, is the difficulty of assigning a quantitative value to an agent's personal belief in a proposition without doing so in an arbitrary way that may lead to the committing of fallacies. However, there may be other ways of defining the notion of probability that could fit with the theory of evidential reasoning put forward in this chapter. There no space here to adequately discuss the controversial question of the various ways of defining 'probability' in relation to evidential reasoning, but perhaps drawing a distinction between two kinds of probability might be helpful.

Cohen (1977) calls the standard kind of probability we are familiar with, that measures probability of a hypothesis on a scale from 0 to 1, Pascalian probability. This kind of measurement of probability proceeds by assigning numbers to all the propositions being considered. It fits the negation rule, the conjunction rule and the disjunction rule of the standard probability calculus. It also fits the Bayesian formula for calculating conditional probability. The Baconian notion of probability is very different. According to Cohen (1979, 389), Pascalian probability grades the probability value of a proposition on the assumption that all relevant facts are specified in the evidence. In contrast, Baconian probability grades the probability value of the proposition based on the extent to which all the relevant facts are specified in the evidence. The Baconian approach favors case specific proof in which an existing body of evidence is evaluated in relation to both what is known and what is not known in a given case (Stein 2005, 43). This distinction has been shown to be vital importance in evidential reasoning reasoning, as shown in Chap. 7, Sects. 7.6 and 7.7 on taking into account negative evidence as well as positive evidence of findings in cases of evaluating evidential reasoning based on knowledge accumulated during an inquiry. According to Anderson et al. (2005, 258) the most important property of Baconian probability is that how probable a hypothesis is depends on how many different tests have been performed, and on how completely the testing has involved relevant matters. They cite the example of testing the toxicity of a drug. Regardless of how many tests a particular drug has passed, we cannot accept it as being non-toxic unless its possible long-run effects have been taken into account and unless it has been tested for its effects when taken with other drugs. In this regard, Baconian probability is based on tests that have been performed, as well as by considering what tests have not yet been performed.

There remains the possibility that a Bayesian framework for argumentation could be developed that fits with the argumentation approach to evidential reasoning taken in this book. But so far, the difficulties with the Bayesian approach suggests that it needs modification in order to cope with the fallacies that arise from attempting applying the Bayesian rules to realistic cases of natural language argumentation. Hence this book has taken another approach.

This alternative approach stems from a body of earlier work on the evidential foundations of probabilistic reasoning (Schum 1994). This work put forward a research program on evidential reasoning that came to be associated with what is called the new evidence scholarship (Tillers 1989, 1226). This program was based on the view that the standard approach to probability, essentially the approach based on the Bayesian rules, does not, on its own, offer a general method that can be used to evaluate for evidential reasoning in law. Schum can be taken as an early exponent of argumentation methods in that he applied argument diagrams of the kind associated with Wigmore charts to examples of evidential reasoning.

Schum's approach led to the analysis of evidential reasoning outlined in Chap. 7, stemming from the epistemology of scientific evidence of Walton and Zhang (2013). Traditional epistemology defines knowledge in terms of personal belief structures, and therefore it fits in with the approach of defining probability as subjective belief. On this approach, knowledge is species of belief, often characterized as justified true belief. The epistemology outlined in Chap. 7 is a different approach. It can be called an evidence-based theory of knowledge. It defines knowledge as a defeasible concept based on argumentation that supports or attacks the hypothesis being investigated. On this view, whether a proposition can properly be classified as knowledge depends on the pro evidence supporting it and the con evidence against it (as well as the lack of such evidence). It is argued in this book that this evidence-based epistemology fits with the systems of argument evaluation recently developed in artificial intelligence.

The new computational argumentation systems can be described as the application of logical systems for defeasible argumentation using the argumentation schemes, forms of evidential reasoning such as argument from witness testimony, argument from expert opinion and inference to the best explanation. These new systems combine argumentation schemes with tree structures for argument analysis and evaluation, and also adopt the hypothesis that important notions of evidential reasoning such as burden of proof can best be modeled using formal dialogue systems. This logical and dialectical approach has combined these tools with the application of a framework in which pro-contra argumentation is defined and evaluated within a tree structure. A key feature of this approach is that it evaluates evidential reasoning by comparison of arguments both for and against a conclusion. Three main systems of this type have already been introduced in this book, DefLog, ASPIC+ (Prakken's system) and CAS.

In CAS the notion of an argument is defined using graph structures, argumentation schemes, the notion of an audience, and formal dialogue systems. CAS models arguments as directed graphs, consisting of argument nodes linked to statement nodes. In CAS-style argument diagrams, statement nodes are shown as propositions in text boxes. Argument nodes are displayed as circles, with a + or − sign inside the circle, to distinguish pro and con arguments, respectively. Argument nodes also contain argumentation schemes. CAS is capable of representing instances of any kind of argumentation scheme, whether deductive, inductive or defeasible. By definition, a CAS *argument graph* is a bipartite, directed, labeled graph, consisting of statement nodes and argument nodes connected by premise and conclusion edges. As shown in many examples in the previous chapters, CAS analyzes and evaluates arguments using argument diagrams to visualize these argument graphs. As explained in Chap. 7, Sect. 7.4, CAS also models argumentation within an overarching formal dialogue structure defined as an ordered 3-tuple $< O, A, C >$ where $O$ is the opening stage, $A$ is the argumentation stage, and $C$ is the closing stage (Gordon and Walton 2009, 244).

Burden of proof can shift from side during the other as moves are made in such a dialogue, moves such as putting forward an argument. Burden of proof is determined by the standard of proof appropriate for an argument and by the determination of which side the burden rests on at a move made in a dialogue, as the burden shifts from one side to the other, according to the rules. Dialogue rules (protocols) of the kind set out and discussed in Walton and Krabbe (1995) define what types of moves are allowed by the parties during each of the three stages.

In this way of defining the notion of argument, we start by seeing how putting forward an argument is a speech act that can be performed for different purposes, depending on the goals of the type of conversation the speaker and hearer are supposedly engaging in. One such type of conversation is a persuasion dialogue, in which the speaker is trying to get the hearer to accept a statement (claim) that the hearer has expressed doubt about. For this purpose, the speaker needs to use an argument based on premises acceptable to the hearer. An argument is an inference from a set of statements used as premises to another statement called the conclusion, a claim that is supposedly in doubt. However, as shown in the previous chapters, arguments are also used in negotiation dialogues, deliberation dialogues, inquiry dialogues and information-seeking dialogues. Seen in this way an argument is more than just a set of premises and a conclusion. It also needs to be seen as something that is used for some communicative purpose in a conversational multi-agent setting. Argument graphs are evaluated, relative to audiences, to determine the acceptability of statements in a stage of a dialogue (Gordon and Walton 2009).

Arguments are evaluated in CAS by using proof standards to aggregate pro and con arguments (Gordon and Walton 2009). The conclusion of an argument is *in* (acceptable) if has been accepted by the audience or it satisfies the proof standard appropriate for the type of dialogue, or if the premises of the argument are *in*, and the conclusion is linked to the premises by an argument fitting the requirements of its argumentation scheme.

The problem is to see how CAS, and other argumentation systems can be extended to take the notion of evidence into account and to model how argumentation can be evidence-based. To begin with this task, a short review of how CAS evaluates arguments will be useful.

## 8.2 How Argument Evaluation Works in CAS

It has already been shown in this book by means of several examples how argument evaluation is carried out. In this section the procedure will be illustrated using a more abstract kind of example. Figure 8.1 displays a typical argument map in which the argumentation contains nine arguments leading into an ultimate conclusion shown at the left of the figure. There are twelve premises in the sequence of argumentation.

Some of the premises in the argument in Fig. 8.1 are displayed in green boxes, indicating that these premises are accepted by the audience. In the printed version of the book, the green boxes will show as darkened (gray) boxes. Starting from the

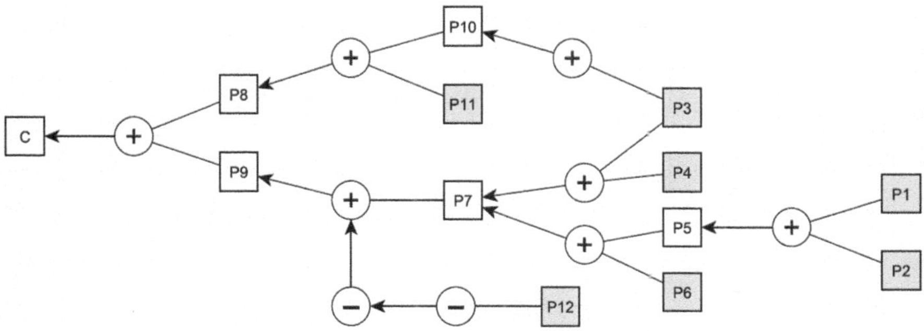


**Fig. 8.1** Propagation step 1

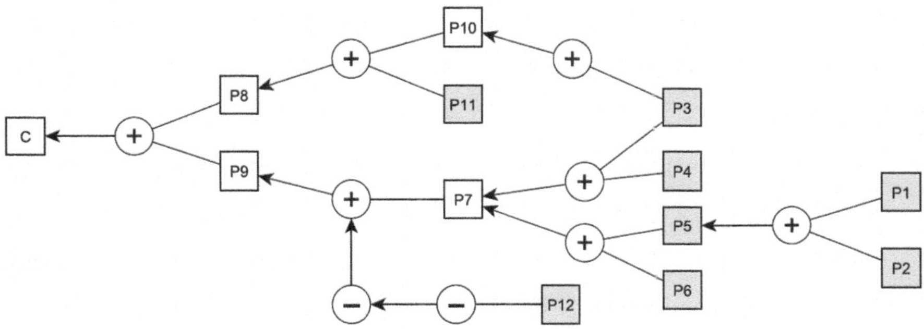


**Fig. 8.2** Propagation step 2

right of the argument diagram and working our way toward the ultimate conclusion at the left, Fig. 8.2 shows the first few changes that will automatically made by the CAS argument evaluation system.

For purposes of illustration, the assumption will be made that each argument represented by an argument node is a valid argument, meaning that it fits the requirements of some argumentation scheme. Now let's look at the rightmost part of Fig. 8.2. Both premises P1 and P2 are accepted, therefore the argument node just to the left of these two premises is applicable, and so it is shown in a round node with a green background. Given these requirements having been met, CAS automatically colors premise P5 as green (accepted). Next, look to Fig. 8.3.

Now that premises P5 and P6 are accepted, and moreover since we know that P3 and P4 have been accepted, CAS automatically calculates that P7 is accepted. Next we look to Fig. 8.4.

Since P3 is the only premise of the single argument leading to P10, the latter proposition is automatically taken to be accepted. Since it was already given that P11 is accepted, it follows that P8 also has to be accepted. This is the state of affairs shown in Fig. 8.4. Next we look to Fig. 8.5.

In Fig. 8.5, since the single premise P7 has already been accepted, P9 must also be shown as accepted. Next let's look to Fig. 8.6.

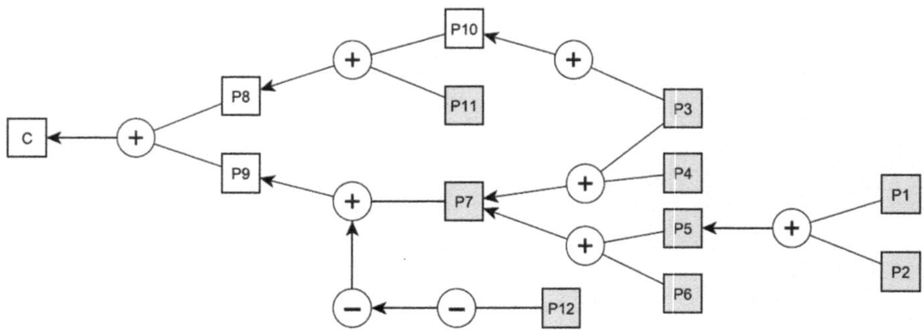


**Fig. 8.3** Propagation step 3

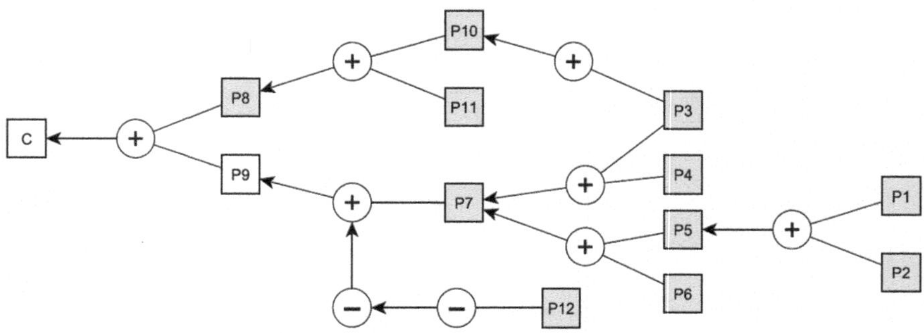


**Fig. 8.4** Propagation step 4

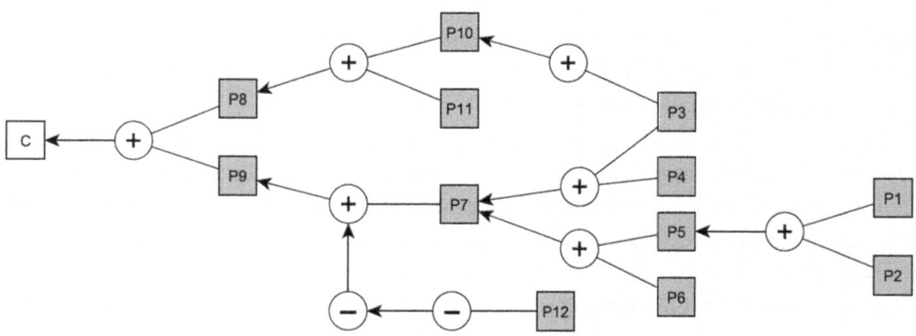


**Fig. 8.5** Propagation step 5

At the bottom of Fig. 8.5, we see that there is an undercutter attacking the argument represented by the circular node containing a minus sign. But we also see that there is another argument with premise P12 that undercuts the undercutter. Normally the presence of a single undercutter is enough to defeat an argument, but in an abstract argumentation framework, if the undercutter is attacked by another

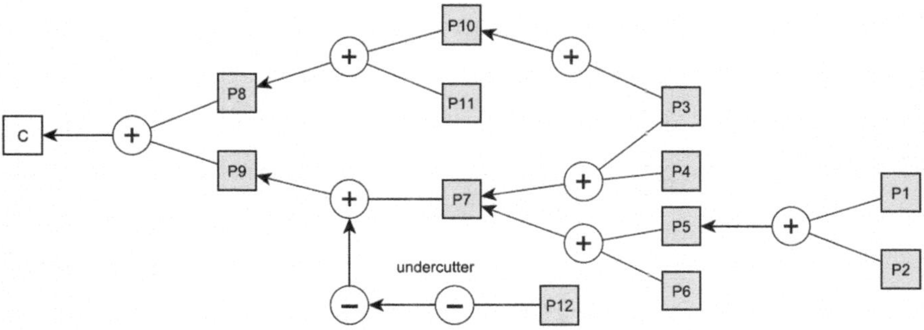


**Fig. 8.6** Propagation step 6

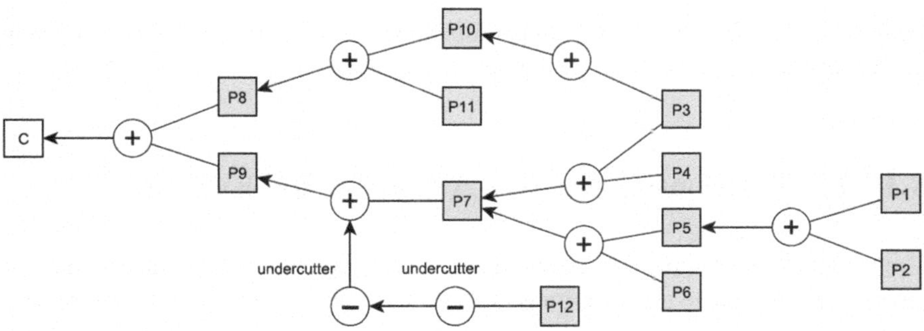


**Fig. 8.7** Propagation step 7

argument, one that has premises that are all accepted, and is an argument that fits an argumentation scheme, that undercutter will be defeated. This is the situation shown in Fig. 8.7.

In Fig. 8.7, the undercutter argument containing premise P12 has successfully defeated the undercutter attacking the argument from P7 to P9. Therefore P9 remains accepted. This takes us to Fig. 8.8.

According to the argument diagram shown in Fig. 8.8 the final argument at the left has both premises P8 and P9 accepted. Assuming that the argument from these two premises to the final conclusion C is an applicable argument fitting an argumentation scheme, CAS automatically shows the conclusion C as accepted. This result is shown by the finished argument evaluation represented in Fig. 8.8. What has been shown is that the evidence provided by the mass of pro-argumentation is not defeated by the counter-argumentation (the undercutter), and therefore the argumentation as a whole is sufficient to prove the conclusion. This outcome also depends, of course, on the standard of proof assigned to the conclusion and to the other elements shown on the diagram, and on the structure of the arguments shown in the circle nodes. Setting these matters aside for the moment, the sequence shown in the eight figures can give the reader a simple but

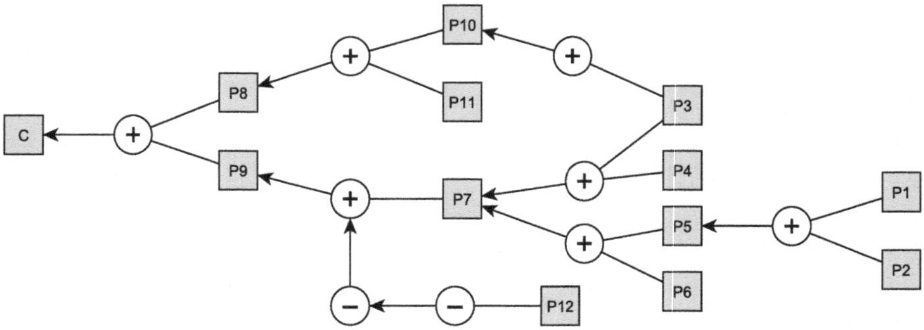


**Fig. 8.8** Propagation step 8

good general idea of how CAS and comparable computational systems can carry out, or help a user to carry out an argument evaluation.

## 8.3 The Relationship Between Argument and Evidence

The way the word 'evidence' is used in everyday conversational speech conceals an ambiguity. One way to use the term is to allow it to comprise any argument presented to support or undermine a claim. This sense of the term makes it equivalent to the term 'argument'. The problem with this wider sense of the word is that it leaves no room to distinguish between argument and evidence as general concepts. In the narrower sense, the term 'evidence' is used to refer to some particular kinds of arguments, such as those based on observations, factual findings, expert opinions of scientists, including statisticians, or experimental results. The problem with this narrower sense of the term 'evidence' is that it makes evidence relative to different fields in which evidences is collected and evaluated.

Legal evidence includes eyewitness testimony, expert opinion testimony, and circumstantial evidence of various kinds, such as physical findings. Rules of evidence in law determine what is admissible as evidence in a trial, and these admissible propositions are known as the facts of the case. In the example of their Wigmore diagram examined in Chap. 1, the evidence, the so-called facts of the case, as well as inferences that can be drawn from them, are represented in a Wigmore chart. Scientific evidence consists of the mass of observations, statistical findings and experimental results used to test a hypothesis to evaluate by scientific methods whether the hypothesis is merely a tentative conjecture or can be proved to be established (or not) in of scientific inquiry. This description of scientific evidence is very broad, but it can be used to contrast scientific evidence with legal evidence. As shown abundantly in the previous chapters of this book, legal evidence is very often based on scientific evidence brought before a court by scientific experts. Even though the two types of evidence are mixed together in such cases, in principle they can and need to be separated as to distinctively different kinds of evidence with different criteria and procedures needed to evaluate them as evidence.

Apart from these two notions of scientific evidence and legal evidence, the use of the term 'evidence' in philosophy is tied to the use of the term 'knowledge', the central preoccupation of the branch of philosophy called epistemology. In Chap. 7, a fallibilistic theory of evidential reasoning and inquiry was put forward that gives an account of how evidence and knowledge are related. Within argumentation theory, comparatively little attention has been given to considering the notion of evidence as fundamental to the subject, while a good deal of attention has been given to the concept of an argument. Indeed, so far in this book, the notion of an argument has been taken as the central tool in the argumentation systems covered.

The upshot is that while the notion of an argument modeled precisely in a formal argumentation system such as CAS, how this relates to the notion of evidence is much less clear. The central problem is posed by the ambiguity of the meaning of the term 'evidence'. In a broader sense, common in everyday conversational speech, the term evidence can simply refer to any argument presented to support or undermine a claim. In a narrower sense, 'evidence' may be taken to refer to specific findings in a particular field. In the narrower sense of the term, what can qualify as evidence varies with the particular field, especially in case of scientific evidence. Accordingly, for example, the way evidence is defined in law can be expected to be quite different from the way the concept of evidence is conceived in a scientific field, such as physics or biology.

So far, the notion of evidence has been underutilized and unexplored in argumentation theory. One part of the solution to the problem is to set standards of what constitutes evidence at the opening stage of a dialogue, so that this standard can be applied to the argumentation that takes place during the argumentation and closing stages of the dialogue. This solution has already been adopted in legal argumentation by legal evidence rules, for example the Federal Rules of Evidence that apply to many trials in the American legal system. But how could this kind of solution be implemented in formal and computational argumentation systems?

In current systems of argumentation technology, premises and conclusions in an argument map can be assigned values such as accepted or rejected, and system can automatically determine whether a conclusion should be accepted based on whether its premises are accepted or not. There is no way of marking certain propositions that should be designated as constituting evidence, and therefore should be accepted for this special reason, and should have special value in supporting other propositions in a network of argumentation. Is there some way of utilizing evidential propositions by adding something new to current systems of argumentation technology?

At the opening stage of a dialogue, criteria for determining what should count as evidence during the argumentation and closing stages can be set in place. These criteria would be used to formulate the protocols governing the speech acts in the argumentation stage. They can also be used to help determine how the dialogue should be terminated at the closing stage. During the argumentation stage, propositions accepted as evidence during the opening stage are held to have a special status in two respects. One is that such an evidential proposition is automatically evaluated as accepted during the argumentation stage. Another is that although evidential propositions are not beyond challenge during the argumentation stage, they have to be challenged in a different way from other propositions that are taken to be accepted during that stage.

This proposal provides an approach to the problems of how to distinguish between argument and evidence is the setting of a formal dialogue, and how to evaluate arguments based on such evidence, but leaves a lot open. The question of how to apply this approach as the basis of a useful working method remains open. To consider how it might be implemented, it is useful to reconsider some of the earlier examples look at a few new examples.

## 8.4 The Chocolate Example Revisited

Two examples are studied in this section. One is the chocolate example presented in Chap. 6, and now re-examined in light of the relationship between argument and evidence. The other is a new example that shows how evidence can play a role in argument evaluation.

When we look back over the examples of arguments from correlation to causation studied in Chap. 6, we see that all these examples were based on scientific evidence that was used to draw inferences from this evidence to support arguments about public policy issues, such as health and safety. The birds example was based on scientific evidence on recent human influenza pandemics and on scientific evidence about weather variations influenced by events in the South Pacific. In this example, one scientific finding suggested that in light of evidence drawn from biology and geography, weather conditions in the South Pacific were combining with bird migration to bring divergent influenza subtypes together in a way that could potentially cause a pandemic. The argumentation in this example followed the typical pattern of the other cases studied in Chap. 6. First there was a body of scientific evidence put forward by publications in one or more scientific fields based on observations and statistical findings suggesting a conclusion that has broad public policy implications. The problem posed is one of the need for public policy decision-makers to interpret and assess the evidence that has been put forward in order to draw conclusions regarding public policy issues. Hence this case, and the other cases as well studied in Chap. 6, raised once again the problem of evaluating arguments from expert opinions. So we have a standard sequence from the scientific evidence, based on statistical, experimental, or perhaps medical findings, to conclusions drawn by inference from these findings by decision-makers who are not experts in the fields of scientific evidence important in the given case. The problems caused by this transference were even more evident in the copper example in that two leading scientific experts who had conducted research on the question of whether the ingestion of copper can lead to plaque buildup in the brain causing Alzheimer's disease disagreed with each other's opinions.

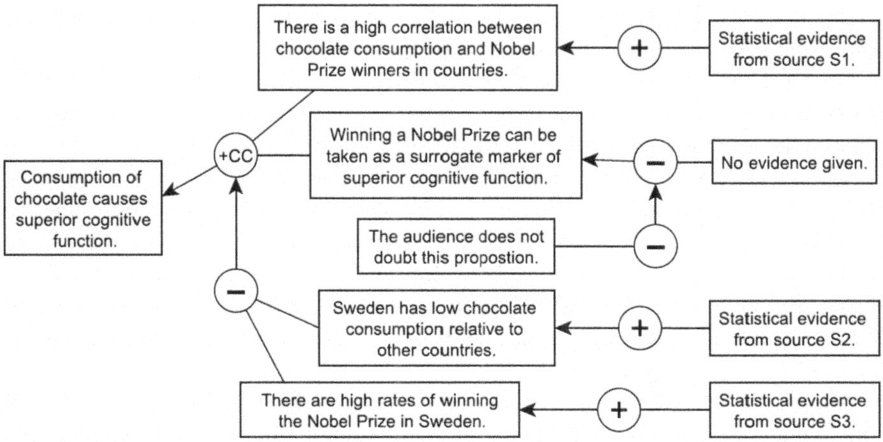


**Fig. 8.9** Evidential structure of the argumentation in the chocolate example

The problem with this kind of case is to figure out how argument is related to evidence over the transference procedure that takes place between the two levels. The first level comprises the part of the argumentation where the scientists present their findings, typically in a scientific journal. The second level comprises the part where inferences need to be drawn from the reported scientific findings by other parties who are not specialists in the research area of the scientific findings originally presented in the journal article.

Some guidance on how to address this problem can be gleaned from briefly reconsidering the case of the chocolate example. The main body of evidence in this case consisted of a scientific article supporting the hypothesis that chocolate consumption can improve cognitive function, based on a reported statistical survey. Let's reconfigure the argumentation in the chocolate example in a different format that fits the basic structure of a CAS argument diagram, but that brings out the evidential structure of the argumentation in case more clearly.

In Fig. 8.9, the ultimate conclusion is shown as usual at the extreme left of the argument diagram. What is different about this way of modeling the argumentation is that a distinction is drawn between the two meanings of the term 'evidence'. The basic scientific evidence is indicated by the three text boxes citing statistical evidence from sources. In each of these three instances, inferences are drawn from the basic scientific evidence to other conclusions. These other conclusions can also be said to be classifiable as evidence, but here the term 'evidence' is meant in a broader sense. Evidence in this broader sense includes not only the statistical evidence but also conclusions drawn from it by inference. For example the conclusion that there is a high correlation between chocolate consumption and Nobel Prize winners in certain European countries is drawn from the statistical evidence cited from scientific source S1. The proposition that there is such a high correlation between chocolate consumption and Nobel Prize winners can also, in the broader sense, be considered evidence. It is taken as evidence in a linked argument that also contains another premise to support the ultimate conclusion that consumption of chocolate causes superior cognitive function.

One problem with using this method of evaluating evidence-based argumentation is that it may not always be so easy to clearly determine in a given case whether a particular proposition should be classified as basic evidence or as a conclusion drawn by inference from the basic evidence. Such a conclusion could be perhaps classified as evidential reasoning, or as secondary evidence derived by inference from the factual evidence in a case. But that would make it different from the basic kind of evidence derived from perceptual data, or from authoritative sources, such as scientific evidence based on expert testimony. Below, further examples encountered in previous chapters of the book are re-evaluated that raise this issue in a sharper way and suggest a way to solve it.

Another aspect of the evidential structure represented in Fig. 8.9 worthy of commentary is the lack of evidence given to support the essential premise that winning a Nobel Prize can be taken as a surrogate marker of superior cognitive function. The situation is somewhat reminiscent of the argumentation scheme for argument from lack of evidence discussed in Chap. 7, Sect. 7.6, on reasoning from absence of knowledge. But the argument in this case is not an instance of that argumentation scheme. What is of interest is that the argument in this case is supported by another argument with a premise stating that the audience does not doubt this proposition. In other words, there is no need to prove this proposition because the audience already accepts it. It is not that the proposition that winning a Nobel Prize can be taken as a surrogate marker of superior cognitive function cannot be doubted. Rather the reason for lack of doubt is that the Nobel Prize in such a prestigious scientific award that it would be generally accepted that receiving this award is a mark of superior cognitive function.

## 8.5 The Smoking in China Example

The next example comes from an article in the *Economist* (The Tobacco Industry: Government Coughers, March 1, 2014, 39–40, no author given). This article argued that China has a serious problem with smoking, and offered a solution to the problem, based on statistical evidence and expert opinion evidence. The article exhibits a complex network of argumentation based on expert opinion evidence from sources such as the British Medical Journal and the World Health Organization. It would be an interesting but lengthy task to analyze the whole network of argumentation in the article, but for our purposes here a point can be made by abstracting out what are taken to be the main arguments in the formulation of the problem in the article and the solution that offers. The main argument can be represented by a set of eleven propositions in the key list below. Let's call this case the smoking in China example.

## Key List

1. China is the world's largest cigarette market.
2. On present trends, 100 million people stand to die from tobacco related illnesses this century.
3. The economic burden will soar as the economy and the costs of healthcare grow.
4. China has a problem with smoking.
5. Many studies show that tobacco taxes are highly effective in reducing consumption.
6. The WHO says that heavy taxation is the most important way to deal with the problem.
7. This approach has worked in poor countries like South Africa
8. It has also worked in rich countries like France.
9. A study published in the British Medical Journal found that nearly 13,000,000 smoking-related deaths would be averted by implementing a policy of high taxes on tobacco.
10. The solution to the problem is for China to implement a policy of high taxes on tobacco.
11. China should implement a policy of high taxes on tobacco.

Without worrying about schemes, the propositions in the key list can be taken as premises and/or conclusions in an argument having the structure shown in Fig. 8.10. The ultimate conclusion, shown at the top, is the statement that China should implement a policy of high taxes on tobacco.

The two main premises supporting this conclusion are the statements that China has a problem with smoking and the statement that the solution is for China to bring in a policy of high taxes on tobacco. Each of these premises is supported by an additional argument that itself has three premises. One of the three premises in the

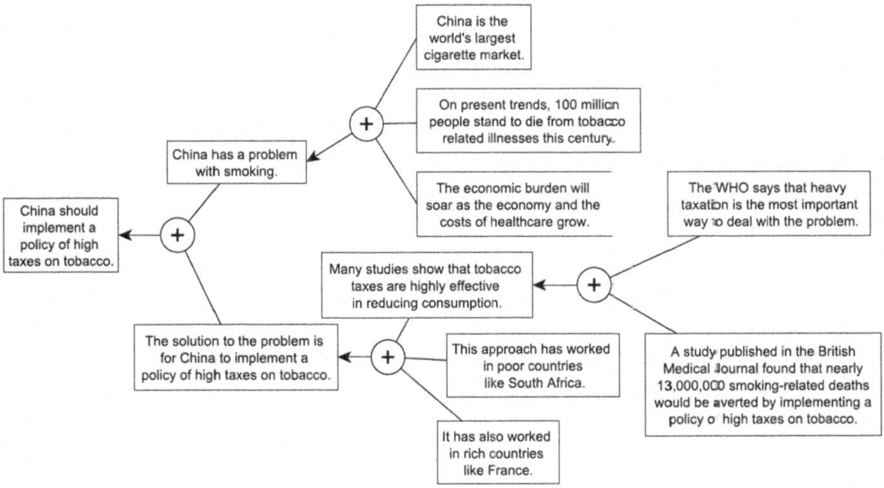


**Fig. 8.10** First argument diagram of the smoking in China example

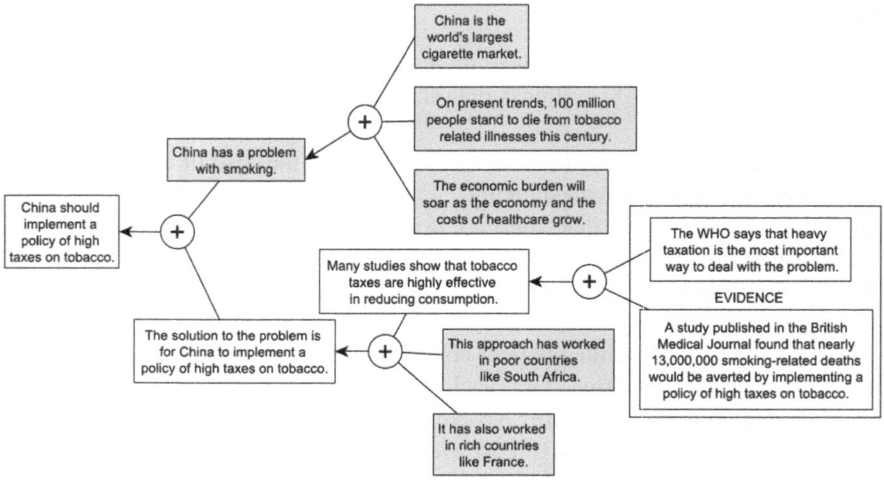


**Fig. 8.11** Second argument diagram of the smoking in China example

argument on the right has an additional argument supporting it where that additional argument uses the two premises shown at the top.

Looking over the argument diagram in Fig. 8.10, we should ask what parts of it can be classified as basic evidence, as opposed to other statements representing indirect evidence drawn by inference from this basic evidence. The two propositions at the right would appear to fit the category of basic evidence, because one of them cites a study published in the British Medical Journal and the other sites a statement attributed to the WHO.

In Fig. 8.11, the two propositions at the right have been placed in a box labeled 'evidence'.

Next we need to see how these two statements can affect the evaluation of the argumentation as it propagates upwards from this bottom level to the ultimate conclusion shown at the left.

For purposes of illustration, let's say that some of the premises in the argument shown in Fig. 8.10 have been accepted by the audience. The propositions accepted by the audience are shown in the green (darkened) text boxes in Fig. 8.11. Let's say as well that all four argument nodes in Fig. 8.11 represent applicable arguments fitting a defeasible argumentation scheme that is valid. Given all this input, the question is how CAS will evaluate the argumentation to tell whether the ultimate claim is proved by the evidence or not. This finding will depend on the standard of proof in the case, but let's not worry about that for purposes of this example. The standard set by default is that of the preponderance of the evidence.

The evaluation of the argumentation in the smoking in China example pictured in Fig. 8.12 shows the outcome once the basic evidence has been taken into account.

The first step in the sequence of evaluation is that the two propositions in the evidence box shown at the right of the diagram are automatically taken to be accepted, once they have been classified under the heading of basic evidence in the system. Since both of these propositions are accepted, and since they are the only two

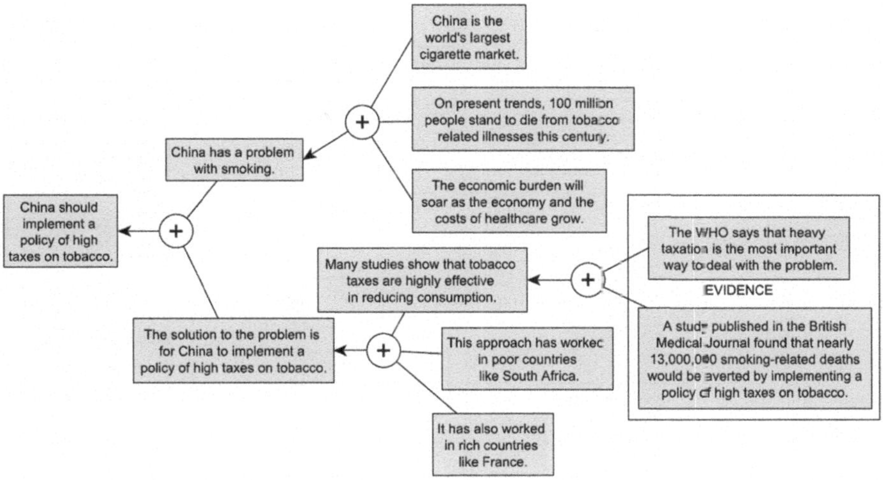


**Fig. 8.12** Third argument diagram of the smoking in China example

premises in a linked argument that is a pro-argument supporting the proposition that many studies show that tobacco taxes are highly effective in reducing consumption, this conclusion is now shown as accepted by the system. So this proposition is now shown in its text box with a green background. Once that calculation has taken place all three premises are now accepted in the next argument, and once again since this argument is defeasibly valid, the conclusion that the solution to the problem is for China to implement a policy of higher taxes on tobacco is also calculated as accepted. Hence this proposition is now shown in a green text box. The next step is that the leftmost argument is a linked argument with only two premises, and both premises have now been accepted by the system. Therefore the ultimate conclusion, the proposition that China should implement a policy of high taxes on tobacco, is shown as accepted. For this reason the system automatically calculates it is accepted, showing the leftmost text box as green. This outcome is shown in Fig. 8.12.

What is shown in Fig. 8.12 is that all of the premises have been accepted by the audience, and since all of the arguments connecting these propositions together into an argumentation sequence represent inferences that also need to be accepted by the audience, the conclusion is proved. But the transitions from Figs. 8.10 and 8.11 has shown that what makes the sequence of argumentation move forward in this way to establish the ultimate conclusion is the acceptance of the two basic evidential propositions shown at the right part of the diagram.

## 8.6 Re-examining the Study in Scarlet Case

The reader might recall that in Chap. 1, Sect. 1.5, in examining how abductive reasoning was used in this Study in Scarlet case, it was noticed that Holmes' reasoning was based on six factual observations that he made when he was first introduced

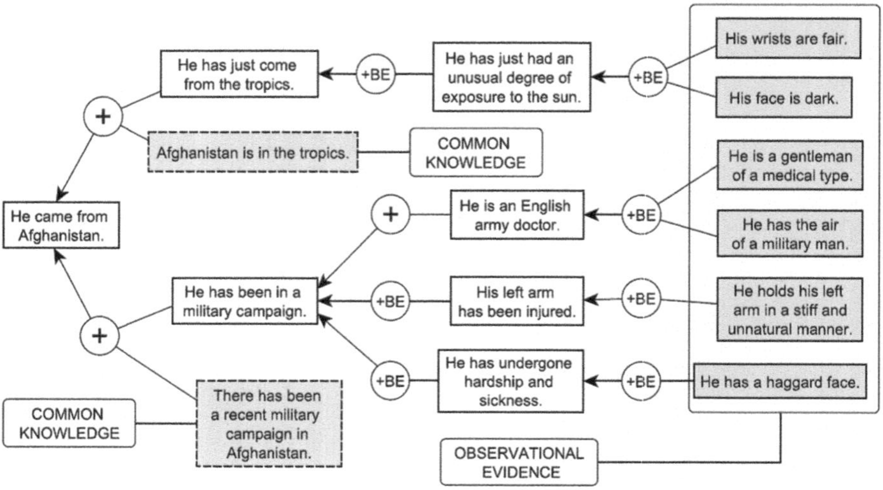


**Fig. 8.13** Evidential reasoning in the study in scarlet case

to Watson. These six observation statements were listed in the right column of Fig. 1.3. They represent items of observational evidence from which Holmes was able to draw conclusions by using inference to the best explanation. Holmes used these conclusions as premises to draw further inferences that eventually led by a sequence of logical reasoning to the ultimate conclusion that Watson came from Afghanistan, the conclusion that Watson found so amazing.

How might CAS be used to evaluate the sequence of reasoning used by Holmes? Evidently Holmes' reasoning was successful in proving the conclusion that Watson came from Afghanistan, based on Watson's reaction to it. But how could this successful sequence of reasoning from the given items of observational evidence to the ultimate conclusion be modeled by CAS? To see how this is done, consider the argument diagram shown in Fig. 8.13.

Holmes was an acute observer, and so let's assume that the propositions shown in the rectangle on the right are all accepted as factual. In Fig. 8.13, they are categorized as items of observational evidence. To indicate that these propositions are all accepted, CAS shows each of them in a green text box. How does the sequence of argumentation run from here in CAS?

Let's start from the top down. Both premises of the top argument, the proposition that his wrists are fair and the proposition that his face is dark, are shown as accepted. Assuming that the scheme for inference to the best explanation applies to the argument, the conclusion, the proposition that he has just had an unusual degree of exposure to the sun, is now automatically calculated by CAS to be accepted. The outcome is the same with the remaining three conclusions in the middle column under the top conclusion. Each conclusion is accepted, because the argument supporting it is based on observational evidence that has been accepted, and the argument fits the scheme for inference to the best explanation, once supplemented with the appropriate implicit premises. Now let's look at the top argument again. The conclusion that he has just had an unusual degree of exposure to the sun is now shown in a green box, because it has been accepted, so the conclusion drawn from it, the proposition that he has just come from the tropics, is also automatically shown by CAS to be accepted. Once again it is assumed that this argument fits the scheme for inference to the best explanation.

Next we need to look at what happens now that the conclusion that he has just come from the tropics has been accepted. It goes along with the other premise that Afghanistan is in the tropics. Should this premise be accepted or not? In Fig. 8.13, this premise is shown as accepted because it is an instance of common knowledge. But notice that this proposition was not explicitly stated in the text of the Study in Scarlet case, as written by Conan Doyle. So we need to represent the argument as an enthymeme, an argument with an unstated premise. To indicate that it is an implicit premise, the border of the text box containing the proposition that Afghanistan is in the tropics is shown as a dotted line. The statement that Afghanistan is in the tropics would be acceptable to Holmes, Watson, and the audience of this argument, and therefore it is shown as accepted. Now these two premises are accepted and shown in green boxes, the conclusion that Watson came from Afghanistan would automatically be calculated as accepted by CAS. This outcome assumes that the argumentation supporting it (just outlined above) going along the top of the diagram is strong enough to meet the standard of proof to establish the conclusion that Watson came from Afghanistan. Let's say that it is not strong enough, considering only this top argument, because the argument that he came from Afghanistan based on the evidence that his wrists are fair and his face is dark would not be strong enough by itself to adequately support the conclusion that Watson came from Afghanistan.

And so in order to evaluate the argumentation in this case adequately, we also have to look at the sequence of argumentation below the first argument. Once we do so, we see the same pattern. The conclusions in the middle column are all supported by the evidence of the six observational statements in the right column, and these conclusions can be reused as premises supporting the conclusion that Watson has been in the military campaign. As in the sequence of argumentation described above, this proposition will be shown in a green box along with the unstated premise based on common knowledge that there has been a recent military campaign in Afghanistan. Assuming that these two sequences of argumentation taken together should be sufficient to support the ultimate conclusion, CAS will show the proposition that Watson came from Afghanistan in a green box. Once all the calculations have been made by CAS, all the text boxes in Fig. 8.13 will be shown with green backgrounds. This evaluation shows how CAS can evaluate the argumentation in the example as successful to prove the conclusion that Watson came from Afghanistan. This outcome assumes however that the argument nodes are weighted appropriately to allow for this result.

## 8.7 Evidential Problems Posed by the Examples

Next let's compare how evidence is managed in the case of the Galapagos finches in Fig. 1.5, displaying the evidence-based structure of the second student explanation. In this argument diagram, the evidence shown at the bottom of the figure contains such statements as Tribulus was the best surviving plant of the drought in 1877. This data represents the evidence in the case. The evidence was used to support arguments, and these arguments were then used to support the explanation that appeared at the top level of the diagram. We have a comparable general pattern of evidential reasoning exhibited in the analysis of the Study in Scarlet case shown in Fig. 1.8, even though the way the components are put together is different. In the Study in Scarlet case, the six items of observational evidence generate four explanations. The way each explanation that is selected as a conclusion inferred from the observational evidence is by means of inference to the best explanation. The four conclusions drawn represent the best explanations of the observational data. The clue here is that inferences are drawn from the observational data to conclusions, and in these conclusions are in turn used as premises to generate further conclusions. Finally these two further conclusions, along with additional implicit premises, are used to draw an inference to the ultimate conclusion that Watson came from Afghanistan.

In the example of the Galapagos finches, the evidence is used to support argumentation, which is in turn used to support an explanation. In the Study in Scarlet example, the evidence is used to generate explanations incorporated into arguments from the best explanation. These initial arguments generate a further sequence of argumentation leading to an ultimate conclusion that is proved by the evidence and the arguments based on it. The role of the evidence is comparable in the two cases, because in each of them, the evidence is used to support arguments and explanations that are woven together, leading through a sequence of argumentation that can be used to prove an ultimate conclusion or to explain some event that needs to be explained.

The evaluation of the Study in Scarlet example using CAS is especially significant with respect to how the evidence is represented in two respects. First, it can be seen that the argumentation in the case traces back to the six items of observational evidence displayed in the rectangle at the right side of Fig. 8.10. Second, several inferences are drawn from these six basic evidential propositions, raising the question of whether the conclusions drawn in these inferences should be themselves be considered evidence. Consider the conclusion that Watson's left arm has been injured. This proposition supports the conclusion that Watson has been in a military campaign. For this reason, the proposition that his left arm has been injured can be taken as evidence to support the proposition that he has been in a military campaign. It seems highly reasonable to take the proposition that has left arm has been injured as evidence in this way. In short, this aspect of Fig. 8.13 brings out the basic ambiguity in the meaning of the term 'evidence'. What can be considered the basic evidence case consists of direct observations. But there is also a wider meaning of the term 'evidence' in which the proposition that Watson's left arm has been injured can also be considered evidence within the mass of evidence that is used to support the ultimate conclusion that Watson came from Afghanistan.

The other aspect of the case worth mentioning is that two of the other evidential propositions in the figure (the two shown in the boxes with dashed borders), are also evidential in nature. But they are implicit assumptions, and can be excluded from the category of observational evidence. This point will be significant in the next sections where different categories of evidence are discussed, as will be already somewhat evident in the discussion of the next example.

The reader might recall from Chap. 1, Sect. 1.1 that Wigmore had some special notations on his chart indicating different kinds of evidence. A round node (circle) is taken to represent an evidentiary fact. The dot in the circle represents the belief that the proposition represented by the circle actually obtains. A square node in a Wigmore diagram is taken to represent testimonial evidence. The infinity symbol placed underneath a square node represents a fact judicially admitted by the tribunal. All these distinctions are interesting, and it could be useful to incorporate then in some form in the new automated systems used to help an argument diagrammer who wants to draw a distinction between argument and evidence and represent it diagrammatically.

Some of these notations are not necessary in a system such as CAS that has argumentation schemes. We would not need the square symbol used in the Wigmore diagram to represent testimonial evidence, because there is an argumentation scheme for argument from witness testimony already available. CAS represents the scheme as a distinctive type of argument displayed in the round node representing an argument. However, it might be useful to have some device for distinguishing between a proposition that has been accepted, and one that has been accepted because it is classified as basic evidence in a case. For example it could be classified as evidence if it represents a fact judicially admitted by the tribunal. In legal argumentation, a decision on whether alleged facts are admissible as evidence during the argumentation stage of the trial is made before the beginning of the argumentation stage of trial. Each side is supposed to inform the other side of the evidence it has collected before the trial begins. In an argument map it could be represented by a particular type of node if it represents an evidentiary fact, as opposed to a secondary conclusion drawn by inference from an evidentiary fact.

One way to represent evidence in a modern argument mapping system might be to simply designate some of the text boxes on the argument diagram as propositions representing statements that can be taken as evidence, meaning propositions that are taken to be factual by the audience. These propositions would be automatically classified as accepted. So for the purpose of evaluating the argumentation in a given case, any proposition in this set would be automatically shown in the argument diagram in a text box with a green background.

This could be shown by modifying Fig. 2.2, and instead drawing a modern style argument diagram of part of Wigmore's argument in the disappearing sailor case. Looking back to Fig. 2.2 it can be seen that the ultimate conclusion to be proved, shown in the text box at the left, is the proposition that D murdered V. Which parts

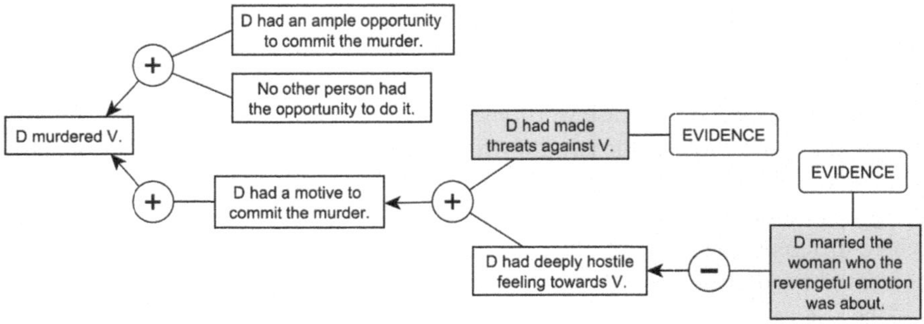


**Fig. 8.14** Reconfiguration of the argument diagram of the disappearing sailor case

of the sequence of argumentation leading to this conclusion could be categorized as evidence? The two most likely candidates are the propositions that D married the woman who the revengeful emotion was about, and the proposition that D had made threats against V. These propositions are shown in green text boxes in Fig. 8.14.

We can carry out an argument evaluation procedure by seeing that once the proposition that D married the woman who the revengeful emotion was about has been accepted, assuming that the argument represented by the circle node containing the minus sign is defeasibly valid, the conclusion that D had deeply hostile feelings towards V will automatically be drawn with green box by CAS, showing it also needs to be accepted. Once this premise has been accepted however, it provides a plausible con argument attacking the proposition that D had deeply hostile feeling towards V. this argument can now be evaluated as a counterargument that attacks or undermines the proposition that D had deeply hostile feeling towards V. As Wigmore (1931, 57) put the point, the fact that the accused did actually marry the woman tends to explain away the revengeful emotion as probably having ceased to exist. For these reasons, the conclusion that D had deeply hostile feeling towards V needs to be shown in a text box with a white background, indicating that the proposition in this text box is not accepted.

Tracking along the evaluation procedure from this point using Fig. 8.14, we can see that the conclusion that D had a motive to commit the murder also needs to be shown in a text box with a white background, because one of the premises in the only argument supporting it is not accepted. Now we no longer have a motive, the argument based on D's having an opportunity to commit the crime, shown at the top of Fig. 8.14, is no longer sufficient to prove the conclusion that D murdered V. What this indicates is that the evaluation of the sequence of argumentation in the case shows that the given evidence is insufficient to prove the ultimate conclusion that D murdered V.

The chocolate case, and also in the other examples of arguments from correlation to causation studied in Chap. 6, showed that there were two evidential levels in such cases. At the first level the results of scientific research were presented in a scientific discipline. At the second level other parties not specialists in that field needed to draw inferences from the reported scientific findings. The problem posed by such cases is to model the transference procedure from the basic level of evidence to the secondary evidence. The problem in such cases is that it may not be so easy to determine where the line should be drawn between the basic evidence and the secondary evidence drawn by inference from the basic evidence.

In the smoking in China example, the same problem came up, but in a different form. This example occurred in an article in *The Economist* arguing that China should implement a policy of high taxes on tobacco, given the evidence showing that China has a public health problem with smoking. The basic evidence consisted of the two propositions shown at the top right of Fig. 8.12. Both of these propositions consist of evidence drawn from sources, one from the WHO and one from a study published in the *British Medical Journal*. In this case, the basic evidence was not empirical evidence put forward by scientists, or even the statements made by the scientists or the WHO. It was a report made describing these statements.

The same problem came up in a different form in the Study in Scarlet case. The six observations that Holmes' made regarding Watson's appearance can be classified under the heading of basic evidence because they are all direct observations of Watson made by Holmes. All the pieces of indirect evidence in the case were derived by a sequence of inferences from these six basic statements, using only the two statements that Afghanistan is in the tropics and that there has been a recent military campaign in Afghanistan as additional premises. This case suggests the importance of direct observational findings as a species of basic evidence.

In the example of Darwin's finches, the difference was that the basic evidence was used to support arguments, which were in turn used as evidence to support the explanation. The scientific evidence provided by Darwin's theory and his description of the evolutionary facts provided the basic evidence. Inferences drawn from this basic evidence were used as arguments to support the explanation. This pattern is characteristic of inference to the best explanation. Here again the problem is one of modeling the transfer of evidence from the basic evidence to other kinds of evidence drawn from it inferentially.

The reader can recall from Chap. 3, Sect. 3.7 that according to Berland and Reiser (2008, 40), the superiority of the second explanation over the first one is that the students presented evidence to support parts of the explanation. As shown in Fig. 3.4, the three components of claim, evidence and reasoning can be clearly differentiated. The structure of this explanation can be modeled by bringing out why this explanation was stronger than the previous one, based on the second criterion of Sandoval and Reiser. Basically the reason is that some parts of the explanation were supported by factual evidence available from the knowledge base that the students were furnished with. The structure of this explanation is shown in Fig. 8.15.

The explanation diagram in Fig. 8.15 combines argumentation with explanation. It shows how the factual information from the knowledge base was employed in the arguments the students used to support their explanation. At the top, we see the explanation given by the students modeled as a story. Note that the story in this explanation is more comprehensive as a script than the explanation modeled by the story diagram in Fig. 3.4. By Sandoval and Reiser's first criterion, it is not as good an explanation as the one in the first example. However, by their second criterion it is

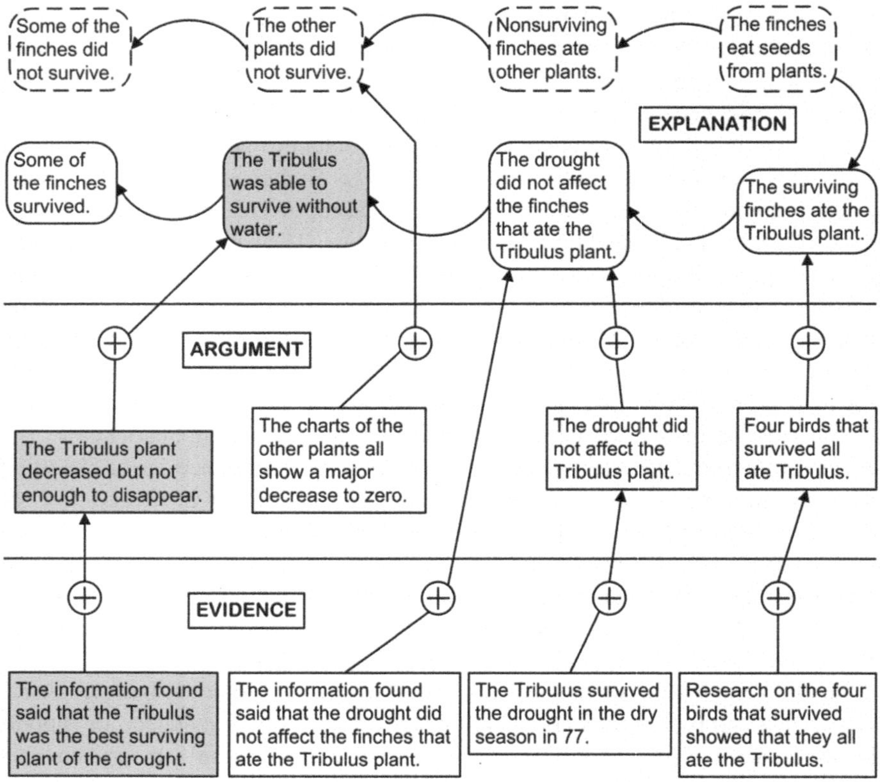


**Fig. 8.15** An explanation diagram combining argument, explanation and evidence

a better explanation because of the argumentation shown in the bottom two levels of the explanation diagram in Fig. 8.15. The four pieces of factual evidence displayed at the bottom level support the arguments shown at the middle level, which in turn support parts of the explanation shown at the top level.

The CAS method of evaluating arguments can be applied to the argumentation structure shown in Fig. 8.15 as follows. The four text boxes shown at the bottom each represent an item of evidence. To say that a proposition qualifies as evidence in a case is to say that is found in the knowledge base in the case, meaning that it has been accepted as knowledge collected from sources admissible as "knowledge" in the case. What qualifies as knowledge is explained in Chap. 7. The three green nodes show and example of how an item of evidence supports an argument, which in turn supports one of the statements in the script.

The problem in the disappearing sailor case was to determine which parts of the argumentation displayed in Fig. 8.14 should be classified as basic evidence, as opposed to secondary evidence drawn by inference from the basic evidence. The diagram in Fig. 8.14 shows only two of the propositions in the case accepted as evidence, the proposition that D married the woman who the revengeful emotion was about, and the proposition that D had made threats against V. Without going into the details of the actual example, let's say that these two propositions are taken as factual evidence in the case. The problem concerns to other propositions not shown in Fig. 8.14 as accepted. These are the propositions that D had ample opportunity to commit the murder and the proposition that no other person had the opportunity to do it. A further description of Wigmore's example would show that both of these propositions were supported by further evidence available in the trial. Perhaps also the two other propositions shown as accepted as evidence in Fig. 8.14 could also be backed up by additional evidence.

These observations about this example show that whether something is to be classified as basic evidence or secondary evidence drawn by inference from the basic evidence, depends on the factual circumstances of the case. In a trial, this evidence is collected and is supposed to be made available to both sides.

## 8.8 Knowledge-Based Systems

What formal argumentation systems such as ASPIC+ and CAS have in common, along with other technologies that have been developed in artificial intelligence, is that they are knowledge-based systems. A knowledge-based system has two main components, the knowledge base and the inference engine. The knowledge base contains a set of propositions formulated in a language suitable for computing, and what is called an inference engine, used to draw inferences from this basic set of propositions using whatever rules of inference are allowed in a given system.

Those working in the field of informal logic tend to see their task as a tripartite one composed of argument identification, argument analysis and argument evaluation. But they see themselves as applying their tools to a given text of discourse that is an example of natural language argumentation. They see their task as working with this text in order to identify the arguments in it, along with their implicit premises and conclusions, to analyze these arguments, and finally to evaluate them (Johnson and Blair 1983). For these purposes, there appears to be no reason to take a knowledge base into account. However, some reasons to do so have emerged from the examples of argumentation already evaluated in this book. What these examples have shown us is that in order to evaluate arguments, decisions have to be made on which propositions the audience to whom the argument was directed can be expected to accept as plausible without further argumentation. Moreover, in order to gain some idea of what the role of evidence should be during this undertaking, decisions have to be made about what standards of proof and kinds of evidence are appropriate for a particular domain. Therefore what we have found through attempting to evaluate so many examples is that in order to distinguish between evidence and argument in such cases, it would be helpful to expand the horizons of argumentation as a field to include the concept of a knowledge base.

Standard knowledge-based systems are typically rule-based computational systems comprised of a set of propositions representing the factual circumstances of

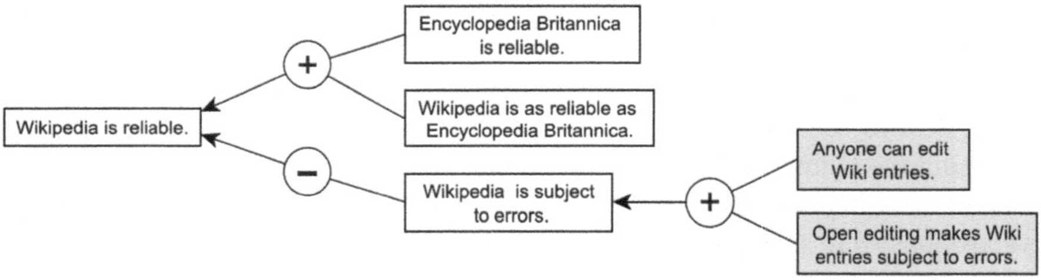


**Fig. 8.16** Diagram of an argument about whether Wikipedia is reliable

the case and a set of rules that can be used to draw inferences from this given set of propositions. For example, DefLog, ASPIC+ and CAS are rule-based systems. One way such systems can include argumentation schemes is to treat schemes as being rules. These rules can be deductive in nature, or probabilistic in nature, or they can represent defeasible argumentation schemes.

CAS uses a knowledge base containing the facts of the case constituting the basic factual evidence known by all parties to the discussion. This feature is useful in assisting the capability of CAS to fill in missing premises and conclusions, and to construct new arguments that can assist a user to prove an ultimate conclusion by inventing new arguments useful for that purpose. It can draw these new arguments from premises that CAS can find by searching the knowledge base. This can be seen as an alternative method of representing evidence on an argument diagram when evaluating argumentation based on evidence in a given case.

To take a simple example, consider a case where there is concern about whether Wikipedia is a reliable source, and whether the audience does not accept the proposition that Wikipedia is reliable. In this case there are two arguments to be considered. One is a pro-argument based on the premises that Wikipedia is as reliable as Encyclopaedia Britannica and Encyclopaedia Britannica is reliable. This argument is shown on the left in Fig. 8.16.

As shown on the left of Fig. 8.16, the audience accepts the premise that Encyclopaedia Britannica is reliable, but it does not accept the premise that Wikipedia is as reliable as Encyclopaedia Britannica. Therefore the argument on the left fails to prove the claim that Wikipedia is reliable. Next consider the counterargument shown on the right. It is based on the claim that Wikipedia is subject to errors. This claim is supported by an argument with two premises, both of which are accepted by the audience. This argument shows that even despite the argument on the left, the claim that Wikipedia is reliable is not acceptable.

Now let's suppose that there is a knowledge base in this case that contains a number of factual propositions and that the evidence in this knowledge base is accessible to the participants in the argument. Let's say, in addition, that CAS has the capability of searching in this knowledge base to find propositions that could be used as evidence to support or attack the arguments and propositions shown in Fig. 8.17. Let's say that two propositions are contained in the knowledge base. One is the proposition that a study in the journal *Nature* found that Wikipedia is as reliable as

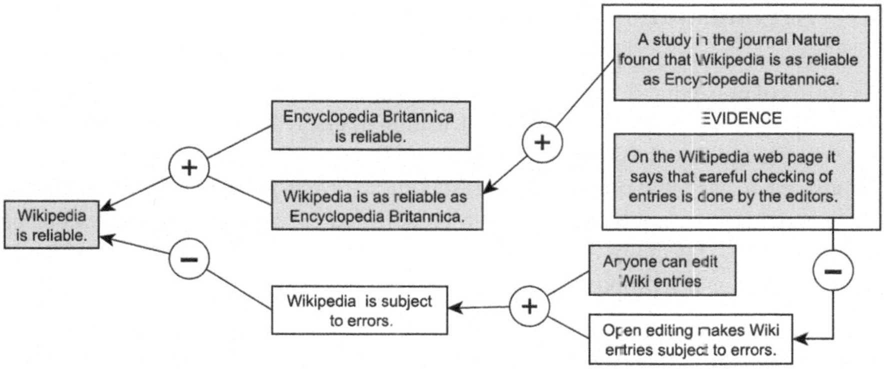


**Fig. 8.17** Finding of evidence on the issue of whether Wikipedia is reliable

Encyclopaedia Britannica. The other is the proposition that it says on the Wikipedia webpage that careful checking of entries is done by the editors.

Once these two propositions are retrieved from the knowledge base, CAS can evaluate their effects on the earlier argument. Let's look at the argument on the right first previously both its premises and conclusion were accepted. But the evidence drawn from the knowledge base stating that careful checking of entries is done by the editors is applied to the argument, showing that the premise stating that open editing makes entries subject to errors is no longer acceptable. Hence CAS automatically shows the text box for this proposition as having a white background. Since this argument is now applicable, its conclusion, the statement that Wikipedia is subject to errors, is calculated to be no longer acceptable. Hence it is shown in a text box with a white background. For these reasons, the argument as a whole fails to prove its ultimate conclusion that Wikipedia is reliable.

Next, let's look at the sequence of argumentation on the left side. The evidence from the journal Nature supports the proposition that Wikipedia is as reliable as Encyclopaedia Britannica. Previously the audience did not accept this proposition, but now, based on this evidence, accept it. Now both premises of this argument are acceptable, and since the argument is applicable, it shows that the ultimate conclusion that Wikipedia is reliable should be accepted. Once the evidence has been retrieved from the knowledge base and applied to the original argument, since the pro argument supports the ultimate conclusion that Wikipedia is reliable, and the con argument is refuted by the evidence, clearly what is shown is that the audience now finds the ultimate claim that Wikipedia is reliable as acceptable.

What has not been explained yet is the mechanism whereby CAS accesses such a knowledge base and applies it to a given argument as evidence that can affect the sequences of argumentation for and against the ultimate conclusion in a given case. But this example explains the task that it carries out.

## 8.9 Argumentation Schemes and Evidence

Six forms of epistemic defeasible reasoning identified in the work of Pollock (1995) have been presented in a succinct and useful manner as rules that can be used in a knowledge-based system by Prakken (2004, 36–37). According to Pollock's account each one of these forms representing a *prima facie* reason to support a claim is defeasible, implying that it can be defeated by counterarguments. Four of these forms are especially interested in connection with the discussion of evidence in this chapter. φ is a proposition.

*Perception*: having a percept with content φ is a *prima facie* reason to believe φ.
*Memory*: recalling φ is a *prima facie* reason to believe φ.
*Temporal Persistence*: φ is true at $T_1$ is a *prima facie* reason for φ to be true at a later time $T_2$.
*General Knowledge*: it is general knowledge that φ is a *prima facie* reason for φ.

The first of these forms has been presented in Chap. 1, Sect. 1.9, and transformed into a scheme called argument from perception. But all four of them, including another two closely related to the study of argument and evidence. The other two are called the statistical syllogism and induction. Their details of their formulation are not significant here, but what is important is to note that they can be taken to represent forms of argument in which statistical evidence is brought forward to defeasibly support a claim. More importantly, the rules for perception, memory and general knowledge correspond to defeasible argumentation schemes that have proved useful, over and over again, in the analyses of the examples in the previous chapters of this book. In the next section, it will be shown how the four fundamental forms above can be configured as a cluster of argumentation schemes that can be used as a basis for distinguishing between direct and indirect evidence.

Redford and Agah (2014) have introduced a new type of computational argumentation approach called Evidentialist Foundationalist Argumentation (EFA) that was inspired by evidentialist epistemology (Conee and Feldman 2004) and that uses ASPIC methodology. ASPIC+ is an example of an artificial intelligence system that fits the ASPIC framework. The ASPIC framework is a comprehensive framework used in artificial intelligence that defines arguments by modeling argumentation in an inference tree formed by applying strict and defeasible inference rules. The aim of EFA is to provide a tool for evidence gathering and evaluation, based around this central notion that certain kinds of evidence can be specified as quantifiable and verifiable. A statement is said to be verifiable (Redford and Agah 2014, 219) if it is produced directly by a sensor, such as a temperature sensor, a device recording wind speed or direction, an air pressure sensor, a digital photograph or a video recording, Using EFA to collect evidence, it is vitally important to be careful about what should be classified as direct evidence, as contrasted with evidence derived from direct evidence inferentially. Redford and Agah (2014, 212) use the following example to illustrate this point [their italics].

> For example, if a temperature sensor reads 35° celsius at the coordinate (54, 45) at time 12:01, this in *not* direct evidence that any of those values actually reflect reality. Perfect

> sensors are, for all practical purposes, impossible. The temperature may have actually been 2° colder, the location may have actually been 2 km further in both directions, and the time may have actually been 12:00:56. But this is direct evidence that the sensor *read* those first values. Sensor data is direct evidence of *what sensors read*, as opposed to direct evidence of *what actually happened*. Arguments about *what actually happened* are defeasible arguments based on sensor data.

The reading of a sensor at a certain point at a particular time can rightly be classified as direct evidence of what the sensor said. This evidence is fixed and verifiable, meaning that it will always be true that the sensor read that particular reading at that time. But it is only indirect evidence of what actually happened.

By way of clarification, Redford and Agah (2014, 212) also consider the example of the statement 'Unicorns exist', typed into a text file or website forum. Because this statement is found on a recording device, does that mean it can be classified as direct evidence that unicorns exist? They say it does not: "[it] is merely direct timestamped evidence that someone *typed* 'Unicorns exist' (or wrote a program to produce the string)". However, this direct evidence could also be put forward as indirect evidence when it is used as a premise in a defeasible argument that has the conclusion that unicorns exist.

A sensor device generally has a reliable memory, unlike human memory which can be highly fallible Loftus (1979) has shown that human memory is highly fallible, and studied cases where false memories have been used as evidence. But in fields such as law and history, much of the evidence is testimonial, based on what a witness claims to have seen in the past. Much time may have elapsed between the visual experience of the witness and his or later recall of what was seen as reported to other parties. Nevertheless, inferences drawn from what a witness claims to have seen or heard represents a kind of argumentation that can be classified as evidential.

In Chap. 7, Sect. 7.2, it was pointed out that evidence is made up of a set of evidential data or items of evidence and inferences to conclusions are reasonably drawn from these evidential data. It was also noted there that one important part of evidence is the perception of data through the senses. For example, if I see something that looks like a red car in the parking lot, my perception of the red car is something that appears to me as data, something that is given. Based on this perception, I can draw a reasonable inference to the conclusion that there is a red car in the parking lot. Here we saw that there is a distinction to be drawn between the evidence, which consists of the visual data of the red car, and the conclusion drawn from it, which is the proposition that there is a red car in the parking lot. Reasonable arguments are based on evidence of this kind. So, for example, if a witness who appears to be trustworthy claims that she saw a red car in the parking lot at a certain time, based on this evidence we might in the appropriate circumstances draw the conclusion, based on a prior premise about what the witness presumably saw, that there is evidence that there was a red car in the parking lot at that time.

The scheme for argument from witness testimony takes the following form (Walton et al. 2008, 310).

Position to Know Premise: Witness $W$ is in position to know whether $A$ is true or not.
Truth-telling Premise: Witness $W$ is telling the truth (as $W$ knows it).

Statement Premise: Witness $W$ states that $A$ is true (false).
Conclusion: $A$ may be plausibly taken to be true (false).

Below are the five critical questions matching argument from witness testimony (Walton et al. 2008, 310).

$CQ_1$: Is what the witness said internally consistent?
$CQ_2$: Is what the witness said consistent with the known facts of the case (based on evidence apart from what the witness testified to)?
$CQ_3$: Is what the witness said consistent with what other witnesses have (independently) testified to?
$CQ_4$: Is there some kind of bias that can be attributed to the account given by the witness?
$CQ_5$: How plausible is the statement $A$ asserted by the witness?

An example of the use of this scheme would be the use of witness testimony as evidence in a criminal trial (Gordon et al. 2007). Witness testimony is generally admissible as evidence is such a trial, subject to exceptions, and so arguments of this form are allowed in by the rules of evidence at the opening stage. During the argumentation stage (the main stage of the trial) this kind of evidence can be critically questioned and subjected to counter-arguments and rebuttals. In law, witness testimony can take two main forms. One is regular witness testimony of a kind based on a claim to have seen, heard, or otherwise perceived something. The other kind is expert opinion testimony, which is treated in a different but comparable way.

It was shown in Chap. 7 Sect. 7.2 that there is an argumentation scheme for argument from perception that was identified in Pollock's theory of defeasible reasoning outlined in Chap. 1, Sect. 1.6. We also saw that this scheme is defeasible and is subject to critical questioning when applied to any given case. It is defeasible because the acceptability of the argument, for example in an instance of witness testimony, depends on such matters as the memory of the witness, the reliability of the witness and the accuracy of the vision of the witness. These aspects of argumentation explained in Chap. 7 shows how there can be evidence supporting a proposition and also evidence undermining or attacking the acceptability of that proposition, at the same time in the same case. For example another witness might testify that he was present in the parking lot at the same time, carefully looked around, and did not see any red car.

Argument from perception is based on the capability of an agent to perceive something and argument from witness testimony is based on the agent's capability for remembering the event so that this agent can communicate with another agent to make statements that the other agent can take away as evidence. The familiar critical questions arise from the possibility that the first agent might be mistaken, lie, have forgotten something or be biased. The critical questions are designed to compensate for the characteristic errors arising from the use of this kind of evidence.

These remarks suggest that there might be a way of dealing with the ambiguity of the term 'evidence' by drawing a distinction between evidence of a more basic kind and indirect evidence drawn by inference from basic evidence. The way of moving

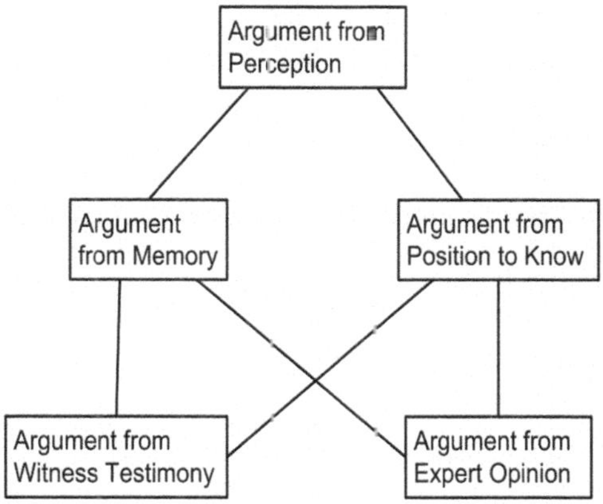


**Fig. 8.18** Cluster of basic evidential schemes

forward is to work toward a classification system for argumentation schemes used in evidential reasoning. So, for example argument from witness testimony, a scheme representing an especially important kind of evidence in law, is based on argument from perception. This suggests that evidence drawn from perception (appearances) is more basic than witness testimony evidence.

The schemes for argument from perception, argument from witness testimony and argument from expert testimony schemes are related to each other forming a cluster (Walton and Sartor 2013). One way of representing the structure of such a cluster is shown in Fig. 8.18.

Argument from perception is based on the capability of an agent to perceive something and argument from witness testimony is based on the agent's capability for remembering the event so that this agent can communicate with another agent to make statements that the other agent can take away as evidence. The familiar critical questions arise from the possibility that the first agent might be mistaken, lie, have forgotten something or be biased. The critical questions are designed to compensate for the characteristic errors arising from the use of this kind of evidence.

The most general scheme, explained in Chap. 7, Sect. 7.6, called defeasible *modus ponens* (DMP), subsumes all other schemes (with some arguable exceptions, such as argument from lack of evidence). DMP is a scheme in DefLog, ASPIC+ and CAS. This scheme can be put in the following form, where *A* and *B* represent propositions.

While all of the above defeasible schemes are general types, covering an open set of reasoning instances, one them, defeasible modus ponens, can be viewed as the most general pattern for defeasible reasoning, subsuming many, or even nearly all other schemes.

Major Premise: *A* => *B*
Minor Premise: *A*
Conclusion: *B*

The connective => in the major premise denotes defeasible implication of the kind defined in ASPIC+. In this sense $A$ => $B$ holds that the conclusion $B$ follows from $\alpha$ provisionally, assuming that there are no exceptions or prevailing reasons to the contrary (rebuttals).

For example, it is possible to see how the scheme for argument from expert opinion formulated so that it fits the defeasible *modus ponens* form.

Major Premise: ($E$ is an expert & $E$ says that $A$) => $A$
Minor premise: $E$ is an expert & $E$ says that $A$
Conclusion: $A$ is true

Note that the minor premise is a conjunction a conjunction that can include other complex schemes whose application requires a set of conditions $A_1, \ldots, A_n$.

For a listing of other schemes that can fit this format the reader is referred to chapter 9 of Walton et al. (2008). These include the following ten schemes that have been applied and discussed in the previous chapters of this book.

1. Argument from Position to Know
2. Argument from Witness Testimony
3. Argument from Expert Opinion
4. Argument from Appearance (Perception)
5. Argument from Lack of Knowledge
6. Argument from Correlation to Cause
7. Argument from Cause to Effect
8. Argument from Evidence to a Hypothesis
9. Defeasible Modus Ponens (DMP)
10. Inference to the Best Explanation

The findings so far in this chapter have led to the general problem of providing a system of classification that will enable these ten schemes to be nested together in a structure that can be used to help an argument evaluator distinguish between the basic evidence and the inferred evidence in any given case of argumentation. This is an unsolved problem, but there is a very recent considerable body of work on argument mining (Mochales and Moens 2011) that is exploring the general problem of how to build classification systems for argumentation schemes.

## 8.10 Conclusions

There are three argumentation technology tools that can be used to show the way to extend the current computational argumentation systems to deal with these problems of how to integrate argument and evidence. The first tool is to apply the new computational approach called Evidentialist Foundationalist Argumentation (EFA) within the ASPIC framework. The second tool is to adapt the six forms of epistemic defeasible reasoning identified by Pollock (1995) that can be fitted into a classification system for the cluster of argumentation schemes most closely related to basic evidence. This cluster of schemes indicates how basic evidence gives rise to inferences that define indirect evidence. The third tool is to use the feature of the knowledge base as found in computational argumentation systems such as ASPIC+ and CAS. Applying these three tools to an argumentation diagram representing a tree structure in a given case, text boxes containing premises of arguments in the tree can be marked as basic evidence. Conclusions drawn from these premise by means of arguments can be identified as indirect evidence.

The problem is posed when the argument analyst confronts an argument diagram that has an ultimate conclusion at the far left and there is a web of connected arguments forming a tree structure leading into the ultimate conclusion. The problem is to designate which parts of the argument diagram are to be taken as representing the evidence in the given case. The examples considered in this chapter suggest the following method. First, we have to distinguish between basic evidence and indirect evidence drawn by inference from the basic evidence. The basic evidence will generally consist of propositions appearing in the right part of the diagram. These are propositions that are premises and arguments, but are not themselves supported by additional arguments that appear to the right of them. Propositions drawn by inferences from these basic evidential propositions can be classified under the heading of indirect evidence.

Second, the analyst needs to look at the argumentation schemes that are represented on the diagram. For example, suppose there is an argument that fits the scheme for argument from expert opinion. Such an argument is of course itself classifiable as evidence supporting the ultimate conclusion. But a particular premise in the scheme can also be classified as evidence. In the case of argument from expert opinion this will be the premise stating that the expert says such and such. This statement represents so-called expert opinion evidence.

Another argumentation scheme that is a common indicator of evidence is the scheme for argument from perception. This scheme is also closely associated with the one for argument from witness testimony. So for example, if a witness states a proposition, the witness's having stated this proposition is evidence, and with what witness stated is also classifiable as evidence.

Another scheme that is a common identifier of evidence is the one for inference to the best explanation. In inference to the best explanation, the arguer considers several competing explanations and selects what is arguably the best one to explain the given facts of the case. So, for example, in the Study in Scarlet case the six observations made by Holmes (the six propositions displayed in the box at the extreme right side of Fig. 8.13 labeled as observational evidence), constitute the basic evidence in the case. The rest of the evidence is drawn by a sequence of connected argumentation from these basic propositions leading to the ultimate conclusion that Watson came from Afghanistan. The four arguments drawn from the six basic propositions shown in Fig. 8.13 fit the scheme for inference to the best explanation. The remaining propositions intervening between these six observational propositions and the ultimate conclusion that Watson came from Afghanistan can all be classified as indirect evidence.

What is classifiable as basic or indirect evidence will vary from case to case. In the kind of evidence typically used in the natural sciences, the basic evidence might consist of recordings from sensors on machines, or recorded results of experiments. In law, visual evidence such as video recordings are common as evidence, but witness testimony is also an extremely common form of evidence. In each field of investigation, there need to be standards determining what kinds of arguments constitute evidence, and standards of proof to determine how strong an evidence-based argument needs to be for its conclusion to be accepted. According to the argumentation framework adopted in formal systems such as ASPIC+ and CAS, these standards are set in the opening stage of the investigation.

The solution to the general problem of distinguishing between argument and evidence is to realize that in a given case what constitutes evidence generally needs to be determined by three main factors. The first is the determination of what kinds of evidence are appropriate for the argumentation in a given case. In terms of formal models of argumentation, this determination needs to be made the opening stage of the dialogue sequence. For example, if the argumentation in the case is about biology, and the outcome is to be determined by the biologists, some agreement is presupposed on what the biologists generally take to be the kinds of findings or calculations that can properly qualify as evidence in their field. Or if the argumentation in the case is about law, and the context is that of a trial, say a civil or criminal trial, the rules of evidence accepted in the jurisdiction as governing the trial procedure are taken to define what kinds of findings are arguments are admissible as evidence.

Once this matter has been clarified at the opening stage, it can help to classify kinds of evidence, such as statistical evidence, experimental evidence, witness testimony evidence, expert opinion evidence, and so forth, depending on the basic kinds of evidence appropriate for the type of inquiry or argumentation the agents are participating in.

The second factor is whether a given argument put forward during the argumentation stage fits a recognized argumentation scheme. During the argumentation stage, arguments are brought forward by both sides and evaluated by means of supporting and attacking arguments that fit argumentation schemes. The issue of whether a given argument fits an argumentation scheme is another finding that can help to determine whether a particular argument should be classified as evidence or not. For example, an argument from expert opinion or an argument from generally accepted opinion (common knowledge) might be acceptable as evidence in one type of inquiry but not in another. An argument from expert opinion might be accepted as evidential in a legal trial, but the same argument might not be deemed evidential by a group of physicists engaged in a technical seminar in physics, or in a paper to be published in that field.

The third factor that is useful in determining whether a proposition can be classified as evidence or not is whether it is found in the knowledge base representing the evidential findings in the case that have been accepted as factual. This knowledge base will take into account not only propositions that fit with type of evidence generally accepted as evidence in a specific field. It will also take into account propositions derived by inferences, especially inferences from identifiable types of argumentation schemes, from the propositions initially accepted as evidence.

This factor applies to formal argumentation models of the kind used in computer science, which generally have a knowledge base from which premises can be drawn to support or attack the claim that has been made. Argumentation theorists other than those in computing may not be so familiar with this aspect of computational models of argumentation. But as it happens, it is a very useful component of argumentation technology for many purposes.

Can evidence be supported by other evidence, on the theory of evidence proposed here? The answer to this question comes in two parts. First, indirect evidence is, by definition, always supported by other evidence. Second, direct evidence, as shown by the examples studied in this chapter, is not normally supported by other evidence, but it can be. For example, statistical evidence taken from the report of an expert statistician would be a typical example of a kind of argument used as basic evidence in a case. But if questioned, it could be based on other evidence that supports it. For example, it might be argued that the figures given by this statistician agree with figures given by another expert statistician. In such a case, what was formerly basic evidence, now that the case has been extended by drawing further information from the knowledge base, has become indirect evidence.

## References

Anderson, T., D. Shum, and W. Twining. 2005. *Analysis of evidence*, 2nd ed. New York: Cambridge University Press.

Berland, L.K., and B.J. Reiser. 2008. Making sense of argumentation and explanation. *Science Education* 93(1): 26–55.

Cohen, L.J. 1977. *The probable and the provable*. Oxford: Oxford University Press.

Cohen, L.J. 1979. On the psychology of prediction: Whose is the fallacy? *Cognition* 7(4): 385–407.

Conee, E., and R. Feldman. 2004. *Evidentialism: Essays in epistemology*. Oxford: Oxford University Press.

Gordon, T.F., and D. Walton. 2009. Proof burdens and standards. In *Argumentation and artificial intelligence*, ed. Iyad Rahwan and Guillermo Simari, 239–260. Berlin: Springer.

Gordon, T.F., H. Prakken, and D. Walton. 2007. The Carneades model of argument and burden of proof. *Artificial Intelligence* 171(10–15): 875–896.

Hahn, U., and M. Oaksford. 2006. Why a normative theory of argument strength and why might one want it to be Bayesian? *Informal Logic* 26: 1–24.

Johnson, R.H., and J.A. Blair. 1983. *Logical self-defense*, 2nd ed. Toronto: McGraw-Hill Ryerson.

Loftus, E.F. 1979. *Eyewitness testimony*. Cambridge, MA: Harvard University Press.

Mochales, R., and M.-F. Moens. 2011. Argumentation mining. *Artificial Intelligence and Law* 19(1): 1–22.

Pollock, J.L. 1995. *Cognitive carpentry*. Cambridge, MA: The MIT Press.

Prakken, H. 2004. Analysing reasoning about evidence with formal models of argumentation. *Law, Probability & Risk* 3(1): 33–50. [PDF].

Prakken, H. 2005. A study of accrual of arguments, with applications to evidential reasoning. In *Proceedings of the tenth international conference on artificial intelligence and law, Bologna, 2005*. New York: ACM Press, 85–94.

Redford, C., and A. Agah. 2014. Evidentialist foundationalist argumentation for multi-agent sensor fusion. *Artificial Intelligence Review* (42):211–243. Accessed on 14 July 2014 at this site. doi:10.1007/s10462-012-9333-3.

Schum, D.A. 1994. *Evidential foundations of probabilistic reasoning*. New York: Wiley.
Stein, A. 2005. *Foundations of evidence law*, 2005. Oxford: Oxford University Press.
Tillers, P. 1989. Review: Webs of things in the mind: A new science of evidence. *Michigan Law Review* 87(6): 1225–1258.
Tversky, A., and D. Kahneman. 1982. Judgments of and by representativeness. In *Judgment under uncertainty: Heuristics and biases*, ed. D. Kahneman, P. Slovic, and A. Tversky. Cambridge: Cambridge University Press.
Vreeswijk, G. 2003. Review of Kevin B. Korb and Anne E. Nicholson, *Bayesian Artificial Intelligence*, Chapman and Hall, 2003. *Artificial Intelligence and Law* 11: 289–298.
Walton, D., and E.C.W. Krabbe. 1995. *Commitment in dialogue*. Albany: State University of New York Press.
Walton, D., and G. Sartor. 2013. Teleological justification of argumentation schemes. *Argumentation* 27(2): 111–142.
Walton, D., and N. Zhang. 2013. The epistemology of scientific evidence. *Artificial Intelligence and Law* 21(2): 173–219.
Walton, D., C. Reed, and F. Macagno. 2008. *Argumentation schemes*. Cambridge: Cambridge University Press.
Wigmore, J.H. 1931. *The principles of judicial proof*. Boston: Little, Brown and Company.

# Index




D. Walton, *Argument Evaluation and Evidence*, Law, Governance and Technology Series 23, DOI 10.1007/978-3-319-19626-8

**F**

## G



## H



## I



## J



## K

**R**



**S**



**T**



**U**

The manufacturer's authorised representative in the EU is Springer Nature Customer Service Centre GmbH, Europaplatz 3, 69115 Heidelberg, Germany. If you have any concerns regarding our products, please contact ProductSafety@springernature.com

Printed and bound by CPI Group (UK) Ltd, Croydon, CR0 4YY
22/09/2026
02221061-0013